Elizabeth Barre

WOMEN IN CULTURE AND SOCIETY

A Series Edited by Catharine R. Stimpson

Elizabeth Barrett Browning

The Origins of a New Poetry

·

Dorothy Mermin

The University of Chicago Press

Chicago and London

The University of Chicago Press, Chicago 60637
The University of Chicago Press, Ltd., London
© 1989 by The University of Chicago
All rights reserved. Published 1989
Printed in the United States of America
98 97 96 95 94 93 92 91 90 89   54321

Library of Congress Cataloging-in-Publication Data

Mermin, Dorothy, 1936–
    Elizabeth Barrett Browning : the origins of a new poetry / Dorothy
Mermin.
        p.   cm. — (Women in culture and society)
    Bibliography: p.
    Includes index.
    ISBN 0-226-52038-2.   ISBN 0-226-52039-0 (pbk.)
    1. Browning, Elizabeth Barrett, 1806–1861.   2. Poets,
English—19th century—Biography.   3. Women and literature—Great
Britain—History—19th century.   I. Title.   II. Series
PR4193.M43 1989   88-28680
821′.8—dc19   CIP

∞ The paper used in this publication meets the
minimum requirements of the American National Standard
for Information Sciences—Permanence of Paper for
Printed Library Materials, ANSI Z39.48-1984.

DOROTHY MERMIN is professor in and chair of the
Department of English at Cornell University.

For David

Contents

Foreword

In 1820, an English girl, blazing with ambition and intelligence, scrutinized herself. In an essay, "Glimpses into My Own Life and Literary Character," she wrote: "I was always of a determined and if thwarted violent disposition. My actions and temperament were infinitely more inflexible at three years old than now at fourteen. . . . At four I first mounted Pegasus but at six I thought myself privileged to show off feats of horsemanship." In love with Greek culture and liberties, the girl summoned steedy classical mythology. For Pegasus, the horse with wings, symbolizes courage, strength, immortality, and poetry. Born from the body of the dying Medusa, he figures, as well, in the wilder stories of the West about the powers of dangerous women.

This prodigous young rider of the imagination was Elizabeth Barrett Browning. For most of the twentieth century, the persona of "Elizabeth Barrett Browning" seemed, not alight with talent, but goopy, droopy, languishing in a dark room with a dog named Flush and counting the ways in which she loved a nameless "Thee." At her most vigorous, she was played by the actress Katherine Cornell in a melodrama about Victorian family life, set on London's Wimpole Street, during which a sweetly virile poet, Robert Browning, pulls and whisks her away from a viciously virile tyrant-papa.

Misleading, hapless, hopeless, false. In 1932, Virginia Woolf, that deep and agile reader of other women writers, lamented the assignment of Barrett Browning to the "servants' quarters" of the "mansion of literature." Having been down-loaded, she can only bang the crockery about and eat peas on the point of her knife. In the 1970s, in debt to Woolf, feminist critics began to reread Barrett Browning and to revise her reputation. Now, in this powerful and elegant book, Dorothy Mermin fully places Barrett Browning's texts in the geographies of writing. Barrett Browning is the originator of a new poetry in two senses: she is nothing less than the first Victorian poet and first major woman poet in England.

To be both, *at once*, demanded all of Barrett Browning's ardor, wit, and will. She grew up in comfort on a family estate, Hope End. When she was a scribbling child, the family petted her. Her father called her the poet laureate of Hope End. Simultaneously, that family taught her the rules of class and gender. Women, like her mother, were to represent the private world of "nurture and mystery." Real women abhorred both Medea and the Medusa. Men, like her father, Edward Barrett Moulton-Barrett, were to dwell in the public world of learning, authority, and judgment. A complex and self-divided man, he may have been sympathetic to the anti-slavery movement, even as his money came from his slave-owning family and their plantations in Jamaica. Girls, like Elizabeth, were to stay at home. Boys, like her beloved brother, were to go away to school. An imaginative boy could dip into cultural tradition and find scads of fathers to overwhelm or to buoy him up. An imaginative girl, like Elizabeth, could ransack cultural tradition and find no "grandmothers." A grandmother is both precursor and grand presence. Women were the poet laureates only of Hope End. Only later, when Barrett Browning rapturously discovered George Sand and comfortably befriended Mary Russell Mitford (who gave her that dog), did she find other literary women to respect.

Sensitively, Mermin describes the strategies Barrett Browning invented to escape from the traps of gender. She was a brilliant student of Greek, the language that the "educated" had to master. She supported Greek deliverance from the Turkish empire, as a cause in itself and as a projection of her own passion for independence. Blurring the categories of gender, she fantasized wearing men's clothing and becoming a female Homer, even "a little taller than Homer." She was fifteen when she first published a poem, on Greece.

At fifteen, Barrett Browning was also negotiating a treacherous passage toward adulthood. Family, friends, literary history, and Victorian ideology cramped a scribbling child who wanted to be the greatest woman writer who had ever lived. She did write. Her first book appeared when she was twenty, two years before her mother's death. By 1838, her fame was growing. By 1844, when she brought out *Poems,* she was established in Great Britain and the United States. The poet without a grandmother had transformed herself into a poetic mother. She was an immense influence on Emily Dickinson. Significantly, however, the lively and active little girl had become an invalid, a perfect Victorian maiden, enclosed in a single room in her father's house, fearful that her father would fear her fame, dependent on the opium she was never to give up.

Re-enacting a mythic narrative, she eventually ran away from her father's house. In 1845, taken with her *Poems*, Robert Browning wrote to her. They corresponded. He called. In 1846, they married secretly and moved, irrevocably, mostly blissfully, to Italy. She doted on their son. If Elizabeth was better known than Robert, he accepted this bubble of a truth and praised her genius. Marriage spurred their minds, conjugality their creativity. For each of them entered "the territory represented by the other." His poems began to explore "the world of normal human feeling." She became more social and political in theme, more hopeful and defiant in tone.

Although Barrett Browning had written protest poetry before her marriage, most notably "The Cry of the Children," her work now leapt toward radicalism. She opposed slavery and supported Italian nationalism. Such poems provoked abuse, in part because they seemed so "unwomanly." Like George Eliot, Barrett Browning was fastidiously aloof from the organized women's movement. Yet she was intensely feminist in idea and feeling. Fighting against the harness of "womanliness," she struggled to rewrite the meaning of gender itself—with prosodic daring, metaphorical grandeur, and some conceptual, class-ridden muddle. She also invented a voice for women's love poetry, for amatory verse, perhaps most excitingly in *Sonnets from the Portuguese* (1850). Her epic, *Aurora Leigh* (1857), interweaves the political and the intimate, the claims of justice and of the heart. So doing, it gives the women's literary tradition in English mass, scope, and reach.

In 1861, Barrett Browning died, probably because her tuberculosis flared up again. *Elizabeth Barrett Browning* revivifies the passionate girl and the courageous adult. It gives us back her poetry. The timorous stable-keepers of literature have hobbled and starved Barrett Browning's Pegasus. The Medusa would laugh as Barrett Browning rides him again, triumphantly.

Catharine R. Stimpson

Acknowledgments

For permission to quote from Barrett Browning's manuscripts I am grateful to John Murray. Manuscripts in their collections are quoted with permission of the Armstrong Browning Library, Baylor University; the Henry W. and Albert A. Berg Collection, the New York Public Library, Astor, Lenox and Tilden Foundations; the British Library Board; the English Poetry Collection, Wellesley College Library; the Huntington Library, San Marino, California; and the Pierpont Morgan Library. For indispensable assistance in my research I am grateful to librarians in these and other libraries, and also—and especially—to Philip Kelley.

Material that first appeared in scholarly journals is reprinted by permission of the editors. I have used all or part of these essays: "The Female Poet and the Embarrassed Reader: Elizabeth Barrett Browning's *Sonnets from the Portuguese*," *English Literary History* 48 (1981): 351–67; "Barrett Browning's Stories," *Browning Institute Studies* 13 (1985): 99–112; "Genre and Gender in *Aurora Leigh*," *Victorian Newsletter* no. 69 (Spring 1986): 7–11; "Elizabeth Barrett Browning through 1844: Becoming a Woman Poet," *Studies in English Literature* 26 (1986): 713–36; "The Damsel, the Knight, and the Victorian Woman Poet," *Critical Inquiry* 13 (1986): 64–80.

My greatest debt of gratitude is to my colleagues and students at Cornell—among many others, Sandra Siegel, Cynthia Chase, Debra Fried, Mary Jacobus, and Paul Sawyer—who helped me think about women writers and write this book; and to David, Jonathan, and Liz.

Chronology

1806 Born 6 March
1809 Hope End
1820 *The Battle of Marathon*
1826 *An Essay on Mind, with Other Poems*
1832 Sidmouth, August
1833 *Prometheus Bound, Translated from the Greek of Aeschylus,*
      and Miscellaneous Poems
1835 London
1838 *The Seraphim, and Other Poems*
1838 Torquay
1841 London
1844 *Poems*
1845 First letter from Robert Browning, 10 January
1846 Married Robert Browning, 12 September
1846 Pisa
1847 Florence
1849 Robert Wiedemann Browning born 9 March
1850 *Poems*
1851 *Casa Guidi Windows*
1857 *Aurora Leigh*
1860 *Poems before Congress*
1861 Died 29 June
1862 *Last Poems*

Introduction

Elizabeth Barrett Browning is for most practical purposes the first woman poet in English literature. She did not spring entirely motherless from the male tradition, Athena from the forehead of Jove, but almost all of the poets who inspired her to emulation were men. "I look everywhere for grandmothers," she wrote in 1845, "and see none" (*LEBB* 1:232), and the homely familial term suggests how intimately she felt the deprivation.[1] A few stepmothers or maiden aunts could be glimpsed now and then, and rumors and echoes of the great ancestress, Sappho, drifted toward her from the dim recesses of ancient time, but that was all. Women had written good poetry in English, had even been published and read, before her—Katherine Philips ("The Matchless Orinda"), Aphra Behn, Anne Finch, and others in England, Anne Bradstreet in America—but in the nineteenth century their works were almost invisible. The popular "poetesses" who adorned the literary scene when she began to write—Joanna Baillie, Felicia Hemans, Letitia Landon, and others of smaller merit and renown—inspired her as both positive and negative examples, but theirs was not the noble lineage with which she wished to claim affiliation. Born in 1806, she was almost a quarter of a century older than Christina Rossetti and Emily Dickinson, for both of whom she loomed as a benign and inspiriting presence, and twelve years older than Emily Brontë. While Rossetti quickly attained a secure but rather small and shadowy niche among minor Victorians, Dickinson's poetry was mostly unpublished until the end of the century, and Brontë's was almost entirely unknown by the Victorians and is not much read even today. Elizabeth Barrett Browning was the first woman to establish herself in the main English tradition (the one that forms the

1

literary consciousness of other poets and educated readers of poetry, as measured by allusions and echoes or, more crudely, representation in anthologies and classrooms). However shaky her tenure in that position had become by the end of the nineteenth century, she was never entirely forgotten, at least by readers of the gift-book editions of *Sonnets from the Portuguese* that proliferate even now. Lacking female precursors (or grand-mothers), she became such a precursor herself.

Her significance as a Victorian poet has been obscured in this century by her erasure from all but the most unselective literary histories and her exclusion from academic anthologies—an exclusion that has recently been mitigated by brief selections from her longer works or a few isolated shorter ones, most of her best poems being too large to squeeze un-mutilated into the narrow room allotted her. But although she has much in common with the other women poets of her era, she belongs even more clearly in the male Victorian line, with poets of comparable stature to her own—and here too, she came first. She was the oldest of the major Victorian poets—Tennyson was born in 1809, Browning in 1812, Clough in 1819, Arnold in 1822, the others later still—and much more often than not, when her poems resemble theirs, hers were written first. Her early poetry of life-weariness, lassitude, emptiness, and alienation from society and nature strikingly anticipates that of Matthew Arnold. The shape of her career, however, is like Tennyson's: they both wrote dreamy, self-enclosed verse and medievalizing and apparently escapist narratives; in 1850 they both published long lyric sequences telling stories undisguisedly based on personal experience; their political poetry was innovative and controversial; and they created new kinds of epics in which to address the issues of the day. There are stylistic similarities too: she insisted that she had acquired the habits decried as Tennysonian before she read a line of Tennyson. Like Browning, she was mocked and chided for being willfully obscure; like Clough, she insisted on dragging poetry into the realms of prose fiction; Meredith after her wrote a tale of modern love in the shape of a Renaissance sonnet sequence; Swinburne cele-brated the Risorgimento in songs that uncannily echo hers; and Dante Gabriel Rossetti extravagantly admired and apparently emulated her me-dievalizing balladry and followed her lead in the amatory sonnet sequence too.

It is as if she held in suspension all the elements of Victorian poetry, all its potential voices, with now one, now another, precipitating into verse—as if she were the great mythic mother of both daughters and sons. She was always looking for a new subject, a generic innovation, a new way to touch the world. Homeric epic, Aeschylean and Miltonic drama, amatory sonnet sequence, novel-in-verse, dreamy fantasies of clouds and islands, political poetry of many kinds on several subjects (poverty in England, slavery in America, the struggle for Italian unification), sonnets, ballads, monologues of sexual obsession, ironical forays into the war between the sexes, occasional verses on her family, friends, birds, and cocker spaniel—nothing satisfied her; she was always moving on.

Nonetheless, her place at the wellhead of a new female tradition remains the single most important fact about her in terms of literary history, whether that history is conceived as simple chronology or as a complex chain of echoes and influence. It was also central to her self-consciousness as a poet. Her anomalousness was constantly present to her imagination, and questions of gender shaped and colored almost everything she wrote. In her most ambitious early writings she assumed the posture of a man among men, while female voices and issues pressed to the fore in small, unfinished, or unpublished works. Then she began covertly to inspect and dismantle the barriers set in her path by gender. Her major works—*Sonnets from the Portuguese, Aurora Leigh,* her best political poems, "A Musical Instrument"—turn difficulty into triumph, incorporating her femininity, her situation as a woman poet, and her increasingly substantial fame into her poetic arguments.

Her life as a woman poet, that is, became part of the meaning of her art. And fortunately, both her personal and her literary development are exceptionally well documented, especially for her formative years. Her family saved many of the productions of her precocious and prolific childhood; she began publishing very early; and her period of poetic growth was exceptionally prolonged. She did not find her own mature voice until she was close to forty, and she continued to experiment and change until the end of her life. The biographical record is unusually full too, although with tantalizing gaps. There are revealing early essays, including autobiographical ones, a diary covering most of her twenty-sixth year, and an enormous number of letters. For several years before her marriage she dealt with the world outside her family mostly through letters, even her courtship being largely epistolary, and after she married and left England her connection with family and old friends was kept up in the same way. Most of her letters, like her childish literary compositions, were treasured by their recipients and still survive.

Biographical approaches have often been injurious to women writers, overemphasizing certain aspects of their lives—especially love affairs,

real, imaginary, or absent—belittling their artistry, and deflecting atten-
tion from their works. It has too easily been assumed that women's pens
are impelled by their emotions, their ink a kind of expressive fluid or
involuntary secretion—men make works of art, women's feelings ooze
out onto the paper—and that the task of composition is simply to channel
the flow. The idea that women should be spontaneous and artless, "sin-
cere" in a very simple and literal way, was taken for granted in the
nineteenth century and has survived into the current feminist era with
new stipulations as to what women should spontaneously express, sex-
uality and rage having displaced the kindlier emotions preferred by the
Victorians. Reinforcing the debilitating stereotypes of women as unre-
flective, unintellectual, unable to shape experience into art, this as-
sumption diverts critics from examining their works in other than expressive
terms. And yet it remains true that we cannot read the major nineteenth-
century women poets without reading at the same time the intricate drama
of engagement and withdrawal through which they encountered the poetic
tradition, declared the validity of female experience as material for poetry,
and created the conditions of their art. The problematic relation of a
woman's life to a poet's work, so different (she rightly thought) from a
man's, was a subject Barrett Browning returned to again and again, never
quite settling it to her satisfaction. She discovered at a very early age
that the poetic tradition was formed by a vision of life seen through men's
eyes, felt on male pulses, and that her own vision, feelings, and expe-
riences were in some essential ways quite different. One of the necessary
tasks of criticism is to trace the shape and consequences of that difference.

But of course a life is not just a set of circumstances imposed from
without. It is also a story invented as it goes along, even if it is not entirely
under the storyteller's control. On the crudest level of plot, Barrett
Browning's is an archetypal romance: a greatly gifted and suffering maiden
is imprisoned as if in a deathly enchantment by her tyrannical father until
a bold poetical lover rescues her, their desperate, thrilling elopement to
a distant paradisiacal land issuing in a marriage of exemplary bliss. This
story of her life was already being retold, with embellishments, before it
was half over; it held the popular imagination even when her poems fell
from grace, and colors responses to her works even now. She herself
found the glamorization of isolation, debility, and pain in the first part
of the story distasteful and was not at all pleased to be celebrated as a
combination of fairy-tale princess and learned monster. But despite its
exaggerations and absurdities, the legend was not only essentially true;
it was also her own creation. Her scholarly attainments really were ex-

traordinary—at least for a woman; her reclusiveness preceded the illness that locked the door on her prison; her poetry was swathed in renunciative gloom long before her most beloved brother's death occurred to explain it; and while her father's morbid despotism bound all her brothers and sisters as well as herself (she was the first, in fact, to break free), her submission was conscious and voluntary. The story of the maiden waiting for rescue had fascinated her from earliest childhood, and the elopement and the strong and happy years thereafter were as much her doing as Robert Browning's.

She enacted old stories as she told them, however, in an exploratory and revisionist spirit, and her revisions became bolder, more open, and more effective as she became more able to imagine and realize, in literature and in life, happy endings. Her poems on the Risorgimento were impelled by her feeling that Italy's restoration from the verge of dissolution to triumphant rebirth would be no less wonderful, but no more miraculous, than the renewal of her own life, and her famously successful career as poet, wife, and mother made Aurora Leigh's extraordinary ambition and accomplishments less implausible than they would otherwise have seemed to contemporary readers. What she had done, she implied with characteristic generosity, others—struggling races and nations, girls who wanted to be poets—could do too. The Brownings' marriage was, for both of them, not only extremely happy (here especially the legend does not lie, although it may strain credulity) but also artistically enabling. A very distinguished feminist poet and critic once asked me if it were not true that Elizabeth Barrett Browning wrote all her best poetry before her marriage; no, it is not true— quite the contrary. Being a happy wife and mother *and* a prolific and successful poet was her most radical revision of all.

Such extensive interdependence of poetry and life is not, of course, exclusive to Barrett Browning, or to women—one has only to think of the great Romantics, especially Byron. But with women it is both more common and more commonly perceived. Since women have found most of poetry's traditional material (male heroism, courtship from a man's point of view, men's relation to other men and to nature) for one reason or another awkward or unsuitable, they have turned to their own experience instead. Furthermore, the personal element tends to appear larger in women's poetry than it actually is. *Sonnets from the Portuguese* has aroused both ardor and revulsion in readers blinded by its aspect as sentimental autobiography to its cunning artistry and its ongoing argument with the tradition of amatory poetry. Still, even if we did not know about the real courtship behind the one in the poem we would probably invent it as we read. For a woman poet will appear as, and will feel herself to be, both the speaking subject who experiences and articulates the world—the poet, traditionally male—and the female object who is seen and addressed but does not herself speak. As both self and other, subject and object, she has a doubled presence in her works. Our correspondingly doubled awareness of her encourages biographical readings; and so does the incongruence with literary convention that the speaker's gender constantly produces: for what is unfamiliar in literature must come, we assume without really thinking about it, from life—and whose life but the poet's own? A female speaker's voice does not blend with those of the past as even the most distinctive and overtly biographical male ones do (Tennyson's, for instance, in *In Memoriam*); we do not hear the voice of tradition speaking through her.

When she ventures to use the metaphors through which certain basic poetic experiences have traditionally been conveyed, the tradition is apt to drop away and leave the naked image as if reborn: fresh, apparently personal, and disconcertingly literal. Such literalization is perhaps the strangest and most disturbing single aspect of Barrett Browning's poetry. It occurs most often in amatory protestations of subordination or dependency (flattery when men use them, but painfully close to the social reality of women's lives); in religious verse, where representation of the soul as female or childlike fits women unparadoxically and all too well; in images for inspiration and creation drawn from sexual desire, insemination, or childbirth; and in self-descriptions, however sketchy and conventional, which bring a speaker before us with painful clarity as an individual woman (who if she did not represent herself as physically unattractive would risk seeming unattractively vain or coy) rather than a representative man.[2] As a Victorian critic explained in an 1840 review of nine women poets—or, as he prefers to call them, nine muses: "when we venture to lift a pen against women, . . . the weapon drops pointless on the marked passage; and whilst the mind is bent on praise or censure of the poem, the eye swims too deep in tears and mist over the poetess herself in the frontispiece, to let it see its way to either."[3] A woman poet is her muse, her text, but above all her picture, and the critic is blinded to her poems—his apparently automatic hostility to them is disarmed—by his response to (what he imagines to be) herself.

And while the obdurate if unconsidered maleness of the English poetic tradition put women poets at a disadvantage, external circumstances hindered them too. They were held back by their exclusion from the classical education that, whatever its value in the actual practise of the poet's craft, was felt to give the key to high culture; by taboos against female self-assertion and self-display that induced timidity, inhibited publication, and limited their subject matter; by the low esteem in which women were held (and held themselves); and by the condescension of reviewers. But the Victorian period also offered new opportunities. Literature was coming to seem less exclusively masculine, and men, too, put their gender identity at risk when they published verse. Prose fiction, which mirrored the diurnal and domestic concerns of contemporary society—the woman's sphere—was becoming the dominant literary genre. Poetry came to be valued largely for expressing and arousing emotions through which it could touch, soothe, and elevate its readers, thereby becoming associated with female subjects, female readers, female attitudes, and even female authors, and dissociated from power and business and work. Men feared the desiccation of the springs of feelings which, they all agreed, were necessary both for virtue and for art, but such feelings were increasingly being relegated to woman's sphere. Growing up in what they grimly conceived of as an industrial, materialistic, postheroic, antipoetic age, moreover, men were hardly more comfortable than women were likely to be in the bardic-prophetic-priestly robes handed down from Homer and Milton, or even from Byron and Shelley, and the examples of Wordsworth and Coleridge could not keep nature alive for them as the grand source of inspiration and art. And within poetry, old generic boundaries, already undermined by Romanticism, crumbled: innovation and anomaly became the order of the literary day, giving Barrett Browning license to seek out new, more commodious vehicles for the new things she wanted to say.

As the reading public grew larger, less elite, and more diffuse, its ear attuned mainly to prose fiction, male poets' sense of their audience became increasingly anxious and insecure and the monolithic masculinity of the literary world began to crumble. There were more places for women to publish: periodicals, gift books, annuals designed for an undemanding and largely female audience—not very prestigious, but offering young women relatively easy access to print. And while reviewers were condescending to "poetesses," they were not unwelcoming: Elizabeth Barrett had no trouble getting published, and reviews were profuse and laudatory. Women poets comprised a recognized category, and one in which it was easy for her to be first, while the interregnum between Romanticism and Victorianism in which she began to publish did not offer much male competition either. Her repuation flourished alongside

Tennyson's and more prosperously than Browning's; in fact, throughout all the years of their marriage Browning was significantly less famous than she. Critical approbation offered immediate gratification and essential encouragement, although it had its problems too: it set low standards for women and discouraged whatever was not overtly tender, touching, fluent, "womanly." Fortunately, such potentially debilitating praise incited her to set herself harder tasks, to try to shock her readers into new notions about Victorian womanhood, and to use her fame for overtly political ends.

Although she quickly found an audience in her day, her works were always considered "difficult," and since criticism has neglected them for so long they can seem difficult still. When I began systematically to read them through (a project greeted by some of my colleagues with open if polite incredulity), I could not match them up with the grids through which I was accustomed to reading Victorian poetry. I had trouble grasping their inner logic and accounting for my own reactions, which varied from exhilaration to bewilderment to positive dismay. Despite their evident complexity of thought and artistry many of them seemed alien and rather thin, their contextual resonances inaudible to my unaccustomed ear—and yet I could discern a powerful intellect and an unfamiliar and very attractive sensibility working in them. Like many other readers, too (including Henry James), I was captivated by her letters. And so I kept looking for an entrance into her obscure but richly attractive world. Now I can see, of course, that there are many entrances: but the main one— the one to which she left the key most visibly in the lock—is through the struggle that began in her early childhood to find woman's place in the central tradition of poetry. Throughout her career this struggle was her main subject, her version of the radical self-reflexiveness and subjectivity of the Romantic tradition, and the model on which she conceived almost all of her poetry on almost every theme. In this book I have attempted, therefore, to show how a girl in early nineteenth-century England grew up to be the first of English women poets: what impelled her ambition, what hindered it, what enabled it, how she used it, and what kinds of poems she wrote and how they can be read.

I have paid especial attention to the roots of her career in childhood, drawing extensively on the materials that are now available in the first volumes of *The Brownings' Correspondence*, on the early writings in which she struggled to find her way and set the course of her mature works, and on the interplay between what she wrote and the world for which she wrote it. I have not aspired to biographical completeness beyond what seems necessary to elucidate her poetry and her poetic career; but in the absence of a female tradition against which to read them, the poems do not seem to me fully comprehensible except in relation to the life that formed and was formed by them, the same imagination controlling both. Similarly, while my primary intention is not to undertake an aesthetic revaluation of Barrett Browning's works (but rather to help make one possible by examining her major poems and the terms of their construction), the unsettled state of the canon and the long lapse of her reputation almost require that each new reading and each choice of works to read be also an evaluation. My emphases fall rather differently from those of earlier writers: in particular, while I have not attempted to assess her political thinking except in its relation to her life and her art, I have given more space than has been usual to her political poetry, which seems to me both integral to her career and of high artistic merit. Her style tends to be expansive rather than lapidary, and like that of Swinburne (another major Victorian poet whom we have only recently learned how to read) has deterred critics from seeking the hard structure of meaning behind its dazzling impulsions of verbal energy. My hope is that others will find, as I did, that the more one understands the inner workings of her poetry and learns to hear its resonances, the richer it will sound and the higher it will stand in one's esteem. Of its importance for literary history as feminist criticism is now rewriting it, there can be no doubt.

I

Childhood and Youth

Elizabeth Barrett Moulton-Barrett was born in 1806, the first of the twelve children of Mary Graham Clarke and Edward Barrett Moulton-Barrett. During her childhood the family lived at Hope End, a beautiful estate in Herefordshire with a grand house designed by Edward Moulton-Barrett in a style of exuberantly orientalizing fantasy rather like that of the Brighton Pavilion. She was a happy, lively, loving child, extremely precocious, petted, admired, and indulged by her parents, and almost from the dawn of consciousness she intended to become a poet. Looking back to her childhood at the age of fourteen in an essay called "Glimpses into My Own Life and Literary Character," she briefly chronicled the first manifestations of the ambition that was to be the driving force of her life:

> At four I first mounted Pegasus but at six I thought myself priviledged to show off feats of horsemanship—In my sixth year [in fact, her ninth] for some lines on virtue which I had pen[n]ed with great care I received from Papa a ten shilling note enclosed in a letter which was addrest to *the Poet Laureat of Hope End;* I mention this because I received much, more pleasure from the word *Poet* than from the ten shilling note. (*BC* 1:349–50)

The literalizing humor and detachment with which she describes her own intense seriousness are characteristic of her self-descriptions throughout her life, especially when they concern ambition. At seven she read for the purpose of "forming my taste" and "to see what was best to write about & read about," at nine she preferred reading to writing, but at ten "I read that I might write" and at eleven "I wished to be considered an authoress" (*BC* 1:350). Many

10

years later she summed up her childhood ambitions in a quasi-auto-biographical account of a ten-year-old girl named Beth who wanted to be "the feminine of Homer," "a little taller than Homer if anything," the greatest woman poet who had ever lived.[1] At eleven Elizabeth Barrett herself, she reports in "Glimpses," thought her own verses better than Pope's translation of the *Iliad;* when she compared the two, however, she recognized her own inferiority, and by the time she was thirteen she had schooled herself (she optimistically supposed) "to throw away ambition" (*BC* 1:352).

She never in fact succeeded in eradicating her poetic ambition, but she usually described it as an aberration from which she had safely recovered and was inclined to mock the self that felt it. She was always entirely serious about the supreme value of poetry itself and never doubted her own vocation, but she was not solemn about her pretensions. For while outdoing Homer (growing taller than a man) was a comically immodest goal, becoming his female counterpart—the first and greatest of women poets—was a rather humble one. Her male contemporaries in the first post-Romantic generation were oppressed by a sense of belatedness, of coming when the great poems had already been written and in times unconducive to poetry. For them, the heroic age was over, in life as in art. But there had never been a heroic age for women, and the great women's poems were all (at least so far as a girl in England knew) still to be conceived. Tennyson could not expect to be another Keats, or Browning a Shelley, or Arnold a Wordsworth, and as they matured they shrank from their great predecessors' shadows. But Elizabeth Barrett could aspire to be the female counterpart of Homer, or Aeschylus, or Byron. No shadow of past greatness darkened her path, and the scope for aspiration seemed limitless.

It was not always clear, however, whether being a woman cancelled or doubled the possibility of greatness, for in other respects a girl who wanted to write poetry found herself facing not only a vast open field awaiting conquest but also a thicket of limits and barriers. The sense of exclusion that countered Elizabeth Barrett's swelling aspirations had little to do with doubts of her own abilities or with worries about the place of a woman poet in the world. On both these questions her courage, her hopes, her ignorance, and the confidence that came from her favored position and evident superiority in the family circle were sufficient to sustain her during her early years. But she had trouble finding her proper relation to poems themselves, a place for herself within them and in the imaginative universe of poetic fictions.

Signs of this radical displacement appear in the earliest literary ex-
perience she ever recorded.

> At four and a half my great delight was poring over fairy phenomenons
> and the actions of necromancers—& the seven champions of Christendom
> in "Popular tales" has beguiled many a weary hour. At five I supposed
> myself a heroine and in my day dreams of bliss I constantly imaged to
> myself a forlorn damsel in distress rescued by some noble knight. (*BC*
> 1:349)

Which was she in these daydreams: the forlorn damsel, or the noble
knight? "I supposed myself a heroine," but "I imaged *to* myself" a damsel
rescued. The knight is more distant—"some noble knight"—and the
fact that the daydreams arose as an escape from weary hours suggests
some identification with the expectant damsel. But she despised senti-
mental young women and the cultivated weakness and passivity that
seemed to be women's lot, and from an early age she wanted to dress
as a boy and run away to be, perhaps, "poor Lord Byron's PAGE" (*LMRM*
2:7)—a daydream of deferring adult sexuality, identification as damsel
or knight. Here, in her earliest daydreams, she hovers between two
mutually exclusive and equally unsuitable literary roles: one precluded
by the need for activity and self-assertion, the other precluded by gender.

The fantasies of ten-year-old Beth show a similar division. Beth wants
to be a warrior armed in steel, singing songs of her own composition
and leading an army down the Danube to rescue Greece, and she also
wants to have hair down to her feet and be "almost as pretty" as Peggy,
the cottager's daughter, and "very much in love" with a poet who will
be called Henry if he is not Lord Byron (*BC* 1:361). She wants to be
both knight and damsel, both poet and poet's beloved; Byron was the
childhood hero of her male contemporaries, too, but for Elizabeth Barrett
he was not only a model to emulate but also a potential lover. It was
many years before she found a story to reconcile the two roles, for even
the dream of becoming the feminine of Homer does not help her find
a place for herself within her fantasies or poems, and it is hard to see
how she can find one so long as she attributes activity and the creation
of poetry to men, and dreaming and waiting to women. It is even harder
to see how, given the kind of stories that fill her imagination and the
literary tradition into which she intends to insert herself, she can imagine
herself as both poet and woman, both the active subject of a poem and
its passive object.

There was an essential lack of congruence between the shapes of her
own experience and the imaginative worlds of the grand tradition running
from Homer to Wordsworth that filled her mind and inspired her constant

emulation: the Homeric heroes engaged in epic conflicts or romantic adventures in which women appeared only as objects of fear or desire; the knights and damsels of romance and their avatars in Romantic poetry; the cultivated masculine society, contemptuous of scribbling women, represented by Pope; and Wordsworth's natural world in which the most significant female presences are his sister, who is subordinate to the poet himself and never speaks, and silent, mysterious Nature. The structure of her own imaginative world was formed from the constellation of family relationships enmeshing a girl in a loving, happy, rich, and rather isolated household in which gender roles were clearly marked and enforced, to the detriment (as she soon perceived) of women. Her sense of herself in relation to other writers, to the genres and subjects of poetry, and to her audience was first formed on the model of her place in her family, and the effort to integrate her own experience with the forms of literature as she knew them challenged and deflected her creative energies for many years. Her experience outside of literature and some mostly epistolary friendships remained almost entirely confined to family life until the advent of Robert Browning in her thirty-ninth year, and her period of maturation as a poet was exceptionally prolonged—except on rare occasions she did not really find her own voice, themes, and poetic forms until she was almost forty. Subjects drawn from family relationships or modelled on them dominate her verse in fairly immediate ways for many years—almost, in fact, forever.

She has little to say, either in letters or in verse, about her mother, whose presence is hardly felt at all in the poetry until after her death in 1828 and even then is generally hidden and inexplicit, glimpsed mostly in the poet's troubled evocations of nature. She wrote to her mother with confident affection, but rarely wrote about her, and could hardly ever bring herself to mention her after her death. But once, in a letter to Robert Browning, she described her in richly suggestive images:

> Scarcely was I woman when I lost *my* mother—dearest as she was & very tender [. . .] but of a nature harrowed up into some furrows by the pressure of circumstances: for we lost more in Her than She lost in life, my dear dearest mother. A sweet, gentle nature, which the thunder a little turned from its sweetness—as when it turns milk—One of those women who never can resist,—but, in submitting & bowing on themselves, make a mark, a plait, within, . . a sign of suffering. Too womanly she was—it was her only fault. (*RB-EBB* 2:1012)

This passage adumbrates the basic mythic structure of her imaginative world—the weak maternal earth, the powerful male heaven—and that this structure was formed very early is apparent from her birthday odes (the writing of which was a family custom) for her parents in 1814. The first, given to her mother on May 1, describes the death of a "wretched Mother" and her "infant Babies," who "died, contented in their Mothers arms," during a winter storm (*BC* 1:11); the unexpressed occasion must have been the death of her three-year-old sister, Mary, a month and a half before. The poem to her father on May 28, in contrast, celebrates (the poet explains) "the recovery of little Arabella [the fourth sister], from a dangerous illness": Death threatened, but God sent an angel to chase Death away (*BC* 1:12–13). A mother embodies nurture and love, but also impotence and death; she is the passive victim of the storm, while the father is allied with power, safety, and God.

Mary Moulton-Barrett's letters show her to have been a lively, clever, sensible woman who was devoted to her children and encouraged her daughter to write. She copied out her childish compositions and sometimes bought and sold them, too, playing at publication. Later she gave eager and thoughtful praise to her properly published works. One of Elizabeth Barrett's first compositions in French was a letter telling her mother that she loved her and wanted to be like her, and in 1817 she dedicated an unpublished poem "to her from whom I have derived the little knowledge I possess" (*BC* 1:39). But Mary Moulton-Barrett could not provide either by precept or by example a coherent model of womanhood suitable for a poet. Instead, her submission to her husband's increasingly tyrannical sway was an example that her daughter pitied, scorned, feared, and for many years—at least outwardly—imitated as well. As a child Elizabeth Barrett despised feminine weakness and harbored "a steady indignation against Nature who made me a woman" (*LMRM* 2:7): for "Nature" here, as Freud has taught us, we can also read, "my mother." For a while her indignation took a political turn: "I used to read Mary Wollstonecraft,—(the 'Rights of woman',) . . when I was twelve years old, & 'quite agreed with her.' Her eloquence & her doctrine were equally dear to me at that time, when I was inconsoleable for not being born a man" (*LMRM* 3:40). In contrast to Wollstonecraft's, her mother's teaching was strangely inconsistent: on the one hand fostering her self-confidence and ambition, and on the other encouraging by example apparently antithetical feminine virtues. She teased her fifteen-year-old daughter good-naturedly and sympathetically about her adherence to Wollstonecraft's "system" and her intention of being an old maid (*BC* 1:132), while she herself was a dutifully subordinate wife who bore twelve children.

In counterbalance with the mother who in her daughter's imaginative life represented love, piety, and submission as well as a covert encouragement to rebellion, Edward Moulton-Barrett embodied power that seemed both oppressive and benign, both hostile and irresistably attractive. "Always he has had the greatest power over my heart," his daughter wrote in 1846, from the other side of the irreparable breach between them, "because I am of those weak women who reverence strong men" (*LEBB* 1:291). He was God the Creator and loving father, and also—increasingly—Jove, whose thunder spoils the milk. Only twenty years old when Elizabeth was born (his wife was four years older), he was a cheerful and affectionate father before time and misfortune hardened him into the infamous domestic tyrant of Wimpole Street. He was most comfortable with his children when they were too young to escape his protective embrace or evade his authority. His fortune derived from a slave plantation in Jamaica, where he had spent the first ten years of his life imbiding a culture of patriarchal autocracy: from her grandmother's companion, Mary Trepsack ("Trippy"), who had lived with the Barretts in Jamaica and thoroughly approved of slavery, Elizabeth heard "infinite traditions of the great grandfather, who flogged his slaves like a divinity" (*RB-EBB* 2:759). The family's slave-owning heritage eventually became hatefully oppressive to her, but it is not clear what she knew or felt about it as a child. It is consistent with the other inconsistencies in Edward Moulton-Barrett's character (and helps to explain his daughter's long loyalty to him) that although he was a great slaveholder he supported the antislavery movement.

He liked to dispose of his family in his own way; he made arrangements for his children's travels, for instance, without consulting or informing his wife, and she did not dare even to ask what he had planned. He was extremely religious, a Congregationalist, and his sublime confidence that his domestic rule was divinely sanctioned no doubt strengthened his apparent likeness in his children's eyes to God. In some very early verses (composed in 1815) Elizabeth Barrett naïvely portrays him as the creator of her world, the fabulously minaretted house and lavishly landscaped estate that were indeed largely his creations.

> These polished walls, raised by y^r tasteful hand,
> These smiling shrubs, these tangled walls & hills;
> These rising rocks,—hewn by your active band
> And drooping flow'rets washed by murmuring rills:
>
> These waters by your hand are taught to glide.

(BC 1:19)

The Morn, she says in similar graceful compliment five years later, welcomes his birthday:

> For half her beauties does she owe
> To him for whom those pillars rise
> Who bade perlucid waters flow
> And waving foliage seek the skies!

> *(BC* 1:93)

While her mother represented a private, inward, hidden world of nurture and mystery, her father stood for—or rather, for many years, stood in place of—the public world which measured, judged, and awarded praise and blame. She thought of her mother as a source of her poetry, her father as its recipient. Both parents were immensely proud of her, but it was her mother who copied her juvenile productions, her father who named her poet laureate of Hope End. In her poems for his birthdays in 1823 and 1824 she attributed the early stirrings of her literary impulse to his promptings and his praise: he "taught my infant fingers first to bear / Th' Aonian lute" *(BC* 1:187), and (changing emblematic instruments a year later) "when the lyre was scarce awake, / I loved its strings for thy lov'd sake. / Woo'd the kind Muses—but the while / Thought only how to win thy smile" *(BC* 1:193–94). Aurora Leigh was to complain that women always have to write with a man in mind *(Aurora Leigh* 5:43–49).

After Elizabeth, the Moulton-Barretts had eleven more children: Edward (called "Bro") in 1807, born when Elizabeth was fifteen months old, Henrietta in 1809, Mary in 1810, Samuel in 1812, Arabella (called "Arabel") in 1813, and then six more boys between 1814 and 1824. Edward Moulton-Barrett sent word that a holiday and distribution of money on the estate in Jamaica should mark his first son's birth, although there is no record of such a celebration for his oldest daughter, and the birth of the third girl occasioned great disappointment *(BC* 1:308, 311). The sisters collectively would have given Elizabeth a sense of female inferiority and vulnerability. Henrietta did not share her elder sister's interests or talents. Mary died at the age of three, the only one of the children who did not live to adulthood, and traces of what must have been a profoundly disturbing experience can probably be found in the uncertain tonalities of her sister's poems on the deaths of little girls and musings on the prospect of dying herself. Arabel lived away from home for much of the time from 1817 to 1820 recovering from illness. Relations between the sisters seem almost always to have been close and affectionate, although as a young woman Elizabeth found Henrietta's conventional ideas and behavior very annoying; but it was Bro who mattered most to her. He was her childhood companion, her second self: they shared interests, pleasures, and affections, she measured and defined herself in contrast to him, and the divergence of the paths that opened to them as they grew older taught her the practical consequences of gender.

For Victorian women of accomplishment, brothers close to them in age were extraordinarily significant, as we see fictionalized by George Eliot in *The Mill on the Floss* and enacted in the lives of Eliot, the Brontës, Harriet Martineau, and Christina Rossetti, as well as Elizabeth Barrett herself. A brother's freedom and opportunities, especially for education, made a girl aware of her own comparatively limited scope: the typical crisis was his departure for school, leaving her desperately yearning for companionship and instruction and resentful of the way his world expanded while hers seemed to contract and empty.[2] A portrait painter who stayed with the Barrett family in 1818 described Elizabeth's "extraordinary genius," "engenuous simplicity," and "airy volatillaty of spirits," observing her to be "idolized by her parents" although in no danger of "being spoilt," and drew the comparison that must have been inevitable throughout her childhood: "Her brother tho by no means difficient has no chance in competition with her" (*BC* 1:319). She made comparisons too, learning to define herself in contradistinction to Bro, and like the painter she saw evidence of her own superiority (although she did not put it quite that way) and differences that did not run along conventional lines of gender. She ruled the nursery unchallenged, since "my dearest Bro tho my constant companion and a beloved participator in all my pleasures never allowed the urge for power to injure the endearing sweetness of his temper" (*BC* 1:349).

She herself was of a more Byronic cast. "I was always of a determined and if thwarted violent disposition" are the opening words of her self-description in "Glimpses into My Own Life and Literary Character" (*BC* 1:349), in which she contemplates with some pride both her success in quelling her passions and their volcanic strength. In an essay written in 1821 entitled "My Character and Bro's Compared!" she attributes solidity, profundity, rationality, and moderation to him, and to herself ardor, enthusiasm, energy, imagination, ambition, and pride. She likes "Poetry Metaphysics & fanciful philosophy"; he prefers history. Both would die for their country, she with "pride indignation and the hope of glory," he with feelings of "honor" and "conscious rectitude" (*BC* 1:357). This comparison is not as straightforward as it may appear, however: the manuscript begins on the same page as a fourteen-line translation from

Anacreon which characterizes Man by his "upright soul" and Woman
by her beauty, and the essay was probably in part a rejection of this
conventional view of gender.[3] Moreover, the virtues she praised in Bro
were not ones she much admired or thought consistent with the poetical
character (Byron being still her poet-hero), although she tried to impose
them on what she felt to be her own dangerously passionate temperament.
Her later assessment of him suggests that she saw in his yielding nature
some of the qualities that disturbed her in her mother: despite his "high
talents," she said after his death, he was "not distinguished among men,
because the heart was too tender for energy" (*LMRM* 1:306).

Apart from the habit of comparison itself, signs of rivalry in her early
writings are rare but not absent. They are elicited by Bro's departure
into the wider world: in a poem lamenting his going off to school which
ominously (he drowned at the age of thirty-three) echoes *Lycidas*, and in
a digressive and melodramatic exhortation in her autobiographical sketch
that he should never "stray from the path of honorable rectitude!" (*BC*
1:354) since she would rather die than hear of his dishonor. This strange
digression (he does not seem to have been inclined to dissipation or
misbehavior) suggests that she is projecting onto him, as a kind of al-
ternate self, her fear of what her own restless and passionate nature
would do if she were allowed to wander freely like a man. She feels so
absolute a difference between a boy's prospects and a girl's that she
imagines him becoming part of the world while she stays home and dies.
One of the first lessons she had learned—in part Byronic posturing,
perhaps, but real and necessary nonetheless—was a self-suppression that
sometimes felt like death.

The difference between girls and boys was most chillingly felt in terms
of education, particularly in the classical languages, which gave access
to the world of power beyond the family. But by seizing every available
opportunity—more than her parents intentionally offered—and applying
herself with steady determination, she managed to override the educa-
tional limits set for girls. Her father forbade her access to such obvious
perils as Gibbon and *Tom Jones*, but it did not occur to him to ban Paine,
Voltaire, Hume, Wollstonecraft, Rousseau, and other difficult but sub-
versive English and French writers whose works she eagerly consumed.
The most extraordinary aspect of her early intellectual life, however, was
her unquenchable passion for Greek, which gave direction to her am-
bition and imaginative coherence to her ideals, her goals, and her ex-
perience. She was enamored—the word is not too strong—of Greek
poetry, especially Homer's; of the ideal of political freedom in ancient

Athens and in modern Greece, where the struggle for liberation was made doubly glamorous by the participation of Byron; and of the classical Greek language. She "had a devil," she said later of her linguistic pertinacity (*LMRM* 2:230), and the characteristic half-humorous exaggeration of her self-descriptions cannot disguise the note of excess both in the descriptions and in what they describe. She imagined Greece itself as a place of noble excess, free effusions of primitive energy: in a draft of a juvenile essay she speaks of the "wild, spontaneous flashes" of Greek genius, of "talent unimpaired & genius unconstrained."[4] Later, in the preface to her translation of *Prometheus Bound,* she describes Aeschylus in terms which match her early descriptions of herself as spontaneous, energetic, and innately rebellious, her passions held down by an iron self-control. Throughout her formative years Greek language, literature, and politics were bound up with most of her major preoccupations, fantasies, fears, and desires.

The language itself had a compelling allure. Education in the classical tongues had been for centuries the gateway both to literary culture and to social and political power, a world that rarely welcomed women. Walter J. Ong describes boys' study of Latin in the Renaissance as a puberty rite designed not only to exclude girls and women but to separate boys from female society and in particular from female language, the mother tongue. In nineteenth-century England at least nominal possession of Latin and Greek marked the higher reaches of power. Since knowledge of Greek was required for matriculation at Oxford and Cambridge, much of secondary education was devoted to attaining it, and some familiarity with the classics was the distinguishing common characteristic of educated men.[5] The fact that it had its own alphabet would have given Greek (like Hebrew, which Elizabeth Barrett taught herself to read some years later) the appeal to a child's eyes of a secret language with a magical key or formula ("open sesame") separating those with access to knowledge and power from those outside the charmed, exclusive circle. Since Elizabeth Barrett's study of Greek was both an incursion into masculine territory and the proof of her right to be there, it is appropriate that Greece for her represented insurgent passion rather than the cool urbanity into which the classical ideal degenerated under the influence of Matthew Arnold.[6]

The exclusion of women from classical studies was made clear even to Elizabeth Barrett, precocious and favored oldest child, by the fact that the only instruction in them that was provided for her came from Bro's tutor, Daniel McSwiney, beginning in 1817 and ending when Bro left for Charterhouse in 1820 and Mr. McSwiney, the job he had been engaged to do completed, left too. Despite her advantages of age and precocity she began studying Latin later than Bro did, and was not enthusiastic about it: "I have begun Latin [. . .]; I do not like it at all, I think it is twice as difficult as French, but I suppose like many stupid things, it is very useful. Poor Bro I believe, has not much more taste for it than I have, but he is now so far advanced in it, as to translate the Latin Bible" (*BC* 1:27). Six months later, however, she was happily learning Greek and looking forward to reading all the great Greek writers. After Mr. McSwiney's departure she worked on by herself, occasionally sending her Greek compositions to Bro at Charterhouse, where Mr. McSwiney, who sometimes visited Bro in London, pointed out errors in them and Bro translated them into Latin when he found time and passed on what he learned at Charterhouse about hexameters.

The efficacy of her self-instruction was such that in 1826 she was able to correspond as an equal with the learned and elderly Uvedale Price on the subject of Greek pronunciation and was welcomed soon afterwards as an exceptionally able correspondent, colleague, and student, although not as an equal, by the scholar Hugh Stuart Boyd. But she felt the inadequacy of her self-teaching. Romney Leigh's patronizing remark that Aurora writes "lady's Greek / Without the accents" (*Aurora Leigh* 2:76–77) adverts to the difference between boys' instruction in the classics and that received by girls, who did not have to pass examinations, and foreshadows the condescension that critics well into the twentieth century have displayed toward Barrett Browning's lack of a schoolboy's training.[7] It is irritating to find her father, many years later, congratulating himself on her unassisted accomplishments and holding them up as an example to one of her younger brothers: "in what snug nook has she obtained all the vast learning & wisdom she posesses—hard work & determined perseverance were her nooks, many a Professor could she dumbfound & what were her advantages—keep her in view & you will go point blank to Helicons Stream—" (*BC* 4:361). Whose fault was her lack of "advantages" but his own?

She makes the link between language and gender clear in her autobiographical essay. Immediately after asserting that her rejection of the "subserviency of opinion which is generally considered necessary to feminine softness" is "not an encroachment on masculine prerogative," she says that "To be a good linguist is the height of my ambition" (*BC* 1:355)—marking by the sequence of ideas the connection between learning Greek and encroaching on male prerogatives. Her linguistic "ambition" (a word always highly charged for her with suggestions of daring and danger) "appears to be innate and rooted in my very nature" (*BC* 1:355). She ascribes it to two motives: vanity, and the thought that knowledge of Greek and Latin would enable her in her literary studies to "come to descision at once on a point which now occupies days in conjecture" (*BC* 1:355), as if language were the magic key to meaning.

> This is tormenting & sometimes agitates me to a painful & almost nervous degree. I well remember three years ago ere I had the advantage of Mr. McSwineys instruction & having found myself entangled in one of these perplexities crying very heartily for half an hour because I did not understand Greek!!!—
>
> It was then I made a secret vow never to pause at undertaking any literary difficulty if convinced of its final utility, but manfully to wade thro the waves of learning stopping my ears against the enchanted voice of the Syren. (*BC* 1:355)

She will have the heroism of Odysseus, "manfully" resisting feminine lures: learning is male, distraction female. And the magic key did indeed open the door to a glorious kingdom, an arduous romance: "To comprehend even the Greek alphabet was delight inexpressible. Under the tuition of Mr. McSwiney I attained that which I so fervently desired. For 8 months during this year I never remember having directed my attentions to any other object than the ambition of gaining fame" (*BC* 1:350–51).

Her ideal of fame, and her first object in the study of Greek literature, was Homer, whom she, like many other eminent Victorians, first encountered in early childhood.[8] For a long time Pope's *Iliad* remained her measure both of poetic excellence and of her own ambition. Beth at the age of ten expected to become "the feminine of Homer" or even a little taller, and Elizabeth Barrett wrote when she was not much older: "Homer I adore as more than human and I never read Popes fine translation without feeling exalted above my self" (*BC* 1:348). But when she compared a composition of her own to Pope's *Iliad* "that I might enjoy my OWN SUPERIORITY," she saw instead her "immense & mortifying inferiority" and wept for an hour (*BC* 1:351). Characteristically, however, mortification led not to discouragement but to more disinterested love and intenser effort: "for a twelvemonth I could find no pleasure in any book but Homer. I read & longed to read again and tho I nearly had it by heart I still found new beauties & fresh enchantments" (*BC* 1:351). Homer became the object of her heroic quest for the beauties and enchantments of romance. She learned Greek "for Homer's sake" (*LMRM*

1:340) and "read Homer in the original with delight inexpressible," tasting "those glorious rewards which I had sought so earnestly" (*BC* 1:352).

Her daydreams of being the female Homer included emancipation from her educational disadvantages. She would no longer be the girl from whom the linguistic key to poetry was withheld, but rather the teacher who resurrected the sounds of the ancient language and made them live again. "When [Beth] grew up she w^d wear men's clothes, & live in a Greek island, the sea melting into turquoises all around it. She w^d teach the islanders the ancient Greek, & they should all talk there of the old glories in the real Greek sunshine, with the right ais & ois" (*BC* 1:361). This commingling of ancient and modern, male and female, writing and speech, land and sea exemplifies the blurring of boundaries, the transcendence of binary oppositions, which to Elizabeth Barrett always meant freedom and power.

Her Hellenism also had a political dimension. She read Greek history and shared the general propensity in late eighteenth- and nineteenth-century Britain to take an historical and political view of the classics. The Homeric poems were almost universally regarded as representing real events, or at any rate a real society, and philhellenic travellers like Byron reported in prose, verse, and drawings on the current state of what Childe Harold called that "haunted, holy ground."[9] Athenian democracy to many (not to all) seemed the glorious prototype of the modern liberal ideal.[10] The political struggle of contemporary Greece for which Byron was to give his life aroused and focussed both her passion for liberty as a political ideal and her probably even more passionate, if to some extent repressed, desire for greater freedom than was allowed to a young girl either presently or in prospect. Sometimes she imagined herself a liberator. Beth planned to "arm herself in complete steel" and ride along the banks of the Danube singing her own poems and attracting an army which would destroy the Turkish empire and deliver Greece. The most important milestones of her early verse—her earliest surviving long poem, her first printed work, and her first publication in a periodical—concern the Greek nation, female weakness, and paternal power.

As a small child she had believed "quite seriously" in the classical gods and (more important) goddesses, especially Minerva, the protector of Athens, and doubts about the reality of "my goddesses" led to some brief skepticism about the Christian deity too (*RB-EBB* 1:392). Her Christian faith revived unimpaired, however, and classical mythology with its abundance of female characters gave her ways to imagine a woman's relationship to the classical world. Her earliest surviving long poem is "The Sorrows of the Muses," written when she was eleven and telling how the muses briefly rebelled against their father Jove's preference of Rome to Greece. This was a preference that Elizabeth Barrett most emphatically did not share, then or later, any more than she had liked learning Latin. When she began studying Greek, she wrote enthusiastically that Greece's glory eclipsed that of Rome (*BC* 1:41), an opinion in which Mr. McSwiney fortunately concurred. She could never make herself appreciate Virgil, whom as a child she scorned as an uninspired plagiarist; she regarded Latin literature as a chilly masculine domain, and Virgil's refusal to let Dido speak in Book VI of the *Aeneid* particularly annoyed her (*LHSB* 22). Her conceptions of Greece and Rome mirror the comparison she drew in 1821 between herself and Bro: she has energy, ambition, pride, and enthusiasm, and loves poetry, while he is reflective, critical, content with mediocrity, and prefers history.[11] In "The Sorrows of the Muses" literary and cultural issues take the shape of the family constellation and the conflict between Greece and Rome is conceived as sibling rivalry: Thalia is Jove's most beloved daughter, but he reminds her that Rome is his son and therefore, apparently, entitled to preeminence. "Rome is my offspring, as fair Greece is thine."[12] The muses' resentment of patriarchal attitudes, however, although intense is easily placated, and they are reconciled to the dominance of the fraternal line by the vague apocalyptic promise that some day Greece will rise again in glory.

The Battle of Marathon, which was the major poetical effort of her childhood, gives a less overt, less perilous version of such rebelliousness. Recently resanctified by Byron, who in the second canto of *Childe Harold's Pilgrimage* (1812) declared it "hallow'd ground" ("As on the morn to distant Glory dear, / When Marathon became a magic word"),[13] Marathon represented triumphant resistance to tyranny, but without any noticeable feminist or unfilial overtones. *The Battle of Marathon* is an Homeric epic in four books written in the style of Pope's *Iliad* and is presumably the work that taught the vainglorious author her inferiority to Homer. The poetry is remarkably good, considering the author's age: the versification is more than competent, the rhythms are varied and interesting, and the story although not very entertaining is well told. Her father, who seems usually to have been most pleased with her translations or imitations of classical or neoclassical texts, the most strikingly precocious and at the same time apparently the most self-effacing of her works, saw nothing subversive in it. He liked it very much, in fact, and arranged for it to be printed when she was fourteen years old. And indeed it seems in every way an act of homage to male values and male culture. "The Sorrows of the Muses" had been dedicated to the poet's mother, "from whom I have derived the little knowledge I possess," but *The Battle of Marathon* is dedicated to her father, "whose admonitions have guided my youthful muse even from her earliest infancy." The mother gives, the father admonishes, and it is the poem for the father that gets into print.

The source of the poet's interest in her subject becomes transparently clear, however, in her lengthy preface. She explains that the appeal of the story is not in its limited set of incidents, but in the feelings it inspires: "Who can be indifferent, who can preserve his tranquillity, when he hears of one little city rising undaunted, and daring her innumerable enemies, in defence of her freedom" (1:6)? She is herself "little" like the (female) city, the child author of what she twice calls a "little Poem" (1:7, 10) although it is actually more than fourteen hundred lines long, "little" only in comparison with a grown-up epic. She herself, one assumes, is asserting her own need for freedom, but she assures her readers that her rebellion is quite innocent, since she is guilty of no "absurd desire of being thought a *genius*" (1:2)—as if she had never secretly dreamed of surpassing Homer. She imitates Homer so closely from timidity, she explains, not temerity: "It would have been both absurd and presump-tuous, young and inexperienced as I am, to have attempted to strike out a path for myself, and to have wandered among the varied windings of Parnassus, without a guide to direct my steps" (1:9). Unlike the protag-onists of her earliest juvenilia, who like to strike out on their own wan-dering paths,[14] she won't leave home alone. The self-protective strategy of hiding ambition under the guise of childishness, which she was to retain long after it was at all appropriate, first appears here. Ambitious women are no longer as vulnerable as they used to be, she says with feeling: "Now, even the female may drive her Pegasus through the realms of Parnassus, without being saluted with the most equivocal of all ap-pellations, a learned lady" (1:2). But she does not present herself as a woman: "how justly then may a child hope to pass unheeded" (1:3). The safest position to take in relation to an audience, she evidently felt now and for a long time afterward, was the one she was most used to, that of a precocious but docile daughter.

But the story she tells has no place for a daughter, or for any girl or woman, except in the epic machinery, remnants of her belief in the Greek pantheon—which explains why there is so much of it. The only women in *The Battle of Marathon* besides some Athenian matrons, who are quickly dismissed as impediments to valor, are Minerva and Venus, representative of two types of womanhood and rivals for their father's love. As in "The Sorrows of the Muses," god is explicitly the father—or rather, perhaps, the father is god. Minerva is warlike, manlike, the defender of Greek freedom; Venus, the goddess of love whose function is to please men, resists freedom on her son's behalf. Although the author asserts in her preface that the epic poet "must suppose himself to be the hero he delineates" (1: 8), it is hard to find anyone in her poem whom she might have supposed herself to be except Minerva (or perhaps Aristides, who politely defers to his elders and consequently has quite a small role). Throughout the preface, in fact, both poet and readers are apparently assumed to be male. She would have sympathized with any young man who was willing to die for his country, a fate she found attractive. Both she and Bro, she wrote in 1821, "would sacrifice our happiness our lives for our beloved country," and she was sure that when she laid her head on the block her soul would swell with "pride indignation and the hope of glory" (*BC* 1:357). Like Christina Rossetti's protagonist in "The Lowest Room," however, she finds no place in Homer's world for an heroic woman. And so her imaginative identification is political and impersonal, not with any particular character but with the struggle of ancient and modern Greece (in her later works it will be Italy) for independence.

The woman or feminine element in her fantasy of Greece is usually Greece itself, conceived as a kind of primal mother or a woman in need of rescue. Although Homer's Greece was regarded in the nineteenth century as a very real place, where civic and manly virtue and political liberty first began, it was also the mythic, magical southern land where the arts were born, mother of beauty and cradle of dreams. The protagonists of "The Sorrows of the Muses" are beautiful young women, and their country includes "fair Arcadia Pans profuse domain / A vale of sweets."[15] For Elizabeth Barrett, Greece was a damsel in distress awaiting deliverance by an armed hero—or rather, by a hero-poet, like Byron—and in her fantasies she herself was the rescuer, Beth delivering "Greece the glorious." In her first poem to be actually published rather than privately printed—"Stanzas, Excited by Some Reflections on the Present State of Greece," which appeared in the *New Monthly Magazine* when she was fifteen—Greece is both a child to whom the speaker will sing her "glory's lullaby" and a mother who has failed the child she had once even in her fallen state inspired to dreams of glory: "Mother of arts, and arms, and liberty! / A lovely corse encircled by a wreath / Of faded flowers" and "beauteous [. . .] e'en in death."[16]

Feminized but less overtly political versions of Greece provide the background for two unpublished early poems in the tradition of second-generation Romanticism, "The Enchantress" and "Leila," which take place in the country neither of Pope's Homer nor of nationalist politics but of nymphs, minstrels, corsairs, and islands set in a turquoise sea. All that we have of "The Enchantress" is what appears to be the introduction to a quasi-mythological tale, told in lush Spenserian stanzas (Byron's stanza also), of two beautiful maidens who are about to have an unfortunate experience on an Aegean island. This island is a place of female youth, pleasure, love, and beauty that, unlike anything else in Elizabeth Barrett's works, might provide a setting for the Sapphic strain in Greek art that compelled the imaginations of such poets as Swinburne and H.D. "Leila: A Tale," also in Spenserian stanzas and acknowledging the evident influence of Byron and Campbell in its epigraphs, tells what it means for a girl to lose (as in "The Enchantress") her father's rule and protection.[17] Leila is the motherless child of a corsair who loves her passionately and had encouraged her to manly virtues; but now, grown from "sportive" youth and wearing "woman's downcast gaze" (I.x), she finds his presence oppressive although necessary to her "bliss" (I.xi). In his absence she discovers that he is holding captive a young minstrel and the minstrel's warlike father, who has only scorn for his delicate son. She befriends the minstrel and frees the father, who promptly kills the returned corsair and vanishes into the sea. The girl and the minstrel, two halves of a woman poet (rather than, as the situation and setting would lead one to expect, potential lovers), have caused the destruction of their brutally masculine fathers. Although they die too—the minstrel of weakness and Leila of remorse—this gloomy outcome is perhaps more encouraging for poets than that of Matthew Arnold's *Sohrab and Rustum,* which also questions crude equations of poetry with effeminacy; in Arnold's poem, the heroic father, falsely believing that his only child had been a daughter, kills his delicate but heroic son. Elizabeth Barrett uses a Greek setting and the most banal materials of a Romantic love story for a rebellion against the dominion of the fathers to which overtly, as in the preface to *The Battle of Marathon,* she willingly submits.

Her dream of female heroism and a female paradise is located mostly in Greece, but heroines (aside from various little girls in her earliest juvenilia) appear in different contexts in some other early unpublished poems too. The first is the singer Catalani, who escaped the convent to which poverty rather than piety had consigned her by being trained to sing. In "Regulus," a brief tragedy written in French when she was about ten years old, the wife and daughter of a captured Roman general die

from sheer sympathy with his misfortune, and a similar family constel-
lation appears in a sketch of scenes between Caroline of Brunswick and
her daughter. Elizabeth Barrett, like Byron, was an ardent partisan for
Caroline during her trial on charges of sexual misconduct brought by
supporters of her husband, George IV. In her dramatization the falsely
accusing husband-father-king is entirely absent; like Regulus, he is merely
the occasion for mother and daughter to express their sorrow, love, and
heroic fortitude. In accordance with Elizabeth Barrett's lifelong habit of
associating geography with gender and imagining England as male and
Greece and Italy (but not ancient Rome) as female, Catalani is Italian
and most of Caroline's misbehavior occurred in Italy.[18]

The female presences that dominate her unpublished early works
almost never appear in her first publications, however, except as Greece
itself. This is less, apparently, a matter of will than of incapacity to imagine
women to fit the classical and neoclassical molds in which her public
poetry was cast. In "Fragment of an 'Essay on Woman,' " written around
1822, she complains in Popean couplets that the Poet sings only of Man.
She blames life, however, not poetry, admitting that female virtues are
insufficiently exalted for the lyre's praise. She therefore sets herself the
task of inspiring women to more ambitious virtues, for "why must woman
to be loved be weak?"[19]—a question she was still angrily pondering when
she wrote *Aurora Leigh*. Her doubt that women can exert themselves
effectively is tellingly if inadvertently revealed by the fact that the "Frag-
ment" itself is addressed to men. There have been women of genius,
she says, but the multinational list of examples with which the poem
breaks off is touchingly far-fetched and uninspiring: Anna Comnena (a
Byzantine physician), Anna Dacier (a French translator of Homer), the
English didactic writer Hannah More, and Madame de Staël, none of
whom could have aroused in her a very passionate enthusiasm. It was
easier to conceive the possibility of female greatness in the mythical
distance of Greece.

Her own life was increasingly unprovided not only with heroic pos-
sibilities but even with literary companionship. Unlike the Brontës or the
Rossettis or the Tennysons, the Barretts were not a generally gifted family;
unlike Emily Dickinson or Matthew Arnold, she had no sympathetic
schoolmates or friends. Bro was no match for her, and in any event went
off to school. Her childhood, she told Robert Browning in 1845, was
isolated and eventless:

> I grew up in the country . . had no social opportunities, . . had my heart
> in books & poetry, . . & my experience, in reveries. My sympathies drooped

towards the ground like an untrained honeysuckle—& but for *one* [Bro]
[. . .] It was a lonely life—growing green like the grass around it. Books
and dreams were what I lived in—& domestic life only seemed to buzz
gently around, like the bees about the grass. And so time passed, and
passed. (*RB-EBB* 1:41)

Despite the pastoral charm of this description, she felt with some bit-
terness that seclusion had made her "in a manner, as a *blind poet*" (*RB-
EBB* 1:41), and from a notebook that she kept from 1824 to 1826 it
appears that she had similar sentiments even then: "I am more & more
convinced that an unagitated life is not the life for a Poet. His mind
should ever & anon be transplanted like a young tree. It should be allowed
to shoot its roots in a free soil, & not vegetate in a corner. Look at the
lives of our great Poets—Shakespeare's, Milton's, Byron's,—& find the
truth of this."[20]

What was happening to her during these apparently uneventful years
is not easy to discern. None of her letters to Bro at Charterhouse survive,
and the relatively few letters that we do have reveal her feelings only
rarely and by indirection. Afterwards she recalled her life at Hope End
as an idyll of pastoral innocence, in terms that screen more than they
reveal. But it is clear that like many other talented and ambitious Victorian
girls she found the passage from childhood to womanhood extremely
difficult, as poems like "Leila" indicate. For her as for others, including
many of Freud's first patients, the psychological crisis was also a somatic
one. When she was fifteen, Elizabeth, Henrietta, and Arabel all fell ill.
Her sisters recovered, but she did not. She was in great pain, it was
feared that she would die, and she was sent for medical treatment to
Gloucester, where she remained for almost a year. Bro had embarked
on a man's career, and she, it seemed, on a woman's.

Her illness was attributed in the family to a spinal injury connected
with riding her pony—that is, to the kind of tomboyish physical activity
that the illness put an end to. One is inclined now to think it the kind
of hysterical phenomenon studied by Freud which afflicted intelligent
Victorian women: Anna O., for instance, like Elizabeth Barrett was strongly
attached to a dominating father and had a striking gift for languages.[21]
There may have been some such suggestion at the time, too: the doctors
were puzzled for a diagnosis, and the single ill-tempered letter from
Elizabeth Barrett to her parents in all of her surviving correspondence
protests angrily against the suggestion that she could get better if she
really tried.

When my dearest Mama I promised to exert myself I spoke sincerely and the promise I made I intended to keep. If it were possible believe me that any mental exertion could shake off bodily torture it should be effected without reluctance as without hesitation. I HAVE exerted all my energy all my locomotive intellects all the muscular power of MIND and I HAVE found that though in some degree bodily anguish may be repressed from AP-PEARING yet it has failed to be overcome. (*BC* 1:127–28)

In fact, however, it was almost certainly a serious organic illness.[22]

Whatever the causes, the consequences were clear enough. An illness need not be neurotic in origin to serve psychological functions.[23] She was separated from her family and apparently did not see her mother at all during her absence from home, although her father visited her. "I do not wish to return home my dearest Mama till I am well" (*BC* 1:128), she wrote in her indignant letter, and her wishes would not have been consulted anyway. A long, close brush with death—her birthday ode to Henrietta for 1822 makes sentimental play with thoughts of death and is subtitled in her fair copy, "Written on the prospect of recovering from a dangerous illness" (*BC* 1:150)—left the possibility of dying always imaginatively present to her thereafter. As a child she had been bold and energetic, but after this she was always more or less fragile physically, her health a perennial object of concern. The child who had dreamed of adventurous activity was becoming a damsel in need of a rescuing knight. The year of illness marked the first stage of the change from a lively, active, self-confident child to a shy, reclusive invalid which con-stituted in her life the outward form of growing up. It is suggestively like the still more drastic disruption of development in Christina Rossetti, who was stricken with a mysterious illness when she was about fourteen and emerged from adolescence having changed, in the words of a recent biographer, "from a passionate, confident child to a repressed and reticent adult," her physical health permanently impaired.[24] Mary Moulton-Bar-rett's encouragement of her daughter's writing is now tempered by worry: in a birthday poem for 1822, she praises her daughter's patience under suffering as worth more than "the charm of genius' magic spell" (*BC* 1:152), and she urges her not to sacrifice her health to extended hours of study (*BC* 1:229). Illness provided both an escape from familial con-finement and an intensification of it, simultaneously taking her away from home and curtailing her ability to act.

More generally, the process of separation from home and family kept an uneven course. About a month after her return from Gloucester in 1823 the family left Hope End for more than half a year's stay in Boul-

ogne, where she perfected her French and was, she said later, happy.
After about six months back at Hope End, she and Henrietta spent the
summer of 1824 in Cheltenham with maternal relatives, and the following
summer the two sisters went to visit their paternal grandmother in Has-
tings for what turned out, for no reason one can see except their father's
iron whim, to be a stay of eleven months. There is no evidence that she
particularly enjoyed any of these visits except the one to Boulogne. At
home, too, she seems to have been less cheerful than before. Bro fre-
quently complains that she does not write to him, and sacred family
tradition annoys her: "I can't bear writing birthday letters" (*BC* 1:173),
wrote the laureate of Hope End in her birthday letter to Henrietta for
1823. Her mother was still having babies more or less biennially, the last
three in 1820, 1822, and 1824, and was more subservient than ever to
her husband. Elizabeth resented her father's habit of keeping his plans
for his children's movements "as inscrutable as if we had all been truants
and adhered to the fourth form" (*BC* 1:235)—as if, that is, she had
deliberately refused to take the road through school to manhood. She
was outgrowing the relations of childhood, but the way to adulthood was
far from clear.

   She led her own life in books, without friends or mentors with whom
to discuss what she read. A record of her reading from 1824 to 1826
shows her working in several directions at once and preparing to write
"An Essay on Mind." She read (among many other things) Hume and
Locke, books on Fox, Pitt, the British Constitution, and Napoleon (ac-
cording the two latter equal enthusiasm), Dunlop's *History of Fiction*,
Southey's *Book of the Church*, Sophocles' *Ajax*, Mary Shelley's *Franken-
stein*, and books on modern Greece. She still thought a lot about Byron,
the poet to whom she felt the greatest affinity—on a list of books she
would like to acquire Byron's works appears first, and she objects to
Madame de Genlis's way of speaking of him—but she begins her en-
thusiastic comments on his poem "The Island" by noting that "The
expression Where summer years & summer women smile! is rather de-
rogatory to the sex!"[25] She read lives and memoirs of such diverse persons
as Marie Antoinette, whom she found a lovable woman and a merely
unfortunate queen, Benvenuto Cellini, Madame de Genlis (in eight vol-
umes), and a Miss Hawkins, whose three volumes struck her as coarse
and unwomanly. She was deeply moved by Cowper's *Letters*, but went
through numerous miscellaneous works of poetry and fiction (almost all
now thoroughly forgotten) without finding much to praise. She cares

about style, about characters of women in fiction and in life, and—over and over again, in all sorts of contexts—about the possible reconciliation of such oppositions as matter and spirit, poetry and philosophy, and perhaps, underlying this, male and female. Similarly, an undated commonplace book opens with an excerpt from Coleridge's *The Friend* on the theme that "Every power in Nature & in spirit must evolve an opposite as the sole means & condition of its manifestation: and all opposition is a tendency to re-union."[26] This concern to reconcile polarities was eventually to issue in the grand reconciliation of poetry and philanthropy, male and female, that concludes *Aurora Leigh*.

She liked the poetry in the *Literary Souvenir* for 1826, especially Letitia E. Landon's "The Forsaken" and Felicia Hemans's "Shipwreck." The living writer who aroused her most intense attention at this time was Landon (known as L.E.L.), who seemed to be claiming the place as first of woman poets which Mrs. Hemans had occupied and to which she herself had aspired. While she was too old now to acknowledge such ambition, she was not too old to feel it. It was an auspicious moment for a new poet. Very little good poetry appeared in the 1820s: Keats, Shelley, and Byron died early in the decade, Wordsworth and Coleridge had pretty much fallen silent, and Tennyson and Browning were still very young. L.E.L.'s thin, fluent Byronism was exceedingly popular, particularly among young men at the universities who admired the unknown poetess with a romantic extravagance that makes one think of Max Beerbohm's Zuleika Dobson.[27] Elizabeth Barrett traces her response to L.E.L.'s swelling reputation with a degree of elaboration, self-consciousness, and uneasiness aroused in her by no other writer and with an acute consciousness of issues of gender. At first she had thought that L.E.L. was overrated, her admiring critics "transformed into swine without a Circe," and "her fair self a very ordinary, poetry-writing young Lady."[28] Then she had seen an attack in the *Westminster Review* which must have struck home hard to her own self-concerns: it derided the *Literary Gazette* for ranking L.E.L. above all poets living or dead, including Homer and Shakespeare—whereas, Elizabeth Barrett says indignantly, the *Literary Gazette* had only said that "by the dint of cultivation she may surpass in practical genius all *female* writers whose works have yet been given to the world!!"[29] In fact, however, the *Literary Gazette*, which regularly published and puffed L.E.L.'s poems, did *say*, whatever the effusive reviewer may have *meant:* "we can adduce no instance, ancient or modern, of similar talent and excellence."[30] Elizabeth Barrett agrees that L.E.L. could be the best of women poets if she would cultivate her powers of execution and write about something besides love.

She seems to be moved, if not by unacknowledged rivalry, at least by a need to assess her competition; by a painful awareness of the gulf between Homer and a female Homer, sharpened by the crude journalistic echo of her own childish ambition; and by a feeling of kinship with an ambitious woman poet who has been unfairly attacked. It is noteworthy that she later defends L.E.L. for what was often criticized in her own verse, the irregularity of her rhymes, which was the chief technical means by which Elizabeth Barrett was to try to make English poetry new, and cites L.E.L.'s example as justification for her own use of double rhymes (*LMRM* 2:43). Inferior as she rightly thought her, she nonetheless felt that her real rival was L.E.L., not Homer or Byron or even Mrs. Hemans, whom she considered too ladylike and deficient in passion to be seriously reckoned with. Some of her works, especially the unpublished "Leila," invite such comparison, although they are immeasurably richer and more interesting than her predecessor's. And her major pieces, like "An Essay on Mind," define themselves, no doubt quite deliberately, as entirely different from the popular writings of women poets.

2

The Development of Genius

An Essay on Mind, with Other Poems (1826) is Elizabeth Barrett's first
 real book, her first serious attempt to address the world as a
poet and find her own voice. It is her threshold volume. But
she stands irresolutely on the threshold, casting anxious glances
behind her, eager yet fearful to cross. The book looks both
ways and is full of contradictions. "An Essay on Mind" asserts
by its manner and matter alike that the author is an adult
treating on equal terms with great thinkers of past and present.
Its dominant voice is impersonal, self-confident, and often
witty: the voice, one might say in Wordsworth's phrase (if not
quite as Wordsworth meant it), of "a man speaking to men."[1]
Elsewhere, however, we hear a young woman who has not yet
emerged from childhood expressing in personal, uncertain
tones her doubts about her vocation.

She hopes for fame, and she fears it. The book is obsessed
with the desire to make her name known, although (like the
first books of Tennyson, Browning, and Arnold) it was pub-
lished anonymously, and it ends with a depiction of the ap-
palling emptiness of Fame. By the fact that it was published
rather than privately printed, it marked her emergence from
the role of poet laureate of Hope End, writing for a small
family circle, although the expenses of publication were paid
by her grandmother's companion, Miss Trepsack. The poems
betray no doubt of her ability to cross the threshold into the
public world and achieve public recognition for work on mat-
ters of serious public concern, but they express considerable
uncertainty about her will to do so. Both within individual
poems and as an ill-assorted whole the book is racked with
conflict about being a poet at all.

We find no such uncertainty, however, in "An Essay on

Mind," a work of remarkable self-confidence for a woman of twenty—
"pertness and pedantry," she called it later with typical retrospective self-
denigration (*LRHH* 160)—offering a bold survey of different kinds of
mental activity (history, physics, metaphysics, poetry) that culminates in
a celebration of poetry. Its heroes are Locke and Byron, linked as eman-
cipators of the mind and spirit from tyrannical external systems. Her
ringingly assertive manner produces stronger praise than she was willing
to defend in cold prose: Locke "is neither 'first in my heart nor noblest
in my song',—and I cannot conceive why I should have said so," she
wrote later (*LHSB* 38), and she excused her adulation of Byron by saying
that "his errors of faith and his errors of conduct" were well enough
known not to need mentioning (*LHSB* 39). Her childish enthusiasm for
Byron as poet and liberator had been moderated somewhat—not much—
by a reluctant acknowledgment of his improprieties. The verse shame-
lessly imitates Pope, but it is a lively and competent imitation, and its
wit and energy can generally carry a reader interested in Elizabeth Bar-
rett's poetic and intellectual development fairly comfortably along.

That development is what interests her, too. By publishing such a
poem, she means to take her place in the intellectual world. As she
modestly explains in the preface, she chose her vast subject not from
"presumption" but because "the subject supports the writer, as much
as it is supported by him" (1:55–56).[2] Her object is most naively shown
in the passage on the kinds and development of "Genius," in which she
must implicitly have been measuring her own precocity against others'.
The tone, derived from Pope and Horace, aspires to be—and often is—
witty, sophisticated, cultivated, and elegant. Weighty matters are treated
in a tone of easy allusiveness that supposes an audience of educated men
(the introductory summary explains, for instance, that part two begins
with "an address to Metaphysicians") and suggests that the writer is
claiming a place among them. It is all the more necessary for her to
assert such a claim, moreover, because the audience is apparently male:
she speaks of and to "Man," and the word carries its full weight of
gender. The poem continuously draws on the classical culture that bound
educated men together, and there is no hint that the writer is not a "man"
too. Many individual men are mentioned, but women appear only as
personifications, and the feminine element is represented by Nature, who
is compared to Milton's narcissistic Eve delightedly seeing her own
"sportive graces, and untutored ways" (977) in the waters: woman as
the unthinking subject of poetry, that is, not its serious and tutored author.
In a similar vein, she began some early notes for the preface by describing

the poem as a "formidable" Rinaldo coming into Armida's garden of imaginative and descriptive poetry.[3]

And yet the qualities that enable her to condescend, as she quite magnificently does, to all the great thinkers she mentions are fully compatible with femininity. She is a Christian, she is (she implies, although her tone may make one wonder) humble, and she is a poet; as such, she can take a higher ground than the men on whose limitations she loftily expatiates. Intellectual work, the poem everywhere suggests (and this seems to accord with her own experience), is exciting but not very difficult. What *is* difficult is recognizing one's own weakness and God's power. But while this was too hard for Gibbon, Buffon, and Leibniz, it should be well within the scope of a nineteenth-century woman. Poetry, furthermore, goes beyond Philosophy: "where Philosophy would fear to soar, / Young Poesy's elastic steps explore" (900–901). Poets with faith to guide them can see, and make others see, what Philosophy can only reason to: "Poesy's whole essence [. . .] / Is elevation of the reasoning mind" (944–45). Poetry is associated with youth and faith, qualities that she possesses but the men of mind do not. Gathering conviction and intensity, the poem moves to the matters she cared most about—Greece, freedom, Byron—and becomes unabashedly personal as she recalls her childhood passion for Greece. It ends by urging the modest hope of leaving

> Some page our country's grateful eyes may scan;
> Some useful truth to bless surviving man;
> Some name to honest bosoms justly dear;
> Some grave t' exalt the thought, and claim the tear.

> (1255–58)

The poem attempts to show that she can do this. The faith she expresses in the absolute preeminence of poetry and its congruence with youth and femininity buttressed the self-confidence that she felt, all her life long, when she thought of herself as a poet.

But the miscellaneous lyrics that make up the rest of the volume show a backward-turning impulse quite different from this modest self-confidence, a nostalgia for early childhood and a fear of growing up that is sometimes explicit and sometimes implied by a strange childishness that forms an astonishing contrast to "An Essay on Mind." Most of them were written before the "Essay," and the fact of publishing them is a reversion to the childishness they display. The first three are revisions of early ones written for family occasions, spoken not by the authoritative speaker of "An Essay on Mind" who takes all knowledge as her province and addresses a large audience of cultivated men, but by the poet laureate of Hope End. Even so, they are addressed only to male members of the family and wistfully recall "th' enchanted world" of her childhood, when she wrote poetry to please her father ("To My Father on His Birthday") and Bro had not yet gone to school. As in many of her poems of the next two decades, the nostalgia springs from regret for lost energies, freedom, hope, and ambition, and for the almost limitless possibilities that had seemed to glimmer before her when she was a child. She dreads the future, which she can imagine only as bringing further loss, and yearns for the comfort of the past. The past is both beautiful and—being itself dead—deathly, a fatal woman whom she nonetheless takes as her muse ("The Past"). "The Dream: A Fragment" moves back in time through Greece to Eden, but Eden vanishes too and leaves only a world spoiled by sin.

When she turns from the past to the future, what she sees besides the loss of happiness is the dubious prospect of fame. Her hesitation about crossing the threshold into poetic maturity focusses on the question of fame and more particularly on naming and being named. As with other nineteenth-century women poets, her version of what was to become a central obsession of Victorian poetry—the fear that art and love are mutually exclusive alternatives—centers here.[4] The question is not whether she can achieve poetic glory, but whether she should even try. She takes for granted as she had since early childhood the immense desirability of fame, but now she nervously counts the cost and wonders if it is not better to be remembered for love instead. "An Essay on Mind" hopefully celebrates a kind of union of the two, fame for writing poems that help one's country and win its grateful affection, but her belief in the public beneficence of poetry did not purge her doubts about her own ambition.

In the nineteenth century fame was frequently associated with loneliness and moral failure, and "ostentatious withdrawal" (in Leo Braudy's phrase) was not an uncommon pose. The two great early nineteenth-century exemplars of fame were the two men who most fascinated Elizabeth Barrett, Byron and Napoleon, and both of them were noted, as she was, for exaggerated shyness on social occasions.[5] Among women, withdrawal was much more frequent. A man who became a poet in the Victorian period might seem to be making a potentially dangerous retreat from the public world into a private, inner space of art, but a woman made an even more dangerous incursion from the private sphere into the public one. Insofar as fame meant publicity or self-display, further-more, it seemed unladylike, almost indecent, for a woman, with overtones of sexual self-exposure that had reverberated for earlier women poets too and become explicit in Elizabeth Barrett's later writings.[6] In the 1820s, however, ambition for fame frightened her more simply as a kind of aggression. She habitually associated it with struggles for freedom and rebellion against tyranny, which in the structure of her imaginative world meant on some level rebellion against her father. At the bottom of a sheet of paper on which she had listed facts about writers and instances of their precocity (presumably to measure herself against them and to use in "An Essay on Mind") she added some striking words: "Callimachus's epitaph on his Father" (Anthologia) where he represents the old man as speaking from the tomb & desiring to be known only as the father of Callimachus."[7] Fame, that is, means usurping the dead father's voice and suppressing his name. Self-liberation would displace her father in one way, and since she habitually defined him (not quite accurately) as her first and best audience, fame would displace him in another. She wards off this danger in the first of the miscellaneous poems, "To My Father on His Birthday," which harks back to the Edenic time when her "proud-est fame" (39) was in his praise and assures him that he is still her "best Maecenas" (44) and that his approbation is the object of the verse she is writing now. In this book obsessed with naming, she names her father first.[8]

When the context is safely unfamilial and distant, however, she can celebrate fame with unimpeded ardor and examine its meaning for women. The volume has three heroes: Byron, a Greek patriot called Riga, and the widow of a Spanish patriot, called simply "Riego's Widow." Byron, Riga, and Riego, poets who died in struggles for national liberation, accord with Beth's daydream of leading an army against the Turks while singing her own songs. Their stories allow her to submerge private mo-tives into public themes, as her later political poems do, and Byron's use of his immense, unprecedented fame to further the cause of liberty and national independence was to become the model for her own later career. As in "An Essay on Mind," Byron is both a great poet and a "great Deliv'rer" (7), on whom both love and fame attended, admired alike for his "generous heart" ("Stanzas on the Death of Lord Byron"), his writ-ings, and his deeds.[9] Riga sings a bold defiance of tyranny on the verge of his execution. But the third hero, Riego's Widow (the only woman in the entire volume aside from the poet herself and personifications of the Past, Nature, and Fame) is only indirectly a rebel and martyr and is not a poet at all. The poem about her is called "On a Picture of Riego's Widow: Placed in the Exhibition"; she is a work of art, not an artist, and while works of art may be expressive, they do not act or speak. In contrast to her husband, a flamboyant popular leader and author of a popular revolutionary song in the Spanish Revolution of 1820, she shows her defiance of tyranny not by proclaiming her feelings but by concealing them: *his* "dying lips gave a free sound" (27), but *her* "calm lip" in the picture "gives no wail" (4). "Silent" (33), "voiceless" (35), and proud, telling her agony only to God, she is a Byron who cannot speak.

Does the poet imagine herself as Riego, or Riego's Widow? Throughout the volume, she is uncertain whether she wants to name or be named: does fame mean speaking or being spoken of, is she the immortalizing poet or the woman whom poets immortalize? For the first time but not the last we see her faced in poetry as well as fantasy with the problem of choosing between complementary gendered roles, the poet's and the woman's. In "The Prayer," she goes so far as to desire an early death so that those to whom her name is dear will outlive her: rather than sing, she says, she wants to die like a song. In "Memory" she imagines her brother grown up and pausing to remember childhood scenes and incidentally her love: "My name, perchance, may haunt the spot" (42)—like Wordsworth's Lucy, who dies so that, for the poet, nature can live.

And the volume ends with a massive display of ambivalence called "A Vision of Fame," in which the poet invites the reader to join her in wholesome thoughts of a pastoral world (suggesting that she herself, of course, is entirely simple and unambitious), and then tells how she dreamed of a beautiful woman who celebrates and personifies fame: who, like a woman, is what she sings. Fame is better than love, she says, because without fame one is forgotten when those who love one die. But the price is youth: at the end of her song the beautiful woman is revealed as a skeleton. Other poems link a larger audience with emergence from childhood, but this one suggests that the desire for fame actually causes the loss of childhood—or, one might say less sympathetically, growing up. The poet anxiously assures us again that she herself does not need to learn this lesson: "She did not sing this chant to me" (73). But the lesson strikes home, and the last words of this initiatory volume are a palinode for the ambition that produced it:

> Alas, alas! I wended home
> With a sorrow and a shame—
> Is Fame the rest of our poor hearts?
> Woe's me! for THIS is FAME.

We can see traces of ambivalence even in the quality of the verse in which she first tentatively reaches out for fame, drawing on traditions as disparate as Popean didacticism and female sentimentalism and veering between grandly impersonal and intensely personal kinds of utterance. The miscellaneous poems show more signs of an original mind and sensibility than "An Essay on Mind" does, but less sustained competence and control and much more unevenness of self-presentation and tone. The didactic impulse and confident expansiveness of the "Essay" remain with her throughout her career, as do the exhortatory tone and the tendency to explain things to her readers and tell them what to think, feel, and do. The self-examination and self-reflexiveness of some of the other verses also anticipate her mature work. But the poems are tonally and stylistically marred, by archaisms, inversions, an overabundance of italics and exclamation marks for emphasis, awkward syntax and diction, and such stock sentimental idioms as the ruined joys, broken heart, and sacred tears of Riego's Widow.[10] The best moments generally come in quatrains, which can sometimes move rapidly and surely, and in wittily intellectualized expressions of feeling that sound both impersonal and deeply felt.

The one short lyric shows some of the volume's faults and most of its virtues, as well as its characteristic drift from moderate hope to apparently inexorable gloom.

> Weep, as if you thought of laughter!
> Smile, as tears were coming after!
> Marry your pleasures to your woes;
> And think life's green well worth its rose!
>
> No sorrow will your heart betide,
> Without a comfort by its side!
> The sun may sleep in his sea-bed,
> But you have starlight overhead.
>
> Trust not to Joy! the rose of June,
> When opened wide, will wither soon;
> Italian days without twilight
> Will turn them suddenly to night.
>
> Joy, most changeful of all things,
> Flits away on rainbow wings;
> And when they look the gayest, know,
> It is that they are spread to go!
>
> ("Song")

Her parents greeted the publication of *An Essay on Mind* with pride and delight, but her mother found the book's extravagant renunciations of ambition somewhat disturbing. The poet's ambivalence was appropriately mirrored in her parents' responses to "A Vision of Fame," which was a particular favorite with her father but stung her mother, whose admiration was otherwise unqualified, to protest: "surely, of all mundane things, justly deserved literary fame, is the most lasting . . . & tho' I much admire the *humility* of the last musical stanza, I think there is more of melancholy in it, than the subject justifies—& it must be acknowledged, that throughout the vol: you leave no corner, wherein poor Earthly Vanity can comfort herself" (*BC* 1:236). Her next major effort perhaps reflected the influence of this encouraging rebuke, given as it is in a voice—sensible, affectionate, gently ironical—very much like her own.

The new project, which she labored over for many months and referred to as "my work respecting the development of genius" (*BC* 1:358), was unlike anything in the volume she had just published. In the preface to *The Battle of Marathon* she had hastened to disavow any absurd desire of being thought a "genius" (1:2), but her temerity was growing. This poem picks up the underlying theme of "An Essay on Mind" to explore a thoroughly Romantic subject—genius rather than intellect, the alienated artist—and speaks in a voice with affinities not to Pope and Horace, although it has Popean moments, but to Romanticism and especially to Byron. The speaker is dramatized as a young man who is unloved at home and therefore wants to wander:[11] the opposite and yet true image of Elizabeth Barrett's restlessness in a household where she felt increasingly constrained and misunderstood. The surviving fragments deal with two main themes, self-expression and ambition, drawing on depths of consciousness that earlier published poems had not approached, the realms of dream and nightmare, and recoiling in almost hysterical moral revulsion. At first the speaker asserts that his experience is representative—"*I* am man!" (1:37)—and as such, interesting and edifying. "I thus unbare / [My heart] unto you, the which ye share— / And bid you meditate your own in mine" (1:49–51). This is the great Romantic credo: in the phrase Keats quoted from Wordsworth, "we have all one human heart."[12]

Perhaps, the poet seems to be thinking, the community of men she had sought in the "Essay" can be found more intimately and with less effort of impersonation; and yet she proffers intimate self-revelation as a male impersonator. "I speak to you, my brothers! come and lay / Your hands upon this pulsing heart of clay" (1:43–44). For this unnervingly concrete and histrionic invitation to be decent, it has to assume the common masculinity of speaker and audience. And the cry for self-exposure—baring the heart to be touched and handled—is immediately followed, as if through the reflux of its own physicality, by an astonishingly violent call to suppress all impulses ungrateful to God:

> Quench we those eyes that burnt with evil thought—
> Chain we those hands whereby ill deeds were wrought—
> Bind we that tongue whereon the falseness sate.
>
> (58–60)

The only fit subject for poetry is the soul, since the maternal earth lives only in a false mythology and nature is fallen like man. But the poet shudderingly imagines the pain that would attend full awareness of one's own life or others' (3:1–36), in a passage that is both reminiscent of Pope's warning that with too great perceptivity we might "Die of a rose in aromatic pain" and proleptic of George Eliot's sense of the terror of hearing the squirrel's heart beat.[13] What she really fears, however, is sin, not just intensity of pleasure or pain—such intensity being in itself, evidently, sinful—and in another fit of revulsion she reverts to the idiom of Pope to mock Romantic self-revelation and gross voyeuristic appetites: "Show us the soul!—insatiate readers cry— / Behold the soul!—indulgent bards reply!" (3:37–38). The soul of such a bard is a "filthy thing" (3:40); poets should show the soul as "Not what it *is,* but what it ought to be!— / What erst it *was*" in Eden (3:170–71). The filthiness of soul most particularly excoriated is that which Elizabeth Barrett felt herself most tainted by: ambition, for which "we put away / The nature's instinct, and th' affections' stay" (2:28–29).

This violent repudiation of ambition was unexpectedly supported, and the poet's no doubt unconscious fear that ambition is aggression against the father was confirmed, in a painful scene that took place in February 1827. She had been working on the poem for "some months" and had once read part of it to her father, who "professed to have heard nothing from the weakness of my voice." "Not discouraged by this, but much disappointed," she worked on, made a fair copy, and asked him to read it himself. This time his displeasure was undisguised. He began much as he had before, blaming the artist's inability to communicate for the audience's refusal to hear: he complained "first of my illegibility, then of my obscurity," and read through less than half of it, reading aloud "in a very hesitating & ridiculing manner, constantly mistaking the words, hardly waiting for my correction, & almost entirely missing the final pause of every line." He told her that her hero was "a madman, & the most disagreeable man I ever heard of," worse than Byron in his insufferable egotism, that the poetry was as bad as the conception, and in short that her ambition had led her to overreach herself. "You see the subject is *beyond your grasp*—& you must be content *with what you can reach.* I cannot read any more—I would not read over again what I *have* read, for fifty pounds—really not for *ten.* I advise you to burn the wretched thing."[14] Robert Browning would have given precisely the opposite advice: "a man's reach should exceed his grasp," says Andrea del Sarto in words clearly endorsed by his creator.[15] But Mr. Barrett did not want his clever daughter imagining herself a genius, and wished to make very clear the limits within which she was expected to confine herself.

Although she was deeply wounded by the extraordinary cruelty of his response (apparently quite unlike his normal behavior in these years) and especially by the first intimation he had ever given her of "how limited" he thought her powers to be, she determined to finish the poem. She does not appear to have done so, however, and the only part of it that she ever published was a passage on nature ("Earth," 1833) that even her father could not have objected to. She also extracted and revised a portion under the title "The Poet's Enchiridion," which she never published. She may have realized eventually that her father's condemnation was not far wrong: unfocussed, bombastic, often out of control, the poem was probably better left unfinished, and she would no doubt have regretted publishing it as much as Browning regretted the publication of the work that has a comparable place in his own development, *Pauline.*

Courage to bear up under her father's grim displeasure came partly from the fact that she had found, in effect, another father. (There is no record of her ever soliciting a response to "The Development of Genius" from her mother.) She had recently made two new friendships, at first simply epistolary, with men who were impressed by "An Essay on Mind" and welcomed her to the community of learned men into which that poem had sought entrance. The first of these was Uvedale Price, a man almost eighty years old who lived nearby and flatteringly asked her to comment on the proofs of his work on the pronunciation of classical Greek. In her record of the painful conversation with her father she notes that Price had approved the subject of her poem and that "Mr. Price's friendship has given me more continued happiness than any single circumstance ever did—& I pray for *him,* as the grateful pray" (*BC* 1:359). In verses written for Price's eightieth birthday a month and a half later, she praised his enabling kindness to Nature (he had written a book on landscape gardening), to Poetry (he had given Greek poetry back its proper sound, as if restoring her tongue to Philomela), and to the poet herself.

> When the tone faltering grew,—the lamp unbright,—
> Thou did'st not still the harp, or quench the light;
> But, patient of my lay,—its harshness borne,—
> Didst spare the minstrel's fault,—the critic scorn![16]

The fact that he had no "personal regard" for her (*Diary* 212) made his esteem if anything more valuable, and when he died in 1829 she mourned him less as a friend than as an irreplaceable audience. "To the Memory of Sir Uvedale Price, Bart." praises him as just such a godlike creator as she had earlier imagined her father to be, referring to his works on gardening and pronunciation:

> Thou spakest once; and every pleasant sight,
> Woods waving wild, and fountains gushing bright,
> Cool copses, grassy banks, and all the dyes
> Of shade and sunshine gleam'd before our eyes.
> Thou spakest twice; and every pleasant sound
> Its ancient silken harmony unwound.

> (41–46)

Price was an important transition figure, partially replacing her father as the benign and godlike audience that gave value to her poetry and freeing her by his relative impersonality to take herself more seriously as a scholar and an adult.

Her relationship with Hugh Stuart Boyd, her other friend of these years, lasted much longer and was much more intense and complicated. Boyd was a classical scholar, blind, married, with a grown daughter, already in his mid-forties when their correspondence began in 1827. Her jealous attachment to him was evidently, as she feared, considerably in excess of his affection for her and aroused resistance and hostility at Hope End. Her relations with his wife and daughter (whom she naturally scorned as unworthy of him) were often difficult. For a long time her father would not let her visit him, although he lived very close by, in Malvern, and her whole family appears to have found her obsessive regard for him puzzling and annoying. They read Greek together—or rather, since he was blind, she read to him and served as his amanuensis, like those models of filial-scholarly devotion, Milton's daughters. Unlike Milton, however, he instructed her about what she read and wrote; after Mr.

McSwiney, he was her only teacher of Greek. He lent her books, and they discussed literature, scholarship, and theology, she with a deference that came first from her acknowledgment of his superior learning, then from her fear of losing his affection, and at last from gratitude and pity.

His view of Greek literature, like his role in her life, was thoroughly patriarchal: while he read the classical poets with her, he also introduced her to the Christian writers (the "Fathers"), whom he admired much more than she did, and he had no sympathy at all with her enthusiasm for the modern Greeks' political struggle, dismissing them as "savage monsters" (*LHSB* 23). Although he indulged himself in writing and sometimes publishing bad verses, he was not a poet and cared more for her scholarship than for her poetry, about which he was frequently inclined to be severe. But the picture of scholarship that he offered her was not wholly attractive. She once wrote down several pages of his anecdotes, consisting mostly of more or less witty insults, about various well-known scholars' vanity, malice, envy, and demands for preeminence—anecdotes entirely antipathetic to her moral and intellectual taste.[17] And she eventually realized that his literary skill and judgment were inferior to her own. Perhaps the most important lessons he taught her— quite inadvertently, and it took her a long time to learn them—were increased self-confidence and independence of the learned world to which since early childhood she had so ardently aspired.

Her dependence on male mentors was all the more intense because there were no women to strengthen her apart from or against them. In 1828 Mary Moulton-Barrett died unexpectedly after a long period of illness, having for some time, apparently, no longer been a source of strength or a model for her daughter's life. Elizabeth Barrett's feelings are poignantly expressed in a brief diary entry written a few years after her mother's death. "How I thought of those words '*You will never find another person who will love you as I love you*' [. . . .] I w^d barter all other sounds & sights [. . .] lay down before her my tastes & feelings each & all, in sacrifice for the love, the exceeding love, which I never, in truth, can find again" (*Diary* 88). This has strange undertones: the mother's desolating words have almost an accusing ring and the daughter's imagined sacrifice suggests that it is the "tastes & feelings" of a poet which, despite all her mother's encouragement, separate her from maternal love as they were separating her from the rest of the female world.

She did not give up her tastes and feelings, but living as a young lady meant that she was often unable to indulge them. Around this time her development received some sort of check. Between 1826 and 1833 she read many Greek texts, but she wrote very few poems. Early in 1828 she said: "my time is continually engaged either in writing, or in reading that I *may write*" (*LHSB* 20), but the quantity of writing seems very soon to have diminished, perhaps partly in consequence of her mother's death. After her exuberant early development came a long period of stasis and frustration which must have been due in large part to the lack of informed and sympathetic encouragement for writing poems that were neither childish nor pious nor self-effacingly imitative. The loss of happiness and of possibilities for happiness, the narrowing of horizons and powers that the poems feared and foretold, seemed to be coming true. As a poet she had reached an impasse, especially after her attempt to find new and more genuine sources and subjects for poetry—ones more in keeping with her own stage of life and with the strongest currents of contemporary literature—within herself, by writing about the development of genius, had been thwarted.

These years are best described in terms of negatives and privations, both literary and emotional. Her mother's death in 1828 was followed by that of Uvedale Price in the following year. In 1832 after a long period of anxious waiting the family home, Hope End, had to be sold as a result of financial losses in Jamaica, and the family moved to various rented houses in Sidmouth. Although she had no major illness, her health was weak, and her susceptibility to colds, exhaustion, and nervous debility detracted from her freedom and her pleasures. At Hope End she had few responsibilities even after her mother's death except for teaching the younger boys and—most onerous and most resented—exchanging visits with a small group of neighbors. She shrank from participation in the uncongenial life around her: "My love of solitude is growing with my growth," she wrote in 1831; "I am inclined to shun the acquaintance of those whom I do not like & love; on account of the *ennui*: & the acquaintance of those whom I might like & love,—on account of the *pain*!" (*Diary* 155).

The most striking fact about these years, if we think of comparable periods in the lives of male poets, is her isolation. This had first made itself felt when Bro went off to school and she lamented that thereafter she would have to "ascend the delightful hill of classical learning" alone, the echo of her lyre dying away unheard (*BC* 1:358). It was not a particularly fruitful isolation, although she had plenty of time to read and work. Apart from Uvedale Price and Mr. Boyd, who were scholars rather than poets and in any case much older than herself, she had no intellectual or literary acquaintances whom she valued, no circle of friends of her own age and interests, and no particular friend to give sympathetic companionship or discriminating encouragement and praise: no Arthur Hallam, Robert Monclar, Arthur Hugh Clough. A few intellectually accomplished older women took an interest in her, but she did not find their friendship satisfying. She found herself with increasing frustration, especially after her mother's death, confined within a narrow circle of women whom she loved but who did not share her interests and who often (her aunt, "Bummy," especially, who lived with them after Mary Moulton-Barrett died, and often Henrietta too) exasperated her: a world of visits to be paid and received, teas and parties that bored, irritated, and exhausted her, hurt feelings, misunderstandings, gossip about matters she had no interest in; and no one she considered a friend.

Like other nineteenth-century women poets, she could escape from this restricted and unsatisfying society only into inner space, not into the wider world. In her diary for 1831–32 we see conflicts with her family arising almost daily, usually about her comings and goings and especially about whether she should be allowed to stay home from church, shirk social calls, or visit Mr. Boyd. For affection's sake and to avoid fruitless quarrels, she always yields, but not without repining. One Sunday, for instance, her aunt wanted her to go to church. (The Barretts were shrewd critics of clergymen and not always regular churchgoers.)

> Feeling convinced as I do, that the gospel is not consistently preached there, & that my time can be more usefully & scripturally occupied at home, am I right in going? I think not; but there was so much thunder & lightening about it that I yielded the point. "Very goodnatured & amiable of me," perhaps Bummy thought; for she kissed me with a smile: "Very weak & wrong of me" I doubted,—for her kiss & smile did not give me as much pleasure as usual. (*Diary* 124)

"My disposition is a yielding one," she reflected the following Sunday when she again attended church and again regretted it. "I have a constitutional dislike of all contention; & therefore I suppose I prefer contending with myself, to contending with other people . . because I am weaker than they are" (*Diary* 131). She has not outgrown the feminist views of her childhood, although she does not use feminist terms: what the world calls female virtue, she calls weakness. The corollary is that being strong would mean renouncing womanhood and love.

She found few compensatory interests or pleasures, especially after leaving Hope End. She followed the events leading up to the Reform Bill with eager attention, but active participation in political affairs would, of course, have been impossible—not that she wanted it. Once she expressed a wish to have been at a political meeting, but only to have heard Bro speak. As for Bro: even when he was at home his life appears to have been centered elsewhere. She found sustenance in books and scholarship—what in her diary she calls her "work," a term normally used by gentlewomen for tasks done with the needle, not the pen—and with Mr. Boyd, and took refuge from the anguish of the family's anticipated departure from Hope End in the study of Hebrew, which she continued at Sidmouth. She knew no young men worth bothering with and was resolved never to marry, and her poems don't condescend to deal with romantic love. She was thus deprived both of conventional young women's main source of amusement and of a frequent subject of most young poets' verse. This deprivation had the advantage, however, of differentiating her from the common run of women poets and protecting her from such easy scorn as that of the reviewer of L.E.L. (the one who had enraged her in 1825) who remarked that "nearly all [L.E.L.'s] poetry relates to love, a topic . . . on which we would engage to manufacture a poet out of any young person, particularly a female."[18]

It was just as well for domestic reasons, too, since Edward Moulton-Barrett would no doubt have disliked his daughter writing love poems at least as much as he disliked her impersonation of a developing male genius. The dark side of his devotion to his family was manifesting itself more than ever in the control that he maintained over his children's lives and in his refusal to talk about his plans for them, behavior to which they had long been habituated but which in the months of miserable suspense before they left Hope End became particularly trying. She did not allow herself to complain much of a despotism that still seemed benevolent, but she wrote rather bitterly to Mr. Boyd in 1831 a reflection that must have occurred to her more than once: "It seems hard upon me that nothing of my childhood, except its tranquillity, should have passed away" (*LHSB* 136). The loss of her home was a wrenching violation of her strong family affection, her memory of her mother, and the deep sense of place that informed many of her early poems: it tore up her roots and ended her childhood. But both male and female worlds seemed closed against her, the paths to adulthood blocked.

It is hardly surprising, then, that an acute sense of limitation and frustration informs her next published volume. *Prometheus Bound, Translated from the Greek of Aeschylus, and Miscellaneous Poems* (1833), like *An Essay on Mind,* has an air of uncertain liminality, but this time both the poet's desire to cross the threshold and her fear of doing so are more intense. The title work, which establishes the mood and theme for most of the others, is not an imitation but a translation, and a hurried one at that. Under the shadow of her mother's death and the impending and then accomplished departure from Hope End, the sense of loss that in 1826 was still a foreboding has become an almost all-encompassing reality. The first two poems, the most interesting ones in the book, describe and enact drastic repressions of will and desire. Instead of the confidence in her energy and self-control expressed in the autobiograph- ical "Glimpses" or the happy if rather stilted thoughts of the mind rejoicing in its own powers in "An Essay on Mind," they carry forward the turbulent feelings of "The Development of Genius" and display the poet's fear of her own passion and imagination as rebellious, murderous, Satanic forces. Most of the "other poems" renounce not only ambition but all earthly joys, including love and fame, and turn at the end to God.

The translation of *Prometheus Bound* was written in two weeks in February 1832, and the poet was so much ashamed of it afterwards ("as cold as Caucasus on the snow-peak, & as flat as Salisbury plain" [*LMRM* 3:76]) that in 1845 she did it all over again. Like the book as a whole, it suggests profoundly equivocal meanings, an uneasy balancing of self- assertion and self-effacement. It celebrates the hero who for Elizabeth Barrett was the Byron of classical mythology, the great rebel for hu- manity's sake against tyranny (Byron himself had been profoundly influ- enced by *Prometheus Bound*), but Prometheus' defiance takes the form of immobility and silence. Insofar as it is a translation the work is an act of homage and obedience to Aeschylus and to classical scholarship, but for a young woman to publish such a translation was an act of considerable daring. Aeschylus, furthermore, was usually conceived in the nineteenth century as a Gothic or romantic artist,[19] and the translator in her preface describes him in terms that suggest an idealized portrait of herself:

> His excellences consist chiefly in a vehement imaginativeness, a strong but repressed sensibility, a high tone of morality, a fervency of devotion, and a rolling energetic diction: and as sometimes his fancy rushes in, where his judgment fears to tread, and language, even the most copious and powerful of languages, writhes beneath its impetuosity; an occasional mixing of metaphor, and frequent obscurity of style, are named among his chief defects. (6:84)

Like Shelley in his preface to *Prometheus Unbound*, she acknowledges Prometheus' resemblance to Milton's Satan, and she explains the moral difference between them in terms that have an obvious relevance to her own situation:

The Satan of Milton and the Prometheus of Aeschylus stand upon ground as unequal, as do the sublime of sin and the sublime of virtue. Satan suffered from his ambition; Prometheus from his humanity: Satan for himself; Prometheus for mankind [. . . .] But in his hell, Satan yearned to associate with man; while Prometheus preferred a solitary agony: nay, he even permitted his zeal and tenderness for the peace of others, to abstract him from that agony's intenseness. (6:85–86)

Shelley sees Satan as tainted by "ambition, envy, revenge, and a desire for personal aggrandisement,"[20] of which his Prometheus is purged. Elizabeth Barrett's comparison of the two great rebels focusses more sharply on what were for her the key oppositions: gregariousness and solitude, ambition and love. She took no interest in Io, the woman who suffers but does not resist. Prometheus defies God the tyrannical father more successfully than the daughters in "The Sorrows of the Muses," whose protest on behalf of humanity ends in pious filial submission, but the translation was published at the instigation of Edward Moulton-Barrett, who evidently saw nothing Satanic or even Byronic about it.

The primary audience for this poem, however, was not Mr. Barrett but Mr. Boyd. It was written in the first half of February 1832, and since from June 1831 to April 1832 Elizabeth Barrett kept a diary we have a unique opportunity to watch the poem emerge from a personal context. During these months she was waiting for what seemed the inevitable losses of Hope End and of Mr. Boyd's company and affection. She wrote her translation in a surge of frantic activity which like her sudden immersion in the study of Hebrew at about the same time was a reaction to prolonged anxiety and frustration. Mr. Barrett was away from home for most of the period covered by the diary, although he returned soon after she began the translations, trying to avert the financial catastrophe that would eventually necessitate the sale of Hope End. He is frequently mentioned, of course—"Dear, dearest Papa"—with much solicitude for what he must be suffering, but the central, almost single, emotional object is Mr. Boyd. The diary is filled with visits to him, successful and unsuccessful schemes for visiting him, and suspicious scrutiny of his words and behavior. She is convinced that his affection is waning and is afraid that he will leave Malvern or that he will not try to find her again when her family moves away. (In the event, he showed his attachment by following her to Sidmouth.)

During these months she appears not to have been writing much poetry, but she was reading a variety of Greek writers, Christian ones especially with Mr. Boyd, and tragedies mostly by herself. On January

20 she recorded that she had now read all the plays of Aeschylus (207). (By the beginning of April she had read all of Euripides too, to Mr. Boyd's astonishment—he "called me 'a funny girl',—& observed, that very few men had done as much" [231].) Many excisions have been made in this part of the diary, including some from the pages that would have recorded the inception of her translation, but by February 2 she had begun, and on February 15 she had finished.

The translation emerges as part of a potential rivalry with Mr. Boyd that she was careful to suppress. For he too was a translator, expecting—and receiving—from her the lavish help and encouragement that she also craved but he refused to give. She knew perfectly well that she was a better translator than he was, besides being a better poet, although she does not quite admit this even in her diary, and she was afraid that her superiority would give offense. From July to October 1831 she helped him to memorize passages from *Prometheus Bound,* and in November he suggested that she translate it into blank verse. She prudently "begged him to do it, instead" (180), however, and the subject dropped. In January he sought her advice on the translation of Saint Gregory Nazianzen that he was working on and asked her to translate it at the same time, but she refused, since she was sure that "the very act of seeming to compete with him, tho' suggested by himself, w^d diminish his regard for me" (210). Her father's affection had been turned suddenly to ridicule and contempt by "The Development of Genius," and she feared a similar reaction from Mr. Boyd to a show of competitive strength. She made a translation of Gregory secretly, however, and although she told herself that she did it "not with the wish of competing with him" but in order to assist him with his own, she could not help gloating that she could accomplish in four days what would take him two weeks (211). The next day she triumphantly recorded that he found the task too laborious to finish, and within five days she had found the "courage" to tell him that she was working on *Prometheus Bound* (212).

But her eager concern for his work was not matched by his for hers. He had a few passages read to him with evident reluctance, and when she visited him in early March, he first "made me read his preface & some additional translations" and then offered criticism and faint praise of her *Prometheus* (222). Her father, in contrast, wanted her to publish it: it did not appear to threaten *his* preeminence. The work comes out of a time, then, when submission was exacted from her in all the small concerns of daily living, when her future was at the mercy of her arbitrary and uncommunicative father's will, and when in her literary and intel-

lectual life she felt that she had to hide her strength to avoid offending
the one person whose friendship supported and validated her as a scholar
and writer. Prometheus gave voice to her own suppressed rebelliousness.

Self-assertion and self-suppression are the themes of most of the
volume. Although almost all the poems inculcate a weary submission to
God, the first two, "The Tempest: A Fragment" and "A Sea-Side Med-
itation," which are the strongest and most interesting and very likely the
latest written, are primarily concerned to express the poet's mingled
exhilaration and terror at her Promethean or Satanic impulses. "The
Tempest" is her most highly charged exploration of the Promethean
struggle as she experienced it within herself. The setting introduces the
Promethean theme: high trees that are called "forest Titans" (8), and
hills that challenge the thunder. The thunder and lightning with which
Zeus threatens Prometheus appear as a storm attacking nature, "Heaven's
wrath / And Earth's despair" (32–33). The terms of opposition are those
by which Elizabeth Barrett defined her imaginative world: Heaven, thun-
der, lightning, energy, wrath, and power on one side, Earth, passivity,
despair, stooping, death on the other: male, one might say, against female,
power against weakness, the Olympian gods against the doomed, rebel-
lious Titans. The attraction of Prometheus must have been that despite
his affiliation with the weak or female side of this pattern of oppositions
he embodies unyielding Titanic power; and in "The Tempest" the
boundary blurs and almost disappears.

For while the speaker sympathizes with earth, she also exults at the
destructive fury of the storm and hails the lightning, which makes "the
face of heav'n to show like hell" (54)—an equation the rest of the poem
confirms—and which suddenly reveals at her feet a dead man whom she
recognizes as her familiar enemy. In a trance of introspection she sees
the doubleness of her own heart:

> Contrary spirits; sympathy with power,
> And stooping unto power;—the energy
> And passiveness,—the thunder and the death!

> (115–17)

She buries the corpse in a scene that blends images of power and passivity,
male and female. There is a Satanically aspiring tree whose "tusky roots"

> Forced for themselves a path on every side,
> Riving the earth; and, in their savage scorn,
> Casting it from them like a thing unclean,
> Which might impede his naked clambering

Unto the heavens. Now blasted, peel'd, he stood,
By the gone night, whose lightning had come in
And rent him, even as it rent the man.

(142–49)

The identification of the dead man with the tree that ravaged and scorned
the earth marks him as both a "forest Titan" and an emulator or false
avatar of heavenly wrath and power. He is the speaker's enemy, but her
hatred of him, her imaginative identity with the lightning that destroyed
both man and tree, and her digging in the earth like the tusky roots to
bury him align her with him too.

She discovers that resistance to power—refusal to stoop (or be turned
like the milk by thunder)—is itself aggressive and yields the tainted
pleasure of asserting power. More than that, the poem suggests that there
is no escape from terms of power: dominance or submission, "Sympathy
with power" or "stooping unto power," are the only and inevitable choices.
There is no world but the father's world of power, in life or after, and
the sweeping energy and exultant horror come from the speaker's dis-
covery that she can imaginatively participate in it. This discovery quickly
leads, however, to a violent revulsion, and the poem ends with a long
evocation of death in many violent forms and hope for peace with God
beyond the "reptile moods" (201) of living flesh. The subtitle "A Frag-
ment" is probably defensive, repelling explication, as well as placing the
poem in the Romantic genre of the "fragment"—poems which mimic in
their broken form both the lack of wholeness or integration in the self
which they express and the dynamic processes of creative genius.[21] Clo-
sure is usually very insistent and often overelaborate in Elizabeth Barrett's
poems, which frequently turn for completion to God, but "The Tempest"
is a poem of self-division, written at a time when the unity of the poet's
life had been shattered.

"A Sea-Side Meditation" is another study of fragmentation and self-
division, the setting and relative maturity of the verse suggesting that it
was written late, in Sidmouth. It is even more explicitly about self-
revelation, enacting the mingled joy and terror of self-confrontation in
the moments when the self seems to crack open and its passion, freedom,
and power flash nakedly forth. It begins by evoking a living, joyful nature
in which human beings can happily participate. But then the sound of
the sea breaks in, both threatening and exhilarating, both alien and (like
the dead man in "The Tempest") deeply familiar—"As memories of evil

o'er the soul" (21)—and also glorious in "his foamy strength [. . .] his life and voice inscrutable" (24–26). Like the storm in "The Tempest," the sea first seems an external, threatening, masculine force, with which the speaker in an exultation that turns into horror recognizes her own hidden affinity. She explains that like other violent forces—"Passions, emotions, sudden changes" (72), and also "trampling tempests" (34)— the sea can burst the chains of habit and reveal the world and ourselves as mysteries. It can "force the mind to view the mind" and by doing so create the "*sublime*" (77–78). We usually resist the sublime, however, as the poem both says and shows. "Ourselves do scare ourselves" (57), and when (as in "The Tempest") we are driven to self-confrontation,

> we view ourselves, and back recoil
> At our own awful likeness; ne'ertheless,
> Cling to that likeness with a wonder wild,
> And while we tremble, glory—proud in fear.

> (94–97)

This is life's poetry (99), as it is the source of Elizabeth Barrett's most vital and individual early work.

But it is poetry that must be renounced. The sea is like the imagination, "casting up / Rare gems and things of death on fancy's shore" (124–25), leading us into dreams that must be broken, "Else should we be like Gods" (131), dreaming our way to the "heights of wisdom" (134). Poetry, dreams, imagination are demonic temptations, and the poem ends with an astonishing apocalypse of the imagination figured as Milton's Satan, the aspect of Prometheus that the preface carefully separates from the classical hero himself: a doomed Byronic-Promethean hero who awakens the storm that Prometheus defies and "The Tempest" ambivalently celebrates.

> E'en so,
> Hell's angel (saith a scroll apochryphal)
> Shall, when the latter days of earth have shrunk
> Before the blast of God, affect his heav'n;
> Lift his scarr'd brow, confirm his rebel heart,
> Shoot his strong wings, and darken pole and pole,—
> Till day be blotted into night; and shake
> The fever'd clouds, as if a thousand storms
> Throbb'd into life! Vain hope—vain strength—vain flight!
> God's arm shall meet God's foe, and hurl him back![22]

The poem begins with a peaceful scene in which the poet's imagination wanders until it meets a power that forces its glance inward. The imagination gathers strength and confidence through identification with that external power until, in the recoil characteristic of Elizabeth Barrett's early poetry, it scares itself with its own lawless daring. Like "The Tempest," "A Sea-Side Meditation" enacts the passage from bold self-confrontation to terror that it describes, brilliantly exposing the dynamics of renunciation and submission.

Many of the poems that follow were written much earlier than these two, but they start, in effect, from their conclusions. They reject earth, which is defined as decaying and worthless, and renounce ambition and desire. Whereas in 1826 fame and love appear as conflicting values, in 1833 both seem empty, with fame on balance the emptier of the two. "Minstrelsy," for instance, associates poetry with the pleasures of childhood and an affectionate familial audience. The speaker says that she doesn't know why she cares for poetry ("minstrelsy") at all, since subjects, audience, and poet will all die, and concludes with the hope that when she is dead those who loved her will forget her poems and remember her love.[23] Heroic songs and the heroes who sang them in 1826 have disappeared, more generalized Promethean or Satanic figures replacing Byron and Riga. There are as many women as men, and the only hero aside from Prometheus is a heroine, Teresa del Riego. But the women are neither objects of the poet's desire nor figures for the poet herself. Rather, they mark her alienation from women both in life (like "Victoire," from whom the speaker feels definitively separated by Victoire's marriage) and in art. "The Picture Gallery at Penshurst" muses on "Sacharissa," the cruel beloved of Edmund Waller's poetry, who is vain and unloving, indifferent to poets and glory, and moreover is seen by the speaker in a painting and is therefore doubly the object of art rather than the artist herself.

In "The Death-Bed of Teresa del Riego" the book's heroine—"Riego's Widow," now (being about to die) with a name of her own—combines the Promethean virtues with those of idealized Victorian womanhood. The result, while rather sentimental, is very interesting. The conception seems indebted to Madame de Staël's *Corinne*, that seminal vision of histrionic womanhood which Elizabeth Barrett had read three times by 1832:[24] like Corinne and like Aurora Leigh later, Teresa del Riego is a passionate woman from the south who learns in cold England to conceal her tumultuous feelings. Unlike Corinne's and Aurora Leigh's, however, her feelings never break forth into words. She is first depicted as a beautiful object, still and silent, an emblem of pious sorrow and of woman as the narcissistic object of her own and others' regard, made to be seen rather than to see—or, to see only herself: "Beautiful form of woman! seeming made / Alone to shine in mirrors" (13–14). In the immobility of her grief she looks like a statue, and when grief kills her at last she becomes—in the words by which Elizabeth Barrett describes Greece in her first published poem—"A lovely corse." Her silence, immobility, and suffering link her to Prometheus, who very noticeably says nothing at the beginning of the play while he is being chained to the rock and whose defiance of Jove is expressed in his refusal to tell what he foresees. Unlike Prometheus, however, but like women in Elizabeth Barrett's later poems who cannot speak until they are dying, her only speech is her death itself, as the epigraph tells us: "Si fia muta ogni altra cosa, al fine / Parlera il mio morire, / E ti dira la morte il mio martire." ("If everything else were mute, at the end my death will speak, and death will tell you my suffering"; the words are spoken by a lovesick swain in Guarini's *Il Pastor Fido*.) She leaves behind her a speaking object (which the poem's speaker has before her as she writes), a lock of hair telling a tale that will echo in "the heart of man, if manly" (44).

Teresa del Riego's silent function is to inspire a male audience, but "To the Memory of Sir Uvedale Price, Bart." laments the poet's apparently irreplaceable loss of an audience. Price's regard had bestowed value on her poetry as her father had done, and she lays her "tuneless harp" (64) on his grave, an emblem like the broken lyre in "Riga's Last Song" of an end to heroic singing. The 1833 poems imagine no possibilities for heroic action or heroic speech or song, with the strange exception of "The Appeal," a grotesque and dreadful poem urging the "Children of our England" to stand together and "Shout aloud" (the phrase is repeated four times) Christian truth to heathens in distant lands; as in Tennyson's *Maud*, much later, the collective shout of the nation is the only valid heroic speech or song.[25] For the rest, these poems reject all earthly things as fleeting and worthless, telling of age, weakness, inadequacy, and loss, and turning for recompense to God. They renounce not only ambition in the world of the father, but also the things of childhood and nature, the world of the mother. "To a Boy" tells the child whose birthday was celebrated in the "Spenserian Stanzas" of 1826 that although he is happy now, he won't be happy much longer. (The mark of transition is that his golden curls were cut off, despite her pleading, a sad prolepsis of what happened to her son when she died and his happy childhood abruptly ended.) "Earth," the only part of the ill-fated "Development of Genius" that she ever published (much re-

vised), evokes earth's beauty and the beautiful pagan myths associated
with it, and then violently rejects mythology as a "heathen dream" (25)
and luridly imagines earth's painful death. The speaker in "Idols" blames
nature for having betrayed her love: an experience very different from
that promised by Wordsworth's assurance that "Nature never did betray
/ The heart that loved her," quoted by Elizabeth Barrett years later in
her essay on the English poets.[26]

> Mine oldest worshipping was given
>   To natural Beauty, aye residing
> In bowery earth and starry heav'n,
>   In ebbing sea, and river gliding.
>
> But natural Beauty shuts her bosom
>   To what the natural feelings tell!
> Albeit I sigh'd, the trees would blossom—
>   Albeit I smiled, the blossoms fell.
>
>   (5–12)

"For *me*, can earth refuse to fade?" she asks in "Weariness" (9). Nor is
there recourse in the human world, since fame and love vanish like
childhood and nature.

    After the self-thwarting energy of the first two poems, the volume
sinks deeper and deeper into renunciation and gloom, the structure of
the whole repeating that of its most significant parts. It ends with "Weari-
ness," which like the endings of individual poems renounces beauty,
love, and earthly hope for the prospect of repose in heaven. The poems
in this volume both individually and collectively portray a poetically de-
bilitating suppression of purpose and will; but the order of composition
as well as the many repetitions of the struggle show the poet fighting the
battle against herself over and over again, never quite acquiescing in her
own defeat.[27]

3
The Seraphim, and Other Poems

The narrowing of life and possibility depicted in the 1833 poems ac-

celerated in the next five years, during which the isolation that had begun at Hope End became the defining condition of the poet's life. The family stayed at Sidmouth in temporary and variously unsatisfactory houses from 1832 to 1835, when they moved to London, first to Gloucester Place and then in 1838 to the house in Wimpole Street that was to be their permanent home. Elizabeth Barrett rather liked Sidmouth, especially the sea and the countryside, and very much disliked the thought of living in London, although the prospect of having her own books and furniture again after years of temporary encampments almost reconciled her to it. A pall of aimlessness and uncertainty hung over the family, revealing behind Mr. Barrett's inflexible will a deep infirmity of purpose. The loss of most of his fortune and his position as the owner of a plantation in Jamaica and a grand estate in England had left him at loose ends, without enough to occupy his time, uncertain where to reestablish his large family, constantly meditating plans but unable to carry them out. "His decisions so often wane away into uncertainties," Elizabeth Barrett said, that even when he talked "decidedly" she did not know what to think (*BC* 3:122). Her loyalty to a domestic tyrant whose faults she saw clearly enough was enhanced by pity for his weakness, but her childlike confidence in a stability upheld by his strength must have disappeared just when the motherless, uprooted family had nothing else to depend on.

The only significant friendship she made in Sidmouth was with George Barrett Hunter, a clergyman and widower whose young daughter she was fond of and who later became annoyingly jealous of her affections and success. Her attachment to Mr. Boyd, who also moved to Sidmouth and then to London, faded with prolonged closer association: his family difficulties, his engagement with patristic texts that did not attract her but with which he expected her assistance, and his evidently greater concern for his interests than for hers, all helped to loosen a tie that could hardly, in any event, have continued with the same intensity. The reclusiveness that had begun in her dreamy childhood grew upon her, becoming by the time she reached London a painful shyness that, augmented by her father's increasing rigidity and aversion to outsiders, prevented almost all social contacts. The first cause of her reclusiveness was not, as people were later to assume, illness: for much of the time she was not in particularly good health, but until 1838 she was not seriously ill.

In London there was some alleviation for her solitude in the friendship of John Kenyon, a distant cousin a little older than her father who composed poetry, participated with genial hospitality in London's literary society, and took a generous interest in his brilliant kinswoman. He induced her despite her shyness to meet Wordsworth and Walter Savage Landor and—most important—Mary Russell Mitford. Miss Mitford was nineteen years older than Elizabeth Barrett and when they met in 1836 had been a famous writer for many years. Never married, she lived in the country with a profligate father who mercilessly exploited her, and she immediately attached herself to the young poet whose ambitions she fostered almost as lovingly and even more boldly than Mary Moulton-Barrett had done. She seems, indeed, to have echoed Elizabeth Barrett's early dreams.

> My love and my ambition for you often seems to be . . . like that of a mother for a son, or a father for a daughter (the two fondest of natural emotions) . . . . I sit and think of you, and of the poems that you will write, and of that strange, brief rainbow crown called Fame . . . . the position that I long to see you fill is higher, firmer, prouder than ever has been filled by woman. It is a strange feeling, but one of indescribable pleasure. My pride and my hopes seem altogether merged in you.[1]

And unlike Mary Moulton-Barrett, she did not just encourage ambition with words; she embodied literary success and showed it to be compatible with womanly qualities, such as devotion to difficult fathers, that Elizabeth Barrett admired. As well as sharing many of her interests, she could offer her younger friend the fruits of extensive practical experience in the literary world. Since she was seldom in London, however, their friendship was chiefly epistolary.

Elizabeth Barrett's isolation was intensified by the physical confinement of a city house and street, where she found "a solitude without the majesty of solitude" (*BC* 3:181). "There is not a being whom I know here, except Mr. Kenyon," she wrote in 1836, "who ever says to me 'I care for poetry'" (*BC* 3:181). And perhaps even worse than solitude, at least for a poet who knew she needed experience to provide aliment for her writing, was the eventlessness of her life. She read, wrote, taught the younger boys Greek. Her *Prometheus Bound* was published and ignored. Once a ceiling fell and almost injured someone; a servant and one of her brothers had mild attacks of smallpox; Mr. Barrett was ill and recovered; Mrs. Boyd, whom she was not fond of, died, and the Boyds' daughter married; her brothers made excursions into the world (Bro and Sam to Jamaica, Henry to Europe) but did not seem to be attaining independence; Henrietta played the piano when they had one; Arabel painted; Mr. Kenyon fell ill but she did not hear about it until he was out of danger. She went to exhibits of paintings. Her pet doves produced an egg that was eagerly attended by birds and poet together and actually hatched (*BC* 3:283). The pervasive sadness of the poems she wrote at this time reflects, not suffering, but the absence of significant engagement, even through pain, with life and the world. Over and over the poems trace an inexorable passage from a pastoral to an urban world, from youth to age, from life to death. Their characteristic attitude toward life is an observer's, not a participant's, and the virtues they celebrate are not Promethean resistance and rebellion, but sympathy and endurance.

Signs that the struggle informing much of her earlier poetry was still going on below the surface, at least in the first part of this period, however, appear in an unpublished poem whose title both asserts and denies its significance: "A True Dream (Dreamed at Sidmouth, 1833)." (Is it truly a dream, or is the dream "true"?) Like other poems too strange or subversive for her to publish, it is a narrative. An unexplicated allegory in ballad form that resembles Coleridge's "Christabel," it expresses a fear like that in "The Development of Genius" of her own passions and creative impulses. Like "Christabel," "The Development of Genius," and "The Tempest," it is in a sense a "fragment," a poem of incompleteness and self-division that does not have the firm closure by which her poems usually contain such impulses.

> I had not an evil end in view,
>   Tho' I trod the evil way;
> And why I practised the magic art,
>   My dream it did not say.[2]

The speaker releases from confinement in magical vials three mysterious figures, one male, one fully shrouded, and one a young girl—a nuclear family, in which the girl is a terrifying demonic double who clings to her with a cold kiss that sucks away her breath. When she breaks the vials to get rid of them, they turn into snakes. Her brother then appears and, with the apparent intention of protecting her, ignores her pleadings on behalf of her detested creations and throws vitriol on them. But instead of dying the snakes shriek and writhe, getting larger and longer and calling her to them, and she falls snakelike on the ground herself. She rises and calls on "The name of sanctity," but the serpents, demonic doubles still, echo and nullify the holy name. An undefined shape of horror arises from them and she flees—but toward it, not away.

> I stood by a chamber door, and thought
>   Within its gloom to hide;
> I locked the door, and the while forgot
>   That I stood on the outer side.
>
> And the knell of my heart was wildly tolled
>   While I grasped still the key;
> For I felt beside me the icy breath,
>   And knew that *that* was *he*.

Without trying to give a name to the nameless evil which resolves into a single male figure ("*he*"), we can see that what she fears, flees, but comes back to as if despite herself is the creative power that releases her own darkest impulses, the lawless, sensual part of herself that is not content inside the safety of a woman's chamber, protected by a well-meaning brother, at home. The major works of both her 1838 and 1844 collections take place outside of a locked door: that, she imagines, is where creative power *is*.[3]

The necessity of going forth from the safety of locked rooms is also enacted in *The Seraphim, and Other Poems* (1838), although the published works generally present the question in more external terms. These poems focus more on suffering than on sin, locate evil outside the self, and imagine the poet not as an evil magician but as a detached observer. The volume depicts a single, coherent vision of the course of human life: loss of Eden, childhood, and pastoral nature; a fall into human society, represented as the city in which people are lovelessly crowded together and all human bonds are broken; and recovery of paradise in heaven. It combines Milton's myth and Wordsworth's, the Christian story of the Fall and the Romantic myth of childhood, and except for its literal belief in a Christian afterlife it foreshadows the equally gloomy presentation of a very similar myth of the progress of human life in the poetry of Matthew Arnold.[4] The fear in her earlier poems that one grows up at the cost of freedom, happiness, and the chance of action seemed by 1838 to have been relentlessly borne out in Elizabeth Barrett's life, and the poems set forth a grim pattern of inexorable loss. Artistically, however, they are remarkably better than what she had published before—more finely wrought, more reflective, more serious, making a virtue of constriction and gaining in subtlety and intellectual force what has been lost in optimism and enthusiasm.

Most of her earlier themes have shrunk back or disappeared, although they will return in later volumes. There are few signs of inner struggle. There are no Byronic heroes—no heroes at all, in fact, except Cowper, from whose misery and madness a spiritual lesson is derived that sums up the experience of the whole volume: "Nor man nor nature satisfies whom only God created" ("Cowper's Grave," 32). The heroic task that had inspired her since childhood of "urging / A captive nation's strength to thunder" is derided, like all other human wishes, since "The storm is cruel as the chain!" ("Vanities," 11). Self-will is gone, and so is worry about ambition, which the poems hardly bother to disavow except in the heavy irony of "The Student," when the unnamed speaker dies leaning on a book in praise of fame (39). Only "The Pet-Name," a reversion to the habit of publishing childish family verse, returns to the theme of naming. This name ("Ba"), she (wrongly) asserts, will never be written in a book—she does not write it here—and she fondly recalls the time when her ambitions were bounded by her father's love, "When stooping down he cared to kiss / The poet at his knee" (49–50); but the poem does not so much disavow ambition as luxuriate in nostalgia. This is the first volume in which her name appeared, the one which began to make it famous, and it is her first sustained exploration of women's place in poetry.

The Seraphim is exemplary of the volume as a whole. It is the Christian antithesis of *Prometheus Bound*, a repudiation of Prometheus, Byron, and the idea of heroic rebellion, conceived (she says in the preface) while she was working on her translation of Aeschylus. It occurred to her that if Aeschylus had known the story of the crucifixion, he would have preferred it to his own; doubtless it also occurred to her that her access to Christian truth lessens her inferiority to the ancient Greeks and that Christian virtues are considerably closer than Promethean ones to the kinds of heroism open to a nineteenth-century woman: "not the Titanic

'I can revenge,' but the celestial 'I can forgive' " (1:165); not defiance of
divine tyranny but acceptance of God's benign chastisements. Chris-
tianizing the classical tradition in effect feminizes it—which may be one
reason why the pervasively religious tone of this volume is accompanied,
despite many apparently unpromising subjects and the inferiority of most
of the overtly religious poems, by an access of power, confidence, and
control.

The Seraphim is *Prometheus Bound* without Prometheus: a lyrical dra-
matization not of suffering and acting, but of watching others suffer and
act. The chorus, one might say, becomes the protagonist. The only actors
who appear as more than disembodied voices are two seraphim who by
witnessing the crucifixion enact the volume's theme: the human necessity,
despite their "shrinking from, and repugnance to, evil" (1:167), to see
and respond sympathetically to the sufferings of the fallen world. The
poem begins, in effect, where "A True Dream" ends: at *"the outer side
of the shut Heavenly gate."* Two Seraphim, Ador the Strong and Zerah
the Bright One (the differences between them inevitably suggest gender
difference, although they are presumably unsexed), linger while the oth-
ers have gone off to earth. Zerah is reluctant to leave heaven and afraid
to revisit earth, which he has not seen since the expulsion from Eden;
but thoughts of the Incarnation, by which Christ chose to participate in
human experience, encourage him, and they go. The second part takes
place in *"Mid-air, above Judaea,"* and is their lyrical response to the
offstage drama of the crucifixion. They learn that "Heaven is dull" (596)
in comparison to earth and to the passions of love that Christ's humanity
embodies and evokes. In the Epilogue, the poet—the observer of angelic
observers—watches her vision fade, apologizes for her temerity in en-
dowing seraphic beings with human speech, and hopes to see in heaven
the angels she imagines hovering invisibly around her (1031–32).

The mythic movement of the volume as a whole—from Eden to crowded
human solitudes and then to heaven—structures *The Seraphim* as well.
Ador and Zerah move from heaven to earth to heaven. Their recollection
of the loss of Eden is augmented by the lament of the fallen maternal
earth. And in the Epilogue the poet herself makes a Wordsworthian
descent from her fading seraphic visions into "the common light" of day
(1010),[5] concluding with a hope or prayer "before [the] heavenly throne"
to "walk in white" (1051). As the Wordsworthian echo suggests, the fall
in these poems is often explicitly associated with the loss of childhood;
many poems trace life through a trajectory that begins in happy childhood
and ends in a happy return to the heavenly Father. Despite the swelling

snakes and ambiguous tonalities of "A True Dream," the fall in Elizabeth Barrett's poems is not so much into sexuality as into gender and the constraints of womanhood. Some poems evoke not just ordinary nature but the paradisiacal isles and seas of her childhood fantasies ("An Island," "The Sea-Mew," "My Doves"). But again and again they enforce the impossibility of any return, except to a paradise within and eventually to heaven. "My spirit and my God shall be / My seaward hill, my boundless sea" ("My Doves," 83–84).

This is the only volume until *Aurora Leigh* that seriously examines the woman poet's relation to nature. Confronting her accumulated losses— of her mother, her childhood, her childhood home, and at last of any congenial natural setting at all when the family settled into a wholly urban and male-dominated life in London—she confronted at the same time her exclusion from the Romantic tradition. Despite her immersion in Greek literature, by 1838 her sense like her contemporaries' of how poetry should sound and feel in the nineteenth century had been decisively formed by the great Romantics, and for her as for the young Matthew Arnold Romanticism meant mostly nature poetry, especially Wordsworth's. Although she kept her enthusiasm for Byron longer than other Victorian poets did, by 1838 he had slipped somewhat, like Prometheus, in her esteem. All the major Victorian poets came to feel excluded in one way or another from Romantic faith and possibilities, but for Elizabeth Barrett this exclusion seems to have come earlier and to have felt more acute and absolute—driving her to such excesses as a long poem with no human characters, not set on earth. For she could see no way for a woman to establish an appropriate poetic relationship with nature.

When nature appears in her poems as anything but inert matter, its meaning is always deeply ambiguous. She continues to conceive of nature as she had in her earliest imaginative constructions, like the Romantic poets, as female and maternal; in *The Seraphim*, for instance, earth has groaned and travailed (818, 823) and is grieved by the grief of her children.[6] As such, nature embodies both remembered childhood and a mythic paradise and represents a double loss: of sensuous and aesthetic delight, and the child's freedom of action and vision of a future limitless in scope. The poems usually assert at the end that this doesn't really matter, because heaven is best, but the assertions contradict the poetry instead of arising from it and carry little poetic conviction. Nature is the lost source of life and the place of death, cradle and tomb ("Earth and Her Praisers," 223). There is an actual mother in the book who also deals both life and death: in "Isobel's Child" a dying infant argues against his mother's prayers to keep him alive for the satisfaction of her "dreary earthly love" (505); Isobel is persuaded, and as if in consequence of her acquiescence the child dies. Such a mixed picture of earth's treacherous beauty and maternal care is a legitimate offspring of Romanticism, although in Victorian poetry by men it is usually sexualized and cultivated for pleasures that Elizabeth Barrett does not aspire to share: it appears in Matthew Arnold's description of the seductress Vivien that closes his "Tristram and Iseult," for instance (a poem that startlingly resembles "Isobel's Child" in language, tone, and narrative technique), and as the fatal allure that Arnold calls "natural magic" and blames for the death of Keats. But for Elizabeth Barrett such ambiguities produce anxiety rather than pleasurable fear, and her poems generally end by renouncing nature for humanity and God.

She had little choice in the matter, since the association of nature with death and deception had disastrous implications for a woman poet. Writing in the Romantic tradition, she would have to situate herself both as the (male) poet and as nature, the (female) object in relation to which he defines himself by his assertion of dominance and his essential difference.[7] Thus she resents Romantic poets' assumptions of imaginative control over nature, mocking in "Earth and Her Praisers" a poet who congratulates himself on having created nature's beauty (actually, she would say, God created it). As a child she had allowed such a godlike role to her father, and later to Uvedale Price, but she would allow it again to no other and could not imagine assuming it herself. But taking the female part in man's relationship with nature would be to identify with subordination, mystery, deception, death—and, since nature does not speak, silence.

She angrily repudiates this consequence of Romanticism in "The Poet's Vow," a long narrative haunted by echoes of Coleridge and Wordsworth. Abandoning humanity because, like the seraph Zerah, he pities the sufferings that the fall of man brought upon earth, a young poet shuts himself up in a monk-deserted, bat-forsaken ancestral hall (rather like Thomas Love Peacock's satirical setting for the Romantic poets, Nightmare Abbey), expecting to purge himself of human sin and be lapped in nature's love as in a mother's. He refuses to make the transition from childhood to experience, from fallen nature into the human world, that the 1838 poems depict as morally essential and in any case inevitable. So, he tells nature,

> my purged, once human heart,
> From all the human rent,
> May gather strength to pledge and drink
> Your wine of wonderment,
> While you pardon me all blessingly
> The woe mine Adam sent.

(1.104–9)

Both theme and diction recall *The Rime of the Ancient Mariner*, giving unmistakable emphasis to Elizabeth Barrett's quarrel with her predecessor: for the poet's crime is not the mariner's violation of love between man and nature but the regressive, infantile love for nature that cuts him off from human affections and makes him, like the Ancient Mariner and many other self-isolated artists or artist-figures in Victorian poetry (Tennyson's "The Palace of Art," for instance), wretched and self-fearful.

The second half of the poem gives a specifically female reaction to this prototypical nineteenth-century figure. Rosalind, to whom the poet had been betrothed until he gave his heart to nature, dies and has her body delivered to his doorstep with a long written message, as if she were a suddenly articulate Lady of Shalott. Unlike the Lady of Shalott, however, Rosalind is not a projection of the male poet, a figure for the fatally self-enclosed artist: instead, she is his victim. The first stanza of her accusatory scroll in effect gives a voice to Wordsworth's Lucy, speaking from the grave to which Wordsworth's poems consign her.

> I left thee last, a child at heart,
>   A woman scarce in years.
> I come to thee, a solemn corpse
>   Which neither feels nor fears.
> I have no breath to use in sighs;
> They laid the dead-weights on mine eyes
>   To seal them safe from tears.

(5.416–22)

The echoes are unmistakable:

> A slumber did my spirit seal;
>   I had no human fears:
> She seemed a thing that could not feel
>   The touch of earthly years.

> No motion has she now, no force;
>   She neither hears nor sees,
> Rolled round in earth's diurnal course,
>   With rocks and stones and trees.[8]

She "neither feels nor fears," like Lucy (who "could not feel," who "neither hears nor sees"). But when she speaks in a Romantic poem, a woman is taking the man's part too, and so she is also Wordsworth's poet-speaker: she does not fear, her eyes are sealed as his spirit was.

Rosalind knows that the poet will attend to her only when her "heart / Is of [his] earth [. . .] a part" (5.427–28), when like Lucy she is one with nature, being dead. She cannot avoid Lucy's fate, silence and death, but she can make it recoil on the poet: receiving the corpse and the scroll, he utters an inarticulate wail and expires, and the two are buried in one grave. Wordsworth and Coleridge imagine nature either as benignly maternal, even her severity helping the child grow to manhood and thus beyond her most habitual sway, or as the responsive object of their creative imagination. Elizabeth Barrett cannot be the poet for whom nature is a mother teaching him to become a man (Rosalind goes directly from youth to death, since she is not allowed to become a woman); but to speak as part of nature is to speak, as Rosalind does, only as one who is dead. The unprivileged position of woman in the Romantic myth of nature makes it impossible for Rosalind to believe that nature is alive; she sees instead a "senseless, loveless earth and heaven" (2.176), and the narrator shares her skeptical view of the poet's "so worshipped earth and sky / That looked on all indifferently" (5.481–82).

Elizabeth Barrett herself, with the literal-mindedness that distinguishes Victorian from Romantic poets when they think about nature, regarded Romantic animism as an error.[9] "Man and Nature" offers as comfort for nature's indifference to human feelings the reminder that human happiness does not depend on nature, and the preface asserts, in effect, that what Wordsworth found in nature was simply put there by God: "The splendour in the grass and fragrance in the flower" (1:165) are the splendor and fragrance of divine love. This is characteristic evangelical resistance to Romantic pantheism and subjectivism: it places the uncertainties of evanescent nature under the firm control of God. And yet the myth kept its hold on her, drawing additional power from multiple associations in her reading and her life. She had to come to terms with it in order to come to terms with the poetry of her great predecessors.

"The Deserted Garden" also links expulsion from the paradise of childhood with the exclusion of women poets from a poetic tradition of antithetical gender roles, women and poets, damsels and knights. As a child the speaker found an abandoned garden, a magical corner of nature's dominion that she entered with a knight's "Adventurous joy" (17) but read and dreamed in like a woman. As she read, her "likeness grew" to "'gentle hermit of the dale,' / And Angelina too" (69–72; the protagonists of Goldsmith's ballad, "Edwin and Angelina," in *The Vicar of Wakefield*). But as if in consequence, the narrative sequence implies, of this impossibly doubled identification with antithetical figures of romance, she "shut the book" (76), grew up, and never returned to the garden. She turns instead—having apparently no other choice—to the God from whom the poet in "The Poet's Vow" resolutely turned away.

The 1838 volume is suffused with the consciousness that children grow up and women can't be nature poets, the poems repeatedly choosing between nature and God, regret for Eden and hope of heaven. Almost always, of course, they choose God. The significant exception is "A Sea-Side Walk," the best nature poem Elizabeth Barrett ever wrote, which discovers an artistically nourishing unity with a nature that despite apparent separation and loss remains her mother. The first two stanzas describe the end of twilight as a transitional moment when things have fulfilled their own being and can pass into their opposites: a moment that by denying the necessity of absolutely separate identities suggests that the separation between mother and child which is at the heart of the male experience of growing up need not always happen.[10] The speaker at first asserts dominion over the scene with elaborate similes in which nature appears grandly self-absorbed, ignoring the observer: "the cliffs permitted us to see / Only the outline of their majesty" (10–11) and "the water grey / Swang in its moon-taught way" (13–14). But nature's apparent separateness and the poet's domination are both illusory, for nature's "heart" (22) is "Bound unto man's by cords he cannot sever" (24) and through the "cord" (28: singular) a "vibration" always runs. The umbilical connection is proved in the last stanza, with its proleptic echo of another poet, Wallace Stevens, beside another sea.[11]

> For though we never spoke
> Of the grey water and the shaded rock,
> Dark wave and stone unconsciously were fused
> Into the plaintive speaking that we used
> Of absent friends and memories unforsook;

And, had we seen each other's face, we had
        Seen haply each was sad.

(29–35)

This conclusion mixes detachment and connectedness: detachment that
allows the poet to render the scene with rich imaginative fidelity and
connectedness that provides artistic nourishment and emotional reso-
nance. Here, separation does not mean inequality, and relations of dom-
inance and submission disappear.

This egalitarian representation of nature is one of many signs that *The
Seraphim, and Other Poems* is a woman's book. There are actually more
women than men in the book as a whole, and while many of the women
are conceived primarily in relation to men, many others are not. It is a
small but significant fact that the poet mentions her sisters as well as her
father and brothers in "The Pet-Name" and even alludes to her mother.
Whereas earlier volumes had little boys, this one has three girls, in "The
Little Friend," "To Bettine: The Child Friend of Goethe," and "A Song
against Singing." There are mothers and infants in "Isobel's Child" and
"The Virgin Mary to the Child Jesus." The only political figure is Queen
Victoria, the only writers Cowper (in his madness), Goethe (as the friend
of Bettine), and three women: Mary Russell Mitford, Mrs. Hemans, and
L.E.L. Other links to the female literary tradition are the ballads, the
piety, and the near-ubiquity of tears.

The tears, which are likely to arouse embarrassment or revulsion in
post-Victorian readers, mark one of the points at which the entrance of
women into the literary tradition in the nineteenth century was made
both easier and more difficult by the valorization of conventionally fem-
inine virtues. We are apt to see tears shed with such facility as signs of
luxuriating in easy emotion, as opposed to serious discriminations of
feeling or rigorous thought. We look for biographical causes and shrink
from the stereotyped portraits of Victorian womanhood that the weepi-
ness calls to mind. But tears serve a serious function. The chief moral
value that the book inculcates is the will to see and sympathize with
human life instead of withdrawing into vision, memory, or dreams. Zerah's
acquisition of this virtue constitutes the dramatic action of *The Seraphim*.
It is characteristic of Victorian literature (we think especially of Dickens)
that the mark of such saving sympathy is tears, especially when shed by
the powerful as signs of connectedness and love. The tears of Jesus
("Memory and Hope," 48, "The Weeping Saviour," *The Seraphim*, 299)
stir human and seraphic hearts to answering emotion. That Victoria

weeps at her accession to power ("The Young Queen," "Victoria's Tears") proves her untainted by ambition and brimming with love for her people: her eyes hold all the nation's "gathered tears" ("The Young Queen," 48). Men are more fortunate than angels in that angels cannot weep (*The Seraphim*, 298, 514).

Furthermore, this volume shares the common Victorian fear, most often and most poignantly expressed by Matthew Arnold, that life in the world dries up the heart and the springs of feeling; as in Arnold's poetry, tears are "the proofs of life" ("The Poet's Vow," 5.432) and the marks of human connectedness.[12] Later, when the sharpest sorrow of her life proved her still alive to pain, the tears in her poems dried up. But in this volume, with its characteristic note of detachment from actual experience and its countervailing insistence on the difficult necessity of feeling with others, the poet encourages their flow. She regards them sentimentally but also with wit: Donne provides the epigraph for "The Weeping Saviour" and the model, surely, for the comment in "The Soul's Travelling" that "Two little tears suffice to cover" the universe (204).

Donne may also have provided the structural model for the end of "The Weeping Saviour" and for "The Mediator." His poetry was not highly esteemed by the early Victorians (Robert Browning was another of its few enthusiasts), and her taste for it is a sign of Elizabeth Barrett's effort to give intellectual toughness to her religious poetry. She says in the preface that she "need not defend" her poems "for being religious in their general character" (1:169)—by which she means, of course, that she does need to defend them—and she proceeds to do so by saying that all great poetry is essentially religious. But very few good religious poems were written in the nineteenth century, and hers are not among them. T. S. Eliot attributed the greatness of Tennyson's *In Memoriam* to the quality of its doubt, not of its faith,[13] and while the two great Victorian religious poets, Christina Rossetti and Gerard Manley Hopkins, do not write a poetry of doubt, exactly, their faith enacts itself poetically through difficulty and struggle. Elizabeth Barrett's religious poems do not doubt, and rarely struggle. Nor do they pay attention to the great religious questions of the time. They give an almost childishly literal picture of a heaven inhabited by a tender Christ, adoring angels, and a paternal deity who reminds us rather too much of Edward Moulton-Barrett. Their universe is comfortably small, unbreached by the scientific movement that was expanding space and time to make the vast inimical emptiness in which Tennyson's imagination had already begun to explore. "Earth and Her Praisers" assumes something very close to the traditional date for the creation of the world, 4004 B.C. (1–2); as does Romney Leigh, who should know better, a few decades later (*Aurora Leigh* 2:167). Her imagination needed the closeness and plenitude of a universe crammed with consciousness and love which spiritualism was later to provide. By the beginning of 1845 she had read or read about Robert Chambers's *Vestiges of the Natural History of Creation* (published the previous year), which summed up with massive particularity the developments in geology and paleontology that cast doubt on the biblical account of Creation and presaged Darwin's theory of evolution, and she found it "one of the most melancholy books in the world" (*LEBB* 1:238).

For Tennyson and Browning the central Christian fact is the Incarnation, the link between humanity and a God who seemed to be drifting farther and farther away. To Elizabeth Barrett, however, God is still close by, and her attention is generally fixed on the Atonement as proof of Christ's love and of the divinity of human suffering. Her imagination does not search for God, as Tennyson's did, nor does she strive to accept God's will as religious poets have traditionally done. In her poems, to accept God's will is to renounce earthly happiness, just as the hope of heaven replaces nostalgia for Eden; but since she does not doubt that happiness is irrevocably lost and earth's beauty just a pale reflection of heaven's, there is no need to struggle. "Earth's greenest place / The colour draws from heaven" ("The Deserted Garden," 107–8). Paradise (in whatever earthly form, real or mythic, remembered or imaginary) is easily relinquished in God's name. "An Island," for instance, elaborates a fantasy of paradise until it imagines a cave for prayer, and then it imagines a prayer ("Thy will be done," 168), which dissolves the fantasy. The poems typically reach closure with references to God or heaven, but the endings do not include or transcend what went before, but simply renounce it. Instead of resolving tensions, they deny them.

One might have expected Victorian women to be comfortable in devotional poetry, where gender would seem not to matter and the speaker more often than not takes an essentially feminine role. Perhaps the trouble is that they are too comfortable, the traditional role of the religious poet reinforcing the self-effacement and self-suppression that threaten their existence as writers. For Elizabeth Barrett as for Christina Rossetti, both the tendency to imagine Christ as maternal rather than masculine (as in "Cowper's Grave") and their ready submission to God the Father push them back into the childishness that Victorian women artists had to fight their way out of in order to write at all. "God, God! / With a child's voice I cry, / Weak, sad, confidingly" ("The Soul's Travelling," 196–

98). George Herbert's recognition that he is God's child does not make him childlike in other ways; the dramatic point, in fact, is precisely that in human terms he is adult and self-dependent. But for Victorian women there is no such saving disjunction between their religious and social roles. Nor could a Victorian woman ask God metaphorically to rape her, as Donne does in "Batter My Heart." In the writings of both Rossetti and Barrett Browning, religion sanctions the life-weariness, the acceptance of inactivity, and the willed subsidence toward death which often appears in the works of male Victorian poets, too, but which the men present with a countering element of resistance that is expressed either tonally or through a dramatic frame: in "Tithonus" and "Tears, Idle Tears," for instance, "Andrea del Sarto," or *Empedocles on Etna.* But in women's religious poems, conventional gender roles match the poetic statement too closely instead of offering an enriching counterbalance and tension. The metaphorical becomes painfully literal.[14]

Another genre popular with women, however, was more flexible and accommodating. Although they have been neglected or reviled by post-Victorian readers because of their apparent acquiescence in the clichés of sentimental romance and feminine self-sacrifice, Elizabeth Barrett's ballads were her most consistently popular poems in the nineteenth century—and not without reason. She found (as did Emily Brontë, Christina Rossetti, and many novelists) that inadmissable feelings and strange ideas could pass unchallenged under a narrative disguise. Beneath their apparent conventionality of plot and sentiment, her ballads—a few published in the 1838 volume, the rest in 1844—offer a covert but thoroughgoing reassessment, often a total repudiation, of the Victorian ideas about womanliness to which they ostensibly appeal. They are her first poems to venture on the topic of romantic love, which is treated in almost all of them simply as one unsatisfactory form of love among many.

The earliest and one of the best and most lastingly popular of the ballads is "The Romaunt of Margret." Henry Chorley, who by his reviews in the *Athenaeum* was to do more than any other critic to advance her reputation, came upon it in the *New Monthly Magazine* in 1836 and was immediately captivated by "an appearance of a strange, seizing, original genius": "I got it by heart," he recalled, "and must have made myself a nuisance . . . by talking of it, in season and out of season."[15] Margret encounters her deadly double, who tells her that everyone whose love she relies on will fail her: her father, brother, and little sister (her mother, not mentioned, is presumably dead) care more for other things, and her lover has just died. She has been a perfect woman in all the appropriate relationships, apparently—trusting, self-abnegating, dutiful, loving—and now she sees how little her virtue was worth, or at any rate how little it was valued. As the poet piously explains in the preface, "the creature cannot be *sustained* by the creature" (1:168). The point is not just that one's lover can die, but rather that the whole cluster of domestic relationships which is supposed to form a woman's existence is radically insufficient. Furthermore, this is a story not of loss, but of recognition, since one's double reveals what one already knows. The use of the double, the sudden recognition of the dark underside of family affection, and the evocation of murky known-unknown regions of the unconscious recall "A True Dream," but like many other poems in this volume "The Romaunt of Margret" is significantly less fearful of evil in the self than of evil or deception in others.

The other ballad published in 1838 elaborates on Margret's discovery. "A Romance of the Ganges" introduces the strong, angry heroine who dominates most of the ballads but is hardly to be found elsewhere in Elizabeth Barrett's poetry until after 1850. Even in the ballads, however, she is distanced and at least partly disavowed by the sorry end she comes to, by the highly improbable plots, and by the characteristic form of the titles: "A Romance . . . ." "A Romance of the Ganges" presents a woman, Luti, whose lover has betrayed her for an apparently younger, more innocent girl. Luti has a deep voice (155), a "dread" laugh (182), and "wild" eyes (183), and blights the happiness of her rival, Nuleeni, with her resentment. The structure of relationships adumbrated in "Margret" recurs here: Nuleeni might be Margret's young sister, and—simply reversing the situation in "Margret," where the lover is dead and the father uncaring—the lover is explicitly associated with Luti's dead father, whose death thus seems both a loss and a betrayal. She had been first with her dying father and then with her lover at the place on the river bank where she is now realizing the lover's infidelity. "What doth it prove when Death and Love / Choose out the self-same place?" (79–80)—a suggestive question, to which we may have more answers than Luti does. Both the near-identity of father and lover and her dominating character are expressed in her recollection of herself as a child cradling her father's head on her knee (75–76). But in Elizabeth Barrett's ballads men prefer weak women.

Distrust of conventional femininity is covertly played out both in the story itself and in its history. It first appeared in *Findens' Tableaux: A Series of Picturesque Scenes of National Character, Beauty, and Costume* (1838), a gift-book annual edited by Mary Russell Mitford for which contributors composed poems or stories to accompany pictures—a reversal of the usual practice of commissioning illustrations for written words which reveals the low value assigned to the writings. She wrote it to please her friend and to help make the volume, the first of several that Miss Mitford edited, a success, since Miss Mitford needed the money. As with her contributions to later issues of *Findens'*, it was anxiously crafted to fit its setting. She did her best with the silly materials she was given to work with, although the requisite banality was beyond her grasp. Miss Mitford's precise instructions reveal some disparity in their tastes: "I want you to write me a poem in illustration of a very charming group of Hindoo girls floating their lamps upon the Ganges . . . . You know that pretty super-stition. I want a poem in stanzas. It must be long enough for two pages . . . within a fortnight or three weeks if possible . . . . [It is] the very prettiest subject and, I think the prettiest plate of the whole twelve.[16]

Although Elizabeth Barrett gave no indication of disliking this as-signment, she takes the fatuity of the picture as her starting point. She frames the story in terms of the inadequacy of natural symbols to express human feeling and the even greater inadequacy of humanly constructed symbols.

> Why, all the stars are ready
>   To symbolize the soul,
> [.   .   .   .   .   ]
> And yet the soul by instinct sad
>   Reverts to symbols low—
> To that small flame.
>
>   (37–43)

The flame is a lamp which young women set afloat on the river in little boats made from carved shells, its continuance symbolizing their lovers' fidelity. Luti's flame goes out, while Nuleeni's burns on. But Luti's fury cancels the happiness of the good omen.

> Frail symbols? None are frail enow
>   For mortal joys to borrow!—
> While bright doth float Nuleeni's boat
>   She weepeth dark with sorrow.
>
>   (209–12)

Enraged by the indifference of the symbolic world to her emotional needs, Luti has destroyed the effectiveness of the symbols that offer themselves, rather as the poet has revised the symbols—the picture—given her to work with. Writing ballads was a way of presenting herself as one woman poet among others, but she used the opportunity to criticize the conventions in which she had to work. Women's poetry mattered to her; it was alive, and could accommodate many of the subjects she most cared about. But although men as well as women wrote ballads, and even Tennyson occasionally published in annuals,[17] it was hardly sufficient for her ambitions, and she strained against it while she used it.

In her elegy on Mrs. Hemans, "Felicia Hemans (To L.E.L., Referring to Her Monody on the Poetess)," she implicitly places herself next in succession to the two most popular "poetesses" of the day, the only ones (despite the fact that she considered Joanna Baillie "the first female poet in all senses in England" [*LEBB* 1:230]) who really mattered to her. She continued to think Mrs. Hemans, while "pure hearted & nobly gifted," "a lady rather than a woman," and L.E.L. deficient in moral and intellectual strength, conventional, and insincere. These judgments are firmly if politely expressed in her revisionary poem of homage, which both imitates and corrects its predecessors.[18] She uses a stanza based on L.E.L.'s, but she turns eight short lines into four long ones and adds a final unstressed syllable to each: the effect is of energy, speed, directness, and a strong note of impatience, as of one sweeping away nonsense.

She places herself in the linked sequence of poets, quoting L.E.L.'s quotation of Mrs. Hemans's "Bring Flowers" (8), and using the repeated words to revise L.E.L.'s revision. But her own revision is not just a compliment and an expansion, like L.E.L.'s; it is a generous addition of real thought to a set of empty phrases (rather like her elaboration of the picture for *Findens'*), and by that very fact a criticism of her predecessor's inanity.

> Yes, flowers, to crown the "cup and lute," since both may come to
>   breaking,
> Or flowers, to greet the "bride"—the heart's own beating works its
>   aching;
> Or flowers, to soothe the "captive's" sight, from earth's free bosom
>   gathered,
> Reminding of his earthly hope, then withering as it withered.

                                                                              (9–12)

But she brushes aside the exhortation to bring flowers for Mrs. Hemans as sentimental and false:

> But bring not near the solemn corse a type of human seeming,
> Lay only dust's stern verity upon the dust undreaming.

$$(13-14)$$

She agrees that suffering and writing poetry are intimately connected
(17–20), but she takes vigorous issue with L.E.L.'s emphasis on Mrs.
Hemans's personal suffering and the concomitant trivialization of her
poetry,

> Which drew, from rocky earth and man, abstractions high and moving,
> Beauty, if not the beautiful, and love, if not the loving.

$$(23-24)$$

Whereas L.E.L. leaves her predecessor comfortably reposing in the
"breast" of "mother-earth,"[19] Elizabeth Barrett waves away this empty
fiction and places her on Christ's "bosom" instead (26). And her last
stanza responds to L.E.L.'s final words—"the quick tears are in my
eyes, / And I can write no more"—with a rather cruel exhortation to
cheer up: "Be happy" (29).

4
Poems (1844)

The Seraphim, and Other Poems appeared in the spring of 1838. Elizabeth Barrett had been anxious about its reception, considering it "more a trial of strength" than her earlier books (*BC* 4:21), but the reviews were gratifyingly numerous and mostly favorable. Although almost all the reviewers found the title work misguided in conception and uneven in execution, they liked many of the others and thought the author remarkably intelligent and talented—for a woman. The book was welcomed by Henry Chorley in the *Athenaeum* "as an evidence of female genius and accomplishment," although unfortunately deficient in the feminine charm of simplicity. Chorley, a distinguished critic of music and mainstay of the *Athenaeum,* was a warm admirer of women's poetry who later published a memoir of Mrs. Hemans, corresponded with Elizabeth Barrett, and became a trustee of the Brownings' marriage settlement.[1] Similar praise came from a reviewer who was struck by "the originality, ideality, earnestness, and masterly power of expression and execution" and also by "the fair author's uncommon learning," and from another who thought the poems "extraordinary productions, and especially, when considered as the compositions of a female."[2] The popularity that her works were to enjoy in America had begun, the *North American Review* devoting several mostly laudatory pages to her three published volumes.[3] She was especially gratified by the favorable attention that John Wilson of *Blackwood's,* the most important of the reviewers, bestowed on "the fair Elizabeth."[4] Good-natured, as always, in the face of adverse criticism, she was roused to defend herself only against accusations that her style was deliberately mannered or obscure. She shared the Victorian taste for poetry that was simple, pathetic, and apparently ingenuous and sincere, although she rarely satisfied it, and indignantly protested to her friends that she wrote "naturally" (*BC* 4:65). But she disputed the assumption of several reviewers and friends, including John Kenyon and Mary Russell Mitford, that religion was unfit for modern verse.[5] And the reviewers' condescension to her as a woman must have annoyed her, as it usually did.

Between 1838 and 1844 she wrote the works that established her reputation, although not the ones for which she is known today. "We learn in suffering what we teach in song," she said, quoting Shelley,[6] in the preface to the poems of those years (2:148). It was a time of intense suffering and also of maturing intellectual and artistic powers. She had a disease of the lungs, probably pulmonary tuberculosis.[7] In the winter of 1837/38 she was too ill to go outdoors, and in August 1838 she went to Torquay, a seaside town with a mild climate thought suitable for invalids. Bro and Henrietta stayed with her and other members of her family, including her father, came and went. She hated breaking up the family that had been so badly damaged already and wanted desperately to go home, but the doctors would not allow it. Except in the summer she remained indoors, usually in bed or on a sofa in her room. It seemed likely that she would not survive, and even at their most optimistic the doctors told her that she would never return to normal health. As her letters show, however, and those of her family attest, she was generally cheerful (at least outwardly) and uncomplaining. But further calamity struck: in February 1840 her brother Sam died of fever in Jamaica, and in July Bro went sailing on the bay at Torquay and drowned. "One stroke ended my youth" (*LMRM* 1:378).

We know very little about Edward Barrett's life from the time he left Charterhouse to his death at the age of thirty-three except that he did not, after all, go out into the world and make a man's career. Probably he had some employment connected with his father's affairs; whatever his occupation, however, it did not prevent his spending months in Torquay with his sister. He wanted to marry, and she wanted to give him her own money, a legacy from her uncle, to enable him to do so, but their father (as became his invariable custom with all his children) would not allow it. She said that his "heart was too tender for energy" (*LMRM* 1:306). He was the only one in her family who shared her interests, she said, the one she loved best in the world, even more than her father, and who loved her best, too. Her grief was exacerbated by a crushing burden of guilt: her father, wanting his children with him, had been reluctant to let her go to Torquay in the first place and reluctant to let Bro stay with her so long, and he had lost his eldest son by yielding to her wishes.

She was grateful to her father for not reproaching her and determined never again to assert her will against him, especially in regard to travelling for her health's sake. She felt more cause than ever to accept his arbitrary rule, although not even remorse could prevent her chafing occasionally against his high-handedness. When she began to recover from the prostration of grief, all she wanted was to escape from Torquay and the hateful noises of the sea and rejoin what remained of the family in Wimpole Street. In September 1841 she returned to London and began the long incarceration which became the stuff of legend and the setting for the most famous literary love story of the nineteenth century.

For the next few years she lived in one room, not leaving it for months at a time. She was usually alone during the day and saw her family in the evenings. Her father, whose room adjoined hers, came every night to pray with her. Arabel slept on the couch. Flush, the cocker spaniel that Mary Russell Mitford had given her, provided a sorely needed element of physical affection, amusement, and even joy. Doctors had prescribed opium some time back to calm her pulse and help her sleep, and she continued to take it.[8]

> The consequence of living through the winter in one room, with a fire, day & night, & every crevice sealed close, . . you may imagine [. . . .] At last we come to walk upon a substance like white sand [. . . .] The spiders have grown tame—& their webs are a part of our own domestic oeconomy,—Flush eschews walking under the bed. (*LMRM* 2:217)

She had two dresses, black silk for summer, black velvet, fully lined, for winter, which she was advised by her physicians never to change. From the disagreeableness—the dirt, the staleness, the smells—that must have lain behind her cheerful descriptions of her mode of living, the imagination shrinks appalled.

But it was a life that could be hallowed, as we know from sentimental fiction and verse, in onlookers' eyes. To her father, she was now the perfect daughter. He had praised her in his stiff and sanctimonious way (so different from his wife's animated, graceful prose) when she was "crushed" by the news of Sam's death:

> But what a Creature she is, I reverence her for the beauty of her character, so happy a specimen of christian submission & devotional feeling never was surpassed—No murmur is ever heard to escape her, no wish uttered to be better, only once or twice have I heard her say, as to any future plan, if it should please God that I should be better &c—Humanly speaking I should say, her health & strength are desirable for the Chest . . . .

But let us never cease importuning the Most High to spare her to us . . . . (*BC* 4:365)

"Humanly speaking," he does not seem to want her restored to normal existence.

And for the secular and literary Victorian imagination, her life was the pure essence of poetry. She was the Sleeping Beauty, Tennyson's Mariana and Lady of Shalott, Arnold's Iseult of Brittany, and the beautiful deathly women who were to dominate the visions of Dante Rossetti, Morris, and Swinburne: enclosed, isolated figures of art and desire, of living death. The domesticated spiders, like the blue fly that sings in Mariana's moated grange, belong in this fairy-tale world. The rooms to which she was confined in Torquay and Wimpole Street felt to her like prisons, her inactivity like being bound and gagged ("Oh, what it is, to lead an oyster's life," she said in lighter mood, "*not* being an oyster" [*LMRM* 2:379). But to the male artists with whom she corresponded she pleasingly figured—although it did not please her to realize it—their fantasy. For the poet Richard Hengist Horne, with whom she had an extensive correspondence, she was an "exotic plant in a greenhouse," "an *Arabian Nights* lady, shut up in a crystal rock afar," and he imagined what might happen if he was permitted an interview with "the Lady in the Iron Mask": "If the instant I entered, you vanished, and left only a large Indian shawl quivering upon the sofa—I should say (taking my breath) 'I thought as much!' "[9] Benjamin Haydon, the painter, was enchanted at the idea that two geniuses (she and himself) knew each other only through letters: "My dearest Dream," he happily informed her, "You are an imagination to me" (*IF* 137). She was artist, object of the artist's desire, and work of art, all in one. During these years of illness she found herself enacting, much against her will, the doubling (tripling, even) of roles inherent in being a woman poet.

Life and art were one for her also in that except for poetry her life seemed to have ended.

All my earthly futurity as an individual, lies in poetry. In other respects, the game is up. If it were not for this poetry which I feel within as a destiny to be worked out, I think I should wish to die tomorrow— [. . .] apart from the pain my dying would give to the few immediately connected with me. But poetry which came first, lingers last, it is like a *will to be written. (IF* 82–83)

The will is not to write, but "*to be written.*" And to John Kenyon a few months later: "All the life and strength which are in me, seem to have passed into my poetry" (*LEBB* 1:178). She seemed in fact more likely to die than to live, and in any event she could imagine no future for herself outside of literature and her family. Change did not even seem likely to come vicariously through her sisters and brothers, since their father took his place in the fairy tale that his daughter's life so painfully resembled not only by exacting complete obedience from all his children but by making it clear that he would never allow them to marry.

> I will tell you [she wrote to Browning in 1845] what I once said in a jest . .
>
> "If a prince of Eldorado should come, with a pedigree of lineal descent from some signory in the moon in one hand, & a ticket of good-behaviour from the nearest Independent chapel, in the other"—?— —
>
> "Why even *then*," said my sister Arabel, "it would not *do*." And she was right, & we all agreed that she was right. (*RB-EBB* 1:319)

Their dependency was exaggerated in Elizabeth's case by illness and reinforced by the attitude of everyone else around her: she both acquiesced in and resented "the universal tendency towards treating me as a baby" (*LBGB* 68) and took comfort in the gentle authority with which her maid, Crow (the name fits the fairy tale), watched over her. Not even her burgeoning fame significantly increased her status at home, since her father was accustomed to laugh "like Jove" at the idea that poetry could be considered serious business (*LRHH* 2:145–46). She seemed doomed to unending childhood.

Through her writing, however, she retained the power of self-assertion, and although the self-sought isolation of her youth was now involuntarily intensified she reached out to the world in letters as well as in verse. Her only visitors were relatives and a few old friends; even Wordsworth was turned away. Visitors distressed and exhausted her, gave her headaches and robbed her of sleep, and she shrank from forming new emotional ties. ("I had observed that I would refuse to know anybody, man, woman, or child, whom I was likely to love and be loved by intensely," she explained in 1843 [*LRHH* 1:65]). The only representative of the outside world who was always welcome was her cousin John Kenyon, who encouraged her as a writer, brought her news of the literary society in which he freely and genially moved, and made no emotional demands. When she wrote, however, shyness and reclusiveness vanished: "I grow insolent when I have a pen in my hand" (*LRHH* 1:64). She continued to write to Mr. Boyd for old affection's sake, to a few old friends of the family, and to some strangers who admired her poetry, including Henry Chorley of the *Athenaeum*. But her most important correspondents were

Mary Russell Mitford and two entirely epistolary friends, Richard Heng-
ist Horne and Benjamin Haydon.

She exchanged very long, very frequent letters with Miss Mitford, the
relationship between them gradually shifting as the younger woman of-
fered not only sympathy but advice in Miss Mitford's various perplexities:
her literary projects, her troubles with publishers, her financial difficul-
ties, her servant's pregnancies, her selfish and extravagant father's illness,
and her efforts to resettle her life after his death. They gossiped about
friends and acquaintances and discussed literary matters with all the
more gusto because they often disagreed. Mitford preferred society to
writing and had somewhat conventional and neoclassical tastes; she dis-
liked both Robert Browning's appearance and his poetry, for instance,
and admired Jane Austen, while Elizabeth Barrett thought Browning a
splendid poet and Austen's novels narrow, worldly, and cold. But they
both read French novels, and Miss Mitford gave her young friend what
she needed: flowers, Flush, letters full of warmth and affection and the
daily bustle of life, and literary encouragement that required no deference
to masculine power or values.

Since 1839 Elizabeth Barrett had been corresponding with Richard
Hengist Horne, poet, critic, traveller, and man of many affairs including
membership on a government commission to investigate the conditions
of children working in factories and mines. This was her first friendship
with someone she considered a poet of true "genius"—she published
an appreciative review of his lyrical epic, *Orion,* in 1843[10]—and almost
all their letters are about literary matters. She contributed a version of
"Queen Annelida and False Arcite" to his modernized edition of Chau-
cer, to which the other contributors included Wordsworth and Leigh
Hunt. They planned to collaborate in a lyrical drama to be called "Psyche
Apocalypte," depicting a man frightened by the confrontation with his
own soul—a sort of cross between "The Tempest," "A True Dream,"
and "The Poet's Vow" (the hero neglects the girl he had loved and
stumbles upon her dead body while fleeing into nature), vaguely set in
Greece. She sketched an outline and some scenes, but the project not
surprisingly languished. And she was the chief and secret collaborator
in his collection of essays on contemporary writers, *A New Spirit of the
Age,* apparently providing most of the sections on Tennyson, Landor,
Wordsworth, Carlyle, and Monckton Milnes and, along with Robert
Browning, most of the epigraphs.[11]

Such unacknowledged labor is the traditional role of women in the
making of men's books, but the relationship was not entirely one-sided.

She advised, encouraged, consoled, and read proof for him; he consulted, praised, and offered to deal with the printers when her *Poems* were coming out. But when he wrote about her in *A New Spirit of the Age*, he exaggerated the ways in which her life was fit for legend, attributing to the woman who had always disliked Latin literature the authorship of elegant Latin verses as well as six or seven years' confinement in one room (actually, she told him, it was only four or five [*LRHH* 1:252]), and presenting her, she said in rueful summary, as "an Hebraic monster who lives in the dark" (*LMRM* 2:400). She was particularly hurt that the essay said almost nothing of her poems, and indeed Horne apologized for having written so poorly about them.[12] But she remained loyal: she defended his odd manners and amatory misadventures against Mary Russell Mitford's complaints, and Mitford's intolerance of Horne's social misdemeanors strained Elizabeth Barrett's regard for her.

Her epistolary friendship with Benjamin Haydon, the historical painter who had been Keats's friend, began in 1842. Haydon wrote to her about his work, the theory and practice of painting, the injustices he had suffered, his hopes (all, in the event, disappointed), Keats, Caroline Norton, Wellington and Napoleon, and his wife and children. He lent her pictures, including a portrait of Wordsworth on which she wrote a sonnet that Wordsworth himself approved when he had fixed one of the lines, and gave her a Keats manuscript. She liked the energy and genuineness of his character, was amused by his appalling egotism, and gently advised him not to imagine conspiracies or to boast or moan in public. That he called her a genius but was interested in no one's genius but his own did not disturb her. His letters were a kind of contact with life although he, like Horne, was charmed precisely by the inaccessibility of his "dear Invisible" (*IF* 155). He committed suicide in 1846 and caused her considerable embarrassment by appointing her to edit his voluminous memoirs, a final ancillary service that she declined to perform.

When she was not writing, she read. She read whatever came to hand—poems, plays, essays, letters and memoirs, novels, periodicals, classical and patristic Greek, and works that for one reason or another despite her age and accomplishments she felt compelled to conceal. At Torquay she made her way through Plato, although her physician told her to avoid mental exertion (her Plato was fortunately deceptive on the outside, looking "as good as a novel" [*LMRM* 1:117]).[13] After Bro's death, however, her interest in Greek seems to have waned, as if the original impulse had worn itself out or lost its reason for being. Instead, she read French novels of a sort that decent Englishwomen did not admit to knowing, Paul de Kock, Hugo, Balzac, and above all George Sand—

the literary version of the dangerous world she had dreaded Bro's going off to, long ago—and when she discovered that Mary Russell Mitford read these books too (although with some trepidation), she arranged to have a steady supply sent to her in the country. There was no one else to whom she dared mention them. They genuinely appalled her: Balzac, for instance, she found "revolting—cold & bitter with the sight & slough of evil . . to be shrunk from, as at the touch of a worm" (*LMRM* 2:124). But they seemed to give her life. "These wicked Gallic geniuses [. . . .] light me up, & make me feel alive to the ends of my fingers" (*LMRM* 2:397). She was increasingly restless, longing to travel, and books were a substitute for experience.

Her turn from ancient to modern literature is marked also in the two series of essays that she wrote for the *Athenaeum* in 1842. Despite the nostalgia for an early paradisiacal literary world with which they begin, they are markedly optimistic, tracing literary history in a way that implicitly leaves a place for herself at the end of the line. The first essay is a lively and entertaining survey of Greek Christian poetry, including about eight hundred lines of original translation. It is a remarkable feat of scholarship, exposition, and—since she found much of the material exceedingly tedious—endurance. She had read this poetry with Mr. Boyd, whose translations she knew were inferior to her own, and the essay is both a tribute and a farewell to him and to classical Greece and the " 'Fathers', as we call them filially" who succeeded to it. It flaunts the superiority she had once attempted to hide. The opening elegiacally evokes the classical Greek language: "No other language has lived so long and died so hard,— pang by pang, each with a dolphin color—yielding reluctantly to that doom of death and silence which must come at last to the speaker and the speech. Wonderful it is to look back fathoms down the great Past, thousands of years away . . . ."[14] She commemorated in prose that mimics what it describes "the subtlety of the ancient music, the variety of its cadences, the intersections of sweetness in the rise and fall of melodies, rounded and contained in the unity of its harmony" (15). This is not the heroic literature of her childhood imaginings, but a lyrical Romantic paradise that mingles death with beauty. Its successors, she says, despite their love, learning, and devotion seldom attained to true poetry, and she regards most of them with amused condescension. In *An Essay on Mind* she had boldly taken her place among learned men; here, she dismisses them from her presence.

Often, however, she seems to be mocking herself too. Some of the translations sound very much like *The Seraphim,* which like many of the works she describes and scorns is after all a Christian version of a classical original. Her witty denigration is particularly nervous and uncertain in regard to a woman, the learned empress Eudocia who in exile "address[ed] herself most unholily, with whatever good intentions and delicate fingers, to pulling Homer's gold to pieces" and turning his poem into a Christian epic.

> For mark the poetical justice of her destiny; let all readers mark it, and all writers, especially female writers, who may not be half as learned, and not half as fair,—that although she wrote many poems [. . .] whose title and merit are recorded, not one, except this cento [the Christianized Homer], has survived. [. . .] This is called Eudocia! [. . .] O fair mischief! she is punished by her hand. (67–68)

Learning, beauty, Christianizing Homer, a woman who *is* her poem ("This is called Eudocia")—the excited tone shows the writer's nervousness about these matters. She insisted that poetry should be religious, although Miss Mitford and Mr. Kenyon and other friends thought otherwise. "We want the touch of Christ's hand upon our literature, as it touched other dead things—we want the sense of the saturation of Christ's blood upon the souls of our poets, that it may cry *through* them in answer to the ceaseless wail of the Sphinx of our humanity, expounding agony into renovation" (23). But she admits that true Christian poetry is not being written. The Greek Christian poets make her uncomfortable because they did boldly and badly the sort of thing she wants to do herself.

This essay ends with the assertion that the English poets are the true inheritors of the Greeks. The other essay, ostensibly a review of two books, an anthology called *The Book of the Poets* and Wordsworth's *Poems of Early and Late Years, including the Borderers,* surveys English poetry from its Chaucerian wellspring to its eighteenth-century nadir and then celebrates the Romantic revival as exemplified by Wordsworth. She presents one author after another, as she did with the Greeks, trying to epitomize the essential spirit of each. She seems to have read everything and liked most of it, and she is especially charmed by the early poets and by the Elizabethans. A true Romantic herself, she looks for genius, passion, energy, and sincerity, and finds Dryden and Pope unpoetical.

Nature and art cannot be separated, she says in some of her clearest formulations of her poetics. "Nature is God's art—the accomplishment of a spiritual significance hidden in a sensible symbol," and human art interprets nature (172). Furthermore (a comforting thought for her urban solitude), the poet finds nature, or "the world," within himself: Shakespeare "was wise in the world, having studied it in his heart" (173).

"Every being is his own mirror to the universe" (174). Nature is not only in the country. "Nature is where God is. Poetry is where God is" (206). They can be found in machinery and steam and "in the foulest street of your city" as well as in the Brocken or Niagara (207). But in her celebration of the birth of Romanticism she reverts from these lofty generalizations back to the image of Nature as the mother who loves only her sons that had troubled her earlier verse.

> Nature, the true mother, cried afar off to her children, "Children, I am here! come to me." (216)

> [Wordsworth] threw himself not at the feet of Nature, but straightway and right tenderly upon her bosom. [. . .] trustfully as child before mother, self-renouncingly as child after sin, absorbed away from the consideration of publics and critics as child at playhours, with a simplicity [. . .], with an innocent utterance [. . .], and with a faithfulness to natural impressions acknowledged since by all to be the highest art. (217)

This is the point of view of someone who is not a son and can no longer be a trusting child, and indeed nature essentially disappears from her own poetry until she returns to the question of maternal betrayal in *Aurora Leigh*. It is peripheral to her final evaluations even of the Romantics. She admires Wordsworth as "a true Christian poet," especially when he is not writing directly about religion (220), and dismisses Byron with surprising harshness because he only expresses passion. She refuses to believe that poetry is in decline, and ends by celebrating Wordsworth because his art (like her own, although of course she does not say so) is his life.

The essays are, then, forward-looking and optimistic, singling out Tennyson and Browning as the gifted spirits of the age and imagining a future for poetry in which she herself (although she does not say this either) could have a part. The "long summer" of classical Greece (13) is over, and the happy boyhood of Romanticism was not for girls. It is a bit chilling to observe that women appear among the English poets only as examples of decline. But true Christian poetry, she persisted in believing, had yet to be written and would come from the heart's experience, and these essays take the essence of poetry to be feeling—fervor, rapture, love—despite their insistence on formal control. The congruence between the empathetic, expressive poetics of Romanticism and the values and experiences available to nineteenth-century women seemed to open the way for women to write poetry. The essay ends with the affirmation that true poets live, as she has done, in and for their art.

Having written these essays, she resolved to waste no more time on prose. By 1842 her health, strength, reputation, and creative powers were all increasing, as if in proof of Victorian pieties about the rewards of suffering. In warm weather she could even go outside in an invalid chair, and while visitors still tired and perturbed her she seems to have become less shy. In 1843 she wrote some of the strongest works she had produced so far, and in 1844 Moxon published the *Poems* in two volumes that established her as one of the leading poets of the age.

Poems (1844) shows Elizabeth Barrett in fuller possession of her powers than ever before. She has not yet, perhaps, quite found her own voice, but she is well on her way to doing so, and this is the last of her volumes that one wants to call transitional. Despite the greatly increased range and versatility, however, a surprisingly large number of the poems seem to amplify or revise those published in 1838. *A Drama of Exile* is an elaboration of the themes and methods of *The Seraphim,* as "The Lost Bower" is of "The Deserted Garden," and "A Vision of Poets" (though less precisely) of "A Vision of Fame" (1826) and "The Poet's Vow." Both the 1838 and the 1844 volumes contain imaginary paradises ("An Island," "The House of Clouds"), pet animals (the sea-mew, doves, Flush), mothers and dead children ("Isobel's Child," "The Mourning Mother"), Queen Victoria, Mrs. Hemans, and L.E.L. Both offer visionary overviews of the course of human life ("Rhapsody of Life's Progress," "The Fourfold Aspect") and several ballads. But on the whole we are reminded more of what will come after than of what went before. The sonnets of psychological analysis and various studies of sexual love anticipate "Sonnets from the Portuguese." The ballads culminate in "Lady Geraldine's Courtship," which carries their themes into the modern world and leads directly to *Aurora Leigh.* "The Cry of the Children" and "Crowned and Buried" point to the later political works. And several poems explore the social and poetical roles of women, reaching toward—and sometimes even demonstrating—the energizing conclusion that modern life offers extraordinary opportunities for women poets.

For although the differences between these poems and those of 1838 may be less immediately striking than the repetitions, they are auspicious of change. In striking contradiction to her actual situation, but with fine proleptic accuracy, the dominant point of view has shifted to that of one who is a participant in life rather than (as in 1838) an observer. Although women's experience is defined mostly as suffering, it is assumed to be a fit subject for poetry. The poet speaks with new confidence, as if she really trusts her own voice, and instead of recoiling from the dreadful brink of self-confrontation she worries about how to express what she has to say. In the dedication to her father, she puts herself forward for the last time in the position of a child, but she asserts as she does so that she is a child no longer and admits that her book is activated by ambition for more praise than his own.

> When your eyes fall upon this page of dedication [. . .] your first thought will be of the time far off when I was a child and wrote verses, and when I dedicated them to you who were my public and my critic [. . . .] Some-what more faint-hearted than I used to be, it is my fancy thus to seem to return to a visible personal dependence on you, as if indeed I were a child again; to conjure your beloved image between myself and the public, so as to be sure of one smile,—and to satisfy my heart while I sanctify my ambition, by associating with the great pursuit of my life its tenderest and holiest affection. (2:142–43)

Ambition still has to be screened and sanctified by filial dependency, but a fleeting appeal to memory—a momentary "fancy," "as if indeed [she] were a child again"—will apparently suffice. And the dedication's brief relapse into childishness is canceled by the preface, which defends her bold dealings with Miltonic subjects and solemnly affirms the seriousness of the occupation that her father regarded with condescending amusement.

> Poetry has been as serious a thing to me as life itself; and life has been a very serious thing: there has been no playing at skittles for me in either. [. . . .] I have done my work, so far, as work,—not as mere hand and head work, apart from the personal being,—but as the completest expression of that being to which I could attain,—and as work I offer it to the public. (2:148–49)

She had justified her emulation of Aeschylus in *The Seraphim* by the fact that she was a Christian. Now, more daringly, she attempts to amplify Milton on the basis of her experience as a woman. In the longest of the new poems, *A Drama of Exile,* she redefines Milton's subject by focussing on Eve's guilt and repentance and redefines the role of the poet by asserting that suffering is a source of knowledge—a source to which even those who lack a classical education or the authority of male ex-perience may have easy access. In "A Vision of Poets," she says in the preface, she tries to show that the "mission of the poet" implies "self-abnegation," and to demonstrate "the obvious truth, above all, that if knowledge is power, suffering should be acceptable as a part of knowl-edge" (2:147). The conclusions are unstated but obvious: women can be poets, and women's lives can be their theme. When she insisted that Christianity belonged in poetry, she did not explain this incidental benefit of the religion of suffering.

A Drama of Exile is Eve's story. It begins, like *The Seraphim* and "A True Dream," outside a closed door—*"The outer side of the gate of Eden, shut fast"*—and takes up where *Paradise Lost* leaves off, just after the expulsion of Adam and Eve from paradise. Formally it is a sort of cross between Greek and Renaissance drama. The writing has verve and variety: the characters speak in blank verse, with Lucifer displaying energy, cleverness, and (what is all too rarely allowed to enter Elizabeth Barrett's earlier poetry) verbal irony, in a way that recalls Jacobean tragedy, while choruses of spirits and angels provide lyric interludes. The plot is minimal, consisting entirely in conversation: Adam and Eve talk first with Lucifer, who cannot tempt them to misconceive their situation and their sin; then with spirits of the earth, who berate them; and finally with Christ, who reconciles them with the earth spirits and promises the redemption of humanity. Adam teaches Eve not to wish to die, Eve teaches Adam humility and patience, and they both learn hope from Christ.

Like *The Seraphim*, *A Drama of Exile* is about learning to accept exclusion from paradise and the necessity of suffering. But the point of view is that of human participants rather than angelic observers: participants, moreover, who are themselves the cause both of the suffering they endure and of that which surrounds them, and whose greatest sorrow (Eve's, at least) is not loss but guilt—not the ambiguous guilt of desire and aspiration enacted in "A True Dream," but guilt for evil clearly and actually done. Eve has to accept a woman's part and replace the lost maternal Eden by becoming a mother herself. "Rise, woman, rise," Adam exhorts her:

> To thy peculiar and best altitudes
> Of doing good and of enduring ill,
> Of comforting for ill, and teaching good,
> And reconciling all that ill and good
> Unto the patience of a constant hope,—
> Rise with thy daughters!

> (1842–48)

She welcomes the prospect of activity, however painful or humble, and willingly takes on "Noble work" in place of "garden-rest" (1899–1900). She emerges from Eden, that is, into adult participation in the world.

As part of this moralized celebration of life outside the locked gate of lost innocence (where the speaker of "A True Dream," too, had inadvertently placed herself), the poem firmly disengages woman from the natural world with which Romanticism had identified her. Nature is a mother who has failed her children (1152), but Eve is "Mother of the world" (1824), and it is she who has betrayed nature rather than nature betraying her. Like the poet in "The Poet's Vow," she blames herself for the curse that blights the earth, but after Adam points out that nature should be subordinate to them (1170) she moves on to consider higher things. Christ explains that earth was created for mankind's "delight and use" (1778), exists only by human law (1786–97), and is repaid for serving humanity by the poet who "extend[s] / Across your head his golden fantasies / Which glorify you into soul from sense" (1811–13). Earlier Elizabeth Barrett had scoffed at the Romantic notion that the imagination half-creates the natural beauty it perceives, but when she separates women from nature she no longer feels compelled to defend nature against male domination. Other poems also assert the power of poetry and religion over nature. The poet in "A Vision of Poets" long ago "claimed for his / Whatever earthly beauty is" (17–18), and moreover "in his spirit bore / A beauty passing the earth's store" (19–20); he learns that poetry beautifies the earth (448–65), just as the foolish people in "The Poet and the Bird" who banish a poet in order to listen to a nightingale discover that without the poet the nightingale doesn't sing. Elsewhere, nature appears simply as a glorified memory ("The Prisoner") or a moral emblem ("Lessons from the Gorse"), more complexly as the setting for the world of childish imagination ("The Lost Bower"). And "The Dead Pan" elaborates the assertion that Christian truth has displaced mythologized nature just as Christ has banished Pan; Christianity, which gives women access to the Aeschylean tradition, also banishes the Romantic idea of nature.

Several poems imagine a woman's life in the social world, although usually at a discreet distance from the present time and place and with considerable obliquity, contradiction, and even, perhaps, disingenuousness. Through narrative she could examine, modify, and criticize conventional ideas about women's place in life and art, and her first major effort to do so occurs in her ballads, all of which, except for those published in 1838, appear here. Aurora Leigh describes the dubiously successful beginnings of her own career: "My ballads prospered; but the ballad's race / Is rapid for a poet who bears weights / Of thought and golden image" (5:84–86). Elizabeth Barrett's ballads prospered too, and like Aurora she did not find their success particularly creditable—a judgment emphatically endorsed by twentieth-century critics. But when Robert Browning told her that he loved her poems, these were the ones he mostly meant; the ballads are almost the only works of hers that he mentions in their correspondence, and he mentions them often. They charmed a diverse and distinguished company of Victorian admirers, including Thomas Carlyle, Harriet Martineau, Margaret Fuller, Edgar Allan Poe, and most of the poet's friends and reviewers, in the years when her reputation was being made.[15] Modern readers are apt to go to the other extreme and find only suspicious fluency, verbal thinness, inept diction, mawkish sentimentality, and the most dreary and conventional female fantasies and repressions. Beneath their apparent conventionality of plot and sentiment, however, these poems add up to a thoroughgoing reassessment—often a total repudiation—of the Victorian ideas about womanliness to which they apparently appeal, and it is in this contradiction that their greatest interest lies.

We can see why they were popular. The stories, although invariably silly, are usually entertaining, and as the poet said, "It is the *story* that has power with people" (*LEBB* 1:247). She herself did not find "the story" the best part of narrative poetry (*BC* 4:109), but she did not scorn its simple appeal, being (she said), a "complete and unscrupulous romance reader": "My love of fiction began with my breath, and will end with it" (*LEBB* 1:234). Sometimes there is amusing dialogue. And while Aurora Leigh deplores the ballad's speed, most of them rush the reader quite pleasantly along: Harriet Martineau felt herself *"swept through"* "Lady Geraldine's Courtship" (*LHSB* 263). But the main appeal is to the feelings. Miss Mitford, whose fondness for such things must have lessened the value of her opinion in her friend's eyes, wrote to her: "I do entreat and conjure you to write more ballads or tragedies . . . poems of human feelings and human actions."[16] The poet told with amused distaste of her ballads' reported effects as evidenced in "a lady falling into hysterics" and "the gush of tears [. . .] down the Plutonian cheeks of a lawyer" (*LEBB* 1:247). Still, she was not immune to the susceptibility she laughed at. "You know how I care for ballads—they *carry* so much .. slight vehicle as they seem to be. All the passion of the heart [if not Aurora's weight of thought and image] will go into a ballad, & feel at home."[17] She even liked Mary Howitt's ballads, which have nothing to recommend them except a kind of watery pathos. Her ballads gave what early Victorian critics of poetry wanted: an apparently simple appeal to common human emotions. That they also undercut the kind of feelings they provoke and ostensibly celebrate, went unnoticed—even, one occasionally suspects, at times by the poet herself.

These poems are particularly revealing because she did not take them entirely seriously. Some were composed, like "A Romance of the Ganges," to accompany illustrations in albums edited under the impulsion of urgent financial need by Mary Russell Mitford, a mode of inspiration (rather like psychological tests which ask one to make up stories about pictures) and a form of publication that would preclude any ambition except to do a decent, professional job.[18] The most popular of them all, "Lady Geraldine's Courtship," was largely written in a day, to meet a publisher's deadline, and the speed of writing reinforces the impression given by the story itself that it represents a relatively uncensored fantasy. She wrote ballads partly because occasions required them, partly because they came easily to her, and partly because she was looking for suitable subjects and genres. Once she had left the empty seclusion of Wimpole Street for a wider world and committed herself to modern themes, she wrote no more of them. In this apparently most innocent, retrogressive, and sentimental of feminine genres, she explored with a passionate heart and a very cold eye the myths and fantasies of nineteenth-century womanhood, and especially the attitudes embodied by the gift books in which the poems appeared. That she satisfied the taste she deftly undermines suggests something of her ballads' strange complexity.

The ballads examine with considerable resentment the virtues of self-repression and self-sacrifice that are seen as heroic in *A Drama of Exile* and associated there and elsewhere in her poetry with mothers. For *Findens' Tableaux of the Affections: A Series of Picturesque Illustrations of the Womanly Virtues* (1839), she produced "The Romaunt of the Page," the story of a woman who succumbs to an ideal of "womanly virtues" that the poet both scorns and shares. The heroine, who met her husband only when they were married at her mother's deathbed, has disguised herself as a page to follow him to the Crusades (enacting the poet's childhood daydream of dressing as a boy and going off as Byron's page) and has three times saved his life in battle. As they ride through the calm woodland she seems to hear her dead mother's prayer and is encouraged to unveil her secret to the knight, who has not recognized her. "Perhaps he [the page] felt in nature's broad / Full heart, his own was free" (40–41: the masculine pronoun is used almost to the end); if so (s)he was mistaken—or betrayed, perhaps, by a nature that is not benign to her daughters—for the knight firmly asserts that wives belong at home. If his wife were to follow him as his page, she would be "Unwomaned" (196) and he would "love her as my servitor, / But little as my wife" (228–29). The page is very angry at this, as Luti was at a similar discovery of what men value in women. She hears the enemy coming, tells the knight to ride on ahead, and dies fighting in his defense, while through the wood echoes a dirge for a dying abbess, another mother. The page is a thoroughly heroic figure whose denunciation of the knight's womanly ideal the poet evidently approves: "False page, but truthful woman" (297); but she chooses a woman's fate—unrecognized, self-sacrificing death— anyway. Nature, which in a contemporary work by a man would be more likely to undermine social and moral conventions, apparently endorses her choice.

A similar choice, expressed with more diffuse and covert rebellion, occurs in "Bertha in the Lane," which might be described as a ballad in the form of a dramatic monologue. The speaker is on her deathbed, telling her sister, Bertha, that she gave up her lover to Bertha when she discovered that he loved Bertha, not herself: like men in the other ballads, he turned out not to admire strong women. Their dying mother had asked her to be a mother to Bertha (35), and this last sacrifice fulfills her promise. The mother's ghost appears, an ambiguous presence ex-pressing heavenly approval but bringing death (her "smile is bright and bleak / Like cold waves" [47–48]). To become like one's mother is to give up everything. "I have given / All the gifts required of me" (38–39), the speaker tells her mother with what sounds very much like re-sentment, and to Bertha she urges the immensity and willingness of her sacrifice in terms that could only be designed to make Bertha miserable. The poem's mawkish and mealy-mouthed tone makes one doubt that Elizabeth Barrett was fully aware of the conflicting impulses it evidently embodies; she made no denigratory remarks about it, and after her own mother's death discourse and judgment tended to fail her on the subject of mothers. One wonders how Robert Browning read it: he refers to it often, but whether he was attracted by its sentiment, or by the skill with which it exploits the ability of the dramatic monologue to reveal more than the speaker intends, is hard to say.

The least successful of the ballads both as a composition and with the reviewers was the rather inchoate "Lay of the Brown Rosary," first published in *Findens' Tableaux: The Iris of Prose, Poetry, and Art for 1840* as "The Legend of the Brown Rosarie" and based on a particularly complicated and improbable picture. This is the one most extensively concerned with family relations. A "sickening farrago of stilted trash," the *United Servœs Gazette* called it, striking a rare note of discord amid the chorus of praise for the ballads.[19] It was popular in America, though: Margaret Fuller liked it less than the other ballads, but she reported that it had circulated extensively in manuscript before the 1844 *Poems* were published in America.[20] The heroine has taken her life into her own hands, giving her soul to the devil to avoid dying before her marriage.

As usual, female self-assertion alienates—here, kills—the lover: he dies at the altar, and then she repents and dies too. Even more than in the other ballads, family affection has sinister undertones: her mother is pleasant but ineffectual, her good little brother watches and accuses her, and her dead father in effect demands that she join him in death. They all in their various ways combine to keep her from her own life. But simply rejecting the family will not do, either: this is the only ballad in which the heroine's behavior is assumed just to be wrong.

"Rhyme of the Duchess May," which despite the irritating "Toll slowly" that interrupts every stanza was extremely popular, gives the same double vision of female self-assertion that the other ballads do but without falling into the complications of mixed familial emotions that make "The Lay of the Brown Rosary" awkward and incoherent. Duchess May escapes from what remains of her family with the poet's approbation although not with impunity: a rich orphan, she elopes with the man she loves, scorning with scathing wit her wicked uncle and the loutish cousin who wants to marry her (like a later heroine, Aurora, she refuses to marry a cousin named Leigh of Leigh). It is somewhat as if Tennyson's Maud were to acquire will and wit and become the heroine of *Maud.* The rejected cousin tries to recover her by force, and when her husband realizes that defeat is inevitable, he resolves in an astonishingly bizarre gesture to end the conflict and save the lives of his people by riding his horse off the top of the castle tower. Duchess May had enjoyed their exciting elopement on that very horse and wants to ride with him this time too. But he, like her uncle and cousin, has a low opinion of female fidelity and courage. She will soon forget him once he's dead, he thinks, and anyway he doesn't want her around when there's man's work to be done. Like the knight in "The Romaunt of the Page," he knows where wives don't belong: "In this hour I stand in need of my noble red-roan steed, / But no more of my noble wife" (319–20). She protests by her "womanhood" (323, 325), leaps into the saddle, and goes with him anyway, in what is in effect a bold, bizarre sexual consummation. The poem insists that her behavior, like the page's, is both womanly in the best sense and unsuitable for a woman. She asserts the strength of a "woman's will" (81), but we are frequently reminded that her hands are small. In the conclusion the narrator meditates on Duchess May's story at the grave of "Maud, a Three-Year Child" (415). "Now, your will is all unwilled," he says to her, "Now, ye lie as meek and mild [. . .] as Maud the child" (425–27). The self-assertive woman is as helpless as a little girl, and the narrator turns for comfort at the end to a paternal God.

Women's rebellions against their lot are always ambivalent, unsuc-
cessful, and misunderstood in the ballads, just as the ballads themselves
were in expressing Elizabeth Barrett's rebellion against social and literary
convention. The use of medieval settings, too, and the implicit medi-
evalism of the ballad form were part of her search for a world which
would give scope for passion and action—a search which she later saw
had been misdirected: Aurora Leigh contemptuously rejects poetry that
sings "of some black chief, half knight, half sheep-lifter, / Some beau-
teous dame, half chattel and half queen" (*Aurora Leigh* 5:195–96). The
rigidly hierarchical social ideal of nineteenth-century medievalism ad-
mitted women only in subordinate and peripheral roles. In Carlyle's *Past
and Present* (1843), as later in Tennyson's *Idylls of the King,* a man's social
and spiritual value is measured by his work, and work is conceived
through metaphors—monastic reform, knightly prowess—in which women
have no part. Carlyle's hero rules a monastery, and all the knights in
Tennyson's Camelot are male: Spenser's Britomart has no Victorian
granddaughters. In the terms that would matter most to women who felt
imprisoned in women's sphere—the relative freedom or fixity of social
roles—nineteenth-century medievalism's dream of order was thoroughly
retrogressive. And in its dreams of love women are passive and remote,
objects of fear and worship but powerless (unless, of course, they are
enchantresses) except to grant or withhold love. Elizabeth Barrett's bal-
lads investigate the resources of medievalism, which was one of the main
imaginative alternatives in the nineteenth century to the constrictions of
modern life, and reject it as nostalgic folly.

The pattern of female fantasy that chivalric romance encourages is ex-
amined in "The Romance of the Swan's Nest," written later than any of
the others except "Lady Geraldine's Courtship." Little Ellie—the dimin-
ishing adjective always accompanies her name—dreams that a duke's eld-
est son will beg for her love. She will send him away to do great deeds and
will require his complete and repeated submission before she accepts him.
The excessiveness of her imagined demands and triumphs shows that this
is a fantasy of power, ambition, and fame, not simply of love. But even in
daydreams her ambition is displaced onto a man, and while she dreams she
loses the one thing she does have: the swan's nest among the reeds with
which, in her fantasy, she will finally reward her knight. The swan disap-
pears, a rat gnaws the reeds, and the nest is left empty. Love, sexuality,
fertility, a cosy Victorian home: while she dreams of annexing male power—
because, presumably, she dreams of it—she loses her one treasure. (Eliza-

beth Barrett herself, she said in 1845, had been rescued only by the "safety valve" of poetry from her youthful habit not just of "castle-building" but of a "consistent living of another synchronal life in the ideal" [*LMRM* 3:61].) Most of the other ballads can be read as variations on the story of the damsel and the knight in which the damsel usurps some of the knight's functions; this one, in contrast, defines the story as a daydream of bliss in which the two roles are fixed and separate.

The loss of the swan's nest is more genuinely affecting than the melodramatic or pathetic catastrophes of the other ballads, and the attack on the destructiveness of chivalric falsehoods is, one would think, unmistakable. And yet it was mistaken. The *Blackwood's* reviewer, for instance, praised the "graceful playfulness" with which it presents the "sympathies and enjoyments of a child."[21] This was how all of Elizabeth Barrett's ballads were received, and she was both amused and disconcerted by the ease with which they touched precisely the chords of feeling that they were meant at least partly to discredit. She called "The Romaunt of the Page" "barbarous," and laughed at it, but Miss Mitford thought it "by far the finest thing" she had ever written, John Forster found it "very sweet and noble," and for the *Athenaeum* reviewer it was "one of the most beautiful things from a woman's hand which has appeared for many a day."[22] "Rhyme of the Duchess May," which was not one of her own favorites, was even more popular. Almost all her ballads cry out to be read as feminist revisions of old tales—"The Romance of the Swan's Nest," most clearly, is an inversion of the story of Sleeping Beauty, like Christina Rossetti's "Prince's Progress," which was similarly misread. Victorian readers took these poems as light and pleasing variations, suitable for women to write and for children to read, on romances and fairy tales as Tennyson and others were retelling them. Elizabeth Barrett told the old stories in a style and tone that gave no hint of revisionary intention, and she discarded the ballad form without discovering how to use it effectively against itself.[23]

Her growing sense that a woman's place was not just in modern times but in the political arena (although not, perhaps, leading armies down the Danube) finds expression in poems of social protest. One stanza in "The Cry of the Human" attacks the Corn Laws, and "Lady Geraldine's Courtship" celebrates with self-consciously radical glee the marriage of a rich aristocrat to a man of peasant birth. But the most important both in popularity and influence and for its place in the poet's development is "The Cry of the Children." Unlike most of her later political poems, it remained within the sphere of women's approved concerns. Like Tennyson's *Maud* in the next decade, it is a horrified response to an official report on social conditions: in this case, to one written by Elizabeth Barrett's correspondent and collaborator R. H. Horne on child labor in mines and factories. We may find the meter awkward, the diction sentimental and false (would one child refer to another, for example, as "little"? [39, 44, 46]), the tears that fall abundantly in almost every stanza too profuse and damp, and the appeal to our feelings inartistically explicit; but we should recognize that for writers without the prophetic-ironic genius of Blake or Carlyle or Dickens it was hard to find an appropriate tone in which to speak of the appalling facts of suffering in Victorian England. Any adequate response was likely to sound, as *Maud* did, morbid or hysterical. "The Cry of the Children" is painful to read, but like *Maud* it attempts to channel emotion through formal complexity, and its moments of wrenching awkwardness seem deliberately to impede too easy a flow of feeling. As a stimulus to the Victorian social conscience it was evidently a success.

Middle-class women's literary protests on behalf of the poor in the nineteenth century, like their work for social reform, reflect the likeness they perceived between their own situations and those of the more obviously disempowered. The feelings given political expression in "The Cry of the Children" are familiar from many of Elizabeth Barrett's other works. Like Isobel's child, the children want to die, and the poet suggests that they would be better off dead. They suffer to the most extreme degree the loss of childhood and of the pleasures of nature that threatens children in Elizabeth Barrett's poems and has already befallen most of the adults. Like several of her apparently autobiographical speakers, they are pale, weary, stricken by loss, unable to answer when action or pleasure calls. This poem, however, does not end in resignation or renunciation, but in accusation and rage and threats of divine vengeance: the last stanza with its violent imagery, angels, and children whose misery incites divine retribution recalls Blake.

> "How long," they say, "how long, O cruel nation,
>   Will you stand, to move the world, on a child's heart,—
> Stifle down with a mailed heel its palpitation,
>   And tread onward to your throne amid the mart?
> Our blood splashes upward, O gold-heaper,
>   And your purple shows your path!
> But the child's sob in the silence curses deeper
>   Than the strong man in his wrath."

The actual, officially documented sufferings of such children, so much worse than anything in her own life or fictions, justify the release of feelings that we may think have been suppressed elsewhere: the children assert that God the Father has deserted them, and they curse the society that makes them suffer. Such open expression of anger, given finer artistic form, will characterize Barrett Browning's most powerful political poetry.

The other mood of her political writings is quite different and aesthetically more attractive: detached, analytical, witty, appealing to a complex range of ideas and feelings. "Crowned and Buried" is a meditation on the return of Napoleon's ashes to France, spoken with a self-assurance, wit, and energy reminiscent of Byron and with none of the rather stilted solemnity that marred her earlier political verse. Off-rhymes ("pyramidal / idle," for instance, or "spice / Ptolemies" [25, 28, 29, 30]), which might grate on our ears at more solemn moments, seem in this lively verse, as they do in Bryon's, pleasing jokes. The poem tries to give an unpartisan view of Napoleon; years earlier Elizabeth Barrett had indignantly likened Napoleon on Elba to Prometheus chained to the rock, and she still cannot help admiring this destructive, flawed Prometheus.[24] In keeping with her early preoccupation with fame, the first thirteen stanzas consider the power of Napoleon's "name," balancing horror at the devastation he wrought against something very like exultation at his power to seize the popular imagination.

> Blood fell like dew beneath his sunrise—sooth
> But glittered dew-like in the covenanted
> Meridian light. He was a despot—granted!
> But the αὐτός of his autocratic mouth
> Said yea i' the people's French; he magnified
> The image of the freedom he denied. (145–50)

Here the unclouded openness and good humor of her letters brightens her poetry too. The ambivalent response to power that formed so terrible a conflict in "The Tempest" has been transferred to a larger, public question, and while love, tears, funerals, graves, death, and even angels are still valorized, they are balanced or even overweighted by the value placed on reason, action, and force.

The intellectual power and emotional control of this poem, although not its rather playful charm, also appear in the twenty-eight sonnets. Most of the sonnets are about grief, but they are analyses rather than expressions of it. They are highly compressed, very carefully organized and crafted, full of thought and a rather Metaphysical wit: elaborate images, similes, metaphors, and logical arguments flourish within the strict Petrarchan form. Sometimes the organization seems mechanical, but often the tight logical structure builds to a powerful emotional climax, as in "Grief," which says that "hopeless grief is passionless":

> express
> Grief for thy Dead in silence like to death—
> Most like a monumental statue set
> In everlasting watch and moveless woe
> Till itself crumble to the dust beneath.
> Touch it; the marble eyelids are not wet:
> If it could weep, it could arise and go.

The sonnets assert that poetry's great theme is sorrow (as in "The Seraph and Poet"), but (content imitating form) they preach patience and self-control ("Patience Taught by Nature," "Cheerfulness Taught by Reason," "Exaggeration"), and they find solace in God's love. Tightly restricted by the Petrarchan form, with no room for the feminine endings that tend to call forth Elizabeth Barrett's most questionable experiments in rhyme, the sonnets have relatively few displeasing eccentricities. Self-control is not, however, art's highest virtue, and it is in channeling feeling in order to intensify it that they are most impressive.

Once again unpublished works dredge murkier depths than the published works acknowledge. Some abortive verses from the early 1840s deal with vexed familial relationships; the speaker in a fragment beginning "She was a fair countess" had been cursed by her dying mother, and another fragment begins: "Dost thou hate my father .. mother? / Hate is running in my blood .. / And I hated my twin brother." In another, the speaker is a hungry child who gives voice not only to feelings like those in "The Cry of the Children" but also to his unhappy satisfaction that the baby who usurped his mother's love is dead. "The Princess Marie" tells how the king of France's daughter became a sculptor and then fell ill and died, destroyed by her art even though a princely lover came to the rescue and carried her away. "Our own works master us / And rising tread us down," the narrator darkly remarks. Princess Marie makes great works and achieves artistic immortality, but (narrator and princely lover agree) her genius kills her. Like "A True Dream," which was also unpublished and also contains statuelike figures that threaten to suck the life from their creator, "The Princess Marie" is concerned with family relationships, the dangerous allure of independence, and the destructiveness of art. Face to face with her pure white heroic statue of

Jeanne d'Arc, "the marble eye & mouth / Fed slowly from her living youth," she pales and pines away.[25]

"De Profundis," formal and stiff with pain, written when she was beginning to recover from her grief for Bro although not published until 1860, recapitulates her earlier visions of the family constellation. The poem falls into three parts: six stanzas about the loss of Bro, eight about her longing for a death conceived as a return to Nature's womb, and ten expressing fealty to God. Bro is remembered as incorporating the creative and sustaining powers she had earlier attributed to her father and Uvedale Price: his face brightened her life like the sun, his tongue brought smooth music from rough stones, his "Good day" made the days good, his heart was her staff of repose. But he is gone beyond recall, and like the old man in Chaucer's "Pardoner's Tale" who (searching for Death) knocks on the ground ("which is my moodres gate") asking "Leeve mooder, leet me in," she "sit[s] and knock[s] at Nature's door" (33).[26] She asks Nature, who gives nests and berries to the birds, to care for her too, to let her "Creep in" (59) beneath the turf, and she imagines what it would be like if Nature relented and gave her maternal welcome.

> From gracious Nature have I won
> Such liberal bounty? may I run
> So, lizard-like, within her side,
> And there be safe [. . . .]?

> (66–69)

"But yet to me she wol nat do that grace," says Chaucer's old man.[27] The totally unexpected lizard (the kind of creature Browning loved to watch and ponder, but she had not met Browning yet) shows that her energizing, literalizing imagination has come wholly alive; while at the same time the Chaucerian allusion and appropriately archaic diction (including "within her side" [118], with its obsolete meaning of "in her womb," as well as "pilgrim shoon" [52] "boon" [47], and "anon" [61]) define forbidden desire in safely traditional and literary terms. But a reproving "Voice"—"God's Voice, not Nature's" (76)—breaks her dream of return, reminding her that God alone reigns everywhere, that no human sorrow can compare to Christ's, and that all happens for the best. She cannot speak to the dead, and Nature does not answer. God, the father, is the arbiter of her imagination, her audience, and the object of her praise.

The published volumes, however, do not stop enmired in old losses or the fear of art. Instead, they are concerned with the practical aspects of accomplishing a poetic vocation, including experimentation with a variety of forms and themes. For while the preface asserts the peculiar fitness of women to be poets, several poems explore the difficulties under which women poets work. Fame, for instance, is still problematic, but more simply than before. "A Lay of the Early Rose" tells of a rose and a poet who come to the world before the world is ready and concludes that poets should sing for themselves and for God, not for worldly praise. The fact that the rose, traditional symbol for woman as erotic object, is the poet's analogue rather than opposite suggests the doubled role of the woman who wants to write her way into the poetic tradition explicitly *as* a woman—which is what Elizabeth Barrett proposes in the 1844 poems to do. The poet may have the vulnerability of a rose, but the problem is not that the rose is fragile but that the weather is cold. The first woman poet will be, precisely, *early.*

But the early world is childhood as well as childish ambition (as the tone and imagery in which Elizabeth Barrett discusses older literature in her essays make clear), and like childhood it is already over as soon as it is nostalgically conceived. A girl's difficulty in growing up to be a poet is most extensively and pessimistically presented in "The Lost Bower," a retrospective narrative based on the poet's own experience that carries the speaker from active, aspiring childhood to impotence and loss. "The Lost Bower" is a much elaborated retelling of "The Deserted Garden." The setting is explicitly named as the Malvern Hills, identified in a note as "the scene of Langland's Visions, and thus [. . .] the earliest classic ground of English poetry"—the setting, that is, of England's Homeric age. As a child, the speaker found herself bored and restless on a pleasant hilltop surrounded by other hills which seemed to represent an exclusively male world, strangely foreshadowing the circle of hills that turn into a not dissimilar band of precursors at the end of Browning's " 'Childe Roland to the Dark Tower Came' ":

> Far out, kindled by each other,
> Shining hills on hills arise,
> Close as brother leans to brother
> When they press beneath the eyes
> Of some father praying blessings from the gifts of paradise.

$$(36-40)^{28}$$

She turns from this vast sunlit realm of brothers and father to nature's secret inwardness, an entangled wood from which the sky cannot be seen, making an incursion that is also an escape: her "fingers / Tore asunder gyve and thong / Of the brambles which entrapped" her (78–80).

This adventure is conceived in specifically literary terms. Thoughts of poets' wanderings inspire her to persist in her explorations until she comes upon the bower, which seems to combine nature and art like a palace made by dryads and fairies, figures from pre-Christian mythic nature. But her wonder and delight end in a sudden recoil, as used to happen when Elizabeth Barrett's imagination threatened to go too far, and she gives herself in "exaltation" (211) to a music finer than Pan's or Faunus' (183) or any bird's—a music that transcends, that is, both myth and nature. The transcendence is quasi-sexual—the music falls on her "like a garment rustling downwards" (215) to her feet, as if she were disrobing—and also an image of birth into a higher life. She is "in a child-abstraction [a nice pun] lifted" back to the open hilltop, which is now heaped with affirmation and praise: "the true mountains," testimony to "the truth of things" and "the beauty of the truth," "Nature's real" (221–35). As at the end of "De Profundis," which moves in a similar fashion from the happy days represented by childhood and Bro, to a thwarted attempt to hide in the heart of nature, to a God beyond nature, she has come back to the world ruled by God.

From this perspective the bower seems innocuously childish, a "lusus, fashioned half in / Chance and half in Nature's play" (238–39), and she assumes that she can return to it whenever she wants. But she can't. For the literary situation requires two people: the quester of romance and the object of his quest, the prince and Sleeping Beauty. At first she ingenuously plans to visit the bower every morning and play both roles: "Henceforth, *I* will be the fairy / Of this bower [. . .] the dream-hall I have won" (241–45). But when she tries to make her way through the thickets and briars back to her enchanted palace, she is, she realizes, taking the role of "the prince who rescued Beauty from the sleep as long as death" (270).

> But his sword of mettle clashèd,
> And his arm smote strong, I ween,
> And her dreaming spirit flashèd,
> Through her body's fair white screen,
> And the light thereof might guide him up the cedar alleys green.
>
> (271–75)

She herself, however, sees no "splendour," has no sword (276–77)—no woman calls her, she is not a man—and so she never arrives, never returns.

"The first of all [her] losses" (300) was the loss of the bower, she says, its primacy marking its causal importance. It was the loss of a poetic world and a poetic subject: the hidden, inward, early world of nature which opened to Ariosto, Chaucer, and Shakespeare but not to her. And since the story in which she has no place is the archetypal tale of sexual awakening, or growing up, she is also excluded from adventure, ambition, and accomplishment ("the dream of Doing / And the other dream of Done" [301–2]), variety of emotional experience, emotional power, and integration in a society which she has seen to be false. The prince's kiss has been preempted by the sexual-mystical experience that carries her from the bower into the world of sexual division in which she is no longer a genderless child or a questing prince. At the end of the poem she is lying on a couch, like Sleeping Beauty, weary and waiting, neither a prince herself nor expecting one to come. As a little girl Elizabeth Barrett had "beguiled many a weary hour" with the daydreams of romance, but now the daydreams are over although the weary hours remain. This speaker can summon up memories of the lost bower, and she can wait (as in so many of the 1838 poems) for the "Eden-land" (367) of heaven, but she cannot conjoin memory and transcendence. She has nothing in the present, nothing in between.

Elsewhere, however, she is somewhat less gloomy about woman's literary place, even if grounds for optimism are hard to come by. In "A Vision of Poets," over a thousand lines of octosyllabic triplets much admired by Robert Browning, a poet is led through a deathly symbolic landscape to see images of great poets and some typical pretenders. Since such vision-poems normally contain a male poet and a female guide, the speaker reverts to the role of observer, as in 1838: instead of having the vision herself, she has a vision of the (male) poet who has it. And as at the end of "The Poet's Vow," male exclusivity is doubled in the conclusion, in which the poet's son celebrates and mourns his dead father, succession passing in the male line. All the poets in the vision except Sappho and one of the typical modern imitators are men. And yet, despite the apparently unadulterated maleness of poetry, the great men have one encouraging feature: "Where the heart of each should beat, / There seemed a wound instead of it, / From whence the blood dropped to their feet" (427–29). The distinguishing mark of even the most early and carefree poets, as of Christ and of mature women, is that they bleed. This is an implicit reply to "The Lost Bower," leading directly to *A Drama of Exile:* the source of poetry is not the prince's quest for the princess, but Christ's vicarious suffering, the capacity for pain.

The pain that women were particularly expected to write about was that of love. Elizabeth Barrett's first published love poem, the great lyrical success of the 1844 volume and the declared favorite of Ruskin and Browning, was "Catarina to Camoens," first written in 1831 and revised several times before publication in 1843.[29] Its popularity marks a perhaps untraversable gap between Victorian taste and our own, which is likely to find the emotion mawkish and thin, the self-abnegation and self-denigration repellent, and the language a painful mixture of awkwardness and cliché. But to the Victorians it was fresh and new: an attempt almost unprecedented in English literature to find a place for a female voice in the central tradition of amatory poetry.

Elizabeth Barrett enters this amatory tradition specifically in response to, not in imitation of, a male speaker. "Reading Camoens last night," she wrote in her diary in November 1831, "suggested what I have been writing this morning" (*Diary* 181). What she read, in a collection of lyrics translated with a biographical introduction by Viscount Strangford, was this, entitled "Madrigal":

> The heart that warm'd my guileless breast
> Some wanton hand had thence convey'd,
> But Love, who saw his bard distress'd,
> In pity thus the thief betray'd—
> " 'Tis she who owns the fairest mien
> "And sweetest eyes that e'er were seen!"
>
> And sure if Love be in the right,
> (And was Love ever in the wrong?)
> To thee, my first and sole delight,
> That simple heart must now belong—
> Because thou hast the fairest mien,
> And sweetest eyes that e'er were seen![30]

In his introductory remarks Strangford recounts the love of Camões, whom he depicts as a rather Byronic poet-hero-warrior-wanderer-lover, for Catarina, a lady of the Portuguese court whose family opposed his suit. "Portuguese delicacy," Strangford says, "suppressed all avowal of her passion,"[31] but on the day he was sent into exile she confessed her reciprocating love. Camões went off to fight the Moors, lost one of his eyes in a sea battle, and lived a gallant and honorable life that ended in penury, disease, and death in an almshouse. He never saw Catarina again before she died at the age of twenty.

Elizabeth Barrett's first important love lyric gives a voice to the woman whom both social and literary decorum had committed to silence, whom the poet adored for her beauty and the translator-biographer admired

because of the poet's adoration and because she died young. ("There
can scarcely be conceived a more interesting theme for the visions of
romance, than the death of this young and amiable being . . . She loved,
she was beloved . . . .")[32] The poem represents Catarina's thoughts on
her deathbed and is conceived as a reply to Camões, the stanzas ending
by (slightly mis)quoting the lover's praise of his lady—"Sweetest eyes
were ever seen"—and addressing the fact that the speaker, as a woman,
exists only to be looked at, not to look or speak. The first version begins:

> Rose o' the cheek it drops away
> Smile o' the lips it flowers no more . .
> Were you near me, would you say
> 'Love, I love you' as before?

(Diary 316)

But the speaker reassures herself that his love creates her beauty, so that
if he looked at her again she would again be beautiful—which makes
him the origin not only of her speech but of the quality in her that
(according to the courtly love fiction of his poem) had inspired his speech
and his love.

> And if you looked down upon them [her eyes],
>   And if *they* looked up to *you,*
> All the light which has foregone them
>   Would be gathered back anew.

(33–36)

He is not, however, correspondingly responsive to her: being absent, he
sees her only in memory, not as she actually is, and when she speaks to
him he does not reply. She is the Sleeping Beauty to whom, like the
princess in Christina Rossetti's sadly sardonic "The Prince's Progress,"
the lover does not come: "On the door you will not enter," the final
version begins, "I have gazed too long: adieu!" (1–2). Strangford reports,
furthermore, that Camões was an enthusiastic and successful lover ("It
is improbable that he remained long constant to the memory of a departed
mistress, when living beauty was ready to supply her place")[33] and Ca-
tarina accepts with sublime unselfishness the likelihood that after her
death he will bestow the same ardor-inspiring beauty on another. "Who
can read without emotion," asked an enthusiastic reviewer, "a picture of
womanly devotion, and self-abnegation like this?"[34]

Her first major love poem, then, defines women in the amatory tradition
as derivative, secondary, powerless, and doomed. Nor can men and women

exchange roles: Catarina conceives of herself as the object of Camões's desire, but she does not conceive of him as primarily the object of hers. A man speaks his desire, which is not diminished—in poetry, it is increased—when its object is unresponsive or absent. But how can a woman speak her beauty, which depends for its existence on the lover whose desire bestows or validates it? Her inability to speak her own diminished beauty is the subject of Catarina's speech. This may account for the obtrusive peculiarity of the poem's language—its sometimes excruciating feminine off-rhymes ("enter / peradventure," "burden / disregarding ," "*Miserere* / weary"), its unattractive archaisms ("I ween / yestreen," "oftly" [rhymed, of course, with "softly"]), odd locutions ("near to go," "unfaintly"), its peculiar and rather graceless stanza, with two short rhymed lines in the middle as well as a refrain, and the tortured syntax of the refrain itself, which reflects Camões's refrain as if in a distorting mirror: "Sweetest eyes were ever seen." These characteristic and controversial tricks of style, of which the first version of "Catarina to Camoens" is an early and extreme example, flout the reader's expectations of verbal beauty and suggest that there are other kinds of beauty, other kinds of music, than sweet smoothness. The poem's thematic statement is that in poetry a woman without beauty can do nothing but lapse into silence and disappear; its form, however, as well as the fact of its existence, suggests other possibilities. (An American reviewer once reminded those who might be repelled by the absence of superficial beauty in Elizabeth Barrett's verse [he pointed to harsh language, defective rhythm, forced rhymes] that while both women and poets should wear graceful drapery, they are not to be judged by their dress.)[35]

The dramatic relation to a preceding work implicitly asserts that the poem is an exploration of poetic possibilities rather than an expression of personal feeling, although it may to some extent reflect the poet's sense of exclusion not just from literary opportunities but from emotional ones too. The day before she wrote the first draft she had exclaimed in her diary: "I never never will marry!" (180). But by one of the splendidly benign ironies that mark Elizabeth Barrett's later years, Catarina's response to a poet who could not hear her was heard and answered by another poet, and *Sonnets from the Portuguese,* named from Robert Browning's delight in "Catarina to Camoens," took up what had by then become an intimate conversation and redefined once more a woman's place and voice in the amatory tradition.

The woman poet who most notoriously wrote of love (aside from Sappho, who may have been an inspiration but could not be a useful model, and Aphra Behn, whose Restoration bawdiness appalled the Victorians) was L.E.L., who worked a romance vein of Byron-and-water rather than the tradition of the amatory lyric and whose passion Elizabeth Barrett thought factitious anyway. "For a woman," asked L.E.L. rhetorically, "whose influence and whose sphere must be in the emotions, what subject can be more fitting?" Fates like Catarina's were the staple of her verse. "Aware that to elevate I must first soften, and that if I wished to purify I must first touch, I have ever endeavoured to bring forward grief, disappointment, the fallen leaf, the faded flower, the broken heart, and the early grave."[36] L.E.L.'s own melodramatic and mysterious death in 1838 provided an occasion to consider not the methods but the desirability of love poetry by women. Earlier that year she had astonished the literary world by marrying an apparently very unsuitable man, the governor of the Gold Coast, and going off with him to Africa, where she seems to have been unhappy. Before her marriage her reputation had been tainted by sexual scandal, and when she was found dead with a bottle of prussic acid in her hand rumor buzzed in England. The question of whether she died by accident, suicide, or murder occasioned much fascinated speculation and was never resolved. Elizabeth Barrett's "L.E.L.'s Last Question" appeared in the *Athenaeum* three weeks after the *Athenaeum* announced the news of the poet's death and is a response to a poem called "Night at Sea," written on the voyage to Africa and published earlier that month. The "question" to which Elizabeth Barrett's title refers is the refrain of "Night at Sea": "My friends, my absent friends! / Do you think of me, as I think of you?"[37]

Unlike Catarina's response to Camões, however, Elizabeth Barrett's poem is not framed as an answer to another poem, even though the reiterated question invites one, but rather, like her elegy on Mrs. Hemans, as a commentary and correction. She engages the male amatory tradition as a voice that has not been heard before, speaking in opposition and response, but she places herself as a continuator of the feminine line. She speaks *of*, not *to*, the speaker in the previous poem, associating herself with the speaker's desire rather than with that desire's object—"We all do ask the same" (9), but she does so only to criticize it: "Not much, and yet too much / Is this, 'Think of me as I think of you' " (55–56). Death parts us; God's love is best. She reverts to the idea that had worried her when she was younger: that fame for a poet, or at any rate a woman poet, comes at too high a price and in the end hardly matters anyway. "She asked not,—'Do you praise me, O my land?' " (27). She defines L.E.L. as the poet of love: "Love-learnèd, she had sung of love and love" (15; the first version read, "of only love"). "And little in the world the Loving do / But sit (among the rocks?) and listen for / The echo of their own love evermore" (11–13). But no echo came.

She must have noticed that both "Night at Sea" and the other poem from the voyage that was published with it, "The Polar Star,"[38] not only are extremely gloomy but also do not mention the husband whose presence might have been expected to provide consolation for the absence of friends. Without adverting to this (she could hardly with decency have done so), she points out that the poet's attempt to realize in her life the romantic visions that had formed the staple of her verse ended in disappointment: she died "With all her visions unfulfilled save one, / Her childhood's, of the palm-trees in the sun— / And lo!—their shadow on her sepulchre!" (47–49). This apparently refers to the description in the *Athenaeum* of the letters "in which she wrote cheerfully of her position and her future literary plans, making the best of her strange and dismal place of sojourn, by saying, that the palms and cocoa-trees reminded her of her favorite book—the Arabian Nights."[39] But "L.E.L.'s Last Question" suggests a more inclusive disappointment.

Despite the immense disparity between the two women in poetic, intellectual, and even moral stature, the older poet remained a significant example as well as a warning for her rival and successor. She anticipated one of Aurora Leigh's most striking accomplishments by living alone in London and supporting herself by her pen. Elizabeth Barrett's ballads, however complex and subversive they may have been, were squarely in the tradition of L.E.L., written for the same kind of publications and twice with the same subject.[40] But her example was hardly encouraging. She did a great deal of hackwork, fought in the tawdry battles of the *Literary Gazette*, which sponsored her, and was mocked as ill-bred and unrefined. Her career luridly enacted the struggle between art and life, fame and love, ambition and femininity that racked Elizabeth Barrett's imagination, and in the end it was a model of failure. Nor were her works strong enough in either conception or execution to offer an alternative to the male tradition.[41]

But whereas L.E.L. was the best England could show in the way of a powerful female voice, a female Byron, France had the real thing. Elizabeth Barrett read George Sand's novels with horror and awe and thought her "the first female genius of any country or age," "the greatest female poet the world ever saw."[42] She objected to "the triumph of sensual tendencies over [. . .] the common virtues of gratitude, friendship, & maternal duties" (*LMRM* 2:127), found *Lélia* a "serpent book," too vile to read (*LMRM* 2:127), and heard the serpent's hiss in other books too. But she was overwhelmed with admiration for Sand's literary style, intellectual power, and impassioned aspiration. Her moral horizons had widened in the last few years: "by the reaction of solitude and suffering, [I] have broken many bands which held me," she wrote in 1845 (*LEBB* 1:243). At least Sand was not, like Mrs. Hemans, debilitatingly ladylike; nor, like L.E.L., did she purvey factitious passions. Elizabeth Barrett expressed her profoundly mixed feelings about her in two sonnets "To George Sand."

George Sand availed herself of a male name, the convenience of male clothing, and male freedom of speech and behavior, but she expressed woman's will and desire with unrivalled lyrical intensity. Elizabeth Barrett, taking for granted a conventional division of masculine and feminine qualities and both exhilarated and appalled by Sand's unification of opposites and blurring of boundaries, thought of her as "man & woman together" (*RB-EBB* 1:159). "A Desire" addresses her as "large-brained woman and large-hearted man," and "A Recognition" admires an even greater paradox: "True genius, but true woman!" But her androgyny, like other transgressions of the bounds of womanhood as Elizabeth Barrett had conceived them, is tainted—here, by sensuality—and the poems urge Sand to transcend both sensuality and gender into realms of sexless purity:

> Beat purer, heart, and higher,
> Till God unsex thee on the heavenly shore
> Where unincarnate spirits purely aspire!

> ("A Recognition")

(In 1844 the last two lines were even more emphatic, if so difficult that they had to be emended: "Till God unsex thee on the spirit-shore; / To which alone unsexing, purely aspire.") Elizabeth Barrett thought earthly androgyny wonderfully impressive but full of danger. Harriet Martineau, she wrote in 1844 when Martineau was ridiculed for insisting that mesmerism had cured her of cancer, "unites to high logic, a deep sensibility to poetry" (*LHSB* 263) and is "the most manlike woman in the three kingdoms—in the best sense of man—a woman gifted with admirable fortitude, as well as exercised in high logic" (*LEBB* 1:196–97). But for these unlikely virtues "men throw stones at her, and [. . .] many of her own sex throw dirt" (*LHSB* 272). The androgynous woman's masculine strength leads her to expose to public view feelings better kept decently shrouded: Sand's "tumultuous senses" are as strong as lions ("A Desire") and roar with corresponding audibility.

Sand is marked as a woman-artist in the sonnets by being herself, like Madame de Staël's Corinne or Harriet Martineau defending mesmerism by her own example, the object she shows to the world. "Thy woman's hair [. . .] / Floats back dishevelled strength in agony"; "We see thy woman-heart" ("A Recognition"). The 1844 poems image self-expression as bodily exposure, highly charged with danger: when the early rose (the poet as flower) displays her beauty, she makes herself vulnerable to physical destruction. But the old spectre of a dreadful self-revelation that Sand evokes is balanced in other sonnets by more pragmatic worries about whether artistic self-expression is in fact attainable at all, and the group of sonnets is organized around this question. The first is "The Soul's Expression," which draws consolation from the poet's unsuccessful struggle "to deliver right / That music of my nature" and "utter all myself into the air," and from the thought that

> if I did it,—as the thunder-roll
> Breaks its own cloud, my flesh would perish there,
> Before that dread apocalypse of soul.

This is the mood of "The Tempest," "The Development of Genius," and "A True Dream," which link the terror of self-recognition with the dangers of ambition, and (recalled by the last three words) "Psyche Apocalypte." "An Apprehension" describes, with the stark physicality that often marks Elizabeth Barrett's metaphors for feeling, her fear of putting her "own heart nakedly below / The palm" of a friend. But the final sonnet, "Insufficiency," asserts that even though the poet's soul "throbs audibly / Along [her] pulses" (like Tennyson's Lotos-Eaters, when "music in [their] ears [their] beating heart[s] did make"),[43] the curse on fallen nature precludes full self-expression.

George Sand, however, has apparently done this impossible thing, and the result is fearful indeed. Elizabeth Barrett marvels at her self-display even while she longs to improve its object:

> I would some mild miraculous thunder ran
> Above the applauded circus, in appliance
> Of thine own nobler nature's strength and science,
> Drawing two pinions, white as wings of swan,
> From thy strong shoulders, to amaze the place
> With holier light!

> ("A Desire")

> while before
> The world thou burnest in a poet-fire,

> We see thy woman-heart beat evermore
> Through the large flame. Beat purer, heart.

("A Recognition")

Self-exposure which is both sexual and redeemed from sexuality by being defined as courage will reappear in Elizabeth Barrett's writings under the image of Godiva, and questions of courage tend to recur when she thinks about Sand. She and Miss Mitford excited themselves for a while with the idea of sending their books to Sand, but the thought of her father stopped her. "He has very strict ideas about women & about what they sh^d read [. . .] & I heard him say once that he could not think highly of the modesty of any woman who could read Don Juan.!!" (*LMRM* 2:462). Still, she was "daring" enough (this was John Kenyon's word [*LMRM* 2:460], and a reviewer spoke of her "moral courage") to publish the sonnets to Sand, thereby displaying her own courage and exposing her own knowledge of, if not implication in, unwomanly impurity. It seems not to have occurred to her that Sand might find the sonnets insulting.[44]

The union of male and female, or poet and object, which is a matter of tortured seriousness in the sonnets to George Sand, becomes an easy fantasy in the last and probably the most popular of Elizabeth Barrett's ballads, "Lady Geraldine's Courtship." It was the final piece written for *Poems* (1844): to make the two volumes of equal length, "there was nothing for it but to finish a ballad poem [. . .] which was lying by me, and I did so by writing, i.e. composing, *one hundred and forty lines last Saturday*! [. . .] Long lines too—with fifteen syllables in each!" (*LEBB* 1:177). In a plot combining elements of the ballad stories with those of "Catarina to Camoens," she attempts to split her identification between a male poet and a female object, to equalize the two figures and participate equally in both. Bertram, the poet, is poor and lowly-born, but he is male, a poet, and the speaker. Lady Geraldine is rich, noble, independent, and the active agent of the plot (it is *her* courtship), but she is the object of the speaker's desire and represents the subjects (nature, beauty, and the like) about which poems are written. She *owns* a garden of art. In the center of that garden, moreover, is a statue of a sleeping woman, representing Silence. Lady Geraldine argues that the statue represents the power of meaning to "exceed the special symbol" (121) embodying it: that is, a silent work of art in female form says more than speech does. Lady Geraldine herself is both a singer and a song: "Oh, to see or hear her singing," sighs the enamored poet-narrator, "For her looks sing too" (173–74). But doubleness here is not a problem. The lovers marry, the two roles merge. This may be the nineteenth-century woman poet's ultimate narcissistic fantasy: she imagines herself enacting both roles perfectly at the same time rather than, as in "The Lost Bower," failing in both. That the poem represents a fantasy of wish-fulfillment is suggested by the fact that it was written so fast and easily, and perhaps too by its enormous popularity. Despite its inordinate length it is perhaps the simplest of the ballads, since the poet's doubled identification means the loss of the articulation and psychological tension that is generated by difference.

"Lady Geraldine's Courtship" is the only one of the ballads with a happy ending. It is almost the only one in which the heroine is not enmeshed in family relationships by bonds of love or hate or both, and—most important—it is the only one with an explicitly modern setting. For the first time in Elizabeth Barrett's stories, the heroine is self-assertive, powerful, guiltless, and free, as well as (of course) virtuous and beautiful. In the final confrontation Bertram acts the parts of both a swooning woman and a knight subdued in combat: "So I fell, struck down before her" (349); and Geraldine "whisper[s] low in triumph" (410), both conqueror and low-voiced woman, while he kneels at her feet. This is the scene little Ellie in "The Romance of the Swan's Nest" had imagined, but Geraldine confers power instead of receiving it. And this revisionary depiction of courtship is matched by the celebration of a marriage that crosses class lines, transforming a commonplace romance plot into a radical social statement. The poet mocks the condescension of aristocracy to genius which for Elizabeth Barrett was one of the disgraceful and alienating aspects of English society.[45]

"Quite low-born, self-educated! somewhat gifted though by nature,
And we make a point of asking him,—of being very kind.
You may speak, he does not hear you! and, besides, he writes no satire,—
All these serpents kept by charmers leave the natural sting behind."

(41–44)

But while Tennyson's "Locksley Hall," which Elizabeth Barrett much admired and which the poem resembles both in the swing and energy of its long lines and in its social radicalism, makes a story of disappointed love the grounds for criticizing the whole modern world, love's satisfaction is attainable in "Lady Geraldine's Courtship" precisely because it takes place in modern times. Where the male poet finds constriction and exclusion, the female poet sees vistas of freedom. This was Elizabeth Barrett's first experiment in bringing together poetry and the novel,

visionary imagination and the modern world. However fantastic it may
seem to us, she herself thought it boldly realistic, "comprehending the
aspect and manners of modern life, and flinching at nothing of the
conventional" (*LEBB* 1:204). With it she triumphantly—like Geraldine—
takes imaginative possession of a new poetic territory.

"Lady Geraldine's Courtship" concludes the first volume; "The Dead
Pan," which deals equally firmly with a fundamental opposition of Eliz-
abeth Barrett's thought, concludes the second. "Lady Geraldine's Court-
ship" reconciles male and female, leaving the woman dominant. "The
Dead Pan," more uncompromising, replies to Schiller's lament for the
banished gods of ancient Greece (a lament lately renewed in some verses
by John Kenyon) by celebrating the absolute triumph of Christianity, the
new age. As in the essay on the Greek Christian poets, her nostalgia is
first indulged (she lists gods and goddesses, stanza by stanza, as elsewhere
she lists poets) and then resolutely dispelled: "We will weep *not!*" (229).[46]
"Earth outgrows the mythic fancies / Sung beside her in her youth"
(232–33), and the poet would like to grow up too. Mythic characters
have rightly given way to angels, as in her own writings, and the modern
age is the firmest ground for Christian art. "God himself is the best
Poet, / And the Real is His song" (248–49). The last stanza is the last
of *Poems* (1844):

> O brave poets, keep back nothing,
> Nor mix falsehood with the whole!
> Look up Godward; speak the truth in
> Worthy song from earnest soul:
> Hold, in high poetic duty,
> Truest Truth the fairest Beauty!
> > Pan, Pan is dead.

> (267–73)

"Nothing . . . truth in" is one of the assonantal double rhymes which,
Alethea Hayter points out, were her main technical innovation;[47] it is
highly appropriate that "The Dead Pan," like "Caterina to Camoens,"
has a lot of them. The language and sentiment of this concluding stanza
are flat and vague ("brave," "truth," "worthy," "earnest," "duty"), quin-
tessentially "Victorian" and rather muscularly Christian—one almost hears
the voice of Thomas Arnold exhorting the boys of Rugby to manly
virtue—but the repudiation of the dead past is borne out by the cou-
rageous if only partially successful attempt to revitalize poetic language,
and in her later works Barrett Browning will fill in the details with vivid
particularity and, by and large, live up to her own exhortations.

5
Courtship, Letters, *Sonnets from the Portuguese*

 The *Poems* were a success. To her gratification and surprise, people bought them, and the first edition sold out in six years. Reviews were numerous and (especially in the less important journals, and in America) laudatory. The American *Christian Examiner*, for instance, spoke of her as "in some important respects the most remarkable poetic genius of this day," with a "union of bold imagination, beautiful fancy, and tender humanity in which she surpasses all other living writers."[1] There was general praise for her intellectual powers, moral and spiritual character, and emotional force. Narrative, pathos, and scenes of domestic and contemporary life pleased most: the ballads (especially "Rhyme of the Duchess May" and "Lady Geraldine's Courtship"), "The Cry of the Children," "The Mourning Mother (of the Dead Blind)," "To Flush, My Dog," "Catarina to Camoens," and the affecting dedication to her father were frequently noticed, as were the sonnets. Her character was discussed with grave respect, and it was remarked that her works were sad because she had suffered, not because she was (in the standard Victorian term of reproach) "morbid"; lachrymosity and gloom were not unacceptable in a woman.

Several reviewers responded to the personal element in her writings and to the stories that had begun circulating about her, attributing what seemed bookish and unnatural in her style to her long seclusion, although Edgar Allan Poe thought that separation from the world had given her "a comparative independence of men and opinions" and "a happy audacity of thought and expression never before known in one of her sex," even while it "seduced her into the sin of imitation";[2] both views, perhaps, were right. Once again, her sex was always noted. "If the poetess does not always command our unqualified approbation [said *Blackwood's*], we are at all times disposed to bend in reverence before the deep-hearted and highly accomplished woman—a woman, whose powers appear to us to extend over a wider and profounder range of thought and feeling, than ever before fell within the intellectual compass of any of the softer sex."[3] "Her poems are certainly remarkable compositions," an American journal said, "especially when considered as the productions of a woman's mind."[4] It was generally agreed that she was or might become the foremost of women poets. The superlatives that flowed with suspicious ease were usually diminished by qualifications in terms of gender, but they did not always issue from male condescension; Margaret Fuller, for instance, found "vigour and nobleness of conception, depth of spiritual experience, and command of classic allusion, above any female writer the world has yet known."[5]

Still, it was a dubious triumph. She would probably have been more pleased, could she have known of it, by the open-hearted enthusiasm of two teen-aged boys, Dante Gabriel and William Michael Rossetti. "Towards 1845, or even 1844." William Michael recalled,

> the poems of Miss Elizabeth Barrett Barrett first caught the attention of my brother and myself. We revelled in them with profuse delight. Our perceptions of poetry were not then of the totally uncritical order, and we found some things which we thought faulty, both in excess and in defect; but in the main our pleasure was unalloyed. *The Drama of Exile, The Rhyme of the Duchess May, The Lost Bower, Lady Geraldine's Courtship, A Vision of Poets,* and numerous other pieces, held us spellbound. In the course of two or three years we must have read some of these more than half-a-hundred times over; and either of us . . . could repeat them with great exactness.[6]

Their sister Christina would probably have read the poems at the same time, when she was about fourteen, and heard her brothers recite them. Barrett Browning's extensive influence on Dante Gabriel and Christina Rossetti began here.

Less ingenuous critics than the young Rossettis tempered their enthusiasm with complaints about deficiencies in artistry and expression: annoying mannerisms, faults of diction, verbosity, obscurity, and especially false rhymes. More than one reviewer was offended by her habit of using adjectives (most annoyingly, "human") as nouns. Her efforts to heighten and vary poetic language were attributed to carelessness, as usual, and such accusations aroused her to defend her deliberate craftsmanship in letters to her friends. Nor did she like having her experiments dismissed as imitations of Tennyson, although she immensely admired him: "What vexed me a little in one or two of the journals was [. . .] the calling me a follower of Tennyson for my habit of using compound words, noun-substantives, which I used to do before I knew a page of Tennyson, and adopted from a study of our old English writers, and Greeks and even Germans" (*LEBB* 1:199). Charges of obscurity, on the other hand, bothered her less, and she generally replied cheerfully that although the difficulties of her verse were much exaggerated she would try to do better.

She insisted that she practised her craft conscientiously and seriously. "My belief is, that very few writers called 'correct' who have selected classical models to work from, pay more laborious attention than I do habitually to the forms of thought and expression" (*LEBB* 1:209). She had reasons for what she did:

> I sometimes fancy that a little varying of the accents, though at the obvious expense of injuring the smoothness of every line considered separately, gives variety of cadence and fuller harmony to the general effect. But I do not question that I deserve a great deal of blame on this point as on others. (*LEBB* 1:200)

> I have a theory about double rhymes for which I shall be attacked by the critics, but which I could justify perhaps on high authority, or at least analogy. In fact, these volumes of mine have more double rhymes than any two books of English poems [. . .] *not comic.* Now, of double rhymes in use, which are perfect rhymes, you are aware how few there are, and yet you are also aware of what an admirable effect in making a rhythm various and vigorous, double rhyming is in English poetry. Therefore I have used a certain licence; and after much thoughtful study of the Elizabethan writers, have ventured it with the public. And do *you* tell me [. . .] *why* you rhyme (as everybody does, without blame from anybody) "given" to "heaven," when you object to my rhyming "remember" and "chamber"? (*LEBB* 1:183–84)

Her defense appeals more to the intellect than to the ear and is to that extent unsatisfying. Still, modern readers will find most of her off-rhymes, like "remember" and "chamber," quite pleasant. The restless formal experimentation springs from her dissatisfaction with the poetic resources available to her—she consistently uses off-rhymes, for instance, in "Catarina to Camoens," "A Vision of Poets," and "The Lost Bower," in which her struggle to find a voice for a woman within the male tradition presses closest to full articulation, and in "The Dead Pan," which calls for new kinds of poetry. These experiments point toward her more radical experiments with genre and subject matter in the next decade.

One reader, however, was captivated by what he called her "fresh strange music." As part of his courtship of Lady Geraldine, the poet Bertram reads aloud from modern poets, including "from Browning some 'Pomegranate,' which, if cut deep down the middle, / Shows a heart within blood-tinctured, of a veined humanity" ("Lady Geraldine's Court-ship," 163–64: the reference is to the series of works that Browning had been publishing under the title "Bells and Pomegranates"). In January 1845 Robert Browning responded with a letter not unworthy in its ex-travagance of Bertram himself. "I love your verses with all my heart, dear Miss Barrett [. . . .] into me has it gone, and part of me has it become, this great living poetry of yours [. . .] the fresh strange music, the affluent language, the exquisite pathos and true new brave thought [· · · ·] I do, as I say, love these books with all my heart—and I love you too."[7] She answered immediately, a lively correspondence ensued, in May he began to visit her, and in September 1846 (her health having continued to improve) they secretly married and set off for Italy.

At the beginning of 1845 Browning was thirty-two years old (she was thirty-eight) and had published *Pauline, Paracelsus,* and *Sordello,* several plays (some of which had appeared on the stage), *Pippa Passes,* and various shorter poems including "My Last Duchess," "Porphyria's Lover," and "Soliloquy of the Spanish Cloister." Her response to his poetry had been as strong and as personal as his to hers, very different from her whole-hearted but calmer admiration for her other great contemporary, Ten-nyson. At first she was repelled by the uncompromising force she felt in him, as she showed in an outburst to Horne in 1843:

> Mr. Browning knows thoroughly what a poet's true work is—he is learned [. . .] original [. . .] his very obscurities have an oracular nobleness about them which pleases me—his passion burns the paper! [. . . .] what has always seemed to me the worst fault—[is] a want of *harmony*—I mean it in the two senses, spiritual & physical. There is a want of the softening power in thoughts & in feelings as well as words—everything is trenchant, black & white without intermediate colours . . nothing is tender . . there is little room in all the passion, for pathos. And the verse . . the lyr-ics . . Where is the ear? Inspired spirits should not speak so harshly; & in good truth, they seldom do.[8]

But she felt, too, the irresistible maleness, passion, and power of "a true soul-piercing poet" (*LMRM* 2:219), "a master in clenched passion, . . concentrated passion . . burning through the metallic fissures of lan-guage" (*LMRM* 2:173). Browning, reciprocating the intensity of her response, not only alludes to but quotes frequently and with intimate knowledge such plangencies of feminine desire as "Bertha in the Lane" and "Catarina to Camoens." In fact, however, despite the highly gendered qualities that drew them to each other, their works were very much alike: learned, innovative, difficult, marked and marred, almost paradoxically, by both prolixity and extreme compression. They shared a fondness for headlong rapidity and for forcing sound and meaning into combinations that annoyed and bewildered ordinary readers. They both wrote long poems in odd forms, full of strange learning. Both were blamed, not unjustly, for obscurity.

Early in the correspondence Browning suggested composing something together, and she agreed, but nothing came of the idea until 1899, when their son published their largely epistolary courtship: a well-constructed story with an exciting if not very original plot in which her intelligence, wit, and charm show more strongly, perhaps, than in any of her other works, while Browning in his dense and tortured prose comes as close as he ever did to direct self-revelation. It has been noted that the theme of epistolary fiction is usually erotic or educational, centering on a woman's response to either a lover-seducer or a mentor and guide (Abelard, of course, being the prototype of both),[9] and the letters begin by moving between these two kinds: she asks him to be her tutor, while he is quietly determined to become her lover. But he was first of all the literary comrade she never had when she was young (the role played also by Horne and to a lesser degree by a poet named Thomas Westwood), discerningly attentive to her work and offering his own in turn for ratification and advice. And she was the enthusiastic and discriminating reader he needed. "I like so much to fancy," he said happily, in characteristically tortuous prose, "that you see, and will see, what I do as *I* see it, while it is doing, as nobody else in the world should, certainly" (1:123). She wrote comments on his work in progress, and her praise—subtle, just, accurate, unstinting—probably helped him more than her criticisms did; her suggested emendations are mostly in the interest of clarity and smoothness, for she was anxious that he succeed with the public. He was eagerly grateful for her corrections and (rather to her alarm) adopted almost all of them. His poetry, rather than hers, was their subject: although she urged him (picking up an unwary suggestion in his first letter) to find fault with her work, he never went beyond an assurance that even her redundancies pleased him ("an instructed eye loves to see where the brush has dipped twice in a lustrous colour" [1:7]). He refused invitations to instruct her: when she asked for help with her new translation of *Prometheus Bound*, he made suggestions about the Greek text but not about her own. Later he asked what she was writing (in fact, *Sonnets from the Portuguese*) and got evasive replies. But he always defers to her judgment, and he quotes her poems more often than she does his.

The progress of their love was shaped by the fact that they were both makers of texts. "I do, as I say, love these books with all my heart—and I love you too." The distinction between a woman poet and her works has traditionally been a blurry one, and was especially so in the Victorian period. The cliché that the style is the man arises more readily and with much greater literalness and force when the stylist is a woman, and it is often, as in Browning's letter, charged with erotic intensity. Edgar Allan Poe remarks in his review of *Poems* (1844) that "a woman and her book are identical." The identification of women with poems was likely to discourage them from writing: Ladislaw in *Middlemarch* tells Dorothea that she needn't write poems because she *is* one.[10] In her letters to Browning, Elizabeth Barrett worries about identity and writing: is she her poems, are they she, which is he in love with? She had become used to saying that the only life left to her was in poetry, and when she reluctantly allowed him to visit her she warned him not to expect a woman who matched the poems. The image she uses, however, admits to a degree of consubstantiality: "If my poetry is worth anything to any eye,—it is the flower of me. I have lived most & been most happy in it, & so it has all my colours; the rest of me is nothing but a root, fit for the ground & the dark" (1:65). Like other Victorian poets, male and female (Tennyson in "The Lady of Shalott," for instance), she feared that art might preclude life and love. But the man who had already written "My Last Duchess," the most famous of several poems reprehending men who turn women into works of art, could make the necessary distinction: "*thro'* what you have written, not properly *for* it, I love and wish you well!" (1:39). What he feared for himself was the opposite—he separated art too much from life, he felt, and he welcomed her help in bringing them together. "This is my first song, my true song—this love I bear you" (1:352).[11]

She dreaded, too, becoming a character in someone else's story, cast in a role she had always disliked and yet seemed doomed to fill: the passive, suffering victim, the damsel awaiting rescue—Tennyson's Mariana in the decaying house, whose lover does not come (to whom she twice wryly compared herself in letters to Browning [1:87, 1:152]), her own Catarina. She was afraid that Browning, like others, wanted to visit her "because I was unfortunate enough to be shut up in a room & silly enough to make a fuss about opening the door" (1:69); she refused visitors partly because "it w^d be unbecoming to lie here on the sofa & make a company-show of an infirmity, & hold a beggar's hat for sympathy" (1:65). His first letter transmutes the simple fact that he had almost visited her a few years earlier into an episode of romance: "I feel as at some untoward passage in my travels—as if I had been close, so close, to some world's-wonder in chapel or crypt, only a screen to push and I might have entered, but [. . .] the half-opened door shut, and I went home my thousands of miles, and the sight was never to be!" (1:3–4). To which she unromantically replies: "BUT . . . you know. . if you had entered the 'crypt,' you might have caught cold, or been tired to death, & *wished* yourself 'a thousand miles off' " (1:5). She rejects the extravagant praise of his early letters as "nailing me up into a false position with your gold-headed nails of chivalry, which wont hold to the wall through this summer" (1:125). And a little later: "I have sometimes felt jealous of myself . . of my own infirmities, . . and thought that you cared for me only because your chivalry touched them with a silver sound" (1:247).

She was right to be nervous about such things, as he more or less admitted: "Nor am I so selfish, I hope, as that (because my uttermost pride & privilege and glory above all glories would be to live in your sick-room and serve you,)—as that, on that account, I would not rather see you in a condition to need none of my service" (2:757). The attitude expressed here in such painfully contorted syntax was only one strand of his affection, but she might well have found it a disturbing reminder of the gratification her father derived from her illness. After his first visit he sent what was evidently a declaration of love, which she tactfully rebuffed as mere generous "fancies" (1:72) and insisted should never be referred to again. In the only ungracious moment in the whole correspondence, he asked her for the letter back and destroyed it, retreating precipitously from her displeasure and assuring her that she had mistaken his meaning. It took him a long time to overcome her suspicion that he loved a creature he had only imagined, and whom she did not wish to be.

For the story that haunted Browning's imagination was precisely the one she wanted to repudiate. A copy of Polidoro da Caravaggio's *Andromeda* hung above his desk at home[12]—Andromeda, chained to a rock like Prometheus but not a Promethean hero, waiting for Perseus to save her. Women threatened by a monster and sometimes rescued, sometimes not, are the radiant centers of Browning's stories early and late, from

"Porphyria's Lover," "My Last Duchess," and "Count Gismond," to *The Ring and the Book* and "Pan and Luna."[13] And Edward Moulton-Barrett confirmed the relevance of the story by unambiguously assuming the part of the monster. In the summer of 1845 her health was better than it had been for years—she even went outside—but the doctor warned that unless she left England she would relapse in the winter. To her utter astonishment and dismay, however, her father refused permission for her to go, and when she and George (the most responsible of her remaining brothers) pressed him to reconsider he said only that she could do as she wished, he washed his hands of her (1:211). "I have no spell," she told Browning sadly, "for charming the dragons" (1:211). She could not let her brothers or sisters incur his displeasure by accompanying her, and she could not go alone.

The episode was decisive in the relations of father and daughter: his nightly visits to pray in her room ceased, and she no longer believed that he loved her. Browning was astounded to find in life so perverse an imitation of romance, "the jewel [. . .] not being over guarded, but ruined, cast away" (1:212), and realized only slowly and with mounting indignation that Mr. Barrett ruled his family in accordance with what his daughter called "the principle of passive filial obedience," "held . . drawn (& quartered) from Scripture" (1:408), and would never sanction their marriage. Edward Moulton-Barrett belongs to his period: Mrs. Gaskell reports that Charlotte Brontë's father, who always disapproved of marriages, refused to walk next door to his own church to give her away; and Mrs. Gaskell was "half amused, half astonished" by the "quiet docility" with which his famous daughter let him treat her as a child.[14] Still, Mr. Barrett cannot be explained away by a false historicism; his cousin John Kenyon rightly spoke of his "monomania" (1:408), and his willingness to sacrifice his daughter's health and even her life for no purpose at all was hardly more justifiable by Victorian standards than by our own. Perseus' intervention was obviously required.

The plot they enacted fit her own stories to some extent, too, although not as well as they fit his. It is pleasingly appropriate that her last ballad-romance summoned the lover who escorted her into the new emotional and literary world the ballad itself heralded: the freedom she imagined for Lady Geraldine became—what when she wrote the poem she never expected—her own. There is a striking reciprocity between her ballads and some of Browning's narratives. His "Flight of the Duchess," written in 1845 and frequently discussed in their letters, tells of a very small woman (like Elizabeth Barrett) whose vitality has been drained away by her arid life with a husband devoted to reviving the Middle Ages (the unsatisfactory dreamworld of her ballads) and who saves herself by running off with the gypsies. "The Glove," also from 1845, celebrates a lady who shows up her lover's empty protestations by asking him to jump into a lion's den to retrieve her glove, and when he and all the court scorn her for imposing such a test marries a plebeian youth who really loves her. "The Glove" is an amusing defense against worldly common sense of the courtly ideal dissected in "The Romance of the Swan's Nest," and the lady and the youth recall Lady Geraldine and her humble poet. Elizabeth Barrett said that "all women should be grateful" for "The Glove," but she excused Browning from a social engagement with the assertion that "Nobody shall leap into lion's dens for *me!*" (1:252, 2:629).

They both wrote about the same kind of women—very unlike the passive, narcissistic figures with whom she feared to be identified—who are at odds with social convention and often actively resist it. Browning valued his heroines for their courage in defying convention, and "The Flight of the Duchess" and "The Glove" forwarded his amatory purpose and answered her poems, not just by exhorting her to courage but by asserting his difference from the men who filled her poems and her life. But his heroines, while they do not just sit around waiting for Perseus, exactly, are more willing than hers are to leave the bold deeds to their lovers. And his versions of the story have more happy endings than hers do. "The Glove" prophesies good fortune for the lady, and Browning explained that the unwritten conclusion to "The Flight of the Duchess" would have described "the life the Lady was to lead with her future gipsy lover—a *real* life" (1:135). Her heroines courageously break forth but—until Lady Geraldine—are defeated in the end. In the story that most closely approximates their own, the Princess Marie dies even though a princely lover carries her off to recover from the debility caused by her art. Her gloomy vision may seem the more realistic one; but when they tested the story in their lives, it was Browning who turned out to have been the true prophet. After they were safely married, he described with playful exuberance in "The Statue and the Bust" two lovers who waste their lives because they never get around to running away from the elderly husband who keeps his young wife shut up in her room; the situation is like what Elizabeth Barrett's had been (the woman even looks like her), and the poem seems to insist triumphantly, "I was right, wasn't I?"

Some of her hesitation can be accounted for by her awareness that in playing out a story she had not chosen, she was allowing Browning's imagination to triumph over her own.[15] Above all, it was the story of

Sleeping Beauty, as she generously acknowledged, frequently reminding him that her life had been over until he came. But she was no longer young or beautiful, and in any case she had said clearly enough in "The Lost Bower" that she wanted to be not Sleeping Beauty but the questing prince. Later, though, when an American journal repeated Horne's "fabulous story [...] about unknown tongues & a seven years eclipse in total darkness" she reflected that the true story was "scarcely less wonderful" (2:703). The myths that proved applicable were richly various. She joked about herself as Cinderella (2:956), since "the Fairy Tales are on the whole, I feel, the most available literature for illustration, whenever I think of loving you" (2:957). And her childish fantasy of a Greek island of poetry, freedom, and joy revived in their shared dream of Italy, which they liked to refer to in the image of the siren isle at the end of Walter Savage Landor's splendid sonnet in praise of Browning: "Beyond Sorrento and Amalfi, where / The Siren waits thee, singing song for song" (quoted 1:274, note). "You ARE the veritable Siren," Browning wrote, "and you 'wait me,' and will sing 'song for song'" (1:352).

He seemed to cherish her song, however, mostly for what she valued least. He saw in her what he missed, as a poet, in himself. He felt that his life had been ominously easy: "for when did I once fail to get whatever I had set my heart upon?—as I ask myself sometimes, with a strange fear" (1:25). But everything he had set his heart upon had not been enough, and he needed something else to want. Despite the disaster of *Sordello*, which had been greeted with incomprehension and ridicule when it was published in 1840, he was confident that success would come, and he declared himself tired of society and even of books. In her situation, her poems, and her letters he read a knowledge born of suffering that was outside his own experience and is in fact conspicuously absent from the poetry he had written so far. In contrast to his scary good fortune, she said bitterly: "everything turns to evil which I touch" (1:305). She felt that she could give him only a burden of sadness—"What could I give you, which it would not be ungenerous to give?" (1:179)—and could teach him "nothing, except grief" (1:87). He had never been touched by death, while she dwelt in its shadow. But what she thought it ungenerous to give was precisely what he wanted: dark experience of the inner life and the means to express it. He said in his second letter: "you *do* what I always wanted, hoped to do, and only seem now likely to do for the first time. You speak out, *you*,—I only make men & women speak [...] and fear the pure white light, even if it is in me" (1:7). Despite the fears of self-expression with which her poems wrestled, to him they seemed enviably transparent.[16]

She, on the other hand, was tired of inwardness. She had worn out her long sorrow, her disease was abating and her strength beginning to return, and she was sick of isolation. Despite her contempt for conventional society and her nervous reluctance to meet people, she had come to value not only cheerfulness but engagement with the world. Browning coveted the knowledge she had drawn from introspection and pain, but she was vivified by his energy, strength, freedom, and experience of life. He said that he wanted to get away from the dramatic mode and write "R. B. a poem" (1:17), but although she classed herself among "poets who write directly from their personal experience & emotions" she considered the dramatic "faculty" such as Browning possessed the "strongest & rarest" in art (2:731). She wanted to turn away from subjectivity and write a "sort of novel-poem" (1:31) about modern life.

Yet despite all the pressures of story and situation to take unequal and opposite parts, they both wanted a balance such as is prefigured in the astonishing likeness between them that is apparent even in their earliest letters. The one story that was peculiarly their own, told just for them, was Landor's brief evocation of the siren isle, and it lent itself to reciprocity ("song for song," Landor had said): once she explicitly imagines him as a male siren, herself as Ulysses (1:540). Browning had a horror of exerting power or imposing his will, to the point that he could not even hold out in an argument against her: when they differed on the morality of duelling, for instance, he wished to concede although he still disagreed with her, and she had to point out that it was not possible to "submit" in a question of opinion (2:609). He admired her for standing up to him in arguments, and she admired his admiration. On literary questions each eagerly deferred to the other. Neither wanted to dominate: at the beginning, each urged the other to set the day for visits, and "think for me" is a recurrent phrase. Both claimed inferiority. Although she despised conventionally "masculine" men (*LEBB* 2:134), she noted the inferiority of women (2:828), while he fell happily into the courtly lover's worship of his mistress (which is not incompatible, of course, with believing her inferior). Both detested the prevailing conventions of courtship and marriage, especially when they involved power. "Generous" and "ungenerous" are the central terms of her self-assessment; she envies him his greater opportunity for generosity (1:178), and he is sympathetically responsive, calling her love a free "gift": "I '*won*' NOTHING (the hateful word, and *French* thought)" (1:335). In worldly terms, there was a balance too: she had an income from legacies sufficient for them to live on and refused to let him squander his genius earning money, while he had youth and health—although even there, the scales were brought closer to balance by his headaches, about which she fussed inordinately. Both still lived with their parents, they had never earned their keep or taken any responsibility for a household, and neither was accustomed to making decisions in the small matters of life—Browning, indeed, asserted with some violence that he preferred to have such decisions made for him (2:960).[17] In marrying him, her escape from the condition of being her father's daughter was complete indeed.

Their search for a paradoxically nonhierarchical relationship found literary embodiment in the love letters, a masterwork in a genre which has been the especial province of women both real and fictional and in which the contradictions that enmeshed Elizabeth Barrett as a poet recur as liberating elements of a harmonious whole.[18] In an exchange of letters each writer is alternately speaker and audience, and a published personal correspondence is inherently anomalous: the private made public. The literary whole is created from parts composed at different times, the temporal gaps between them being essential and significant. Each letter, once dispatched, escapes from the author's control and becomes subject first to the recipient and eventually to the editor who selects, interprets, annotates, and chooses its context and frame. Barrett Browning's editors have made various kinds of volumes. There are collections of her letters to one person, presented with different degrees of completeness, accuracy, and annotation; Frederic G. Kenyon's turn-of-the-century selection, covering most of her life and many correspondents, but drastically pruned and radically incomplete; and the first part of Philip Kelley and Ronald Hudson's massive project (they anticipate at least forty volumes) that will subsume if not replace all the existing collections and add many other voices to her own. Kelley and Hudson's *Brownings' Correspondence* will eventually include all surviving letters from and to both Elizabeth Barrett and Robert Browning, in chronological order, along with related documents and data, extensively annotated. But Elvan Kintner's edition of the love letters is the most tightly unified of the published epistolary works and the one with the most compelling plot, subtlest characterization, and best writing. It is also the most complete: only the indiscreet declaration of love that Browning destroyed when she returned it to him is missing, and its absence is an integral part of the story.

This text is doubly a collaboration, between the two writers and between them and the editor. The collaborations are subtle and delicate: the writers maintain a finely balanced reciprocity, and Kintner's editorial control is of a very different kind from that of Kenyon, who trimmed away not only redundancies and what he considered trivia but also domestic and personal queries and information, gossip, scandal, and ill-will, and a great deal about spiritualism—whatever, in short, might have blurred the outline or marred the decorum of the portrait he wanted to draw. Kintner gives us not only the writers' final texts but everything they crossed out which remained legible, as well as noting more effectual cancellations, and his elaborately informative presentation, with visually obtrusive marks scratched all over the elegant surface of the texts and endnotes separating one letter from another, establish them as documents to be quarried for information as well as the components of an aesthetic object, a story to be read. We are constantly aware of his intervention and of ourselves as readers whose presence violates, one might think, the essential privacy in which the letters had their being.

And yet this meticulous presentation is less unsuitable than it might seem. One thinks of familiar letters as (except for the diary) the most private of literary forms, the farthest removed from the activities of a professional writer—and therefore, of course, the most suitable for women. Like lyric poetry as the Victorians typically conceived it, their essential charm requires the appearance of having sprung spontaneously out of a particular moment, concentrating entirely on the intended recipient and unaware of any other prospective reader. But Elizabeth Barrett's spontaneity is the result of long practice, "encouraging [her]self in writing naturally" (*BC* 2:303). Letters like lyrics artfully enact sincerity, and her rare lapses from candor can be detected only by juxtaposing correspondences that were not meant to be read by the same person: her denial to Thomas Westwood, for instance, of her collaboration with Horne in *A New Spirit of the Age*,[19] or the affectionate effusions about Mary Russell Mitford's prospective visits that she coldly belies when she writes to Browning. The impression of spontaneity suffers somewhat, too, when we find the same lively sentences reproduced for different correspondents. Nor was she unaware of other readers lurking in the eventual distance. By the mid-nineteenth century, writers who hoped to interest posterity could expect their letters to be published after their death, and perhaps even before, unless they took preemptive action.[20] Harriet Martineau commanded her friends to destroy all her letters, but Elizabeth Barrett considered this a "conventional excess of delicacy" and a wanton denial of pleasure to those (like herself) who loved to read letters: "As if . . when we have seen God, we shall care for man seeing *us*!" (*LMRM* 2:371).

Those who read our letters see ourselves ("*us*"). Barrett Browning's letters are not just records of her life; they are part of it, and by 1845 they seem also to have become, like her poems, a substitute for it. Letters had long been her preferred form of social intercourse except with her immediate family. She did not really enjoy Mary Russell Mitford's occasional visits, and for a while even Browning seemed "nearer" (1:360) to her as a disembodied correspondent than in the flesh. Their meetings did not staunch the epistolary flow, and there are remarkably few moments at which nonepistolary communications or events seem to have made a gap in the written story. She worried that his feelings sprang from his imaginative response to her writings and her situation rather than to herself, and she worried all the more because of her own feeling that she was more herself in words than in the body.[21] His presence inhibited her, she said, because she feared that his love was "all dream-work" and would vanish when he awoke and saw her—whereas "the dear letters took me on the side of my own ideal life where I was able to stand a little upright & look round" (1:360). In correspondence she could choose her posture ("stand upright") and see ("look round"), while being seen only in her own self-depiction. (Browning, who never tried to master the art of apparently self-revelatory letter-writing, replied that he felt safer in letters, where he could always stop himself, while in person he might go too far [1:364].)

Like Catarina, she could not reconcile her physical self, which she shrank from displaying, with the self that existed in words. She was a very small, very thin person, and she spoke in a very soft voice and wrote in very small characters on tiny pieces of paper, giving her words the least possible physical embodiment. Her consciousness of herself as a physical object was manifested in paralyzing shyness, as Catarina's is in humility. The disparity felt irreconcilable, and not just in an amatory context—the ambitious young poet whose sonnet in praise of himself Wordsworth graciously emended, for instance, would become in his presence just an awkward young woman.[22] This shyness disappeared as soon as she changed her status and validated herself as a woman through marriage.

In letters, however, such doubleness necessarily exists, regardless of gender, and so can be used and mastered. Unlike most literary forms (epitaphs carved on tombstones are the other obvious exception), letters themselves—and especially love letters—are both reproducible verbal creations and, in a very important sense, unique physical objects. Their function is not completed until they have passed from the writer to the intended recipient, and they can be lost or stolen or fall into hostile hands—or, like Browning's first declaration of love, be reclaimed by the writer and destroyed, lost forever. Felt to partake of the writer's physical presence, they are preserved by recipients, heirs, collectors, and libraries. Although he abhorred the thought of showing his private self to the world, Browning could not bring himself to include the love letters in the general destruction of his correspondence that he carried out before he died; he left them to his son, who described them with moving redundancy and elegiac precision as things imbued with the life and death of their authors: "Ever since my mother's death these letters were kept by my father in a certain inlaid box, into which they exactly fitted, and where they have always rested, letter beside letter, each in its consecutive order and numbered on the envelope by his own hand."[23]

Since the contradictions inherent in letter-writing—between speaking subject, object, and audience, between ingenuousness and the high self-consciousness of art, and between the intimate immediate audience and a potential public one—were those that Elizabeth Barrett wrestled with in her poetry, it is perhaps no wonder that she attained to a very high order of epistolary skill. The birthday odes she had composed as a child present themselves as letters, combining (often as a joke) literary convention and intimate address. Her earlier letters are sometimes marred by signs of effort and uncertainties of touch, but she learned to seem more spontaneous.[24] Her self-presentation is always deft and usually humorous. She almost never allows herself to express, except in detached retrospect, the misery that frequently consumed her, and her reports of cold weather and winds, ill health, and other misfortunes are often very funny. Before her marriage her letters come from a small, self-contained, almost entirely private and domestic world which lent itself to artful representation not for its own sake but for what, in the way of art or intimacy, could be made of it.

When the range of her relationships was very narrow, she could focus intently on her auditor, and her different correspondences achieve considerable tonal and thematic unity. Later her correspondents became more numerous and she wrote more often to maintain than to establish intimacy, and—especially as her life became more eventful and more involved with impersonal matters—to communicate information and argue public questions rather than for the pleasure of writing or the act of self-creation. Letters from her married years that do try to establish new intimacies, like those to Mrs. Gaskell, are not part of sustained correspondences. Although few of her letters are simply pragmatic in intent—invitations, appointments, lost umbrellas, and the like—they satisfy as Victorian novels do our appetite for small matters of daily life. The proximity they were meant to create for one reader is now accessible to us all, spiced with the pleasures of blameless eavesdropping. They establish a sense of physical as well as emotional closeness through precise although not terribly personal details about her thoughts, friends, activities, and surroundings, and especially through lively reports (attractive to those who are fond of dogs and children although tedious, no doubt, to others) of Flush and (later) her son, Pen—in particular, their gestures of love. Frequent expressions of concern for her correspondents' plans and doings, and especially their health, work to make them physically present in the letters too.[25]

She portrays feelings and states of mind, her own and others', with extraordinary delicacy. The syntax, while always perfectly under control, is loose and open, relying heavily for punctuation on dashes or ellipses—it is often hard to tell which—and imitating the impromptu, exploratory quality of speech. And there are wonderful images everywhere, very lightly brushed in but cumulatively rich in suggestiveness and physical presence. For example (to choose almost at random): she tells Browning that she would be wrong to let him take "the step of wasting, in a sense, [his] best feelings . . of emptying [his] water gourds into the sand" (1:178). And farther on in the same paragraph she says that if he withdraws she will continue to "feel, as those do who have felt sorrow, (for where these pits are dug, the water will stand), the full price of [his] regard" (1:179). These parenthetical images swiftly and delicately sketch the shapes of male and female anatomy within a vaguely biblical symbolic landscape, first conveying her sense of his fertile sexuality and her own irremediable barrenness, and then imaging herself as a receptacle in which the water although unused will not be lost, her "sorrow" for him added (presumably) to that for Bro. (Ten years later she writes in a very different tone to another correspondent, thinking of a different liquid, that she has been so shaken that she bubbles: "If I had much of the milk of human kindness I should have the butter of it by this time.")[26] She wrote an enormous number of letters, in health and sickness, pleasure and sorrow, excitement and tedium, and they have charmed almost every reader. Henry James, most memorably, found in them "a nameless intellectual, if it be not rather a moral, grace."[27] Less concerned, apparently, to record her life than to remake it, at least in the uneventful years before her marriage, she needed a reader (she kept a diary only briefly); and in Robert Browning she found the best reader of all.

The other major literary product of their courtship was *Sonnets from the Portuguese,* a sequence of forty-four Petrarchan sonnets that has been the most enduringly popular of Barrett Browning's works among non-academic readers, and the most consistently undervalued by the few post-Victorian critics who have stooped to notice it at all. It is her first major work to bear no marks of immaturity, uncertainty of touch or purpose, or a reach that exceeds her grasp. It mirrors themes and allusions from the letters, explores ways of conceiving an unconventional pair of lovers within traditional poetic fictions of romantic love, and discovers how a woman can speak as a poet to a lover who is a poet too. Anomalies that epistolary form comfortably encompasses reach more difficult and precarious resolution here.

This is the first long poem in which she writes directly about her own experience. It is also the first with a workable form and a subject that is not too grandiose to be interesting. After more or less unsatisfactory experiments with Homeric epic, Popean didactic verse, Christianized Greek tragedy, and a hybrid combination of Renaissance dramatic verse and Miltonic epic, she turned to lyric, the most inward, personal, and expressive of major poetic forms. She published twenty-eight sonnets in 1844 and fourteen more in 1850, and had recently been translating Petrarch. The tradition of the sonnet sequence encouraged the tightly wrought psychological analysis at which she excelled, and it also allowed for a strong narrative line. Its unabashed depiction of a contemporary setting and small events of ordinary life, furthermore, make *Sonnets from the Portuguese* her second approach, after "Lady Geraldine's Courtship," to a novelistic poem of modern life. And it is the first long work since *An Essay on Mind* in which she seems to be speaking in her own person and in her natural voice.

Sonnets from the Portuguese inaugurated both the nineteenth-century revival of the amatory sonnet sequence, which had been in desuetude in England since the Renaissance, and also (with *In Memoriam*, published a few months earlier) a major Victorian innovation: the long poem telling a story through a series of individual lyrics. More narrowly, it is the first of the semiautobiographical, lyrical or partly lyrical amatory sequences in modern settings of which there are distinguished examples by almost every important Victorian poet except Browning: Tennyson's *Maud*, Arnold's *Switzerland*, Clough's *Amours de Voyage*, and Coventry Patmore's *The Angel in the House* in the 1850s, Meredith's *Modern Love* in 1862, Dante Gabriel Rossetti's *The House of Life* in 1870, and (most directly influenced by *Sonnets from the Portuguese*) Christina Rossetti's *Monna Innominata*, probably written in the 1860s but not published until 1881. Honoring the great social imperative of early and mid-Victorian literature,

its movement like that of *In Memoriam* subsumes a life-denying attach-
ment to death into a new, living love, a gradual reconnection with the
natural cycles of regeneration and the human community; its structure,
in fact, resembles that of elegy. Like almost all Victorian amatory se-
quences, and unlike most Renaissance ones, it assumes that marriage—
the social affirmation of love, the affective bond holding society to-
gether—is love's proper end: *In Memoriam*, too, ends with a marriage.
By surrendering to love, the speaker is repudiating (as many Victorian
poets felt it necessary to do) art bred in isolation: "I lived with visions
for my company / Instead of men and women, years ago," but the visions
have faded (as, in Victorian literature, such visions do), and the lover
replaces them, "to be [. . .] what they seemed."[28] And as in most Vic-
torian sequence poems, lyric utterance is set in a context of humdrum,
unromantic, unheroic, everyday life.

Barrett Browning transforms the Renaissance sonnet sequence by
immersing it in Victorian life and values, and even more by having a
woman as speaker: a woman, furthermore, who does not just respond,
like Catarina, to a male voice, filling the space left by its absence and
telling the other side of the story. She takes the male poet's place too.
She is the reluctant object of a poet's courtship, but she is also the
sonneteer: both Catarina (the "Portuguese" of the title) and Camões,
both poet and poet's beloved.[29] This is not a reversal of roles, but a
doubling of them. There are *two* poets in the poem, and *two* poets'
beloveds, and its project is the utopian one of replacing hierarchy by
equality. The plot, too, doubles gender roles, subject and object: the
awakening of the isolated, self-enclosed heart is the quintessentially Vic-
torian male poet's story, as in *In Memoriam*, but it is also what happens
to Sleeping Beauty, and what Renaissance sonneteers hope to make
happen through their verse.

The sequence begins with the speaker unexpectedly seized by love:

> a mystic Shape did move
> Behind me, and drew me backward by the hair;
> And a voice said in mastery, while I strove,—
> "Guess now who holds thee?"—"Death," I said. But, there,
> The silver answer rang,—"Not Death, but Love."

(1)

Although this may seem helplessly feminine, the source of the image is
Homer's Achilles being pulled back in his wrath by Athena,[30] and the
speaker's plight is like that of a Renaissance lover pierced by Cupid's

arrow or a dart from his lady's eyes. Still, she is the object rather than the initiator of courtship, and the first fifteen sonnets record the (very unconventional) reason for her apparent unresponsiveness: her belief that loving her would do him harm. And so she "stand[s] unwon, however wooed," resisting like the woman whose heart is figured as a besieged fortress in courtly romance, with "a most dauntless, voiceless fortitude" (13). At last, however, she surrenders:

> And as a vanquished soldier yields his sword
> To one who lifts him from the bloody earth,
> Even so, Belovèd, I at last record,
> Here ends my strife.

> (16)

This masculine martial image casts her in the suitor's role again, even if at the very moment of abandoning it: poets who describe courtship in metaphors of "winning" and "conquest" do not usually go so far as to image women as defeated soldiers.

The doubling of roles is more pronounced and disturbing, however, when the woman speaks both as the traditionally humble lover and as the object of desire whose beauty is a necessary premise of the sonnet sequence. The result is a devaluation of the erotic object that casts the whole amorous and poetical enterprise in doubt. She says, in effect, *Look at me, and you will cease to desire me,* and many readers, so solicited, turn away. They turn from a sight that violates both literary and social decorum: an unmistakably Victorian woman in the humble position of a courtly lover. She is a "poor, tired, wandering singer" looking up at the beloved's window (3), a Keatsian "acolyte" who "fall[s] flat, with pale insensate brow, / On the altar-stair" (30). The traditional poet-wooer, insofar as he describes himself at all, is pale and weary from unsatisfied desire. Barrett Browning in her essay on English poetry quotes with affection a passage from Stephen Hawes that includes these typical lines: "With your swete eyes behold you me, and see / How thought and woe by great extremetie / Hath changed my colour into pale and wan."[31] "Why so pale and wan, fond lover?" Sir John Suckling asked, simultaneously mocking and perpetuating the convention. In *Sonnets from the Portuguese* the speaker's pallor and weariness violate decorum both because they are signs of male desire, as in the images of minstrel and acolyte, and because they present as object of desire an ill and aging woman.

The speaker's self-portrait is uncompromisingly contemporary, detailed, and unflattering. In one of many vivid scenes of nineteenth-century courtship, she gives her lover a lock of hair and reminds him that her hair is no longer dressed with rose or myrtle like a girl's:

> it only may
> Now shade on two pale cheeks the mark of tears,
> Taught drooping from the head that hangs aside
> Through sorrow's trick.

> (18)

She has "trembling knees" (11), "tremulous hands" (28), and "languid ringlets" (27). The metaphorical becomes literal with particularly disturbing effect in women's love poems, detached from the context in which they are recognized as merely metaphorical.[32] Allegorical images of manly defeat look like feminine weakness, as in the opening sonnets, and the description of the poet is meant to be taken as literally true (unlike, presumably, Shakespeare's picture of himself marked by extreme old age in the *Sonnets*), as early readers would guess and later ones, expecting factual accuracy from a Victorian poet and recognizing Barrett Browning's unfashionable ringlets and characteristic droop of the head, would know.

As usual in poetry, there is much less description of the man. When his appearance *is* described, it is always imaginatively transformed. *Her* hair is just "brown" (18), but *his* is fit for verse: "As purply black, as erst to Pindar's eyes / The dim purpureal tresses gloomed athwart / The nine white Muse-brows" (19). His colors are purple and gold: purple denoting royalty, with which he is frequently associated, gold including in its manifold associations the golden hair of women sung by sonneteers. His merit, in the manner of Petrarchan hyperbole, knows no bounds. She apologizes for her ineptness in portraying him:

> As if a shipwrecked Pagan, safe in port,
> His guardian sea-god to commemorate,
> Should set a sculptured porpoise, gills a-snort
> And vibrant tail, within the temple-gate.

> (37)

No apology is necessary, however, for this witty comparison to a sexy sea god, or for the delightfully erotic porpoise. When she herself is imaginatively transformed, however, it is into an object that repels desire: the inhabitant of a desolate and broken house (4) like that of Tennyson's Mariana (with whom Elizabeth Barrett was wont to compare herself), or "an out-of-tune / Worn viol" (32).

But the speaker's humility and self-denigration should not be taken quite at face value. They are the signs of the desiring subject, and it is as subject that a poet speaks—something the two poets knew, no doubt, when they competed in their letters for the lowest place.[33] She soon realizes, furthermore, that her desire is the source of her own attractiveness. For what, after all, does a lyric lover offer as an inducement to love except his love itself? Her poem can survive her being humble, so long as she is not cold.

> Yet, love, mere love, is beautiful indeed
> And worthy of acceptation. Fire is bright,
> Let temple burn, or flax; an equal light
> Leaps in the flame from cedar-plank or weed:
> And love is fire. And when I say at need
> *I love thee* . . . mark! . . . *I love thee*—in thy sight
> I stand transfigured, glorified aright,
> With conscience of the new rays that proceed
> Out of my face toward thine. There's nothing low
> In love, when love the lowest: meanest creatures
> Who love God, God accepts while loving so.
> And what I *feel*, across the inferior features
> Of what I *am*, doth flash itself, and show
> How that great work of Love enhances Nature's.
>
>   (10)

This is one of the finest poems in the sequence, with its quick and subtle reasoning through analogy and image, the flexibility and control with which the verse bends to the argument and to the rhythms of thought and speech, and the final sonorous generalization. The metaphors of fire and light are literalized with a forceful vividness that stresses without actually stating it the destructiveness of fire (to the outworn self of the poet, one assumes, and to the lover whose primacy is threatened),[34] and convey both amatory and artistic confidence. Like a character in a Victorian novel, the speaker sees herself through another's eyes, but she insists that what glorifies her is the fire of her own love. Love me, she says later, "for love's sake only" (14).

To express desire she finds new kinds of images and a new voice, sensuous, witty, and tender, encompassing a wide range of nuance and tone. The sixth sonnet, for instance, says that she will always stand in her absent lover's shadow, and then shifts to something altogether stranger:

> The widest land
> Doom takes to part us, leaves thy heart in mine

With pulses that beat double. What I do
And what I dream include thee, as the wine
Must taste of its own grapes.

(6)

The tone is tender, but the images of incorporation carry menace, and grapes must be crushed to make wine. A later image of inclusion and enclosure is even more surprising:

Let the world's sharpness, like a clasping knife,
Shut in upon itself and do no harm
In this close hand of Love, now soft and warm,
And let us hear no sound of human strife
After the click of the shutting.

(24)

Love enfolds, rather than casting out, what opposes it. And perhaps most striking of all:

When our two souls stand up erect and strong,
Face to face, silent, drawing nigh and nigher,
Until the lengthening wings break into fire
At either curvèd point.

(22)

As souls, they are equal.

Renaissance sonnet sequences often record the struggle of reason and religion against desire; but while Barrett Browning's speaker asserts in the early sonnets that God opposes her love, having made her unfit for so splendid a lover, it never occurs to her that desire itself might be sinful.[35] On the contrary: the lover is godlike (not simply "divine"), while she was as "dull" as "Atheists [. . .] Who cannot guess God's presence out of sight" (20) when she did not detect his existence before she knew him. She prefers his company to that of angels (22) and almost suggests that he is more to her than God: "I who looked for only God, found *thee!*" (27). There is no hint that such exaltation of the human might be wrong. Her doubling of roles makes her peculiarly aware, however, that desire can conceal the object it transforms, and one of the most surprising sonnets urges him to break free from her entwining imagination. The imagery suggests a Bacchic invocation of divine presence, rising to a climax that is simultaneously playful, witty (in the Metaphysical sense), and joyously erotic:

> I think of thee!—my thoughts do twine and bud
> About thee, as wild vines, about a tree,
> Put out broad leaves, and soon there's nought to see
> Except the straggling green which hides the wood.
> Yet, O my palm-tree, be it understood
> I will not have my thoughts instead of thee
> Who art dearer, better! Rather, instantly
> Renew thy presence; as a strong tree should,
> Rustle thy boughs and set thy trunk all bare,
> And let these bands of greenery which insphere thee
> Drop heavily down,—burst, shattered, everywhere!
> Because, in this deep joy to see and hear thee
> And breathe within thy shadow a new air,
> I do not think of thee—I am too near thee.

(29)

She asks him to reclaim his own subjectivity, as she had reclaimed hers.

For the poem never forgets that it is about two poets, recording with loving exactness the play of the balance between them. One of the conventions of the Renaissance sonnet sequence is that the lover is explicitly a poet writing poems, and the uses and value of poetry, particularly to immortalize the beloved, have always been among its preoccupations. Despite Barrett Browning's early concern with fame and naming, however, when she writes in the genre which traditionally thematizes that concern she ignores it, perhaps because the beloved is a poet too and, the sonnets say, a better one. Instead, she works out terms of reciprocity between poet-lovers, starting with the assumption that lovers must be peers (9), giving and taking equally. "What can I give thee back, O liberal / And princely giver" (8)—"Can it be right to give what I can give?" (9) ("What could I give you," she had asked Browning, "which it would not be ungenerous to give?" [*RB-EBB* 1:179]). In the end the balance rests surprisingly close to even.[36]

She writes the poems, but he draws them forth, both arousing her desire by his own in an endless circle, a seamless reciprocity, and validating her as desire's object. He is the prince whose kiss made her fit to be in a love poem—where, as in fairy tales, women draw power from their beauty. He "kissed / The fingers of this hand wherewith I write; / And ever since, it grew more clean and white, / [. . .] quick [. . .] / When the angels speak" (38). His imagination has the "power" and "grace" to penetrate appearances; through "this mask of me" he sees her "soul's true face" and "all which makes [her] tired of all, self-viewed," and still "Nothing

repels" him (39). She contrasts him to lovers whose rapacious sensuality
scorns everything touched by pain or time:

> Mussulmans and Giaours
> Throw kerchiefs at a smile, and have no ruth
> For any weeping. Polypheme's white tooth
> Slips on the nut if, after frequent showers,
> The shell is over-smooth,—and not so much
> Will turn the thing called love, aside to hate.
>
> (40)

But despite her deference to his initiating imaginative energy and oc-
casionally to his words as well—which she quotes, however, only once—
she is the one who speaks. She asserts that his poems are better than
hers, but we never hear them.

At first she presents both of them as singers, but unequal ones. He
is a court musician, she a "poor, tired, wandering singer, singing
through / The dark, and leaning up a cypress tree" (3). He is a
"gracious singer of high poems" who "let[s] [his] music drop here
unaware / In folds of golden fulness at [her] door"; in response, her
"cricket chirps against [his] mandolin," and she asks him to stop:

> Hush, call no echo up in further proof
> Of desolation! there's a voice within
> That weeps . . . as thou must sing . . . alone, aloof.
>
> (4)

Here again she imagines them knowing each other only as disembodied
voices, but now she is afraid that his song will reduce hers to an echo,
or silence it altogether. The best she can offer him, she says, is silence:
"let the silence of my womanhood / Commend my woman-love to thy
belief" (13). And when she yields to his love, she offers to yield herself
to his song too.

> How, Dearest, wilt thou have me for most use?
> A hope, to sing by gladly? or a fine
> Sad memory, with thy songs to interfuse?
> A shade, in which to sing—of palm or pine?
> A grave, on which to rest from singing? Choose.
>
> (17)

As in "The Poet's Vow," she reminds us that a poet's ideal objects are
always absent and usually dead; she offers, one might say, to be his
Rosalind. But of course she goes on speaking.

Later poems invite or respond to his words with similarly doubled feeling and intention. She asks him to say that he loves her, but the words she requires are only the simplest ones, mechanically repeating like an echo or a bell: "Say thou dost love me, love me, love me—toll / The silver iterance!" (21). She meditates on a letter from him which she paraphrases but does not quote (23); later she does quote him, but only the formulaic words, "*Dear, I love thee*" (28). She will be his instrument, "an out-of-tune / Worn viol" (32); but "perfect strains may float / 'Neath master-hands, from instruments defaced" (32), and although he is the musician, she is the instrument that produces the music, just as she writes the poems stimulated by his love. Later she thanks him for his silence—for dropping his "divinest Art's / Own instrument" to listen to her (41); "Instruct me how to thank thee," she adds, but there is no sign that he acts the teacher's part any more than Browning did. And the last sonnet defines their relationship with quiet but brilliantly doubled images of amatory exchange. He brought to her "close room" flowers which, flourishing there, made that room the enclosed garden that traditionally has symbolized a woman's heart; and in return she gives him flowers from her heart's garden: her poems.

In a poetic sequence the speaker need not be trapped in any one structure of relationship. The space between poems provides room to move around: to reconsider a formulation, explore its ramifications, or drop it and try another. And so the speaker takes a part at least briefly in several stories besides that of courtly love. She is the damsel saved from death, for whom "the face of all the world is changed" since she heard "the footsteps of [the lover's] soul" steal up beside her (7); the Sleeping Beauty restored to life by the prince's kiss (38); the girl covered in the king's purple robe (16) or given a great ruby and set upon a throne like the beggar maid chosen by King Cophetua (12), a favorite character of Victorian art and allusion. She is a vanquished soldier (16), and a prisoner whose chains have been struck off (20) like Andromeda's by Perseus. Conversely (although with some muffled irony), she condescends like Lady Geraldine to a lover of low degree:

> As brighter ladies do not count it strange,
> For love, to give up acres and degree,
> I yield the grave for thy sake, and exchange
> My near sweet view of Heaven, for earth with thee!
>
> (23)

Sometimes she is a child again (33, 34). And her long acquaintance with angels provides images of a more equal and passionate relationship (22).

The opening sonnets establish through multifarious allusions an extraordinarily wide range of contexts for love. The first begins: "I thought once how Theocritus had sung / Of the sweet years." The reference is to the song in the fifteenth idyll which anticipates Adonis' return from death to the arms of Aphrodite, foreshadowing both the speaker's movement from death to love and the coming of the lover; as in the prose essays, classical pastoral embodies her nostalgia for both historical and personal loss. She "mused" Theocritus' story "in his antique tongue," she says, establishing her cultural credentials. And as she mused, the "mystic Shape" from the *Iliad* took hold of her as if she were Achilles. The allusions are deft and easy, the voice that of one who lives familiarly with Greek texts. The second sonnet draws with the same casual confidence on Milton and Shakespeare. Only she, her lover, and God heard the word "Love"—and God "laid the curse / So darkly on my eyelids, as to amerce / My sight from seeing thee—a more "absolute exclusion" than death itself. "Amerce" recalls Milton's Satan "amerced / Of heaven," an appropriate allusion in the context of "all God's universe," "absolute exclusion," and a blinded poet, while the idea of blindness recalls Elizabeth Barrett's remark that her isolation from the world had made her, "in a manner, as a *blind poet*" (*RB-EBB* 1:41). In the sestet we hear echoes of Shakespeare:

> Men could not part us with their worldly jars,
> Nor the seas change us, nor the tempests bend;
> Our hands would touch for all the mountain bars:
> And, heaven being rolled between us at the end,
> We should not vow the faster for the stars.
>
> (2)

("Let me not to the marriage of true minds / Admit impediments. Love is not love / Which alters when it alteration finds, / Or bends with the remover to remove.") Greek pastoral, the rebirth of Adonis, Achilles' injured love and pride, Satan's banishment from heaven, Shakespeare's celebration of human love—these are the contexts in which *Sonnets from the Portuguese* first establishes itself.[37]

The third and fourth sonnets introduce the metaphor of court musicians, and the fifth returns to the Greeks.

> I lift my heavy heart up solemnly,
> As once Electra her sepulchral urn,
> And, looking in thine eyes, I overturn
> The ashes at thy feet.

In Sophocles' *Electra,* Electra is given an urn said to contain the ashes of her brother Orestes by a stranger who then reveals that he is Orestes himself. The comparison suggests that the lover is like a brother returned from the dead, and also that if he were to cure the speaker's grief he would be taking the brother's place—which may be why the speaker warns him that the ashes will flare up and burn him (as if in recognition of rivalry: later she will ask him to "Be heir to" the dead [33]). While we cannot help reading in this the poet's sorrow for Bro, it functions without biographical reference as another allusion to the return of the dead: not the mythic return in Theocritus, but the complex relations of new love and old grief.

From these vast literary spaces the poem contracts into smaller ones, including homely and domestic interiors, and ends in the speaker's "close room." The space is symbolical and highly schematic, tightly constricted on the horizontal plane but open to heaven above and the grave below. At worst, the speaker is like "a bee shut in a crystalline" (15). As a child she had run from one place to another (33, 34), but the movements she imagines for the future are almost always vertical. Typical repeated words are *down, fall, deep, rise, beneath,* and especially *drop,* used eleven times in the forty-four poems, and *up,* used fifteen times. Even marriage, leaving one home for another, means that her eyes would "drop on a new range / Of walls and floors" (35). The reader may feel uncomfortably hemmed in, but the speaker usually imagines enclosure as protective, openness as allowing separation: "the widest land / Doom takes to part us" (6). "Open thine heart wide," she tells her lover, "And fold within the wet wings of thy dove" (35). And in the last sonnet, her "close room" becomes a garden of art.

Within that small space, she enacts some of the main themes and images of Victorian art. The pictorial equivalent is Dante Gabriel Rossetti's painting *Ecce Ancilla Domini,* an Annunciation scene nearly twice as high as it is wide in which the Virgin (for whom Christina Rossetti was the model) sits on the bed pressed against the wall, as if cowering away from the tall upright angel who reaches almost from the top to the bottom of the picture and takes up a full third of its horizontal space. The speaker also resembles the women shut up in houses or towers in Tennyson's early poems, recurrent figures for the poet. She is like the Lady of Shalott, who sings unseen in her tower: people outside the "prison-wall" heard her music, paused, and went on their way (41). Like the soul in "The Palace of Art," she has "lived with visions [. . .] Instead of men and women" (26). She inhabits a figurative dwelling like Mariana's moated grange: "the casement broken in, / The bats and owlets builders in the roof" (4). Her unspecified sorrows belong to the poetical character as Victorian poets typically conceived it; Matthew Arnold's Empedocles, for instance, renounces poetry because isolation and empathy hurt too much. Love comes to her as to Tennyson's bookish, imaginative heroes as an escape from self-imprisonment in a world of shadows.[38] Like the heroes of *Switzerland* and *Amours de Voyage,* the speaker finds that her lover is more passionate and alive than she is herself and can draw her back to life. She is the Victorian poet as introverted self-doubting lover; and she is also one of the female figures in which Victorian poets embody the artist's isolation.

Similar doublings occur wherever *Sonnets from the Portuguese* anticipates the Pre-Raphaelites. Here as elsewhere, Barrett Browning is the precursor, although we are likely to read her through expectations formed by those who followed.[39] Sometimes her wit, quickness, cleverness, and variety call to mind Meredith, as in the tenth sonnet, "Yet, love, mere love." Sometimes the poems resemble Dante Gabriel Rossetti's *The House of Life* in their marmoreal cadences, personifications, archaisms, and heated slow simplicities ("Very whitely still / The lilies of our lives" [24], or "What time I sat alone here in the snow" [20]) and, more pleasingly, in their striking use of Latinate words ("lips renunciative" [9], "Antidotes / Of medicated music" [17]). The speaker is like the tortured husband of *Modern Love* in her subtle psychological analysis, intricate arguments and images, and variations of tone and rhythm that can shift in a flash from formal intensity to broken phrases of the speaking voice. Her dark allusions to untellable sins and sorrows somewhat resemble those in *The House of Life.* But if she speaks like a Pre-Raphaelite poet, she speaks also as such poets' favorite erotic object, the fatal woman: narcissistic, self-enclosed, deathly. Like Morris's Guenevere or Rossetti's Lilith, she seems to look at herself in a mirror (10, 18, 32). Like the wife in *Modern Love,* she breathes poison (9). From the lover's point of view, she is at first silent and unresponsive. And yet she lacks the fatal woman's guile and mystery: being the speaker, she must always let the reader, at least, hear her, while her bent for self-analysis and formal commitment to lyric self-expression preclude duplicity.

Despite (or perhaps partly because of) its enormous popularity, *Sonnets from the Portuguese* has often inspired repugnance and ridicule. This may be partly a reaction to the sentimental legend that grew up around it and partly a simple reflex of distaste for expressions of female desire, but it is more than that. The doubleness and dislocations produced by the female speaker make the poems seem awkward, mawkish, and indecently personal: in short, embarrassing. The embarrassment arises from the clashing of apparently incompatible roles; we are made uncomfortable by the appearance of a woman where we expect a man, by the fact that as subject of desire she denigrates her attractiveness as desire's object, and by the manifold incongruities between amatory convention and Victorian courtship. Readers don't seem to be disturbed by the most strongly erotic passages, which use images—grapes, androgynous angels, palm trees, dolphins, and the like—that evoke neither the literature of courtly love nor the domestic realities of Victorian life. But the disparity between the woman's situation and the traditional poet-lover's, between this speaker and the half-remembered voices we dimly hear behind her, makes us continuously aware that nothing quite fits the generic conventions, and we assume without thinking about it that what is not conventional is autobiographical, merely personal, mawkishly "sincere."

The problematics of convention and sincerity came inevitably with the genre of amatory verse. The poet's convention-defying sincerity is a convention of the sonnet sequence: "Look in thy heart, and write," Sir Philip Sidney's Muse admonished him at the beginning of *Astrophel and Stella:* a famous and witty line that Elizabeth Barrett singles out in her essay on English poetry as "the completest 'Ars Poetica' extant" (the joke, which she does not appear to have noticed, is in demanding spontaneity by way of the creaky machinery of the Muse and the familiar conceit that the lover's heart enshrines the beloved's picture). Nor is it surprising to find autobiographical material in a lyric sequence, or at any rate to find critics intent on finding it there. *Astrophel and Stella* and Spenser's *Amoretti* seem to contain a great deal of such material, and the compelling strangeness of Shakespeare's *Sonnets* has persuaded generations of readers that they must be based on life. "With this key / Shakespeare unlocked his heart," Wordsworth said of the sonnet, to which Browning (master of disguises) replied tartly: "Did Shakespeare? If so, the less Shakespeare he!"[40] Barrett Browning greatly valued the appearance of sincerity in art, as most Victorian readers and writers did, and had the skill to achieve it.

We know, furthermore, that the story the *Sonnets* tells is in fact true, and this knowledge is inevitably part of our experience of reading it. The parallels between the love letters and the poems tempt us to assume (although there is no good reason to do so) that the poems were the spontaneous products of the moments they appear to describe. It is worth noting, though, that the letters themselves don't embarrass us: only the poems do. We are disturbed by the incongruity between the sentiments and the genre, not by the sentiments themselves. Little scenes from Victorian life and characteristically Victorian modes of feeling and turns of phrase give a strange context to the sonnets' erotic intensities, formal language, and traditional form. They seem to belong to prose fiction instead.

> My letters! all dead paper, mute and white!
> And yet they seem alive and quivering
> Against my tremulous hands which loose the string
> And let them drop down on my knee to-night.
>
> (28)

The speaker recalls her dead mother's kiss (18) and her own childish play among the cowslips (33). She sometimes addresses her lover ("Dear," "Dearest," "Beloved") more like a Victorian wife than a courtly lover: "I lean upon thee, Dear, without alarm" (24). She asks him to call her by the "pet-name" of her childhood (33). They exchange, as Victorians liked to do, locks of hair (18, 19). She wonders if she will miss, when she marries, "Home-talk and blessing and the common kiss," the "walls and floors," even, of home (35). Alethea Hayter, who is an exceptionally sympathetic and discerning reader of Barrett Browning, finds *Sonnets from the Portuguese* too intimate, "emotionally . . . naked"—and yet Hayter's well-chosen examples of unduly intimate passages all refer to self-descriptions or incidents, not feelings: the speaker's pale cheeks, the locks of hair, the pet name, letters and kisses.[41] The events of a Victorian woman's courtship don't seem to belong in a sonnet sequence—at least, we haven't seen them there before—so they must (we assume) be personal, particular, trivial.

Barrett Browning hesitated to publish the *Sonnets*, showing the poem to her husband for the first time three years after their marriage: "all this delay," Browning reported in 1864,

> because I happened early to say something against putting one's loves into verse: then again, I said something else on the other side . . . and next morning she said hesitatingly "Do you know I once wrote some poems about *you?*"—and then—"There they are, if you care to see them,". . . . How I see the gesture, and hear the tones . . . . Afterward the publishing them was through me . . . there was a trial at covering it a little by leaving out one sonnet which had plainly a connexion with the former works: but it was put in afterwards when people chose to pull down the mask which, in old days, people used to respect at a masquerade. But I never cared.[42]

This is simple and straightforward enough. But Edmund Gosse's silly, apocryphal version of this episode, which has accompanied the *Sonnets* through many printings, transfers the reader's embarrassment to the poet herself. She came up behind her husband, Gosse reports, "held him by the shoulder to prevent his turning to look at her, and . . . pushed a packet of papers into the pocket of his coat. She told him to read that, and to tear it up if he did not like it; and then she fled again to her own room." Afterwards, says Gosse, she "was very loth indeed to consent to the publication of what had been the very notes and chronicle of her betrothal."[43] But Browning makes it clear that her reticence had been mostly the deferential reflex of his own. In 1846 she had answered his question about what she was writing (almost certainly these sonnets) with a self-possession absolutely antithetical to Gosse's emblematic tale of coyness, self-dramatization, and shame. "You shall see some day at Pisa what I will not show you now. Does not Solomon say that 'there is a time to read what is written.' If he doesn't, he *ought*" (*RB-EBB* 2:892–93).

Poetic sequences by Victorian men use the poet's own experiences, too, and also invite biographical readings by their oddities of form.[44] *Sonnets from the Portuguese* differs from most other such poems in that it apparently makes no attempt to fictionalize the characters or story, although the title is a half-disguise and the sonnet (42) that would have identified the author by a reference to one of her earlier poems was omitted in 1850. Male poets, however, could present their experiences (fictionalized or not) as exemplifying those of modern man, or at any rate of the sensitive modern poet-intellectual. Meredith did this with his title, *Modern Love*, and Tennyson said that the speaker of *In Memoriam* was not always the poet himself, "but the voice of the human race speaking thro' him."[45] But the modern woman's personal experience could not easily be made to carry so heavy a contextual burden, and Elizabeth Barrett was not yet quite ready to try. There were no ancestral female voices to validate her own and define by contrast its particular quality. Nor, as she knew, were readers disposed to see a woman as representative of the human race, or a poet as a representative woman. Women can't generalize, Romney smugly explains to Aurora Leigh, and therefore can't be poets (*Aurora Leigh* 2:183–225), and Lady Waldemar repeats the common assumption that "artist women" are "outside [. . .] the common sex" (*Aurora Leigh* 3:406–7).[46] The situation of a female poet in love with a male one is particularly abnormal.

Still, she tried to generalize and distance this situation. The use of the sonnet sequence, which seems an obvious choice now but was not so at the time, placed her experience in a wider tradition, even if in the event it also showed how untraditional, in poetic terms, it was. The crowd of allusions in the opening sonnets serves much the same function. She reminds us that she is composing poems, not love letters, when a poem represents what she does not say to the lover (13) or suppresses words of his letters that are too private to repeat (28). And the title is a witty doubling of private and public: in fact a private allusion to Barrett Browning's Catarina, it suggests that the sonnets are translations of someone else's published words.[47]

She might, of course, have taken the opposite tack and demonstrated the insufficiency of old bottles for new wine; but although there are obviously rich possibilities for irony in the disparity between literary convention and a modern woman's life, she does not seem to notice them. Nor does she call attention to anomalies and contradictions even without irony, as she sometimes does in the ballads. This above all distinguishes her from her male contemporaries. The juxtaposition of traditional amatory poetry and the Victorian idea that love should be fulfilled in marriage, combined with the desire of almost every important Victorian poet to write about contemporary life, inevitably opened up the disjunction between the passionate certainties of literature and the flawed complexities of life, between the amatory intensity of poetic lovers and the confusion and distractedness of modern ones. Sometimes modern settings produce unintended comedy, as in much of Patmore or the description of Maud's dress ("the habit, hat, and feather" and "the frock and gipsy bonnet"—"nothing can be sweeter / Than maiden Maud in either").[48] More often, though, Tennyson, Clough, and Meredith exploit the disjunction between literature and contemporary life through self-denigrating irony. *Sonnets from the Portuguese* might well have been the same sort of poem; at any rate, the love letters, kisses, pet names, childishness, and ringlets rest uneasily with Maud's dresses on the dangerous edge of bathos.

But Barrett Browning does not want to show up disparities. She wants to take her place in the tradition, not to prove herself an outsider. Nor can she mock the sonnet tradition from within as Shakespeare and Sidney did, since she has first to assert her right to use it at all. *Sonnets from the Portuguese* is organized around the double discovery that love's seeming illusions are realities and that one can be both subject and object of love, both poet and poet's beloved. Because she does not use irony to mark the points at which the old and the new come together—she wants to create fusion, not show incongruity—she risks leaving us disoriented and uneasy instead of releasing us, as Clough and Meredith do, into the ironical recognition of a familiar failure. The predominance of heavy rhythms and slightly archaic, "poetical" diction work to seal the poem against anything that might break the lyric spell. But since success for the poet in this poem requires a happy ending for the lovers, or at least not an unhappy one, there is no release such as Arnold and Dante Gabriel Rossetti give us into the lyrical pain of loss.

The jolt to our expectations and the transfixing power of what appears to be autobiography have made it very difficult to see what is going on in the poem, especially for those who assume that these intricate and artful sonnets are spontaneous and sincere, simple and artless.[49] But when we take the poem on its own terms, we can appreciate the emotional and intellectual complexity, the richness of reference, the elaborate and ingenious conceits, and the subtle ways in which images are used both for their emotional power and to carry an argument. We can appreciate, too, the way the poet keeps to the difficult Petrarchan structure, eschewing odd rhymes almost entirely in her effort to claim her place within the lyric tradition but allowing herself freedom for enjambment of lines and of the boundary between octave and sestet and capturing tones and rhythms of speech. Even the uncharacteristic simplicity of "How do I love thee? Let me count the ways" (43) is less simple and more satisfying when we see it as the culmination of such themes as the definition of space ("I love thee to the depth and breadth and height") or the relation of new love to the past ("I love thee with the passion put to use / In my old griefs"—a libidinal economy first figured in the comparison to Electra, further adumbrated in later sonnets, and now plainly defined). That she is at last forthrightly answering his question, speaking her love, is her triumph as a poet and his as a lover. And the repetitive structure (six lines begin, "I love thee," and the phrase appears three more times as well) forms a striking contrast to the other sonnets, while thematically it echoes with triumphant elaboration the "silver iterance" of "I love thee" that she had earlier asked of him.[50]

Sonnets from the Portuguese records unexpected successes in both poetry and love, and the two kinds of success are as inextricably connected as the comparable failures are in Christina Rossetti's *Monna Innominata*, where the speaker says at the end that she has lost her lover and her ability to sing: "Youth gone, and beauty gone . . . . Silence of love that cannot sing again." For both Rossetti and Barrett Browning, woman's place in love poetry has to be sustained by male desire, and *Sonnets from the Portuguese* ends with a quiet formulation of the reciprocity that made the poem possible.

Belovèd, thou hast brought me many flowers
Plucked in the garden, all the summer through
And winter, and it seemed as if they grew
In this close room, nor missed the sun and showers.
So, in the like name of that love of ours,
Take back these thoughts which here unfolded too,
And which on warm and cold days I withdrew
From my heart's ground. Indeed, those beds and bowers
Be overgrown with bitter weeds and rue,
And wait thy weeding; yet here's eglantine,
Here's ivy!—take them, as I used to do
Thy flowers, and keep them where they shall not pine.
Instruct thine eyes to keep their colours true,
And tell thy soul their roots are left in mine.

Barrett Browning has revised her early letter to Browning: "my poetry [. . .] is the flower of me [. . . .] & so it has all my colours; the rest of me is nothing but a root, fit for the ground & the dark" (*RB-EBB* 1:65). The desire expressed through his flowers nourished the root of self from which her poems grew.

6

Marriage and Italy: *Poems* (1850) and *Casa Guidi Windows*

Barrett Browning had always had a low opinion of marriage, especially for women, but her own was an unqualified success. She finally yielded to Browning's patient and passionate insistence that she protect her recovering health from another English winter and allow him to (as she could not but feel it) burden himself with her care. They were married secretly in London on September 12, 1846, returned to their homes for a week, and then set out for Paris and Pisa. Hoping to spare her sisters some of their father's inevitable wrath, she kept the secret even from them until she had left. When they reached Paris she was very happy but dangerously exhausted, and they immediately threw themselves on the maternal care of Mrs. Anna Jameson, a writer and friend of them both, who was also on her way to Italy and agreed to travel with them. "I have . . . here," she wrote, "a poet and a poetess . . . . Both excellent; but God help them! for I know not how the two poet heads and poet hearts will get on through this prosaic world."[1]

In fact, they got on very well. They set up housekeeping first in Pisa and then in Florence, and the risk of the arduous journey was almost immediately vindicated by a remarkable improvement in her health. Living together only increased their affection and their high regard for each other as paragons of noble selflessness and delightfully good-natured companions. After eight months of marriage Browning praised her "entire generosity and elevation of character" and "sweetest of all imaginable sweet tempers." "I solemnly affirm," he wrote to her sisters, "that I have never been able to detect the slightest fault, failing or shadow of short-coming in her" (*TTUL* 48, 50). She described his admiring solicitude less solemnly, with her usual lively sense of the ridiculous:

147

> Even the pouring out of the coffee is a divided labour, and the ordering of the dinner is quite out of my hands. As for me, when I am so good as to let myself be carried upstairs, and so angelical as to sit still on the sofa, and so considerate, moreover, as *not* to put my foot into a puddle, why *my* duty is considered done to a perfection which is worthy of all adoration. (*LEBB* 1:306)

> Every word I say is something right and bright, let it be ever so dull: and if I say nothing, why then, I am sure to be looking right, or pouring out coffee right, or listening divinely to something said to me, so that mine is not a difficult part by any manner of means. (*LS* 46–47)

Some women, she notes (but she is not one of them), "might not like *the excess*" (*TTUL* 25). She fears that he will injure himself, carrying her, and is "quite seriously angry": "Sins of this sort are his only sins against me" (*LS* 109). The only danger she feared was that of sliding back into loving dependency.

The simplicity and cheapness of housekeeping in Italy facilitated the creation of a new life on their own terms. Elizabeth's maid Wilson, who had replaced the more appropriately named Crow, had accompanied them from England, and with a few Italian servants she took care of everything very satisfactorily. Except for deciding where to live and negotiating with landlords, which was Robert's work, neither Elizabeth nor Robert took any responsibility, then or later, for household affairs, even for ordering dinner, although Robert enjoyed poking about the markets for furniture and paintings at a time when what might even be "Old Masters" could be found in odd corners for very little money. For Elizabeth, the details of ordinary diurnal life had both the glamor of romance (attractive little dinners simply appeared, for instance, from the restaurant below) and an immensely satisfying reality. They had the pleasures of domesticity without domestic cares—her happy letters describe what sounds more like playing house than housekeeping—and lived very much alone, almost always together, gradually making friends among the small group of like-minded English and American residents in Florence but resolutely avoiding "society." Except for occasional outbursts of political excitement Florence was a quiet place, so quiet that they often thought wistfully of moving to Paris. Books were hard to come by, and the reading room where Robert looked over the new periodicals was closed to women. But she liked the climate, the comfort, and the freedom from social obligations and thought with horror of the cold weather, drafty houses, and formal and expensive social life in England. They intended, they said, to visit England in a warm season, but for one reason or another they did not actually do so until 1851.

Back in London, Mr. Barrett was too angry even to open the letters she kept hopefully dispatching. This was expected; what she had not expected was that her brothers would take his side:

> it pained me that [George], [. . .] who knew that the alternative of making a single effort to secure my health during the winter was the severe displeasure I have incurred now, and that the fruit of yielding myself a prisoner was the sense of being of no use nor comfort to any soul, papa having given up coming to see me except for five minutes a day [. . .] that [George] should now turn round and reproach me for want of affection towards my family, for not letting myself drop like a dead weight into the abyss, a sacrifice without an object and expiation—this did surprise me and pain me—pained me more than all papa's dreadful words. (*LEBB* 1:287)

She was naïvely surprised that her brothers did not applaud her escape from the despotism by which they themselves remained bound. In fact her sudden assertion of independence and sexuality was a nasty shock to them, spurring George to complain that she had "sacrificed all delicacy & honour"[2] by her decorous elopement. Nor did they consider Browning a desirable brother-in-law. He was the son of a bank clerk, with no income and no apparent intention of earning one, and poetry could not appease men with small regard for literature. Her father's accusation that she had sold her soul for "*genius* . . . mere genius" (*TTUL* 6) was more amusing than her brothers' assumption that Browning had married her for her money. She refused to be reconciled with her brothers until they accepted her husband too, and although George held aloof until 1851 they all—unlike their father—eventually gave in. She was painfully conscious of the insult to Browning, who for her sake was conciliatory.

Her aunt Arabella Graham-Clarke ("Bummy"), who had lived with the family after Mary Moulton-Barrett died and was never much in sympathy with Elizabeth, also disapproved. But her sisters were as affectionate as ever, and in 1850 Henrietta followed her example by marrying a man who had been courting her for years. (Henrietta asked her father's permission first, which was of course refused, and was duly cast off in her turn.) Mr. Boyd was delighted, all the more, no doubt, because he disliked Edward Moulton-Barrett. Mary Russell Mitford concealed her chagrin at the loss of her friend to a man she did not admire. John Kenyon tried to fill the place her father had left empty: he told them they had behaved perfectly, took over the management of her investments, and a few years later gave them an annual allowance. Browning's parents and sister made no objections. But none of their close relatives or friends except Mrs. Jameson, who travelled for her own purposes, ever visited them in Italy, and apart from her sisters, left to bear the brunt of the paternal displeasure, there was nothing to make her regret England.

The deepening lights and shadows that fell on their Italian idyll were cast mostly by a series of miscarriages, beginning in 1847 (she had not even realized that she was five months pregnant, having assumed that she would be unable to conceive a child), and by the birth of their son Robert Weidemann (first called Penini, then Pen) in 1849. Pen proved a delightful child, happy, lively, and affectionate, and the Brownings were astonished and devoted parents. One anecdote among the hundreds that throng her letters may serve to illustrate the new relationships in the household:

> Robert is very fond of him [the baby], and threw me into a fit of hilarity the other day by springing away from his newspaper in an indignation against me because he hit his head against the floor rolling over and over. "Oh, Ba, I really can't trust you!" Down Robert was on the carpet in a moment, to protect the precious head. He takes it to be made of Venetian glass, I am certain. (*LEBB* 1:421)

She sees his outburst of paternal protectiveness as touching but comically naïve, the baby being primarily her own responsibility. During her pregnancy she bought herself a thimble, emblem of the woman's work she had always detested, to sew baby clothes, and reduced her dependence on morphine; afterwards she entered enthusiastically into the society and preoccupations of mothers of young children and filled her letters with reports of Pen's doings. The pleasures of motherhood were enhanced by the fact that the actual work of caring for him was done by servants, including (to her great regret but at the doctor's insistence) a wet nurse.

But domestic satisfaction, beautiful surroundings, and freedom from social and economic pressures did not conduce to artistic productivity as much as the two poets had expected. In the first years of their marriage they wrote very little. She was not bothered on her own behalf—unlike Browning and Mary Russell Mitford, she found writing relatively pleasant and easy and was content to let life displace art for a while. But for the penniless husband of a famous wife whose family refused to acknowledge him, with reputation and fortune still to be made, there was more urgency. He was acutely conscious of the difference in this respect between them, as he rather stiffly told his publisher in 1847: "I say nothing of my wife's poems and their sale. She is, there as in all else, as high above me as I would have her."[3] As the months passed she became increasingly worried about the strange cessation of his fluency, especially since his mother's unexpected death had plunged him into a long, almost incapacitating depression right after the birth of the baby. "I scold him about it in a most anti-conjugal manner," she wrote in 1849, adding protectively that "his spirits and nerves have been shaken of late; we must have patience" (*LEBB* 1:422). They had been married almost a decade before her patience was rewarded by the publication of his finest work, *Men and Women*, in 1855. In 1849 he brought out a revised edition of his poems, and in 1850 published *Christmas-Eve and Easter-Day*, which was not successful with reviewers or the public and has pleased few readers since. Barrett Browning herself did a little better: besides revising her earlier work, she wrote some new poems—not many, but a few of them very good— and published old and new together in the two-volume *Poems* of 1850.

These volumes contained most of the 1838 poems, many of them heavily revised; those from 1844; the new translation of *Prometheus Bound; Sonnets from the Portuguese* and thirty-six other poems that had not appeared in book form before; and some translations. She felt somewhat ashamed (as well she might) of republishing so much bad early work, and her excuse in the "Advertisement" has a trace of her old childishness toward the public: her readers "may use the weakness of those earlier verses, which no subsequent revision has succeeded in strengthening, less as a reproach to the writer, than as a means of marking some progress in her other attempts"—like parents recording a child's growth on the wall. Nor were many of the new poems very new either. Some (including "A Sabbath Morning at Sea," "Calls on the Heart," and "Wisdom Unapplied") had been written many years earlier and recently expanded and improved. Before leaving England she had sent "a heap of verses swept from my desk" (*LMRM* 3:195) to *Blackwood's*, which published them in 1846 and 1847, and these were included too. Many of the more recent ones were about love, which emerges for the first time as a main theme in her works, and when some of these appeared in *Blackwood's* she had worried that they might offend her father as seeming to bear on her own situation. In fact, however, the presentations of love take a generally disillusioned view of it. "Maude's Spinning" (later called "A Year's Spinning") is a dramatic lyric telling the balladlike tale of a girl seduced and abandoned, "Change upon Change" is also about an unfaithful lover, and "A Woman's Shortcomings" and "A Man's Requirements" comment ironically on relations between the sexes. Six poems ("Life and Love," "A Denial," "Proof and Disproof," "Question and Answer," "Inclusions," and "Insufficiency") that appear in the British Library manuscript of *Sonnets from the Portuguese* are variations on the themes of the *Sonnets*, but without the emotional intensity and thematic richness derived from being part of a larger narrative whole. There are sonnets, poems about poetry, and tributes to her sisters, to Flush (already celebrated in 1844), and to Hugh Stuart Boyd, who died in 1848.

Technically, the new poems take a new interest in the uses of dramatized speakers, especially when the topic is love. "The Mask" separates the poet from the speaker—a woman who hides bitterness of unspecified origin behind a joyful face—by the simple device of inserting "she said" twice in each four-line stanza. "Confessions," on the other hand, is a rather awkwardly oblique dialogue between a mysterious accuser and a woman who has loved human beings more than God and not been loved equally in return—the theme of Elizabeth Barrett's first ballad, "The Romaunt of Margret," as well as a response to her father's and brothers' coldness after her marriage—written with a verbal inventiveness and force that resemble her husband's work more than her earlier ballads. She may have learned something about dramatic speakers from Browning, but she seems more concerned to set a distance between the speakers and herself than to create a dramatic character or (except in "A Man's Requirements," which owes as much to Donne's "Go and Catch a Falling Star" as to Browning and belongs in a long tradition of women poets' satire on male attitudes) invite ironic readings.

Her readiness to write in new ways appears less in these fairly timid experiments than in various repudiations of nostalgia for childhood. Two uplifting and rather banal sonnets take issue with Wordsworth. "Mountaineer and Poet" scolds presumptuous poets: "Ye are not great because creation drew / Large revelations round your earliest sense, / Nor bright because God's glory shines for you." "The Poet," more simply celebratory, asserts (presumably against Wordsworth's "Immortality" ode) that poets retain their first vision: "The poet hath the child's sight in his breast / And sees all *new*. What oftenest he has viewed / He views with the first glory." For a writer who had been obsessed with loss, "The Poet" offers the comfort that creative vision, at least, endures, and the idea of the poet as "godlike, childlike" conveniently effaces the necessity of being a man or a woman. In "Hector in the Garden," however, which works through story rather than statement and is consequently much more subtle in its analysis, the persistence of childhood's visionary powers is a source of terror rather than delight.

"Hector in the Garden" was probably written in 1844, the same year as "The Lost Bower," and like "The Lost Bower" it describes an imaginative impasse that actually occurred (she said) during the poet's childhood. At the age of nine, the speaker recalls, she conceived her life in Homeric terms and lived in magical connection with nature, learning pleasure from the companionable sun and possessed of a charm against rain. She lavished her creative energies on a flowerbed laid out as a giant figure of Hector: a combination of Homer and nature that balanced the sun's friendly power over her with her own magical control of natural forces. This supine floral hero, of "passive giant strength," whose brow she raked and cheeks she weeded, was a grotesque mixture of threat and charm.

> Eyes of gentianellas azure,
>   Staring, winking at the skies:
>   Nose of gillyflowers and box;
>   Scented grasses put for locks,
> Which a little breeze at pleasure
>   Set a-waving round his eyes:
>
> Brazen helm of daffodillies,
>   With a glitter toward the light;
>   Purple violets for the mouth,
>   Breathing perfumes west and south;
> And a sword of flashing lilies,
>   Holden ready for the fight.
>
> (49–60)

But the power and passivity, magic and threat, of life-in-death (the eyes stare and wink, the locks wave, the mouth breathes) were fearfully intensified when she imagined the soul of Hector himself "Rolling up the thunder-roll" (72) in "a dreary joy" (70) to inhabit the representation. Since as a child Elizabeth Barrett had regarded control over nature as a paternal prerogative and was terrified of thunder, it is not surprising that Jovian thunder accompanies Hector's arrival. Sound or movement from the floral figure aroused in the young poet the kind of "terror" (89) that is associated with the animation of the inanimate or revivification of the dead and could be allayed only by the example of birds singing in a pear tree, their song untainted by ambition or will.

But as she recalls all this, the experience repeats itself in the present. That comforting natural world now partakes of death too, and threatens a dreadful revivification: birds, pear tree, and flower garden "revive" in her memory "like Hector's body" and "stir again" (95, 96).

> And despite life's changes, chances,
>   And despite the deathbell's toll,

They press on me in full seeming
Help, some angel! stay this dreaming!

(97–100)

As in "A True Dream," or Mary Shelley's *Frankenstein*, fear of imagi-
nation is expressed as fear of bringing things to life: the Greek heroes
of Barrett Browning's childhood fantasies, nature, and the childhood that
Homer and nature represent. She is afraid that they will drag her back
into dreamy oblivion—into death—as things returned from the dead
traditionally do. And so the last lines, which assert the irrevocable loss
of her childhood, are reassuring although syntactically concessive: she
will "wake up and be doing," "Though [her] past is dead as Hector, /
And though Hector is twice dead" (105, 107–8). "Hector in the Garden"
enacts a shuddering revulsion against the romantic desire to give life to
nature or resuscitate the personal or literary past. It declares her readiness
for a new literature and a new life.

Her actual experience in Italy is used directly only in an ambitiously
baroque but rather ineffectual elegy, "A Child's Grave at Florence," and
in the first part of *Casa Guidi Windows*, which was written in 1848 but
not published until 1851. In 1850 her new freedom and energy are most
apparent in "The Runaway Slave at Pilgrim's Point" and "Hiram Powers'
'Greek Slave,' " which are political rather than personal—or rather, per-
sonal in a new, political way. They repudiate the cultural tradition with
which *Sonnets from the Portuguese* had made brilliant accommodation,
taking from American racial conflict and the issue of slavery a potent
image for the rebelliousness she had never expressed so directly before.
She wrote three poems about America (the third was "A Curse for a
Nation," some years later), and all three are denunciations of slavery in
which the central figure is a woman exposed to public view who represents
both slavery's helpless victim and its invincible opponent—both the dis-
tressed damsel, that is, and the rescuing knight—and also the woman
poet.

The double and apparently antithetical meanings of this figure, charged
with helplessness and terror but also with bold defiance, emerge from
an incident that served as a prelude to the American poems. Early in
1845 the Anti–Corn Law League had asked Elizabeth Barrett for a poem
in support of their cause.[4] She wanted to comply, thinking it her duty
to speak out against injustice, and Mary Russell Mitford apparently agreed.
A storm of masculine opposition, however, immediately broke upon her:
her father disapproved, her brothers enraged her by jeering at the very

idea of women (or poets, for that matter) meddling in politics, and even John Kenyon sided with the other men—all of them blatantly revealing, she said bitterly, their "contempt" for women (*LMRM* 3:80). Being unwilling to vex her father, she yielded and did not write the poem, but she was very displeased with herself afterwards. The terms in which she described her dilemma do a lot to explain both her hesitation and the violence of the male reactions. At first she had qualms on grounds of modesty, wondering "whether it is not & whether it might not be considered by some of my friends, undesirable to take such a prominent post in the political ground, harp in hand & petticoat down to the ankles." But after this self-denigrating irony she immediately added: "But I am writing ungenerously [the word that recurs in her letters to and about Browning]—I feel I am. *Not like a Godiva*" (*LMRM* 3:63).

This comparison would have come quickly to mind because in the last few months she had been watching with horrified fascination while the role of Godiva was being earnestly but not very successfully enacted by—of all people—Harriet Martineau, who thought that she had been cured by mesmerism of a uterine cancer and reported her cure as public testimony in the current controversy about mesmerism. The press ridiculed her, and the doctor who had been treating her (who was also her brother-in-law) published a detailed gynecological account of her illness in a shilling pamphlet to prove that she had not had cancer at all, and therefore not been mesmerically cured.[5] Elizabeth Barrett was appalled by the idea of mesmerism—a psychic force, apparently, by which one will could unclothe and bind another: "there is something horrible & cold to me in the whole matter & mystery—like the undressing of the soul from its familiar conventions & the plunging of it, shiveringly, into a new element."[6] Still, "if [Martineau] believed that her sufferings were in any way connected with the *conditions of her womanhood*, she was *not* a coward, but on the contrary very brave indeed, in drawing her case into the daylight—perhaps even, . . too brave" (*LMRM* 3:31). She wrote a letter of sympathy to Martineau, who replied, "I took my part deliberately,—*knowing privacy to be impossible*, & making up my mind to *entail publicity* as the only course faithful to truth & human welfare. I cannot tell you how the thought of *Godiva* has sustained & inspired me" (*BC* 4:326). Elizabeth Barrett was deeply impressed: "She says, she was prepared for the publicity; *& she thinks of Godiva*. She is a noble creature indeed. I admire her more than ever. I always did admire the *moral heroic* beyond all things . . next to genius!" (*LMRM* 3:33). "We must praise her for 'moral courage'—as the Westminster Review [in regard to her

sonnets about George Sand] does *me*" (*LMRM* 3:27).[7] The same as-
sociation of political controversy, sexual exposure, and publishing poems
appears in her report of the warning conveyed to her from Henry Chorley
of the *Athenaeum* that if she gave the league a poem she would be "ruin[ed]"
forever, her "poetical reputation" destroyed, and her "utility" "circum-
scribed, shackled, undone" (*LMRM* 3:75): it is not clear whether "ruin,"
"reputation," and "undone" are her words or Chorley's, but the sexual
overtones are in any case unmistakable.

The idea that for a woman publication is a kind of bodily display, best
clothed in pseudonyms or anonymity if it is to be hazarded at all, has
been a common one. "I would as soon undress in public," said Emily
Dickinson, "as to give my poems to the world."[8] We usually associate
such a notion now with confessional or otherwise peculiarly personal
poetry. But Barrett Browning did not worry about exposing herself in
Sonnets from the Portuguese, even though readers have found that poem
emotionally naked and Edmund Gosse imagined her hiding from her
husband's gaze when she showed it to him. And while the story of Lady
Godiva has many layers of meaning, including erotic ones, she rode
naked through the streets of Coventry because her husband had promised
to remit the heavy taxes he exacted from the people if she did so. Her
nakedness is a political protest and an exercise of power: Tennyson's
"Godiva" (1842) presents her as someone who loved the people and
acted effectively on their behalf, and Peeping Tom (in the nineteenth-
century version of the legend that Tennyson uses and Barrett Browning
knew) was struck blind for looking at her. Godiva's story represents the
politics of social class in terms of the politics of gender: with hair that
protects her and power to blind those who look at her, she is an avatar
of Medusa and of Diana seen naked by Actaeon, threatening castration,
dismemberment, death.[9] To Elizabeth Barrett in 1845 Godiva was an
heroic example that she failed to live up to.

She felt that her refusal to write a poem for the Anti–Corn Law League
would be "a remorse to [her] for life" (*LMRM* 3:97), and she did not
allow herself occasion for such remorse again. Instead, she always af-
terwards took pride in anticipating angry responses, especially on touchy
political or sexual themes. When the Anti-Slavery Bazaar in Boston asked
her late in 1845 to write something for them, she agreed to do so, although
it was not until February 1847 that she sent them "The Runaway Slave
at Pilgrim's Point," which was apparently the first poem she wrote in
Italy. She no longer had reason to avoid vexing her father, having irre-
parably done so already, and it pleased her to think her poem too ferocious

for the Americans to print. In fact, however, they did print it—in *The Liberty Bell* in Boston in 1848, among works by Bayard Taylor, Theodore Parker, Frederick Douglass, James Russell Lowell, and others. It is a long dramatic monologue that she referred to as a ballad (*LMRM* 3:310), like her earlier narratives about women. The speaker is a black American slave who after being separated from her slave lover and raped by a white man kills her newborn child because it is too white, like its rapist father. Like Godiva, she challenges oppression, political, economic, and sexual, by simultaneously exposing herself to be seen and punishing aggressive eyes. The child had *looked* at her with "the *master's* look, that used to fall / On my soul like his lash . . . or worse!" (144–45). As she speaks she finds (or perhaps imagines) herself surrounded by a ring of men who have hunted her down, and—empowered although not quite in Godiva's way by the rightness of her cause—she defies and threatens them.

> Keep off! I brave you all at once,
>   I throw off your eyes like snakes that sting!
> You have killed the black eagle at nest, I think:
> Did you ever stand still in your triumph, and shrink
>   From the stroke of her wounded wing?
>
>   (206–10)

"I see you staring in my face— / I know you staring, shrinking back" (219–20); but she forces them to look at her, to see the marks of her suffering and hear her curse. The poem is meant to do the same.

Barrett Browning would have found it both easy and very complicated to associate herself with this protagonist. She was one of the first women writers in Britain to take up slavery as a feminist issue, recognizing that the oppression of black women (especially in sexual terms) offered a grim commentary on the angelic purity that was supposed to enshroud white women. But slavery was not just a metaphor for the position of women. She knew it all too saliently as a political fact, her family's money having come from slave plantations in Jamaica.[10] "Cursed we are from generation to generation," she had told Browning in 1845 (*RB-EBB* 1:333). To Ruskin ten years later she wrote, "I belong to a family of West Indian slaveholders, and if I believed in curses, I should be afraid" (*LEBB* 2:220). She was unequivocally happy when Britain abolished slavery in 1833, even though her father—who had actually favored the antislavery cause—predicted irreparable ruin for the West Indian plantation owners. His fears were exaggerated, but the insurrection in Jamaica in 1832 that preceded abolition, along with extensive litigation about slaves and cattle, contributed to the financial difficulties that led to the loss of Hope End. (Browning also had a familial connection with slavery in Jamaica, but one to be proud of: his father had been sent out at the age of twenty to help manage his mother's family's plantations, where he "conceived such a hatred to the slave-system" that he gave up his prospects and incurred his father's wrath by returning to England.)[11] Surtees Cook, whom Henrietta eventually married, heard Edward Moulton-Barrett discourse on the "passive obedience" owed by children to parents, "particularly in respect to marriage," and meekly asked "if children were to be considered slaves" (*RB-EBB* 1:408–9); no negative reply is recorded. The consequences, Elizabeth Barrett thought, were disingenuousness and cowardice—the "vices of slaves" (*RB-EBB* 1:169). When she married she became in the eyes of her father and brothers a "runaway" herself.

Her belief that every adult had the right to free choice in marriage went squarely against her father's views, which are enacted in the poem as the killing of the speaker's slave lover. More generally, "The Runaway Slave at Pilgrim's Point" expresses her fury at a tyranny that presents itself, as her father's did, in the guise of benevolence. The speaker invokes the shades of the Pilgrim "fathers" and curses America because America vaunts itself as the land of freedom. The oppressors Barrett Browning had known were familiar and familial ones, not just her father but her whole family, herself included, who had flourished on the proceeds of slavery. And so the oppressor whom her protagonist murders is not an alien or a stranger, a rapist or a white man, but her own child: the fruit of her own body, part of herself. Like the speakers in "A True Dream" and "Hector in the Garden," she has given life to an inimical being, and by displaying herself to her pursuers she makes them see both their victim and a murderer whose unsated rage mirrors their own murderousness. For Barrett Browning as for Godiva, oppression is an intimate— a family—matter; and her sensitivity to the political bearings of the personal and the tangled links between oppressor and oppressed enriches, here and elsewhere, her political writings.

"Hiram Powers' 'Greek Slave' " bestows on a Godiva figure the accusatory force that its first creator had withheld. Hiram Powers was an American sculptor with whom the Brownings became very friendly in Florence, and Barrett Browning was not the only one on whom his statue called "The Greek Slave" made a profound impression. It was a huge success at the Great Exhibition in London in 1851 and at the first World's Fair in New York in 1853. Copies of it toured America (Powers himself made five more full-sized versions, as well as smaller ones), and it was reproduced in many media. The statue is a nude figure of a young woman in the pose of a classical Venus, representing a Greek Christian who has been captured by the Turks in the Greek war of independence (the struggle that had excited Elizabeth Barrett's youthful imagination) and is being exposed for sale in a Turkish slave market.[12] In emphatic contrast to the woman's nudity, the post on which she rests her hand is swathed in carefully modelled drapery, a cross conspicuously displayed upon it; she looks soulfully downward, absentmindedly protecting her modesty with what Barrett Browning's sonnet refers to as "enshackled hands."

The word "enshackled" resonates ironically from Chorley's warning against publishing an anti–Corn Law poem, the "utility" (in the words she attributed to Chorley) of the Greek slave for Barrett Browning's purposes coming precisely from the fact that she is "circumscribed, shackled, undone." She would seem to be the opposite of the murderous runaway slave; but she is also her counterpart. The poem stresses her whiteness and her silence, her "passionless perfection"; and yet like her passionately speaking black predecessor, she bodies forth (the poem says) a condemnation of slavery everywhere.

> Appeal, fair stone,
> From God's pure heights of beauty against man's wrong!
> Catch up in thy divine face, not alone
> East griefs but west, and strike and shame the strong,
> By thunders of white silence, overthrown.

Her exposure in naked weakness will overthrow "the strong" with her paradoxically speaking visual presence: "thunders of white silence."[13] The synaesthetic, oxymoronic last line was itself an offense against reviewers' taste for female clarity and simplicity, "passionless perfection."

What strikes a modern eye about the statue, however, is not its denunciatory potential but its genteelly pornographic appeal. It was the first of many representations of captive women by nineteenth-century American sculptors, to whom the subject offered the great advantage in prudish America of justifying nudity.[14] The Godiva story offers similar justifications: her husband suggested it, it was in a good cause, she didn't intend to enjoy it, and so on. Barrett Browning, however, thinks that what requires explanation is not the figure's nakedness, but its impassive acquiescence. The sonnet begins by noting that the woman does not seem to be distressed, explaining this in terms of a theory (not the poet's own) of art: "They say Ideal beauty cannot enter / The house of anguish." Her emphasis on the statue's whiteness and her effort to imagine it as an actual woman actually experiencing the fictional situation suggest that for Barrett Browning (who did not pretend to much knowledge of the visual arts, although she preferred sculpture to painting) it is an image of a naked woman rather than a "nude," a narrative fact that the drapery beside her and beneath her feet makes it impossible to ignore. The sculptor has tried to soften the nakedness by supplying a narrative context that suggests historical distance and high moral purpose and by casting over it the veil of classical allusion and the associations of high art, and in one of his many attempts to desexualize what is only too obviously an erotic object he explained the figure's lack of expression as a sign that she was thinking about higher things and was therefore unconscious of her nakedness—*she* was not in a lascivious mood, that is, whatever the spectator might be.[15]

Barrett Browning suggests that the artist's failure to give his statue an appropriate expression may have a legitimate function:

> as if the artist meant her
> (That passionless perfection which he lent her,
> Shadowed not darkened where the sill expands)
> To so confront man's crimes in different lands
> With man's ideal sense.

But she finds passive confrontation insufficient and urges the statue to "pierce," "appeal," "strike," "shame," and "overthrow." She would like to turn the artist's still, withdrawn figure into a Godiva armed with moral purpose, casting off the impassivity and unselfconsciousness that are essential to Hiram Powers's success in making nakedness respectable and inoffensive and using the unrespectable and highly offensive power of the naked (not "nude") woman: to make her nakedness speak. This, of course, is what the poem does. "Beth" had dreamed of liberating Greece the glorious, singing songs of freedom; now Barrett Browning tries to give words to a representative figure for Greece as she had to the runaway slave. Both are victims who are potentially their own rescuers, whose weakness is their strength. These poems create a modern, female Prometheus in reaction against Olympian culture: the false liberty of the Pilgrim "fathers" as well as the cool, exclusive, essentially misogynist version of classicism that was to be promulgated most effectively by Matthew Arnold and had been debased into genteel pornography by Hiram Powers.

The main effect of their marriage on the Brownings' poetry was, in general, to open up for each of them the territory represented by the other. Broadly speaking, her poems augment inward, abstract, or personal scenes and subjects with social and political ones, often dramatically presented, and replace weary resignation with defiant hope. His, on the other hand, move from monstrous psychological realms inhabited mostly by fanatics and murderers into a contiguous but notably different world of normal human feeling. The change is most marked in what appear to be the first poems they wrote in Italy, in which each seems half to assume the other's identity and speak in the other's voice. "The Cry of the Children" had given a voice to generalized victims of oppression, but the runaway slave is a fully realized dramatic character who tells her dreadful tale with the hallucinatory vividness, swinging energy, and crazily self-justifying logic of Johannes Agricola or Porphyria's lover, Browning's earliest dramatic monologuists.

> My little body, kerchiefed fast,
>   I bore it on through the forest, on;
> And when I felt it was tired at last,
>   I scooped a hole beneath the moon.
> Through the forest-tops the angels far,
> With a white sharp finger from every star,
>   Did point and mock at what was done.
>
> Yet when it was all done aright,—
>   Earth, 'twixt me and my baby, strewed,—
> All, changed to black earth,—nothing white,—
>   A dark child in the dark!—ensued
> Some comfort, and my heart grew young;
> I sate down smiling there and sung
>   The song I learnt in my maidenhood.

(176–89)

Against this we can set Browning's "The Guardian Angel: A Picture at Fano," apparently the only short poem he wrote in the early years of their marriage,[16] which by a curious reciprocity is suffused with infantile yearning for a masterful, protective maternal figure. The speaker addresses an angel in a painting by Domenichino, asking to take the place of the praying child in the picture.

> And wilt thou bend me low
> Like him, and lay, like his, my hands together,
> And lift them up to pray, and gently tether
>   Me, as thy lamb there, with thy garment's spread?

(18–21)

Whereas "The Runaway Slave" is a dramatic monologue, "The Guardian Angel" identifies the speaker as the poet through references to Browning's wife, excursions, and friend. He seems finally to be speaking out in his own voice, as they had long ago agreed he should. But the voice sounds like a parody of Elizabeth Barrett's, with its paraphernalia of angels, wings, and children, the thinness, the stiff archaisms, the near-bathos of the diction, and the depressed and inhibited tone.

> O world, as God has made it! All is beauty:
> And knowing this, is love, and love is duty,
> What further may be sought for or declared?

> (33–35)

This recalls Elizabeth Barrett's worst moments, things like the end of "The Dead Pan," for instance ("Look up Godward [. . .] Hold, in high poetic duty, / Truest Truth the fairest Beauty." *Christmas-Eve and Easter-Day* (1850) is much the same: a vision of Christ appears in "a sweepy garment, vast and white" (*Christmas-Eve*, 438), to which the speaker clings as he travels from one church to another and which saves him at the end, when he is "lapped again in its folds full-fraught / With warmth and wonder and delight" (1231–32), like the happy baby of a full-skirted Victorian mother. This is the last of Browning's poems on which his wife's work seems to have had a deleterious influence, however, and the influence is in any event not simple. Although she is usually blamed for its unattractive form and doctrine, she disliked its asceticism (*LEBB* 1:449); and while Browning was writing about the yearning to be enfolded in maternal garments, she wrote about a mother who uses her clothing to suffocate her child.

The 1850 *Poems* provoked less attention than her preceding volumes, perhaps because so much of the contents had already been published, perhaps because the competition was keener. Earlier in the same year Tennyson had definitively established his preeminence with *In Memoriam*, which provided a very superior version of the kind of emotional experiences readers expected from women. Browning's reputation was still in partial eclipse, but reviewers who noticed the Brownings together thought his work stronger, if not always more successful, than hers.[17] Almost no notice was taken in America, where only a pirated edition appeared. Still, her American reputation remained high. A laudatory but highly inaccurate essay in an American journal published in 1851 reported, among other contributions to the swelling legend of her life, that her correspondence with Browning had been conducted entirely in classical Greek.[18] In Britain she was again accused of diffuseness and carelessness of style, although improvement in this respect was sometimes noted; her scholarship was rather condescendingly praised, and her pathos and "pure" and "womanly" spirit were much admired.[19]

Not all the reviews were favorable. One found the new poems disappointing and her style inadequate to her ambitions, while another in similar vein liked the "human feelings" in her "simpler lays and ballads" but chided her for treating subjects too high for a woman.[20] Still, these were minority opinions. Henry Chorley in the *Athenaeum* was full of praise as usual, mostly for qualities that modern readers may find less attractive than he did: "The ardour of woman's individual devotion, her self-sacrificing love, her sympathy with the victims of wrong, and her faith in a presiding good that consecrates and chastens affection," the strength of feeling, and the "morals" the poet draws. Chorley naturally admires the ballads and "Catarina to Camoens" and concludes that "Mrs. Browning is probably, of her sex, the first imaginative writer England has produced in any age:—she is, beyond comparison, the first poetess of her own"—an opinion he had already expressed by recommending after Wordsworth's death in April 1850 that she be appointed poet laureate, a female laureate in compliment to a female ruler.[21]

Others, too, praised her specifically as a woman: "the best poetess . . . whom England has yet produced"; combining a "delicate, pure, and intense . . . spirit of womanly love" with a "masculine and far-reaching intellect"; an exception to the general rule that women's poetry is "doleful or morbid . . . weak and diffuse."[22] In general, the same poems were popular as had been before, especially the ballads, but some reviewers also liked *Sonnets from the Portuguese.* Her usual equanimity in the face of reviews pleasant or otherwise was augmented by the fact that journals reached Italy very slowly if at all, but signs that her reputation had declined somewhat would not have perturbed her. She was still without question—for whatever the distinction was worth, based as it was on the valorization of women's poetry for emotional and spiritual rather than intellectual or artistic qualities, and on the not-always-tacit assumption that it was inferior to poetry by men—the foremost English "poetess."

Casa Guidi Windows, published eight months later, exploits and risks that position for Italy as Byron had exploited his fame for the cause of Greece, taking for granted that fame is now hers to be used. The poem is a meditation in two parts on the political situation in Tuscany, in which the speaker defines herself explicitly both as a woman and as a poet. The first part, which the usually hospitable *Blackwood's* refused to publish on the grounds that English readers were not sufficiently interested in Tuscan politics, was written in 1847, the second in 1851, and the two together represent her first full poetic response to Italy. In Italy she found warmth, light, art, beauty, freedom from familial and social restraints, love, motherhood: rebirth, a new life—or, in the word that belonged to the Italian political struggle, *risorgimento*. Being in Italy to share the hopes of the Risorgimento was in itself a kind of rebirth, a renewal of childish dreams and ambitions which had been simultaneously personal, literary, and political. Like Greece when it first entranced her, Italy was a beautiful southern country with a grand artistic heritage struggling for national independence, inevitably personified as a woman in need of rescue, offering splendid possibilities for heroic action and song, and gloriously championed by Byron, who died for Greek independence but spent the last several years of his life in Italy, of which he had memorably written. In Florence her early dreams returned as reality.

And because the liberation she had accomplished for herself seemed to prefigure that toward which Italy was struggling, she found for the first time in her poetic career that she could, like her male contemporaries, generalize her own experience to that of the age. The high new vocation—to write in modern terms about modern times—that "Lady Geraldine's Courtship" and "The Dead Pan" had announced in 1844 is realized in *Casa Guidi Windows*. It is a book, in Lawrence Lipking's terms, of poetic initiation: "the starting-out, the gathering-in," a rediscovery and reinterpretation of her past, and a new beginning. "In almost all initiations," Lipking says, "the excitement derives from the same source: the poet realizes that his own personal history, reflected in his poems, coincides with the universal spiritual history of mankind." Such an initiation restores the poet to history, transforming the time and place he lives in from a provincial backwater to "the focal point of all civilization" from which, "Making sense of history at last, he sees into the future" and makes "a prophecy of greater works to come."[23] What had happened to her was more than a liberation. The pattern of her life had changed, the meaning of the past altered; dream had become reality, what was lost returned. After her life had apparently ended, she had circled back to her beginning, and now she could push forward to new life.

And so to the defiant energy of the antislavery poems *Casa Guidi Windows* adds a moderating confidence and joy. The poetry itself—iambic pentameter firmly but unobtrusively rhyming ababab—is confident, graceful, flexible, easily accommodating changes of tone and relatively free of mannerisms. The poet seems perfectly at ease, in control of her medium and of the didactic public voice she had not used for a major work since "An Essay on Mind." Despite the suggestion of the title that she has returned to the observer's stance of the 1838 poems (although the windows she looks out from are right in the center of things), she is in fact actively engaged both with the world she describes and with an activist artistic tradition of which she self-consciously presents herself as a continuator. The poem takes an engaged delight in Florence, its art, its traditions, the surrounding countryside, and its people, all of which the speaker describes with close and loving knowledge. It is highly significant that *Casa Guidi Windows* refuses to valorize suffering (except for heroic death in battle), and despite the terrible disappointment recorded in part two it expects an eventual real, not just heavenly or fantastic, happy ending. The decline into impotence and loss that from an early age she had perceived as the necessary pattern not only of her own life but of all life had been miraculously reversed (even the displacement of nature by the city ceased to be loss when the city was Florence), and in 1847 the pattern of restoration and rebirth seemed about to be enacted for Italy too.

At a time when movements for national identity and independence were attracting widespread liberal sympathy (even Matthew Arnold, who deplored practical applications of poetry to politics, wrote a "Sonnet to the Hungarian Nation" in 1849), the Brownings found themselves at a center of excitement. In 1847, Grand Duke Leopold II of Tuscany seemed to be opening a way to the Risorgimento by offering some civic liberties, and happy crowds celebrating his generosity flowed under the Brownings' windows in Casa Guidi to the Pitti Palace just across the way. The first part of *Casa Guidi Windows* describes events in Florence and expresses the poet's somewhat dubious enthusiasm for the hopes raised by the grand duke and by the recently elected and apparently liberal-minded Pope Pius IX, Pio Nono. The second part, written when the revolutions of 1848 had ended in disappointment for liberals all over Europe, responds to the betrayal of these hopes.

The carefully articulated analysis of the political situation and of the artist's political responsibility has been all but obscured, however, by Barrett Browning's inability to speak with the same mature confidence *about* her work as she does within it. The "Advertisement" that she

unfortunately prefixed to the poem suggests that it is just another of the
tourists' reports produced in large numbers by nineteenth-century trav-
ellers to Italy.

> This poem contains the impressions of the writer upon events in Tuscany
> of which she was a witness. "From a window," the critic may demur. She
> bows to the objection in the very title of her work. No continuous narrative
> nor exposition of political philosophy is attempted by her. It is a simple
> story of personal impressions, whose only value is in the intensity with
> which they were received, as proving her warm affection for a beautiful
> and unfortunate country, and the sincerity with which they are related,
> as indicating her own good faith and freedom from partisanship.

These are the unassuming virtues (artlessness, spontaneity, affection,
sincerity) and defects (lack of sustained thought or organizing purpose)
that critics expected in women poets and that she had not learned to
disavow in her dealings with the public, perhaps because she herself
could not help feeling them intrinsic to womanliness. One recalls her
excuse for reprinting bad poems in 1850—that they will show how much
she's grown—although here she offers her mistakes as exemplary of
human as well as of feminine fallibility.

> The discrepancy between the two parts is a sufficient guarantee to the
> public of the truthfulness of the writer, who, though she certainly escaped
> the epidemic "falling sickness" of enthusiasm for Pio Nono, takes shame
> upon herself that she believed, like a woman, some royal oaths, and lost
> sight of the probable consequences of some popular defects. If the dis-
> crepancy should be painful to the reader, let him understand that to the
> writer it has been more so. But such discrepancies we are called upon
> to accept at every hour by the conditions of our nature, implying the
> interval between aspiration and performance, between faith and disillu-
> sion, between hope and fact.

She seems to be trying to disarm in advance the kind of objections she
had run up against in England when she wanted to write controversial
political poetry.

This denial of serious purpose, artistic unity, or intelligent political
analysis, which until very recently has been taken by most critics at face
value, makes it necessary to point out that the poem is neither foolish
nor naïve.[24] Even when the English liberals in Florence had fallen com-
pletely under the spell of Pio Nono, she never trusted him to be more
than a pope could be—which was not, she thought, very much (1:888–
1052).[25] However "good and great / [. . .] Most liberal" (1:1029–31) he
might be in some ways, she says (with something of an Evangelical and

reformist Englishwoman's prejudice, perhaps), he cannot avoid acting as a prince and a priest: he's "only the Ninth Pius after eight, / When all's praised most" (1:1033–34). She had more hope of the grand duke, who was said actually to have wept (sure sign of virtue) at the Florentines' demonstration of gratitude, but here too her confidence was hardly immoderate.

> I like his face; the forehead's build
> Has no capacious genius, yet perhaps
> Sufficient comprehension,—mild and sad,
> And careful nobly.
>
> (1:564–67)

He seems at best a good kind of duke, as dukes go, "while dukes reign" (1:573). The Carlylean hero whom the first part of the poem calls for is not likely, she thinks, to be either the duke or the pope. She has been derided for looking for a hero at all; but however innocent her hopes may seem now, we must remember not only that they were shared by sympathizers with the Risorgimento throughout Europe, but that in due course they were realized.

The post-Romantic view that art should not condescend to the level of practical politics, most powerfully set forth in the mid-Victorian period by Matthew Arnold, has doubtless also contributed to later devaluations of *Casa Guidi Windows*. But Barrett Browning did not share that view. Instead, she places herself in the tradition of Byron's poems about Italy, not only *Childe Harold's Pilgrimage* (with which she takes vigorous issue) but also the forecast of Italy's renewed greatness in "The Prophecy of Dante." She carries forward the inspiration to revolution in Shelley's "Lines Written among the Euganean Hills" and "Ode to Naples," and she repeatedly invokes Dante and Michelangelo as the great Florentine examples of politically engaged artists. In "The Dead Pan" she had asserted that the actual and the present were the proper sphere of poetry, and the poet's role as she defines it in *Casa Guidi Windows* is not to mourn the heroic past but to inspire the present and call forth new heroes. The inspiration of Michelangelo's art and deeds is still active (1:73–144), and the people of Florence gathered to begin their celebration of freedom at a stone sacred to the memory of Dante (1:581–606). She herself, in turn, depicts the state of Florence and summons a leader to save Italy (1:765–72).

> Come, appear, be found,
> If pope or peasant, come! we hear the cock,

> The courtier of the mountains when first crowned
> With golden dawn; and orient glories flock
> To meet the sun upon the highest ground.
> Take voice and work! we wait to hear thee knock
> At some one of our Florentine nine gates.

(1:1052–58)

The second part deals with the aftermath of her disappointed hopes, asking what poets who were fooled by false promises should do next (2:16–27). The answer, as the rest of the poem demonstrates, is that they should themselves inspire fresh hope and new deeds. Although she "repents," she says, of her "woman's fault" of "put[ting] faith in princes" (2:58–75), she has by no means lost confidence in her poetic vocation and authority, her place as one of "We thinkers," "We hopers," "We poets" (2:17–19). She mordantly describes ("I saw and witness" [2:287]) how Leopold, who had fled in fear that a republic might be declared, returned to Florence with an escort of Austrian troops, a grim parody of the happy procession described before. This sorry spectacle is invested with the grandeur and terror of classical myth:

> Sword and bayonet,
> Horse, foot, artillery,—cannons rolling on
> Like blind slow storm-clouds gestant with the heat
> Of undeveloped lightnings, each bestrode
> By a single man, dust-white from head to heel,
> Indifferent as the dreadful thing he rode,
> Like a sculptured Fate serene and terrible.

(2:301–7)

In a different key, she mocks "the people," who tamely acquiesced in their own defeat.

> If we did not fight
> Exactly, we fired muskets up the air
> To show that victory was ours of right.
> We met, had free discussion everywhere
> (Except perhaps i' the Chambers) day and night.
> We proved the poor should be employed, . . . that's fair,—
> And yet the rich not worked for anywise.

(2:154–60)

She diagnoses the problem as that very unheroic one which Matthew Arnold was to lament a few years later in "The Scholar-Gipsy" as the disease of modern life: "want / Of soul-conviction," "aims dispersed, / And incoherent means, and valour scant / Because of scanty faith" (2:527–30).[26] And she knows the cure: the people need, as Carlyle said people everywhere did, a leader.

She addresses the rest of Europe, asking the nations that sent their treasures to the Great Exhibition at the Crystal Palace in London whether they cannot also produce cures for social wrongs: the ignorance of the poor and the oppression of women (especially prostitution) in England, repression all over Europe, slavery in America. She speaks most directly to her own country—reasonably enough, since that is where she is most likely to be heard—calling on England in lines that anticipate Tennyson's *Maud* and echo *King Lear* not to choose a peace which cares more about the profits of trade than about suffering and wrong, "which is not fellowship / And which includes not mercy" (2:399–400),

> a Peace that sits
> Beside a hearth in self-commended mood,
> And takes no thought how wind and rain by fits
> Are howling out of doors against the good
> Of the poor wanderer.
>
> (2:407–11)

Better, she boldly asserts in images that combine epic scope and precise, surreal detail, "the raking of the guns across / The world" or "the struggle in the slippery fosse / Of dying men and horses, and the wave / Blood-bubbling" (2:401–5).[27] The call to bloody battle and heroic death recalls Elizabeth's and Bro's enthusiastic notions of dying for their country and for freedom, "Beth" leading an army to rescue Greece, and Riga and Riego who sang and died: the ambition renounced in "Vanities" (1838) of "urging / A captive nation's strength to thunder," renounced because "the storm is cruel as the chain" (7–8, 11). *Casa Guidi Windows* movingly urges just that.

> So let them die! The world shows nothing lost;
> Therefore, not blood. Above or underneath,
> What matter, brothers, if ye keep your post
> On duty's side? As sword returns to sheath,
> So dust to grave, but souls find place in Heaven.
> Heroic daring is the true success.
>
> (1:1210–15)

But the poem begins and ends with a child, a new promise of peace.

The question of how to speak of Italy is first of all a question of plot, since the situation inevitably and in accordance with long tradition takes shape as the story of a woman in need of rescue. Barrett Browning starts with a scornful review of the roles in which Italy has been cast by poets, especially Byron: childless widow, fallen woman, Cybele, Niobe, Juliet (1:14–42)—"images / Men set between themselves and actual wrong, / To catch the weight of pity, meet the stress / Of conscience" (1:43–46) in songs so musical that "pity scarcely pained" (1:19).[28] Rejecting these soothing images as she rejects the untroubled perfection of Hiram Powers's statue or the allure of death in *Sonnets from the Portuguese*, she offers in their stead a description of the actual beauty of Florence and an anecdote of Michelangelo's forward-looking art that shows how the past can inspire the artist with something more than pleasant gloom. She will not "croon the dead or cry / *'Se tu men bella fossi, Italia!'* / 'Less wretched if less fair' " (1:167–69). Here again, that is, she rejects a tradition that requires for its object a passive, deathly, beautiful woman, and she also rejects the political quietism it implies. Her highly particularized description of the hopeful scene she had just witnessed in Florence stands as an example of how Italy should properly be depicted, without luxuriating in nostalgia but encompassing a past that provides heroic inspiration and example, the hopeful if uncertain present, and the hero yet to come. This places the poet herself at the center of the plot: neither victim nor rescuer but a third character, who wakens, exhorts, inspires.

Rejection of the strongly gendered traditional plot is part of a larger and also gender-related refusal to valorize the past at the expense of the living present—"O Dead, ye shall no longer cling to us [. . .] And drag us backward" (1:230–32)—that extends the movement from death to life recounted in *Sonnets from the Portuguese* from the personal sphere into that of history, politics, and art. She insists that art improves and can continue to do so (a bold position to take in Florence, of all places): that there is room for new kinds of art, new artists, and—implicitly but unmistakably—women poets. Barrett Browning's optimism about artistic progress owes much to the fact that, unlike her male contemporaries, she could imagine great untapped ranges of possibility. She had less reason to lament a past that gave so little to women artists. When the human race has progressed beyond war, she says,

> The poet shall look grander in the face
> Than even of old (when he of Greece began

To sing "that Achillean wrath which slew
　　So many heroes")—seeing he shall treat
The deeds of souls heroic toward the true,
　　The oracles of life, previsions sweet
And awful like divine swans gliding through
　　White arms of Ledas, which will leave the heat
Of their escaping godship to endue
　　The human medium with a heavenly flush.

(1:731–40)

The poet who will be greater than Homer is pronomially male, but his visionary powers are imaged as Leda's reception of Jove. In a higher state of civilization a woman—and a sexually adult woman at that—will embody heroic vision. All the more reason for the female artist to work for social progress.

The poet of *Casa Guidi Windows* is explicitly a woman. In the second part she is also a mother, regarding politics, history, and art from a point of view, foreshadowed in *A Drama of Exile*, that is unprecedented in English poetry. The poem's themes converge in images of parents and children: the relationship between past and present, as between individuals, is conceived in terms of "generations" linked not just in temporal sequence but by familial connection, and progress in life and art becomes a matter of inheritance willingly yielded, preeminence lovingly conceded, to posterity. "All great men who foreknew / Their heirs in art, for art's sake have been glad" (1:373–74): Cimabue welcomed Giotto, Fra Angelico welcomed Raphael, while Margheritone showed his inferiority by his jealousy of Cimabue. And "heirs in art" have a reciprocal obligation to honor the memory of their precursors, or else the future will only "sadden and confuse; / If orphaned, [they] are disinherited" (1:440–41). Likewise in politics: the Italian people are depicted as disinherited, fatherless, and (as in Barrett Browning's letters) childish (2:9–15). Although the grand duke won the poet's guarded confidence when she "saw the man among his little sons, / His lips [. . .] warm with kisses" (2:93–94), he did not offer "fatherly" (2:278) forgiveness to the Florentines and proved a treacherous parent to the "filial South" (2:435). Even Garibaldi could not protect his pregnant wife and unborn child, who died in 1849 during the retreat from Rome. Garibaldi's wife

Outfaced the whistling shot and hissing waves
　　Until she felt her little babe unborn

> Recoil, within her, from the violent staves
> And bloodhounds of the world,—at which, her life
> Dropt inwards from her eyes and followed it
> Beyond the hunters.

(2:679–84)

Out of the elements of "The Runaway Slave at Pilgrim's Point"—disempowered lovers, a dead infant, a defiant, hunted woman—Barrett Browning now makes a story of paternal failure and maternal love.

And both Italy and the poet are maternal too. Although the poet scorns "Bewailers for their Italy enchained [. . .] childless among mothers, / Widow of empires" (1:21–23), she predicts that "one clear word" from Italy "would draw an avalanche / Of living sons around her" (1:197–98). The image of Italy that frames the poem, scornfully rejected in the first part but reluctantly accepted at the end, is that of Niobe (1:32, 2:726), the mother who lost all her beautiful children. The poet herself has abandoned the filial attitudes of her earlier writings, rejecting the false paternal claims of pope and duke[29] and thrusting off the clinging hands of the dead so that her generation can become parents themselves, "to be invoked / By future generations, as their Dead" (1:248–49). In this morally acceptable reformulation of the will to fame, ambition means displacing the father in order to become a father—or mother—oneself.

The poem begins and ends with happy children, in relation to whom the poet defines herself and her song. "I saw last night a little child go singing," she begins, *"O bella libertà, O bella!"* (1:3). It is this vision, rather than those of "rhymers sonneteering in their sleep, / And archaists mumbling dry bones up the land, / And sketchers lauding ruined towns a-heap" (1:148–50), that she chooses to follow. She can catch up the child's song because Italy has given her back her own childhood, enhanced by a more than English proximity to the springs of poetry. "Milton's Fiesole" is "dearer" even to the English than "Langlande's Malvern," where England's poetry, and her own, began (1:1127–28). She and her "beloved companion" (1:1130) have seen Vallombrosa, which seems unchanged since Milton "sang of Adam's paradise and smiled / Remembering Vallombrosa" (1:1161–62): the early world, the remembered paradise, that she and her beloved rediscover. They remember, too, how as children they had loved "Sorrento vines in picture-book," "Rome's wolf with demi-gods at suck," "the classic hill and brook, / And Ovid's dreaming tales and Petrarch's song" (1:1191–96); and because of those happy early associations, she says at the end of part one, they support Italy's cause now (1:1190–1202).

In part two the dream of regaining a paradisiacal childhood and fulfilling that childhood's dreams has been disappointed, but becoming a mother has made her look forward instead, with a new kind of hope. She begins part two by recalling that the child's song could not, after all, carry the weight of a woman's heart. "I leant upon his music as a theme, / Till it gave way beneath my heart's full beat" (2:3–4). At first she protects her "two-months' baby" from awakening to the sound of Austrian troops that represent "the world's baseness" (2:297), but eventually (motherhood having aroused an unwonted Wordsworthian faith in the wisdom of infants) she recognizes him as "Posterity [. . .] smiling on our knees, / Convicting us of folly" (2:774–75) and instilling courage and hope. The generational image of society set forth in part one is fully realized, fully literal, in her own life, and her child restores her confidence in the political future. Italy may indeed be Niobe, but instead of Niobe's children who were killed by the "most dazzling arrows" (2:727) of the sun, she shows us, in a bold and terrifying defiance of Niobe's fate, her own child whom "The sun strikes" (2:742) only to glorify, making a "glittering nimbus" (2:760) of his hair. *Casa Guidi Windows* is, finally, a hymn to progress and human possibility that is also, and not coincidentally, a song of motherhood.

In England the Risorgimento aroused considerable sympathy.[30] Even so, however, a complicated account of an abortive reform in Tuscany did not (as *Blackwood's* had predicted) greatly interest English readers, and the reviews of *Casa Guidi Windows* were sparse and rather cool. Her friends seemed "mystified" and "disgusted" (*LEBB* 2:60), although the poem did not "prevent everybody [. . .] from speaking" to her (*LEBB* 2:5), as in her hope of provoking a violent reaction she had half-anticipated. To Mary Russell Mitford, who heard reports in London that Mazzini wanted to have it translated as a political pamphlet, it was simply dull. Some kindly reviewers praised its combination of male and female virtues: "womanly faith and trust" and "a manly power of analyzing events and facing disagreeable truths," showing "something at once manly and womanly in the character of her mind—energy large, and feeling deep."[31] On the whole, though, political engagement and even her marriage were perceived as injurious to her writing. The change in her personal circumstances was noted with mixed feelings by a reviewer who regretted for art's sake the loss of Miss Barrett in that unpoetical being, "the happy wife and mother,"[32] and the *Guardian,* which had prefaced high praise of the 1850 *Poems* with a disquisition on women writers' proper sphere, pronounced *Casa Guidi Windows* "an unmistakeable and complete failure" because of its subject matter.[33] A year later Browning's French friend and admirer Joseph Milsand published an admiring survey of her works in the prestigious *Revue des deux mondes* which dwelt approvingly on her feminine qualities while proclaiming *Casa Guidi Windows* powerful but chaotic and politics an unsuitable theme for poetry.[34] Even her old friend Chorley, who was drawn to women's poetry by its womanliness, was cooler than usual and complained that her husband had had a deleterious influence on her style.[35] George Eliot, however, liked it very much—in 1862 she read it again "with great delight"—but she did not review it.[36] The reviews were neither sufficiently favorable nor sufficiently outraged to encourage Barrett Browning to write more in the same vein; but as usual, she did not much care.

Overtly political concerns, however, became less important to her during the next several years. After the failed revolutions of 1848 things were quiet in Tuscany, where the disappointing grand duke was dismissed with good-natured contempt by the Florentines as *il gran ciuco* ("the great ass").[37] In the first half of the next decade her attention was fully occupied by her son, her family and friends, spiritualism, and the composition of *Aurora Leigh.* At the same time Browning was writing the collection of (mostly) dramatic monologues published in 1855 as *Men and Women,* the greatest of his books. They were busier, more distracted, less harmoniously absorbed in each other now—they were living more like ordinary people—and for both of them, this was the most significantly productive period of their lives.

The passion of belated motherhood was lavished on Pen. She had always been drawn to children, assuming for years that she would never have any, and almost to the end of her life she yearned for a daughter. But other pregnancies miscarried, and by 1852 she was sure that there would be no more. The more unusual aspects of Pen's upbringing can be traced to her refusal to honor the rigid distinctions of gender, nationality, and class that she hated in the English. She refused to indoctrinate him in class consciousness or British patriotism, pleased whenever he was taken for an Italian or insisted that he was Florentine, not English. "I try to bring up my Peni without national prejudices," she said, "as a citizen of the world."[38] Her letters record (with the charmed particularity with which she had once chronicled the doings of Flush, now almost forgotten in her letters until the report of his death in 1854) the peculiar language he forged for himself from a combination of Italian, English, and an admixture of French. When he had straightened out these three languages he began to learn German, but initiation into the serious business of Latin was deferred, since by now Barrett Browning thought the living languages more important for a citizen of the world than the language of male culture. His early religious experiences were even more dramatically eclectic than his linguistic ones, ranging from rapturous forays into Catholic churches to a happy Swedenborgian belief in the proximity of friendly spirits.

Above all, she refused to respect gender differences. Being a mother released her to enjoy directly or vicariously aspects of womanhood that she had previously spurned. "My whole personal vanity is absorbed in that child," she confessed rather proudly to Mrs. Gaskell in 1853, "I look at him for halfhours together as the Lady Mathildas look in the glass."[39] She dressed him in a rich and fanciful style that carried to an extreme and to an unusually late age the androgyny permissible for boys' attire. He had long golden curls and wore lace and silk and velvet with embroidery done, despite her lifelong hatred of the needle, by her own hands. Her own dress was rich and modest, her ringlets were unfashionable, and Browning was occasionally roused to protest about her hats, but she lavished adornments without compunction on Pen and encouraged him in what she considered feminine self-display. "There's a great deal of girl-nature in the child," she remarked complacently, describing how nicely he danced and accompanied himself on the tambourine, and she was always gratified—although Browning was not—when people turned to look at him in the street and asked whether he was a girl or a boy.[40]

She relived many elements of her own childhood through aspects of Pen's: his enterprising and affectionate nature, the admiring love with which he was surrounded, his mastery of languages, and the enforced prolongation of his childhood. Like her own father, she did not want her child to grow up. "I have but one [baby], & must keep him as long as I can," she wrote when he was six years old (*LMO* 132). And once again she found herself in bondage to love. When Wilson left the Brownings on their own for a while in London, Barrett Browning complained not entirely in jest of her "slavery" to the child who demanded her constant presence (*LS* 138), although she concluded that "the filial despotism is better than the 'paternal' " (*LMRM* 3:371). Her husband firmly resisted her willingness to be tyrannized over, but despots flourished around her—

even Flush was remarkable for his imperious ways—and Pen soon learned how to rule her through love. "Such a darling, idle, distracted child he is," she wrote rather desperately in 1855,

> not keeping his attention for three minutes together for the hour and a half I teach him, and when I upbraid him for it, throwing himself upon me like a dog, kissing my cheeks and head and hands. 'O you little pet, *dive* me one chance more! I will really be dood,' and learning everything by magnetism [. . . .] Oh, such a darling that child is! I expect the wings to grow presently.[41]

As she had once struggled to subdue her self-willed and passionate nature, so now she had to cope with Pen's frighteningly intense enthusiasms and some wilful evasions of discipline, mostly in regard to lessons. The storybook aspects of her life were transferred to him, too; the oppressive coloration of romance and even the fairy-tale atmosphere of the happily-ever-after had faded into the pleasant light of common day, but now Pen was her beautiful fairy prince. "Penini sounds like a fairy's name—and he looks like a fairy—he has been called twenty times a fairy-child by different strangers."[42] The re-experiencing as a mother of some of the deepest issues of her own childhood and her self-displacement as the central character of her romance are reflected in the subjects, and especially the perspectives, of *Aurora Leigh.*

In late spring of 1851 the Brownings, with Wilson, a manservant, and Flush, finally ventured north, stopping briefly in Venice and for a month in Paris and reaching London in July after an absence of almost five years. Barrett Browning was happy to see her sisters, to be reconciled with her brothers, and to meet Tennyson, Carlyle, and other luminaries and old friends. But her father responded to a conciliatory letter from Browning and a beseeching one of her own with a reply (addressed to Browning) that put an end to any lingering hope of forgiveness, and he took the occasion to return, unopened, all the letters she had sent him since her marriage. Social engagements exhausted her, emotional stress and the inhospitable physical climate wore her down ("Airs and hearts, all are against me in England" [*LEBB* 2:13]), and after two months she was glad to escape to Paris for the winter.

They both enjoyed Paris, where they frequented a more varied and interesting society than their narrow Florentine circle and the climate and apartments were more comfortable than in London. Less conventional in social matters than her husband, she then and later found "the half artist half gypsey life one can lead there" very much to her taste.[43]

They called on George Sand, although Browning's enthusiasm by no means matched her own. She kissed Sand's hand—Sand kissed her on the lips—and tried not to be shocked at her masculine company and unladylike deportment, but despite Barrett Browning's "gypsey" proclivities the two women were too disparate to be friends. There was political excitement, too, Louis Napoleon's *coup d'etat* in December 1851 arousing her enthusiastic partisanship against her suspicious compatriots: he embodied the will of the people, she said, and the people could choose whom they pleased. Some domestic arguments ensued, since Robert tended to share the British distrust of Louis Napoleon, and she enjoyed shocking her friends with her radical opinions.[44] On the whole, Paris encouraged her radicalism and her alienation from England and accentuated her divergences from her husband's views.

In July 1852 they returned to London and were met once again by a wrenching paternal betrayal. Browning's father and his sister Sarianna had welcomed them warmly, and Robert Browning senior proved an affectionate grandfather. But the recently bereaved and presumably heartbroken widower had been courting a rich widow, a Mrs. von Muller, and when at his son's instigation he not only tried to end the relationship but accused Mrs. von Muller of bigamy, she sued for defamation and breach of promise. His love letters were read out in court, where his counsel defended him as "a besotted old man," "a poor old dotard in love," and he was ordered to pay £800 in damages. These humiliating proceedings were duly made public in the *Times*.[45] For Browning, who had been shaken to the depths of his being by his mother's death and for whom eternal fidelity in love was a central tenet of both art and life, and who in addition was observant of the proprieties and tender of his reputation, this must have been an exceedingly unpleasant experience. And it would have confirmed Elizabeth's disillusionment with fathers and with England. To avoid paying the damages, which came to more than twice his annual salary, Mr. Browning and Sarianna moved to Paris. Robert and Elizabeth left them there in October and returned, after almost a year and a half away, to Florence. Robert preferred the liveliness of London and Paris, but for Elizabeth the apartment in Casa Guidi was home, and in the warmth and quiet of Florence—despite the stirrings of her "gypsey" blood—she was happy. They spent a summer at the hillside resort of Bagni di Lucca, outside Florence, and the winter and spring of 1853–54 in Rome (where, as in Paris, Browning went out in the evenings while she stayed quietly at home), and did not return to Paris and London until the summer of 1855.

Their domestic peace was most ruffled, and her growing impatience with England and patriarchal culture most perplexingly expressed, by her addiction to spiritualism. The spiritualist craze began in America in 1850 and quickly made its way to England, and in the spring of 1853 almost everyone the Brownings knew in Florence was dabbling in it or quarrelling about it. Spirits of the dead answered questions and delivered messages by means of rapping noises or through the voices of mediums, tables and other large objects moved without apparent human agency, and disconnected hands and arms touched people or floated luminously.[46] Some mediums practised levitation, and all sorts of people, including Wilson, discovered themselves capable of transcribing spirit messages. On one occasion Wilson's writing indicated the presence of Mary Moulton-Barrett, but her mediumistic powers proved disappointingly weak. Barrett Browning's common sense and her sharp eye for the ridiculous did not wholly fail her and she laughed at particularly egregious examples of credulity and fraud; still, she believed most of what she heard. She expected from spiritualism "the solution of some of the deepest mysteries of our double nature" (*LMO* 108), and the inanity of the spirit messages did not disturb her: "I care less about what [the spirits] are capable of communicating," she said, "than of the fact of there being communications" (*LEBB* 2:104).

For some time she had been an ardent reader of Swedenborg, seer and prophet of the world of spirits. Her interest in Swedenborg seems to have begun in the 1840s, although she said that her Swedenborgianism preceded her reading of his work, and it intensified at the beginning of the next decade. "He is wonderful," she wrote in 1853; "his scheme of the natural and spiritual worlds and natures appears to me, in an internal light of its own, divine and true [. . . .] If he was not *taught* it, if we are to consider him a common man and no seer, then I maintain that, of all makers of systems and dreamers of ideal philosophies, from Plato to Fourier, he stands first . . a man of genius beyond all their genius."[47] Increasingly scornful of the narrowness of the Protestant churches, she found Swedenborg's system attractively open and accommodating while still centered on the divinity of Christ. She would have found his inclination to think more about heaven than hell particularly congenial and must have liked his kindly view that to live well on earth is not really very difficult. For Swedenborg, the object of this life is individual development, with opportunities to continue developing provided in the afterlife. Stressing the virtue of charity, he is contemptuous of asceticism and seclusion, imagining heaven as a richly populated kingdom with houses and palaces, streets, squares, and gardens, marriage and giving in marriage, and all the bustle and business of life that Barrett Browning had long been deprived of and now delighted (at least from a quiet distance) to contemplate. The author of *The Seraphim* and *A Drama of Exile*, with their small casts of solemn spirits and vast empty settings outside the gates of heaven or Eden, could not but have admired the ease with which Swedenborg crossed the barriers that had been obdurate to her own imagination and conversed familiarly with varied multitudes of spirits. Swedenborg's idea of correspondences and influences, connections between the material and spiritual worlds and between this life and the next, also pleased her. But it was probably the exuberant fullness, the matter-of-fact particularity, and the pleasant zaniness of Swedenborg's visions that kept her reading and rereading his books.

When spiritualism and Swedenborgianism erupted into English consciousness in the early 1850s they fit naturally and easily, as if they were what she had always been looking for, into Barrett Browning's life. She had been fascinated and terrified by mesmerism, which was closely allied to spiritualism and apparently responsible for many of its effects, ever since she saw Harriet Martineau act the part of Godiva as witness to its power. She had thought mesmerism then, as she did spiritualism later, a rising force in the world, but she hated and feared the subjection of will that mesmerism seemed to imply.[48] With an imagination singularly untainted by the scientific movements of the age, she had always been fully convinced of the immortality of the soul and the reality of the spirit world—guardian angels, seraphs, and the like—that Swedenborg described with infinite elaboration, and spiritualism gave material proof of the existence of the beloved dead. Convinced that infidelity was rampant in England, she greeted the sudden outburst of spiritual manifestations as the inauguration of a new antimaterialist age, a spiritual version of the Risorgimento. She detested barriers of nation, class, sect, and gender, and spiritualism seemed to be dissolving not only these but also the greatest barriers of all: between life and death, the human and the divine.

In her own life, however, spiritualism threatened to create divisions as well as break them down. For a while Browning seems to have taken a reasonably good-natured interest in what was engrossing not just his wife but many of their friends as well, including men whom he respected (William Wetmore Story, for instance, who had been a distinguished legal scholar at Harvard before becoming a sculptor and whom no one could accuse of weak-mindedness); but after a seance with the most eminent of the mediums, Daniel Dunglas Home (or Hume), in the summer of

1855 his patience gave way.[49] Barrett Browning's description of the seance demonstrates how her critical intelligence plummeted to the level of bathos where spiritualist matters were concerned in regard to all but literary questions, and tolerated it even there:

> We were touched by the invisible, heard the music and raps, saw the table moved, and had sight of the hands. Also, at the request of the medium, the spiritual hands took [. . .] a garland [. . .] and placed it upon my head. The particular hand which did this was of the largest human size, as white as snow, and very beautiful. It was as near to me as this hand I write with, and I saw it as distinctly. I was perfectly calm! not troubled in any way, and felt convinced in my own mind that *no spirit belonging to me* was present on the occasion. The hands which appeared at a distance from me I put up my glass to look at—proving that it was not a mere mental impression, and that they were subject to the usual laws of vision. These hands seemed to Robert and me to come from under the table, but Mr. Lytton [at an earlier seance with Home] saw them rise out of the *wood of the table* [. . . .] The music [played by spirits on an accordion under the table] was beautiful.
>
> I think that what chiefly went against the exhibition, in Robert's mind, was the trance at the conclusion during which the medium talked a great deal of much such twaddle as may be heard in any fifth rate conventicle. But according to my theory (well thought-out and digested) this does not militate at all against the general facts. (*LS* 220)

While she was completely persuaded by what she saw, Robert's report of the same event was skeptical and sarcastic, seeing nothing beautiful in either the hands or the music, describing one air performed by the spirits as "commonplace . . . , but played with expression enough."[50] A few days later Home called on the Brownings and was treated very rudely by Robert. For a while Elizabeth had to warn her correspondents not to mention either spiritualism or (a taboo that lasted longer) Home, since the subjects were not discussible between them. But she does not seem to have tried very hard to avoid provoking him: the garland the spirits had given her hung on her dressing table until it withered and Browning in a fit of temper threw it out the window.

The tawdriness and absurdity of Home's performance disgusted Browning, but they may almost have been attractions to his wife, despite her moral and intellectual fastidiousness. It was not just that she habitually explained away the "twaddle" talked by the spirits as showing only that foolish people remained foolish after death or that she thought mediumistic powers could be independent of moral character. The fact that most professional practitioners of spiritualism (as opposed to amateurs and believers, who represented a much wider range of social and intellectual strata) were outsiders to high culture—Americans, servants, women, the uncultivated and undereducated—would have appealed to her rebellious and democratic sentiments. Women performed mediumistic functions, although churches barred them from sacerdotal ones, and receiving spirit messages was something women could do in their spare time at home.[51] She tolerated imperfect mediums, as she tolerated imperfect political leaders, and she derived considerable enjoyment from the spectacle of eminent men of science apparently unable to discredit men—and women—whose intelligence they despised. Her calm acceptance of rawness and crudity was of a piece with her other refusals to disdain the present as inferior in grandeur and beauty to the past. Spiritualism was too thin and tawdry to provide her directly with material for poetry, but the hope of a freer and finer age that it inspired in her is suffused throughout *Aurora Leigh,* which in its own way was just as offensive to "good taste" and as hostile to high culture.

Other apparent impediments to peaceful composition also stimulated her creativity. For most of her life she had suffered from a surfeit of leisure, freedom from responsibility, and rooms of her own that she did not appreciate as more harassed and distracted women might have done. The rooms felt like prisons, and she pined for experiential grist for her poetic mill. *Aurora Leigh* shows that her instinct about what was best for her art was right. In the 1850s her life was filled with the multiform distractions of travel, society, spiritualism and the marital misunderstandings consequent upon it, and above all Pen. "I don't know how my poem is ever to be finished," she complained when they were in Paris in 1855; "It's as much as I can do, to get through Peni's lessons"—and then she cheerfully praises his learning and his velvet hat (*LS* 233). Browning reported that she "used to write it, and lay it down to hear our child spell, or when a visitor came—it was thrust under the cushion then."[52] (This was not unusual for women writers: Jane Austen, Elizabeth Gaskell, and many others wrote under similar circumstances.) She no longer had a room of her own, although she always tried to provide one for Robert, who enjoyed writing less than she did and so presumably needed one more.

Much of *Aurora Leigh* was composed not only under practical difficulties, however, but also in somewhat darkened circumstances. A serious illness in 1854 cast the first shadow on the wonderful restoration of her health. There were money worries, for Mr. Kenyon did not always remember to pay their allowance, the ship in which she owned shares was sometimes delayed, and poetry was hardly profitable. Although she had laughed at Browning's unpoetical insistence that bills be paid promptly, she was forced to take money seriously when the lack of it kept her from going to England or visiting Henrietta and her babies once she got there. For a time she had the satisfaction of knowing that while she was composing her most ambitious and important work, Robert was writing too. There was some friendly rivalry, especially when she realized that his book would be finished before hers, but there was also the great pleasure of mutual encouragement and their pride in each other's work, which they showed each other only when it was done. She recognized the singular greatness of his new poems, and they were both confident that this time the public would recognize it too. But when *Men and Women* appeared in 1855 few readers understood or appreciated it, and the incomprehension of such a reader as Ruskin, even, was a bitter—for a while, almost a crushing—disappointment to Browning and clouded his wife's pleasure in the completion of her own major work.[53]

7
Aurora Leigh

Aurora Leigh is Barrett Browning's longest and most innovative work, expressing, as she says in the dedication, her "highest convictions upon Life and Art" (4:1), imagining how a woman could become the feminine of Homer and perhaps, through imagining it, doing so. It is her epic: of epic size (longer, reviewers pointed out, than *Paradise Lost*) and epic scope, with a woman poet as hero and her country's destiny hanging in the balance of her deeds. Its argument is that writing a poem can itself be an epic action that leads, like an epic hero's, to the creation of a new social order. And the heroine's poem mirrors the one in which she appears: Barrett Browning wanted *Aurora Leigh* to work for change in British society, and it was sufficiently provocative—this time she managed to shock people almost as much as she intended—to make her publication of it a significant act of courage. The epic deed is not fighting at Marathon to preserve a city but writing a poem that will build a new one.

Aurora Leigh is the story of a girl who was born in Florence of an Italian mother and an English father, brought up first by her widowed father in Italy and then by a rigidly conventional aunt in England, and who grows up to become a poet. Aurora falls in love (although it takes her many years to admit it, even to herself) with her high-minded cousin Romney Leigh, who loves her; but she agrees to marry him only after she has established herself as a self-supporting and successful poet and his misguided philanthropy has collapsed into the destruction of his work, his hopes, his ancestral home, and his eyesight. There is also a virtuous lower-class girl, Marian Erle, whom Romney plans to marry as part of his project of social renovation and class reconciliation, who is lured away

183

and raped and then rescued with her child by Aurora. And there is a beautiful aristocrat, Lady Waldemar, who deceives Marian and tries to ensnare Romney. The center of the story, however, is Aurora's literary development and her struggle to reconcile the warring claims of work and marriage, art and love. Barrett Browning's uncertainties about women's place in poetry are argued, analyzed, dramatized, and triumphantly resolved in the traditional happy ending, marriage.

This sounds like the plot of a novel rather than an epic poem, and *Aurora Leigh* is best described as a novel-poem (the term Barrett Browning sometimes used), or verse-novel, or novel in verse—the only one of its kind, except for some very minor works, in nineteenth-century English literature. Like all the other great long nineteenth-century poems, it is a generic anomaly.[1] The closest resemblance is to Byron's *Don Juan*, one of the many books her father thought unfit for women to read and the one model she acknowledged. Despite a good deal of high-minded solemnity, it is Byronic in range, scope, and tonal variety—wit, travel, politics, celebrations of nature, social satire, passions of many kinds, and what she called "philosophical dreaming & digression" (*LMRM* 2:49), all jostling comfortably against each other. The heroine's name may suggest Byron's half-sister Augusta Leigh and Aurora Raby in *Don Juan*, although the most important resonances are with Aurore Dudevant (George Sand) and, more simply, the goddess of morning who shines through Elizabeth Barrett's juvenilia.[2] Like Wordsworth's *Prelude*, published in 1850, it is a first-person account of a poet's development, but with a fictional protagonist and a more novelistic interest in plot, characterization, social life, and manners.[3] It is a long continuous narrative with a contemporary setting told in installments by a single speaker: as the fictional autobiography of a woman by a woman, its only significant Victorian counterparts are Charlotte Brontë's *Jane Eyre* (1847) and *Villette* (1853).

The plot teems with incident, falling into three main overlapping parts: the lovers' misunderstandings, estrangement, and marriage; the disaster befalling a lower-class girl who has the misfortune of attracting the attentions of a gentleman (the standard Victorian seduction plot); and more generally, the *Bildungsroman* or *Kunstlerroman*, the story of the education of an artist. It has affinities with many particular novels, including Mme de Staël's *Corinne*, George Sand's *Consuelo* and its sequel, *The Countess of Rudolstadt*, Mrs. Gaskell's *Ruth*, Charles Kingsley's *Alton Locke*, and above all *Jane Eyre*.[4] Like Victorian novels, it is attentive to the ways in which character develops and relationships change through time; it relies heavily on dialogue and effectively differentiates characters' voices; it presents with considerable realistic detail a social world that encompasses England, France, and Italy, aristocrats, artists, and tramps; and it takes up the kinds of political, social, and religious questions that novelists dealt with too.[5] But its heightened, highly charged feeling and language, especially the elaborate metaphors and ostentatious epic similes, are overtly "poetical"; and the fact that it is a poem is an essential part of its meaning. It is about writing poetry, and it *is* the kind of poem it describes. The fusion of two apparently incompatible genres gives it a startling originality and allows for a scope and flexibility that neither genre alone could provide.

It must also have given Barrett Browning the confidence of writing for the first time in a strong female tradition, even though she denied what might seem like specific indebtednesses. Unlike Charlotte Brontë's Mr. Rochester, she pointed out, Romney is not disfigured when he is blinded and his house burnt (*LEBB* 2:246). By mid-century the novel had proved to be the most hospitable to women of all the literary genres. Being relatively new and only loosely connected to traditional high culture, it was not tuned exclusively to the male voice, even though in hope of a fairer hearing some women set forth on their careers with the protection of male pseudonyms. Nor was its audience predominantly male or even presumed to be so. Women read novels, women's concerns inhabited them, women wrote them, and sometimes (at least in France) they even wrote about women artists. Barrett Browning had found no grandmothers among the English poets, but the family resemblances between Aurora Leigh, Corinne, Jane Eyre, and Consuelo, or between Marian Erle and Mrs. Gaskell's Ruth—aunts and cousins, if not grandmothers—suggest similar ties among their authors. And the fact that Sand, Brontë, and even Gaskell (a Unitarian minister's wife of unimpeachable respectability) had all been reprehended for their treatment of sexuality, as she expected to be, must have cheered her with the feeling of being in brave company.

She had always been an indiscriminately voracious reader of novels. The *Poems* of 1844 closed with a ringing repudiation of the literary past ("Pan is dead"), and both the ease with which "Lady Geraldine's Courtship" flowed from her pen and its enthusiastic reception encouraged her to penetrate still further into the realms of modern prose fiction. Although readers charmed by her letters have sometimes regretted that she did not actually write novels, however, it seems never to have occurred to her to do so. From early childhood she had defined herself as a poet, placed poetry highest in the hierarchy of literary genres, and aspired to the composition of the highest kind of poem, an epic. She wanted poetry to deal with life as fully as prose fiction did, but without sacrificing its generic superiority. Since much of her worldly experience derived in the first instance from novels, she would probably not have felt knowledgeable enough to write them herself even if she had wanted to, and it is just as well that she did not. She had no gift for inventing plots, and her fondness for absurd melodrama, distressing enough in her poems, would have been intolerable in prose. The wit and stylistic elegance and the moral and intellectual grace of her letters, which can make small domestic events and nuances of behavior shimmer with significance, may remind us of Jane Austen, but she thought Austen's novels narrow and cold and would never have tried to write anything like them.

Nonetheless, *Aurora Leigh* was first conceived in terms of genre rather than character, theme, or plot. In October 1844 Barrett Browning announced that she had "a great fancy" to write a poem "comprehending the aspect and manners of modern life, and flinching at nothing of the conventional" (*LEBB* 1:204), and in December and again in February she declared more decidedly that she intended to write "a sort of novel-poem" but was looking for a story (*LMRM* 3:42; *RB-EBB* 1:31).

> You see nobody is offended by my approach to the conventions of vulgar life in "Lady Geraldine"—and it gives me courage to go on, & touch this real everyday life of our age, & hold it with my two hands. I want to write a poem of a new class, in a measure—a Don Juan, without the mockery & impurity, . . under one aspect,—& having unity, as a work of art,—& admitting of as much philosophical dreaming & digression (which is in fact a characteristic of the age) as I like to use. (*LMRM* 3:49)

She liked to think that writing a poem could be an act of courage (even though as yet "nobody is offended"), and Byron not only provided a generic example but was also her model of a revolutionary poet-hero. She wanted her poem to be revolutionary, too, violating poetic decorum and speaking (without "impurity") about matters on which respectable women were expected to be ignorant or silent—in 1844 she was probably thinking both of politics (like the agitation against the Corn Laws, or Lady Geraldine's defiance of class distinctions) and of sex, and *Aurora Leigh* has a good deal to say about both. She imagined her poem "running into the midst of our conventions, & rushing into drawing-rooms & the like 'where angels fear to tread'; & so, meeting face to face & without mask the Humanity of the age, & speaking the truth as I conceive of it, out plainly" (*RB-EBB* 1:31). *Aurora Leigh* rushes fearlessly not only into drawing rooms, but into slums and a brothel.

Her ballads showed that to imagine women's empowerment Barrett Browning needed modern settings, as in "Lady Geraldine's Courtship" and *Sonnets from the Portuguese*. The speaker in "The Runaway Slave at Pilgrim's Point," the first narrative Barrett Browning wrote after formulating her hopes for a novel-poem, is in her way active and powerful too, and her world although utterly disjunct from English drawing rooms is no mock-medieval dreamland. *Aurora Leigh* brings into lurid collision Lady Geraldine's aristocratic milieu and a grim underworld like the runaway slave's of cruelty and rape. Both Lady Geraldine and the runaway slave, however, are in their different ways idealized fantasy figures; and while *Aurora Leigh* has elements of fantasy too, especially in its nightmarish depictions of the lower classes, the heroine and her social background are drawn from the poet's experience. The settings are the places she knew best—the Malvern Hills, London, Florence, Paris—and even for the scenes in the London slums she drew not only on novels, newspapers, and parliamentary reports like that written by her correspondent R. H. Horne in 1843, but also on the memory of a bold foray she had made in 1846 into a den of dog thieves to ransom Flush.[6]

The heroine's empowerment is enacted mainly through decisive revisions of the chivalric quest and rescue story which had structured Barrett Browning's imagination since childhood and which she uses here for the first time in a long poem. Much of the plot consists of thwarting Romney's grim determination to be a rescuing knight, the people he tries to rescue one after another repudiating his assistance. Tormented by an unrelenting awareness of human suffering, Romney throws himself into the task of reforming society and ameliorating the conditions of the poor, and he asks Aurora to marry him and join in his work. She refuses partly because she would rather write poetry than labor for the poor, partly because of his irritating assumption of superiority, and partly because she thinks he doesn't love her—she assumes that like the men in most of Barrett Browning's ballads he would prefer a less assertive woman. She thinks, too, that he wants to save her from prospective poverty, and she recoils from the humiliation of being bought and paid for like patient Griselda and thereby, she thinks, losing her independence and her right to speak (2:785–94). Instead of encouraging him to fight on her behalf, she arms herself against him, and wins her first victory in a comically legalistic argument (marked as an heroic battle by unusually formal epic similes [2:1120–24, 1162–68]) through which she foils his ingenious attempt to give her money.

Thus decisively rebuffed, Romney turns his chivalrous attentions to Marian Erle, whom he saves from abject misery and arranges to marry. But he is swiftly punished for this second attempt (which is genuinely quixotic, since he loves Aurora) to help a woman: having invited a pre-posterous mixture of aristocrats and slum-dwellers to celebrate their exemplary wedding, he is left to face an enraged mob when Marian does not appear. He then collects poor people to live out a socialist ideal with him in his ancestral home, Leigh Hall, but another angry mob burns the house down and in the confusion of the fire Marian's father strikes the blow that blinds him. Meanwhile Aurora has found Marian, who has been drugged and raped in a Parisian brothel, and carried her and her child off to Italy. Romney follows them, offers again to marry Marian, and is again rejected. Marian wants to devote herself to her child and (like Aurora) refuses to take generosity for love. She left him in the first place because Lady Waldemar persuaded her that he should have "a wife more level to himself" (6:1027), and she has learned to appreciate equal-ity and independence.

> "I think I did not give you anything;
> I was but only yours—upon my knees,
> All yours, in soul and body, in head and heart,
> A creature you had taken from the ground
> Still crumbling through your fingers to your feet
> To join the dust she came from."
>
> (9:373–78)

This is a self-respecting beggar maid's answer to King Cophetua, Cin-derella's to the prince, the damsel's to the knight. It is the final and definitive refusal to let Romney rescue anyone.

For Aurora such a refusal is an assumption of poetic as well as personal power, recalling the poet's fear in *Sonnets from the Portuguese* of being glorified by her lover's chivalric imagination and her assertion of the primacy of her own desire. Aurora's struggle to become subject rather than object in relation to Romney, like that of the poet in the *Sonnets*, is also a struggle to have him recognize her as an artist rather than a work of art. This struggle begins in the first scene between them. Aurora has crowned herself with ivy in playful anticipation of posthumous glory, but when Romney comes suddenly upon her he sees the wreath as just an adornment, a sign of female vanity that flatters his sense of male superiority, his contempt for mere artists, his love, and his hope of marrying her. She is embarrassed:

> I stood there fixed,—
> My arms up, like the caryatid, sole
> Of some abolished temple, helplessly
> Persistent in a gesture which derides
> A former purpose. Yet my blush was flame.

> (2:60–64)

Under his amused, admiring gaze her aspirations dwindle into girlish narcissism. Instead of an artist she becomes a work of art, and an archaic, useless one at that; and the flush of embarrassment that marks the conflict between her intention as an artist and the self-consciousness sparked by his desire makes her the literal embodiment of her name: Aurora.

Romney inadvertently drives home the meaning of the incident by asking her to marry him and explaining that women cannot be poets, and despite her firm refusal she is pursued by the ramifications of his gaze. She seems to be surrounded by curious, hostile eyes. The servants observe her in the private acts of daily life, the neighbors come to look too, and "The very dog / Would watch me from his sun-patch on the floor, / In alternation with the large black fly / Not yet in reach of snapping" (2:886–89). Her aunt's gaze probes so surely to her unacknowledged sexual responsiveness that she blushes even in retrospect: "I feel the brand upon my forehead now / Strike hot, sear deep, as guiltless men may feel / The felon's iron" (2:698–700). Death alone averts the terrible eyes that see only repressed desire: having wished that everyone in the house would sleep rather than look at her (2:909–10), Aurora finds her aunt dead. "And did I pray, a half-hour back, but so, / To escape the burden of those eyes . . . those eyes?" (2:949–50). Yes; and her prayer achieved its aim. Now she can go off to London and write.

In the end it is Aurora who captures Romney with a transfixing gaze. His arrival in Florence is heralded by her dreamy vision of a "sea king"— a male version of the mysterious, half-natural half-human erotic object that men have figured as a mermaid. "Flooded" with shadows, Florence looked one evening like

> some drowned city in some enchanted sea,
> Cut off from nature,—drawing you who gaze
> With passionate desire, to leap and plunge
> And find a sea-king with a voice of waves,

And treacherous soft eyes, and slippery locks
You cannot kiss but you shall bring away
Their salt upon your lips.

(8:38–44)

This vision, strange and sexy as anything in *Sonnets from the Portuguese* (like the images of seagod and porpoise, it locates eroticism in the sea) establishes her as the speaking subject whose desire elicits its object: Romney immediately appears. But these lovers do not achieve the complicated reciprocity of those in the *Sonnets*. He comes like the prince to Sleeping Beauty—on one of the many evenings when she "did not write, nor read, nor even think" (7:1306), her selfhood "Dissolving slowly, slowly, until lost" (7:1311)—and bestows the kiss of sexual awakening. By the time the traditionally gendered rescue plot is consummated, however, he is not only helpless, dispossessed, a failure in everything he tried to do—whereas all *her* efforts have succeeded—but blind. Now she sees *him* as a work of art, "pale and patient" like a statue (8:1100), but he will never look at her—never objectify her—again.

While the plot which had haunted Barrett Browning's imagination from early childhood is so relentlessly discredited, moreover, a similar plot intersects and displaces it: the daughter's quest for the mother. Here women are both subject and object, men little more than distractions. Except for some obscure images of alienation and betrayal, Barrett Browning had had little to say about mothers until the joyful celebration of maternity in *Casa Guidi Windows*. *Aurora Leigh*, however, is replete with the presence or felt absence of mothers, babies, feeding, and eating: having "breasts / Made right to suckle babes" is proof of being a woman (6:1183–84). All the women except Aurora herself, as well as such personifications as Nature, Italy, and the modern Age, are conceived primarily as mothers, good or bad, and filial perspectives are augmented by maternal ones.

The mother whose early death filled the world with the "mother-want" (1:40) that suffuses the poem was, like Barrett Browning's own, an ambiguous figure, simultaneously encouraging and quelling, of whom Aurora recalls only six words: "Hush, hush—here's too much noise!"— an ominous legacy to a poet-daughter, but for the fact that as she spoke them "her sweet eyes / Leap[t] forward, taking part against her word / In the child's riot" (1:17–19). She died when Aurora was four, and her death seems to have been somehow (not in any obvious way) a consequence of love. Like Mary Moulton-Barrett, she was too womanly and tender: "She was weak and frail; / She could not bear the joy of giving life, / The mother's rapture slew her" (1:33–35). Or, in an even more elliptical formulation: Aurora's father looked at her, "he loved. / And thus beloved, she died" (1:91–92). It is not surprising that a portrait painted from her dead face haunts her daughter as an image of perplexing ambivalence:

> Ghost, fiend, and angel, fairy, witch, and sprite,
> A dauntless Muse who eyes a dreadful Fate,
> A loving Psyche who loses sight of Love,
> A still Medusa with mild milky brows
> All curdled and all clothed upon with snakes
> Whose slime falls fast as sweat will; or anon
> Our Lady of the Passion, stabbed with swords
> Where the Babe sucked; or Lamia in her first
> Moonlighted pallor, ere she shrunk and blinked
> And shuddering wriggled down to the unclean.
>
> (1:154–63)

These are images of virtue and power thwarted, self-contradiction and defeat, even though we know that love will return to Psyche and our Lady will ascend to heaven. Teaching that women are bound to sorrow, the mother appears to her daughter as both tender and malign. She becomes the shifting embodiment of everything the daughter "read or heard or dreamed" (1:148) about women, the object of worship, desire, repugnance, and fear. The milk that streams through the poem in an astonishing flood of imagery, signifying love, flows first from the slime of Medusa's snaky hair.[7]

The first substitute for the lost maternal presence is nature, a familiar symbolic equivalence that here becomes unflinchingly literal. Aurora's father takes her to live in the mountains, "Because unmothered babes, he thought, had need / Of mother nature" (1:112–13) and of "Pan's white goats, with udders warm and full / Of mystic contemplations" (1:114–15). But at the moment of her departure the maternal hills of Italy withdraw from her, as her mother had withdrawn into death: from the ship taking her to England she looks back and sees

> The white walls, the blue hills, my Italy,
> Drawn backward from the shuddering steamer-deck,
> Like one in anger drawing back her skirts
> Which suppliants catch at.
>
> (1:232–35)

She returns to Italy, years later, still yearning for maternal love.

> And now I come, my Italy,
> My own hills! Are you 'ware of me, my hills,
> How I burn toward you? do you feel to-night
> The urgency and yearning of my soul,
> As sleeping mothers feel the sucking babe
> And smile?

$$(5:1266-71)$$

Put so literally, Aurora's question can have only one answer: "Nay" (5:1271).

Into the vacancy left by her mother's death her father pours (all he has to give) a boy's education in the classics. But he dies when she is thirteen—at puberty, when gender distinctions come inexorably into play— and she is inducted into femininity by the unaffectionate aunt who represents not the nurturing mother of infancy but the one who betrays her daughter by inculcating subservience to men. Under her aunt's supervision she receives the lessons proper for a girl: music, drawing, dancing, and needlework, formalistic and inhumane religious instruction, a little French and German and a bit of mathematics, treatises on the inferiority of women, and a variety of disconnected facts (1:392–455).[8] She performs without pleasure but without complaint the social duties that had galled Elizabeth Barrett when her own aunt imposed them. Her aunt tries to consummate her education in feminine subordination by persuading her to marry Romney, telling her (the most painful lesson of all, being true) that she is in love with him. But at this point—she is twenty now, her adolescence over—Aurora asserts her own will, and the aunt dies and leaves her to go her own way.

The composite maternal image in the portrait then splits into two opposite figures: virtuous Marian Erle and wicked Lady Waldemar, the victimized innocent and the predatory sophisticate, the good mother and the bad. They retain traces of mythic doubleness, their oxymoronic names linking them to nature and the preternatural: *Marian Erle*, virgin mother of Christ and pagan fairy, Lady *Waldemar* (wald-e-mar), the forest and the sea. And while Marian eventually becomes a mother herself, virgin in spirit if not in fact, she first appears as a daughter, the object of repeated maternal betrayals—the definitive ones being, like the aunt's attempt to give Aurora to Romney, sexual. Her mother tries to sell her to a man; and Lady Waldemar, the "woman-serpent" (6:1102) whose beautiful milk-white breasts are bared only for display (5:619–27), hands her over under the pretense of maternal affection to a still more depraved woman who in turn delivers her to a Parisian brothel. All this, says Marian, is "only what my mother would have done, [. . .] A motherly, right damnable good turn" (7:9–10).

As a mother herself, however, Marian becomes the object of Aurora's hunger and quest, "Whom still I've hungered after more than bread" (6:454). Having fled to Paris to escape from Lady Waldemar, the false mother she thinks Romney is going to marry, Aurora catches sight of Marian's face, which rises into her consciousness like that of a drowned person rising to the surface of the water—"a dead face, known once alive" (6:239), charged with the contradictions of the mother's portrait: "old" and "new" (6:240), familiar and fantastic, spectral and real, innocent and apparently (since she is holding a child) sexually impure.[9] This momentary vision inaugurates a dreamlike, directionless search through the streets of Paris that is Aurora's version of a knightly quest. When she finds Marian, she immediately offers her "a home for you / And me and no one else" (6:458–59), as if proposing marriage.

Her attempt at rescue is more effective than any of Romney's, since it does not imply domination, and it is not punished like his. It does not work, however, quite as she plans. First she escorts Marian in proper knightly fashion, "As if I led her by a narrow plank / Across devouring waters" (6:482–83); but Marian wants to go home to her child, and so in turn (repetition stressing the reversal) "she led / The way, and I, as by a narrow plank / Across devouring waters, followed her, / Stepping by her footsteps, breathing by her breath" (6:500–503), like a child following her mother. The "home for you / And me and no one else" must have room for a baby, for although Marian is indeed a loving mother, Aurora is neither her husband nor her child. And insofar as Aurora thinks that she is pursuing the bad mother rather than the good, hoping to save a fallen woman (a favorite preoccupation of Victorian men and a charitable activity engaged in by many Victorian women, including Christina Rossetti), she is thwarted by the discovery that Marian did not acquiesce in—was not even conscious of—her sexual violation and is therefore not morally "fallen" at all. They settle down together in a little house in Italy, but she remains outside the charmed circle of mother and child into which she had hoped "to creep [. . .] somewhere, humbly" (7:392). Marian cannot satisfy her restless longing, and the vision of the sea king that summons Romney replaces Marian's drowned face as subaqueous object of desire.

Marian is the last and most benign of the large company of rejecting mothers who crowd the pages of the poem: Aurora's mother and aunt, Marian's mother, Lady Waldemar and her agent, as well as Marian's friend Lucy's horrible grandmother and the various passing sights, voices, and images that stain the fabric of the text with the colors of maternal cruelty. When Lucy dies her grandmother "Scream[s] feebly, like a baby overlain" (4:63)—as if she were simultaneously an evil mother and an abused child—to avoid being mistaken for the corpse. Among the pro- letarian guests at Romney's wedding Aurora sees "babies, hanging like a rag / Forgotten on their mother's neck,—poor mouths, / Wiped clean of mother's milk by mother's blow / Before they are taught her cursing" (4:576–79). She hears a woman describe herself as "tender": "I never banged a child at two years old / And drew blood from him, but I sobbed for it" (4:821–23). At the other end of the social scale, Lady Waldemar talks of "babes [stretching] at baubles held up out of reach / By spiteful nurses" (5:991–92), and Romney says bitterly that "things went smoothly as a baby drugged" (8:922). Marian generalizes: "God, free me from my mother, [. . .] These mothers are too dreadful" (3:1063–64), and "When mothers fail us, can we help ourselves?" (6:1229). Like Aurora, Marian received parental love among the hills, from nature, and is forced to leave them by a sexual awakening; when her mother tries to sell her to a man, the hills become tainted and terrifying, like the mother, and she cannot return. In the most dreadful of all the images of maternal corruption, Aurora compares natural innocence to "babes / Found whole and sleeping by the spotted breast / Of one a full day dead" (4:1064– 66). Nurture is most typically imagined, as in Aurora's dream of Italy, in terms of breasts and milk—"mother's breasts / Which, round the new- made creatures hanging there, / Throb luminous and harmonious" (5:16– 18). The imagery defines the quest for the mother as a yearning for the paradise of infancy (or perhaps one should say, makes explicit what lost Edens in poetry are apt to mean): a quest that by definition has to fail.

The representation of motherhood and the loss of Eden is marked as a woman's not only by its extreme literalness but also by the extraordinary balancing of the rejected child's pain on the one side by maternal am- bivalence on the other: impulses of exceeding tenderness, and fear that motherhood costs a woman, figuratively or literally, her life. "Our Lady of the Passion" is "stabbed with swords / Where the Babe sucked" (1:160– 61). "The mother's rapture slew" Aurora's mother (1:35). Pregnancy makes Marian an outcast, and after her child is born she is dead to everything but him. "I'm nothing more / But just a mother" (6:823–24). "This ghost of Marian loves no more / [. . .] except the child" (9:389– 90). A fine emblematic set-piece shows mother and child in the Flor- entine garden: Marian knelt,

And peeled a new fig from that purple heap
In the grass beside her, turning out the red
To feed her eager child (who sucked at it
With vehement lips across a gap of air
As he stood opposite, face and curls a-flame
With that last sun-ray, crying "Give me, give,"
And stamping with imperious baby-feet,
We're all born princes).

(8:8–15)

The kneeling mother and haloed child are like figures in a Florentine painting, a "madonna of the fig," but the child's imperious demand to suck what the mother withholds (a fig instead of a breast) gives an odd turn to the sacred story. Even Marian, who gives everything, does not give enough.

Visions of filial tyranny (inspired partly, no doubt, by the poet's own experience, although the more lurid version in "The Runaway Slave" precedes the birth of Pen) occur much less frequently than those of maternal hostility. Nevertheless, they are obviously interdependent, and they reinforce Aurora's resistance to marriage. While daughters without exception suffer from maternal withdrawal or treachery, male children (like Marian's, or a male poet to whom Aurora compares herself [5:524], or the prospective suitor who is "a good son [. . .] To a most obedient mother" [5:883–84]) command maternal attention—they all seem to have "the master's look" that provoked the runaway slave to murder her infant son. Aurora thinks that children are "given to sanctify / A woman" (6:728–29)—that is, to make her perfect in self-sacrifice. And like the speaker in "Bertha in the Lane" she assumes that children demand their mother's lives, if not their deaths as well.

Had she married Romney when he first asked, she thinks after she has been in London for a while,

I might have been a common woman now
And happier, less known and less left alone,
Perhaps a better woman after all,
With chubby children hanging on my neck
To keep me low and wise. Ah me, the vines
That bear such fruit are proud to stoop with it.
The palm stands upright in a realm of sand.

(2:513–19)

She is "a printing woman who has lost her place / (The sweet safe corner of the household fire / Behind the heads of children)" (5:806–8). She takes for granted that if she had children she would not write, but she regrets the children she does not have. Her delight in Marian's son is like Barrett Browning's extravagant baby-worship. While she was writing *Aurora Leigh*, Barrett Browning's friendship with the great singer Adelaide Kemble Sartoris, who had retired from the stage when she married, showed her precisely the predicament that Aurora fears. "The artist has revived in the woman," Barrett Browning reported in 1854, and "the domestic life, though perfectly happy, seems narrow for the soul. She tells me that she feels like a healthy person whose feet & hands are tied—& she suffers yearnings towards her great lost public career, even under the eyes of her beautiful youngest child who has the face of an angel."[10]

The traditional metaphor that poets give birth to poems holds no solace for a woman racked by doubts about maternity: quite the contrary. Aurora is the murderous poet-mother of stillborn children.

> I ripped my verses up,
> And found no blood upon the rapier's point;
> The heart in them was just an embryo's heart
> Which never yet had beat, that it should die.

(3:245–48)

When she felt something greater burning within her, she could not give it birth (3:251–60), although later she "felt / [Her] heart's life throbbing in [her] verse to show / It lived" (3:338–40). Later still, however, she compares herself with Niobe (5:413–20), all her poem-children dead. Images of creativity as failed maternity are part of her more general realization that metaphorical satisfactions cannot replace real ones, just as the satisfactions of art do not suffice for life.

This is what Barrett Browning herself had found. Aurora's experience of the fruits and failures of a literary career roughly parallels her creator's, although it is much compressed in time (she is twenty when she goes to London, thirty at the poem's end) and is less idiosyncratic and more like that of an ordinary hardworking woman of letters. She is well read but not remarkably learned, and no particular importance is placed on her knowledge of Greek. Instead of translating Aeschylus or learning Hebrew, she writes prose for a living—anonymous pieces "for cyclopaedias, magazines, / And weekly papers" (3:310–11), reviews, light tales—as well as composing poems. She dismisses her youthful works as "lifeless imitations" (1:974): odes, bucolics, didactics, epics, elegies, and love songs, a varied list that encompasses Barrett Browning's early productions as well as kinds more typical of other women writers. She starts her adult career with ballads (as popular as Barrett Browning's, evidently), sonnets, and a long descriptive poem (5:84–133), and then composes the poem of modern life that establishes her success—a success like Barrett Browning's in 1844, one imagines, and a poem like *Aurora Leigh*.

Like Barrett Browning, Aurora moves to London to establish her literary career, shuts herself up in a room to write, and arouses a good deal of public attention. Unlike her author, however, she lives alone (except for a servant, of course) and earns most of the money she lives on. If we think only of the major nineteenth-century women poets— Emily Brontë, Dickinson, Rossetti, and Barrett Browning herself— or the aspirants to art who had no rooms of their own to write in and whose names we do not know, this may seem more revolutionary and fantastic than it actually was. Felicia Hemans and Letitia Landon lived by their pens. So did Caroline Norton, who was paired with Barrett Browning in Horne's *A New Spirit of the Age*. So did her friends among women writers: Mary Russell Mitford, Harriet Martineau, Anna Jameson, Margaret Fuller. And of course there was George Sand, who went to Paris to live in a garret, forge a career, and move with a man's freedom through the world.[11]

But none of these women offered her acceptable models for living. Mrs. Hemans, Mrs. Jameson, and Mrs. Norton were separated from their husbands, and Mrs. Norton's most effective works were her attacks on the divorce and custody laws by which she was herself oppressed. The names of Landon, Sand, and Norton were tarred by sexual scandal, and Harriet Martineau's uterus became a matter of public debate. It is part of the boldness of the poem that although Aurora is young and beautiful she lives alone in London and is apparently immune to scandal, as Barrett Browning pointedly has her explain: "I am a woman of repute; / No fly-blow gossip ever specked my life; / My name is clean" (9:264–66). Her affections having been usurped by her cousin, in an unimpeachable attachment sanctioned by her aunt and both their fathers, during her ten years in London no other romantic issues ever arise, and she gives Marian a highly disagreeable lecture on the wickedness of sexual sin. Barrett Browning's awareness of what people would be likely to think of Aurora's independence without such safeguards is clear in her remark in 1854 that the young American sculptor, Harriet Hosmer, living alone in Rome, "emancipates the eccentric life of a perfectly 'emancipated female' from all shadow of blame by the purity of her's" (*LMRM* 3:409). The heroine of a story that deals with rape and prostitution would have to guard her own name with especial care. Still, Swinburne remarked that "a young lady of family who lodges by herself in Grub Street, preserves her reputation, lives on her pen, and dines out in Mayfair is hardly a figure for serious fiction."[12] *Aurora Leigh*, however, is not just "fiction," but a poem, and as such obeys different rules of seriousness.

Barrett Browning used sometimes to remark that few women writers were "womanly" or happy. It struck her as sadly ironical that the first names of both Felicia Hemans and Letitia Landon mean "happiness" (*LMRM* 1:170), and when Margaret Fuller and her husband and child were drowned she consoled herself with the thought that the "socialistic" book Fuller was writing about Italy would have drawn such ferocious attacks that "it was better for her to go": "Was she happy in anything, I wonder? She told me that she never was" (*LMRM* 3:309). Barrett Browning gives a distinctively Victorian articulation of the Romantic commonplace, particularly associated with Byron, that artists are unsociable and miserable. Her early works had been shadowed by the widespread Victorian conviction that one cannot have both art and life, both love and fame, and until the end of the poem Aurora fears this too. As a girl the tastes that make her a poet also make her shrink from ordinary social intercourse, as Barrett Browning's had done, and later they separate her from Romney. When Lady Waldemar asserts that "You stand outside, / You artist women, of the common sex" (3:406–7), "your hearts / Being starved to make your heads" (3:409–10), or Romney accuses Aurora of having lost her "natural instinct (like a beast) / Through intellectual culture" (8:1230–31), they articulate the paradigmatic fear of the Victorian poet—Tennyson, Arnold, Clough, and often Browning, too—that art means isolation and intellection kills the feelings. This fear was even stronger for women, whose nature (they were authoritatively told and usually believed) was essentially emotional. Despite the immense satisfaction of leading her own life and doing her own work, she feels cut off from experience. Romney is "sunburnt by the glare of life" (4:1140), while she is pale (4:1143–45), and grand assertions that art is "life upon the larger scale" (4:1152) do not alleviate her loneliness.

"The end of woman (or of man, I think) / Is not a book" (7:883–84). Aurora says this, although not until she has published her book. Elizabeth Barrett had also felt the desolation of a life apparently destined to issue in nothing but print, and Aurora's problem is not so much how to write—success seems to come to her inevitably, if not exactly easily, as it did to

Barrett Browning—but how to be happy. She does not enjoy dealing with readers or the professional literary world, although she describes them amusingly enough, and fame brings satisfactions but not happiness. No matter what metaphor she turns to, art and life remain distinct and she cannot make success in one feel like success in the other. Poems are not living children, and unlike Pygmalion she cannot create an object fine enough to love (5:400–413). There is no straightforward connection between her life and what she creates. Shedding her "life-blood" (5:356) into her work does not make it live, while pain still hurts even if it is transmuted into art (5:365–73). "I cannot love: I only find / The rhyme for love" (5:895–96).

Nor, despite conventional identifications of women with works of art, is love for her poems enough.

> How dreary 'tis for women to sit still,
> On winter nights by solitary fires,
> And hear the nations praising them far off,
> Too far! ay, praising our quick sense of love,
> Our very heart of passionate womanhood,
> Which could not beat so in the verse without
> Being present also in the unkissed lips
> And eyes undried because there's none to ask
> The reason they grew moist.
>
> (5:439–47)

This was not just Aurora's experience, either: Mrs Gaskell set these lines as the epigraph to her *Life of Charlotte Brontë,* and Mrs. Hemans's Properzia Rossi, a sculptor, not only acknowledges the worthlessness of fame but actually dies of unrequited love.[13] But Aurora tries to scold away her self-pity: "it's pitiful / To wail like unweaned babes and suck our thumbs / Because we're hungry" (5:488–90) for love. And despite the proven insufficiency of fame, she does not, as Barrett Browning had grandly if rather prematurely done in 1833, renounce it.

She resolves to be self-sufficient.

> We women are too apt to look to one,
> Which proves a certain impotence in art. (5:43–44)

> Yet, so, I will not.—This vile woman's way
> Of trailing garments shall not trip me up:
> I'll have no traffic with the personal thought
> In Art's pure temple. Must I work in vain,

>   Without the approbation of a man?
>   It cannot be; it shall not.
>
>   (5:59–64)

But it is. "Books succeed, / And lives fail" (7:704–5), and without Romney she is miserable.

She complains bitterly that independence is against woman's nature:

>   we yearn to lose ourselves
>   And melt like white pearls in another's wine,
>   He seeks to double himself by what he loves,
>   And make his drink more costly by our pearls.
>
>   (5:1078–81)

Envying male writers the mothers, wives, and children who sweeten their success (5:519–40), she assumes that a woman with a family would melt her life into theirs—milk for babies, milky pearls for men—and so liquefied, could not write. Being orphaned is the precondition of her literary existence, just as Barrett Browning could not have written *Aurora Leigh*, with its luridly imagined forays into lower-class life, pointed criticism of social customs, and rapturous celebrations of marriage, if she still feared to vex her father.[14] She yields to the love she had shrunk from as feminine weakness only after establishing herself as a poet, creating an indissoluble identity, and redefining her relations with Romney so as to ensure her autonomy. At the end we know—because Romney says she will, because she has so firmly defined herself as a poet that we cannot imagine her as anything else, and because we know that Barrett Browning did—that she will go on writing.

Romney's jumbled heap of conventional notions about women coalesce into a mirror that shows Aurora a distorted but all too recognizable image of herself. At first he is reverential and infuriating:

>   "Mere women, personal and passionate,
>   You give us doating mothers, and perfect wives,
>   Sublime Madonnas, and enduring saints!
>   We get no Christ from you,—and verily
>   We shall not get a poet, in my mind."
>
>   (2:221–25)

In his proposal of marriage she reads contempt for women ("Anything does for a wife" [2:367]), and although she is mistaken in thinking that he does not love her, she is right about his contempt, kindly as it is. It hurts her because she shares it, just as Elizabeth Barrett did when she admitted in 1846 that women "as they *are* (whatever they *may be*)" are inferior in "instruction, capacity, wholeness of intellect" to men (*RB-EBB* 2:828). She acknowledges that the trivial occupations gentlewomen call "work"—decorating slippers, stools, cushions—deserve the low valuation men put on them (1:455–65), and much of her self-development consists of efforts to overcome the characteristic weakness of her sex. Years after she has angrily repudiated Romney's condescension she still sees herself through his eyes and despairs of deserving his esteem. "It seems as if I had a man in me / Despising such a woman" (7:213–14).

She frequently accuses herself of behaving like a woman, especially when she fails in self-control. "O woman's vile remorse" (2:523), she says, or, when she scolds her maid, "what a pettish, petty thing I grow,— / A mere mere woman, a mere flaccid nerve" (3:36–37). "Put away / This weakness" she tells herself sternly, "the poor conscious trouble of blood / That's called the woman merely" (7:228–32). Women can't control their bodies: they blush (2:701–4), or weep for tiredness (7:204–10), or (metaphorically) can't open their hands with life-giving openness (3:254–55). Feminists talk but don't do anything, "prate of woman's rights, / Of woman's mission, woman's function" (8:819–20)—proving what men already knew, that women talk. "*Que la femme parle,*" Browning had said of George Sand.[15] After her first literary successes Aurora feels "the silent finger of [Romney's] scorn / Prick every bubble of my frivolous fame" (3:234–35). His imagined scorn diminishes even her best work into something "foolish, feeble, and afraid" (8:273).

And if she agrees with Romney that women are weak, she also agrees (as most mid-Victorian feminists did) that they should be loving and tender, what Barrett Browning called "womanly." She blames herself for having abandoned him (as she thinks) to the snares of Lady Waldemar:

> Now, if I had been a woman, such
> As God made women, to save men by love,—
> By just my love I might have saved this man,
> And made a nobler poem for the world
> Than all I have failed in.
>
> (7:184–88)

But then she turns on herself again and mocks women's foolish quixotry (7:215–27). Barrett Browning had long suspected that many womanly virtues (her mother's submissiveness, her own churchgoing to please her aunt) were only weakness by another name, and Aurora refuses to sacrifice her independence for them. Her tenderness is bestowed only on those who, like her dead father, cannot threaten her autonomy; and while her assertions of the primacy of love may be antifeminist and retrogressive even in her own terms, she never in fact chooses love at the price of art or self-fulfillment.

For although she doubts her own strength and worries that she is deficient in tenderness, she does not for a moment accept Romney's denigration of poetry and women poets. They agree on the overriding importance, for both men and women, of work ("heaven itself is only work / To a surer issue" [8:724–25]—a creed in which many eminent Victorians would concur), and eventually he acknowledges that her work is more important than his. Art and love, vocation and marriage, ambition and womanliness are reconciled through a series of revisions of the power relations between men and women and concomitantly, between poetry and social action: between, that is, different ideas about what constitutes valid and powerful work. The Carlylean imperative to *work* that resounds through Victorian England is applied here to women as well as to men and includes, as for Carlyle it usually did not, writing poems. This is a highly topical anticipation of the feminist campaign to provide employment for women, as both a financial and a moral necessity, that began in 1857 with the publication of Barbara Bodichon's *Women and Work*.[16] Romney does not doubt that women should work—when he asks someone to marry him, he hastens to point out that he wants her to work with him—but he offends Aurora by asserting not only that women cannot be very good poets, but that alleviating human suffering matters more than poetry anyway. She retorts that she has her own "vocation,—work to do" (2:455), and furthermore that only poetry can effect real social change. To the charge that women care only about individuals and cannot generalize, she replies that while poets, like women, work through the particular, "a poet's individualism" is necessary to accomplish the philanthropist's universal goals (2:478–79). "It takes a soul / To move a body: it takes a high-souled man, / To move the masses, even to a cleaner stye: / [. . . .] your Fouriers failed, / Because not poets enough to understand / That life develops from within"(2:479–85).

Victorian writers' faith in the social function of literature was grounded in their belief that art can arouse in individual readers the feelings that bind humanity together. In *Hard Times* Dickens appeals to the loving heart against the cold abstractions of utilitarianism, and Tennyson in *In*

Memoriam shows how feeling counters religious doubt ("the heart / Stood up and answered 'I have felt' ")[17] and confirms social ties. Barrett Browning draws the logical but unusual conclusion that women's expertise in the sphere of the emotions should make them especially good artists as well. It was commonly thought around mid-century that by bridging with sympathy the gap between the classes writers could further the cause of social reform: Disraeli (who described in *Sybil* an England divided into two nations, the rich and the poor), Kingsley, Gaskell, Carlyle, Dickens, and others took upon themselves the responsibility of making the sufferings of the poor visible and palpable. Barrett Browning particularly admired the courage and effectiveness of Gaskell and of Harriet Beecher Stowe, irreproachably respectable wives and mothers who took on the dangerous topics of seduction and slavery, and she did her own part with her "Cry of the Children," her poems against slavery, and *Aurora Leigh*.

Aurora is appalled by the poor in general—baffled by their brute misery, terrified by their hostility and violence. They haunt the poem with the demonic vitality of nightmare. But she indignantly champions poor women when they become the sexual victims of men and the objects of virtuous women's scorn. Despite a sojourn in a Parisian brothel and an illegitimate baby Marian turns out (when Aurora stops scolding and lets her tell her story) to be transcendently pure, and we are even invited to sympathize, although from a discreet distance, with Marian's friend Rose, who has become a prostitute. Here, too, Barrett Browning is in tune with the feminists, for whom prostitution was becoming a central issue.[18] Like the feminists, she wanted to make respectable women see, sympathize with, and ameliorate the ills of women who were considered unfit for them even to read about, "a book," in the words of Dante Gabriel Rossetti's "Jenny," "In which pure women may not look."[19] Prostitution is the social evil that the poem cares most to cure, and Aurora asserts that if art teaches men to reverence the body they will cease to "Make offal of their daughters for its use" (7:866). Since Romney directs his materialistic philanthropy toward "the body's satisfaction and no more" (8:416), *his* efforts to help prostitutes (3:550–52) are bound to fail.

Artists lead the way in the most practical sense, then, to a better world. Barrett Browning thought that the French socialists from whose ideas Romney's are derived, while often "full of pure and noble aspiration, the most virtuous of men and the most benevolent," would have to impose their ideal society as a crushing despotism, since human nature can advance only by inner impulse and one step at a time (*LEBB* 2:61).

Aside from socialism, however, Aurora thinks that they order these things better in France; she shares both Matthew Arnold's fearful contempt for popular movements and his admiration for the rationality and seriousness of the French, their dreaming after "some ideal good" (6:56), and like Barrett Browning she has high hopes of Louis Napoleon and democracy. Poets, she says, should be democrats, not averting their eyes from ugliness, poverty, and pain. She shares Romney's robust scorn for the timid pleasures of pastoral art and resolves to look boldly, as he does, on common, ugly, diseased, distorted human forms and find the divine within them; the scenes among the poor are Barrett Browning's own attempts to do this. But the new life that Romney thrusts on people who don't want it only heaps fuel on their incendiary rage, and he finally realizes that people can only be affected through their souls, and that poetry does this best. Women and poets, not political theorists or practical men of affairs, will change the world.

Such claims for the grand renovating force of poetry are for the most part Victorian commonplaces derived from Romanticism: poets, Shelley said, are the unacknowledged legislators of mankind, and in the preface to *The Battle of Marathon* the young author explains that poetry, which "elevates the mind to Heaven, kindles within it unwonted fires, and bids it throb with feelings exalting to its nature" (1:2), is "the parent of liberty" (1:9). Barrett Browning revives these commonplaces with considerably more verve and confidence than other Victorian poets were able to muster, and with the genuinely revolutionary addition of an implicit claim that poetry's true subjects belong to women's sphere. It is not just that poets *can* write about contemporary life, instead of the old male-dominated themes, but that they *must.* "All actual heroes are essential men, / And all men possible heroes: every age, / Heroic in proportions" (5:151–53).

> [Poets'] sole work is to represent the age,
> Their age, not Charlemagne's,—this live, throbbing age,
> That brawls, cheats, maddens, calculates, aspires,
> And spends more passion, more heroic heat,
> Betwixt the mirrors of its drawing-rooms,
> Than Roland with his knights at Roncesvalles.
>
> (5:202–7)

In drawing rooms, of course, there are women; but although there is indeed a fine and funny scene in a drawing room (Lord Howe's party, where men chatter about politics and religion with comic inanity and gossip about their betters), the spheres occupied by women in the poem reach far beyond domestic walls. Barrett Browning always refers to heroes, like poets, as generically male—even in this poem about a heroic woman poet—but the modern world itself is marked as female in an image borrowed from Tennyson: the "Mother-Age," an inert phrase from "Locksley Hall" that Barrett Browning makes shockingly literal and alive.[20] "Hide me from my deep emotion, O thou wondrous Mother-Age," Tennyson's hero innocuously cries; but Aurora Leigh, astonishingly, urges poets to

> catch
> Upon the burning lava of a song
> The full-veined, heaving, double-breasted Age:
> That, when the next shall come, the men of that
> May touch the impress with reverent hand, and say
> "Behold,—behold the paps we all have sucked!
> This bosom seems to beat still."
>
> (5:214–20)

Poets should instill reverence for the mother-age instead of scorning it as men are apt to do, and should display its essential heroism instead of showing up its lack of heroes or indulging in the retrogressive medievalism which depicts men as "half knight, half sheep-lifter" and women as "half chattel and half queen" (5:195–96). *Aurora Leigh* argues that modern poets should celebrate modern heroes, and it does so.

The other grand abstract subject of the poem, nature, is female too, but not quite as it had been for the Romantic poets. At the beginning of book 5 Aurora hopes to speak "in mysterious tune / With man and nature": with the "lava-lymph / That trickles [. . .] adown the finger of God" into the world, the impassioned life of nature's seasons, and the seasons of the human heart, which include "sexual passion," "mother's breasts," and the ecstasy of death (5:1–24). She wants her words to be "imperious as the primal rhythm / Of that theurgic nature" (5:29–30). Insofar as the things on this list other than the inseminating God are gendered, they are female. Nature and impassioned humanity will be her theme, imperious primal nature her inspiration; she will reclaim the heritage of Romantic nature poetry, Christianizing and feminizing it as she does so. Tennyson and Arnold, with eyes informed by science, recoiled from their visions of a nature untouched by moral values and indifferent to human concens. But Barrett Browning, whose imagination still finds God immanent in creation, held on to the Romantic vision of living nature even when its life seemed most obscure and treacherous, and her pain at being unable to see nature as a benign mother at least meant that the Romantic vision was not a dead convention for her.[21]

For Aurora, as for Barrett Browning, nature is officially subordinate to God, but it is untouched by the curse that had prompted the deadly sympathy of the poet in "The Poet's Vow." God is the "supreme Artist" (5:435), the world his living art, and earth is alive not in the "unnatural vampire-uses" (5:116) of pagan mythology but with a real life bestowed by Christ. Nature is "the body of our body [. . .] / Indubitably human like this flesh" (5:117–18) and (in a rare irruption of overt Sweden-borgianism) "allied / By issue and symbol, by significance / And correspondence, to that spirit-world / Outside the limits of our space and time" (5:121–24). And yet despite several wonderful descriptions of nature and ecstatic formulations of its meaning Aurora declares that cities make better poems: no one sings on Sinai or Parnassus (3:190–93), and "forests chant / Their anthems to themselves, and leave you dumb" (3:193–94). On the patriarchal heights nature is too grand, and lower down, where the women are, it is too exclusive.

For the nature that corresponds to her deepest experience and inspires some of her richest poetry represents female self-sufficiency rather than maternal generosity or redemption by God. It is embodied in the self-absorbed Tuscan forests that enchanted Barrett Browning with their "fresh, unworn, uncivilised, world-before-the-flood look" (*LEBB* 2:130) rather than the English earth and hills of "The Tempest" and "The Lost Bower" that are stricken by storms and owe fealty to God. Instead of access to heaven, it offers the dream of a prelapsarian earthly paradise. But such a paradise is by definition gone forever. When Aurora returns to Italy the "old miraculous mountains" (7:468) first rise into sight as "ambassador for God" (7:466), the parent she seeks is her father, and she roams and writes more about Florence than about her beloved hills. Without her "irrecoverable child-innocence" (7:1104) she has returned only to an empty nest (7:1109), where the creatures with whom she had once shared Edenic fellowship "all seemed farther off, / No longer mine, nor like me" (7:1099–1100). And yet nature's elusiveness is also the sign of an invigorating potency. Nature is even less responsive to her desire, she tells the hills, than

> when in heat
> Vain lightnings catch at your inviolate tops
> And tremble while ye are steadfast. Still ye go

> Your own determined, calm, indifferent way
> Toward sunrise.
>
> (5:1271–75)

Instead of dreadful manifestations of divine paternal power, Jove's thunder that turns the milk, there is only heat lightning trembling harmlessly against the hills. Milk is withheld, but it is not spoiled.[22]

Nature provides Aurora, then, with an image of female potency that she finds nowhere else, and in which she can participate by becoming (like Marian, another rejected daughter) a mother herself. Barrett Browning had been afraid that being a mother and writing poetry were mutually exclusive alternatives—the one requiring self-sacrifice, the other self-assertion—and before her return to Italy Aurora has the same fear. But Barrett Browning was a mother when she wrote *Aurora Leigh*, her boldest and strongest work, and since it is taken for granted throughout the poem that children are the inevitable consequence of marriage, we can assume that when Aurora finally accepts Romney she is accepting motherhood too. By writing *Aurora Leigh*, moreover, she joined the company of women novelists, a stronger and bolder group than women poets. In England Aurora remembered Italy as

> My multitudinous mountains, sitting in
> The magic circle, with the mutual touch
> Electric, panting from their full deep hearts
> Beneath the influent heavens, and waiting for
> Communion and commission.
>
> (1:622–26)

Barrett Browning's relations with other women writers and with women readers, like Aurora's sisterly partnership with Marian as second mother to her child, may perhaps be said to place her in such magical communion, and it is pleasant to think that (although Barrett Browning never knew it) Emily Dickinson was extensively and minutely influenced by passages like this one. And Aurora herself is the object of younger women's rather embarrassing emulation. Her example teaches Kate Ward, newly engaged to the painter Vincent Carrington, to (in Carrington's words) "Grow insolent [. . .] against men" (7:615): an insolence neatly symbolized by Kate's covering her "nude harmonious arm" (7:597), which Carrington wants to paint, with a cloak patterned on Aurora's. All Aurora's friends, curiously enough, are men, but the sororal bond with Marian is deeper than the differences of class and education that circumscribe friendship, and as a poet she too effects something like a "magic circle" of female connection.[23]

The power of mothers is heightened by the weakness or absence of fathers and the comparative impotence of men in general. Marian wants no father for her child. Aurora's father seems never to have accomplished anything, and we learn little more about Romney's than that he was cursed with the unpromising name of Vane Leigh. Nor do the men have the imaginative appeal that the women—Aurora's mother, Marian, Lady Waldemar—do, her father and Romney being the objects of rather chilly and superior satire and depending on women for their substantial life. Her father "was flooded with a passion unaware, / His whole provisioned and complacent past / Drowned out" (1:68–70) by sudden desire, but his wife's early death left him one "Whom love had unmade from a common man / But not completed to an uncommon man" (1:183–84). Like Romney, he is ineffectual and incomplete alone.

The unusual distribution of strength and weakness between women and men does not, however, point toward an androgynous ideal. Maternal functions are strictly reserved for women, and men who try to preempt them ignominiously fail. Aurora's father proves an awkward and unsatisfactory mother, and Romney recapitulates his disastrous career as a social reformer through a series of perverse images which show him trying even less successfully to be a mother to the world. He had imagined the poor as prisoners inside the "Phalarian bull, society" (8:388), which simultaneously holds them in its male womb and tramples them with its hoofs (8:385–93). Then he saw them as the "great famishing carnivorous mouth" of a "huge, deserted, callow, blind bird Thing" which he tried to feed with worms (8:396–400). Philanthropy, he says, puts up as its sign "Some red colossal cow with mighty paps / A Cyclops' fingers could not strain to milk," but all it produces is a "saucerful / Of curds" (8:849–52). The objects of his misguided maternalism are not grateful, and fears that he will try to nurture his poor neighbors impel the local population to destroy the ancestral house which he has turned into a phalanstery and, the description suggests, a womb: it has covered floors, "Carved wainscots, panelled walls, the favourite slide / For draining off a martyr (or a rogue) [. . .] stairs [. . .] slippery darkness" (8:967–75). He returns to Aurora stripped of maternal attributes, "like a punished child" (8:362).

What Romney properly represents is the paternal line, patriarchal culture, and patriarchal power, and he represents them at their best.

Driven by a noble sympathy for human suffering to acts of self-defeating excess, he is superior to his smug neighbors and even to his generous friend, Lord Howe, who is protected by his wayward and self-indulgent intellect and his immensely comfortable life from committing himself to any line of action at all. Despite a good deal of programmatic and self-dramatizing foolishness (summed up in the aborted wedding through which he had planned to make an edifying symbolic spectacle of himself), we like him for his fits of discouragement and self-doubt, his tart, sad wit, his generous affection, and his indefatigable altruism. But his virtues cannot make male privilege tolerable. He bears the family name (which Aurora can retain only by marrying him), inherits the family fortune, receives a man's education and easy access to the world (for want of which "A woman's always younger than a man / At equal years" [2:329–30]), sits in Parliament, smiles with the superiority of one who has been to school at Aurora's "lady's Greek / Without the accents" (2:76–77), and laughs like Mr. Barrett at the idea of taking poetry seriously. His first gesture of affection is to touch the head of the lonely child, "Bent down on woman's work," and her first rejection of him is to shake off "The stranger's touch that took my father's place" (1:543–46). One father was enough.

Romney, male culture, and England are the Roman side of the opposition between Greece and Rome that Elizabeth Barrett had formulated when she was a child. She had identified herself with Greece and Bro with Rome, and although she loved Bro, she did not warm to Roman virtues. Italy is Aurora's mother country, where nature is mythic and alive, passion flourishes, and the poem originates and is resolved. England is her father's country, always somewhat alien and cold, and bears the father's culture. In England God and nature maintain the conventional hierarchy of gender. Aurora "drew / The elemental nutriment and heat / From nature, as earth feels the sun at nights, / Or as a babe sucks surely in the dark" (1:473–76). English nature is "tamed / And grown domestic," like a cackling hen (1:634–35), and the Malvern Hills, where Marian grows up, are less unambiguously female and nurturing than the Italian countryside and as in "The Lost Bower" are explicitly subject to a God that transcends nature. The hierarchy holds in language, too: Italian is Aurora's mother tongue, English her father's, but despite her nostalgia for the sweet soft Tuscan sounds she writes in English and in England. Since the only words of her mother's that she remembers ("Hush, hush—here's too much noise" [1:17]) enjoin silence and belie the speaker's feelings, there is no mother tongue for her to use.[24]

Except for the futile teachings provided by her aunt, she gets all her significant education from her father, from whom she learns Greek and Latin until puberty, like Elizabeth Barrett from Mr. McSwiney (who left Hope End when she was about fourteen). Like Elizabeth Barrett in the library at Hope End she steals the rest of her education from her father's books, which she consumes with "terror, haste, victorious joy" (1:840)— language that recalls the note of excess with which the young Elizabeth Barrett described her incursions into classical territory. She finds boxes of his books (paternal food) in a garret:

> where, creeping in and out
> Among the giant fossils of my past,
> Like some small nimble mouse between the ribs
> Of a mastodon, I nibbled here and there.
>
> (1:835–38)

Nibbling at this vast parental fossil, she learns the taste of poetry. Eventually, however, she sells his books for the money that takes her to Italy.

And yet, although she helps herself to what she wants from the books and discards the rest with apparent ease, she has still to locate a woman poet's place in the poetic tradition inherited—or stolen, like Promethean fire—from the fathers. She explores the roles traditionally allotted to women in the metaphorical structure of poetry and finds that she fits none of them. Romney tells her that poets, like Miriam, should not sing until Moses has destroyed the power of Egypt (2:171), an injunction to wait upon the deeds of God and men that she repudiates when she says that although poets do not destroy armies, they can have grandly destructive visions (such as London disappearing in the fog, drowned like pharoah's army). Such visions make them "feel as conquerors though [they] did not fight" (3:201) and enable them to sing. But while she easily refutes the idea that poets should celebrate male heroism (as she had done in *The Battle of Marathon*), similar ideas are more insidious. Lady Waldemar calls her a muse, as if a woman artist has to fill all the female roles in a poem and be her own inspiration, and although she denies that she is even so much as a sybil (3:363–64), the highly wrought opening passage of book 5 has the tone and structure of an invocation and is addressed not to a muse but to herself: "Aurora Leigh, be humble" (5:1).

The most compelling images of the poet, however, depict poetic inspiration as sexual subjugation by a male muse. The poet is a pipe blown by her precursors (1:887–91), like Syrinx by Pan, or Ganymede (a boy in a female role) "ravished" by Zeus's eagle (1:918–25), or Io (in whom Barrett Browning had not been interested when she translated *Prometheus Bound*) pursued by Jove (7:829–30). Aurora figures the artist most elaborately in her friend Vincent Carrington's two images of Danaë receiving Jove, one reaching upward, "overbold and hot" (3:122), an insufficient because self-seeking artist, the other prostrate and passive, representing the true artist whose self is annihilated in passionate receptivity. Lord Howe in satiric vein offers another version, likening the pains of writing poetry to those of the Delphic oracle: "the god comes down as fierce / As twenty bloodhounds, shakes you, strangles you, / Until the oracular shriek shall ooze in froth!" (5:943–45). The gender of the poet, and also the fact that the plot is impelled by sexual passion and has at its center an actual rape, foreground the literal meaning of these metaphors in a very disturbing way. Lord Howe's grotesque description of Apollo and the oracle is literalized in Marian's experience in the brothel, which drives her temporarily mad but also endows her with wisdom. And Danaë receiving Zeus with "the long hair swathed about her to the heel / Like wet seaweed" (3:129–30) foreshadows Marian, "drenched and passive" under her "waterfall" of hair, "blinded" by "all that stream / Of tresses" (3:1046–50), offered for sale (Jove's shower of gold) to a man. Aurora apparently accepts the implication of these images, which stand outside the plot to suggest that for women, writing is a kind of sexual submission, and the plot reinforces them by the fact that while Marian's narrative of her early life has to be retold by Aurora, after she has been raped she speaks eloquently for herself. Eventually, however, the images are reversed, Aurora descending in imagination, like Jove to Danaë, to the sea king with "slippery locks" (8:42).

At first there seems to be no place in a poem for a woman like Aurora except as the object of male desire, like Danaë and the muse, either speechless or speaking like Catarina only her need for love. By rejecting Romney's love and suppressing her own, Aurora repudiates that position. Instead, she explores her relationship to the usual female inhabitants of poetry, the erotic objects and mysterious Others who are neither poets nor epic protagonists. Are they possible selves, since she's a woman too? Or objects of her desire, since she's the poet? The endlessly reiterated, narrowly defined images of women in Italian art deeply impressed themselves on Barrett Browning when in Italy, for the first time in her life, painting and sculpture assaulted her senses. The multitudinous depictions of the Virgin seem to have issued in her picture of Marian, and portraits of more worldly women (especially, no doubt, those in the Pitti

Palace, where she often wandered when the Brownings rented an apart-
ment in the palace itself or across the way in Casa Guidi) in that of Lady
Waldemar. They all merge in the phantasmagoric portrait of Aurora's
mother. But eventually her relationship to all these women, who encom-
pass the normal female population of poetry as well as of Renaissance
painting, fades away. She learns that she is not one of them and that she
does not, after all, have to define herself in relation to them. She is
neither the female object of a male poem, nor the male subject for whom
they are objects of desire. This discovery frees her to marry Romney.

Alone among heroines of English *Bildungsromanen* in the nineteenth
century, Aurora follows the male pattern of development as Jerome Ham-
ilton Buckley describes it: she leaves the provinces, goes to the city, has
(in effect) two love-affairs, one debasing and one ennobling (Lady Wal-
demar, that is, and Marian Erle), and returns to her place of origin to
measure the distance she has gone.[25] The last two books compute that
distance through a reevaluation of the past in which the amatory-poetic
competition for the lowest place in the Barrett-Browning love letters and
Sonnets from the Portuguese is transferred into the realm of ideas, each of
the lovers claiming to have been wrong and denying the other's self-
denigration. They agree, however, that Romney was considerably *more*
wrong. He denounces the "male ferocious impudence" (8:328) with
which he had proposed marriage ten years before and says that he has
come "to abase [him]self, / And fasten, kneeling, on her regent brows /
A garland which I startled thence" (8:1219–21). He agrees that women
must do their own work, and that hers has been excellent. She, conceding
a good deal less, says that although she was "right upon the whole"
(8:536) she could have been gentler and less arrogant (8:497). He ac-
knowledges that his views were programmatic and materialistic and there-
fore doomed to fail; she does not dispute this, but adds that they both
erred in leaving "too small a part for God" (8:555). They agree that
spirit is more important than matter, although the material basis of life
can't be ignored.

But if he was wrong about abstract matters, she was wrong about
emotional ones. Not recognizing that "No perfect artist is developed
here / From any imperfect woman" (9:648–49), she "would not be a
woman like the rest, / A simple woman who believes in love" (9:660–
61). Having reached the level of accomplishment that she refused Rom-
ney in the first place precisely to attain, she is free to accept the demands
of love—now that they will cost her nothing. (She sounds like the young
women in Charlotte M. Yonge's immensely popular novels who learn to

value self-forgetful service to others, however trivial it may seem, more than the masculine accomplishments they yearn for; but Yonge's heroines actually do sacrifice their ambitions.) "Our work shall still be better for our love" (9:925), says Romney, who articulates the decisive reversal of gender roles that makes her acquiescence possible: "work for two, / As I, though thus restrained, for two, shall love" (9:911–12). Writing poetry, which neither Romney Leigh nor Edward Moulton-Barrett had taken seriously, is now defined as the real "work" of the world.

And the basis of that work is marriage. Aurora's quest for maternal nurture and Romney's attachment to philanthropic systems are both replaced by "the love of wedded souls": the "counterpart" of God's love, which includes "Loves filial, loves fraternal, neighbour-loves / And civic" (9:882–89). One of the most extraordinary aspects of the poem is its outspoken celebration not just of "love" but of "sexual passion, which devours the flesh / In a sacrament of souls" (5:15–16). This love is figured in an image that recalls both the Greek slave and Aurora as a blushing caryatid, but here it glows with its own free, self-generated, unembarrassed fire:

> a love so fiery hot
> It burns its natural veil of August shame,
> And stands sublimely in the nude, as chaste
> As Medicean Venus.
>
> (3:703–6)

The fusion of matter and spirit into which their conflicting philosophies resolve themselves, like the belief that God is immanent in nature and souls perceptible through flesh, teaches reverence for the body and for "sacramental," "eucharistic" (1:90–91) love. Part of the work of poetry, as of this poem, is to convey this sacramental notion of sexuality in a way that will change men's attitudes toward the social evil the poem cares most about, prostitution. By celebrating love, poetry *is* philanthropy.[26]

The conflict between love and work fades away when Aurora's work is redefined as including (rather than, as he had originally proposed, being included by) Romney's. Her clarion-blast will "blow all class-walls [Romney's main target] level as Jericho's" (9:932). Renewal in individual hearts will create "new dynasties of the race of men; / Developed whence, shall grow spontaneously / New churches, new oeconomies, new laws / Admitting freedom, new societies" (9:945–48). The poem ends with a vision of the New Jerusalem, "Beyond the circle of the conscious hills"

(9:954), which draws on the imagery of the Book of Revelations and combines in a transcendental unity Romney's vision of a new social order and Aurora's dream of nature, Barrett Browning's hopes for Italy and the fruits she expected from the spiritualist awakening. Having claimed poetry for women and women's values, it goes on to assert the supreme power of poetry even in territories still controlled by men. Female heroism has ascended through self-dependence, self-conquest, and an act of knightly rescue to the founding of a new world.

The price of female triumph, though, is male abasement. Romney's punishment seems excessive to most readers who respond to the characters and the story rather than to an abstract formulation of its meaning; he may have been wrong, but not *that* wrong. "To mean so well and fail so foul" (8:797) may be the essential human antithesis, as he says, but it seems hard nonetheless. Barrett Browning (herself inclined to allegorize the story after she had written it) explained to a friend who protested on Romney's behalf that "He had to be blinded, observe, to be made to see; just as Marian had to be dragged through the uttermost debasement of circumstances to arrive at the sentiment of personal dignity. I am sorry, but indeed it seemed necessary" (*LEBB* 2:242). But while the connection between abasement and dignity is really cause and effect, that between physical blindness and spiritual vision is at best symbolic, at worst a crude literalization or a play on words. His fate is ennobled by echoes of Milton, who also presents blindness as both a punishment and a spiritual gift.[27] But the blindness seems consequent on her needs rather than his. It is ominously linked to her name—"Shine out for two, Aurora" (9:910)—as if her light can dawn only in his darkness, and indeed it is through her words that he sees, at the end, the New Jerusalem. Punishing him for his objectifying vision ten years earlier and rendering him incapable of objectifying her again, his blindness is part of the thoroughgoing destruction of all the forms of male power that he represents: familial dominance and inheritance ("The House went out" [8:1014] with the destruction of Leigh Hall, from which nothing survived but an ancestral portrait of a woman who looks like Aurora); male control of culture (Aurora sells her father's books, and those in Leigh Hall are burned); male political and social power, which is seen as ineffective at best, destructive at worst; male contempt for women and for poetry; men's desire to make women's work the handmaid of their own. And insofar as Aurora represents Italy ("My Italy of women," Romney calls her [8:358]), the conclusion is charged with Barrett Browning's burning desire to see Italy free and powerful and her anger at

Britain's refusal to help. Since the forces Romney represents are too strong to be kept down without a tremendous exertion of force, her success requires his subjugation.

It also requires transcendence of the norms of both Victorian poetry and Victorian fiction, made possible by the union of the two. Perhaps the oddest thing about *Aurora Leigh*, after all, is the triumphantly happy ending—happy for the heroine at any rate, if not for her disempowered and humiliated lover. She gets much more than the nineteenth-century marriage plot usually allows its heroines: love *and* work *and* fame *and* independence *and* power. *The Idylls of the King, The Ring and the Book, Empedocles on Etna, Modern Love, Amours de Voyage*—all the other great long Victorian poems end in failure or loss except *In Memoriam*, which begins with loss and ends by accepting it, and heroines of novels do little better. Even Jane Eyre has no real independence and no vocation comparable to Brontë's or Barrett Browning's, and while Lucy Snowe in *Villette* has her vocation, Brontë cannot quite bring herself to let her have her lover too. George Eliot's Maggie Tulliver dies and her Dorothea Brooke exerts an unacknowledged influence as the wife of a political reformer, precisely the sort of life that Aurora indignantly spurns. It has often been remarked that women novelists do not imagine lives for their heroines that are as successful, in terms of achievement or scope for achievement, as their own.[28] But in her strange mixture of genres, Barrett Browning did what neither novelists nor poets in the Victorian period seemed able to do. The contemporary setting and novelistic elaboration of plot allow Aurora to work her way out of the passivity and subordination to which women had been relegated in poems, while at the same time the poetry establishes a context in which freedom and the heroic triumph of the spirit feel not only appropriate but possible and proves (if the poem is successful for us) by its energy, zest, and exuberance, the heroine's vocation. Barrett Browning retains the conventional identification of woman with the inner, spiritual, emotional, and subjective sphere: with poetry, and with poems. Instead of switching gender roles she switches the locus of power within them, the novelistic story concluding with an assertion of the primacy of poetry over the novel and of women over men. If power resides in the inner life, it belongs to poetry, and to women, and so to the woman poet most of all.

So tremendous a victory over custom and convention is easier to achieve in plot than in the texture of the work itself, where the mingling of poetry and prose (like the novelistic incidents in *Sonnets from the Portuguese*) is liable to produce what may seem embarrassing absurdities.

To write a novel-poem, Elizabeth Barrett had said in 1844, would mean rushing in where angels fear to tread—being, that is, a fool—and her characteristic willingness to risk making a fool of herself was an essential qualification for writing it. Perhaps the greatest inadequacy of Victorian poetry was its narrow range of diction, which usually could not accommodate simple prosaic things—dialogue, the mechanics of narrative, the details of common life—except to make an ironic contrast between the vulgar present and the glorious past. King Arthur's mustache is named in Tennyson's solemn verse by a comical circumlocution: "the knightly growth that fringed his lips."[29] Barrett Browning does not altogether avoid such risible effects; we are rather taken aback to read, for instance, that Aurora asked the Paris police to find a girl with "hair in masses, low upon the brow, / As it were an iron crown and pressed" (6:400– 401). The diction, although less eccentric than in some of her earlier works, offers an occasional jolt like "angerly" (1:370), some archaisms that awkwardly belie the insistence on modernity, and rather too many apostrophes to life (1:666), poetry (1:915), the reader ("Mark, there" [1:702]), or other characters ("Sweet holy Marian!" [6:782]). Such exuberance is usually to the point and under control, but jarring nonetheless.[30] The dialogue is often, as Virginia Woolf points out, preposterously unrealistic,[31] although it is often witty and always energetic and pointed. Unless it is ironical, poetry of this sort works best at the highest intensity, when we can call it "operatic" (as with Tennyson's *Maud*, which has also been scolded for indecorous behavior) and exempt it from the canons of realism.[32] *Aurora Leigh* does maintain a high level of intensity: conversations even on such dry matters as the laws of inheritance carry a high emotional charge, the narrative is always densely suffused with feeling, and the mixture of poetry and prose generally works.

Complaints about lack of realism most often center on Marian's excellent standard English. But Barrett Browning is not interested in a realistic portrayal of uneducated speech—why should she be? What matters is that Marian speak and be understood: that the trade in women's bodies be removed from the protective obscurity bestowed on it by false ideas of modesty and shame, and that the claims of even the most apparently degraded women to attention and respect be forced on the notice of women who think it virtuous to ignore them. Lady Waldemar is neither modest nor virtuous, but she refers to prostitutes as women "we could not name / Because we're decent" (3:551–52), and Marian knows that if she spoke plainly about being drugged and raped she would give offense ("we must scrupulously hint / With half-words, delicate reserves, the thing / Which no one scrupled we should feel in full" [6:1222–24]). The poem, however, speaks of these things plainly enough to be understood. When Barrett Browning says that poetry should deal with "life," she really means it; as the husband in Meredith's *Modern Love* (another long poem about sex and marriage that shocked mid-Victorian readers) says to his almost-adulterous wife when she objects to French novels, "Unnatural? My dear, these things are life: / And life, some think, is worthy of the Muse."[33] The extraordinarily insistent evocations of breasts, babies, and sexual desire are part of the poet's determination to make female experiences that are usually silenced speak loudly and unmistakably from the heart of her poetry.[34] Her insurgency against rules of gender and genre is enacted in an indifference to superficial realism and in repeated assaults on literary decorum and that most vulgar of idols, "good taste."

Aurora becomes, in effect, the feminine of Homer, and so, by writing Aurora's bold modern story, does Barrett Browning—and also, since her poem visits the underworld, points the way to the founding of a new city, and ends in a vision of the New Jerusalem, of Virgil or Dante. The poem is enlivened by the exhilarating consciousness that she is fulfilling her earliest ambition. The heroic strength celebrated in epic is preempted by the heroine, while the softer virtues that adorn poems by nineteenth-century women, including some early ones of Barrett Browning's own, are viewed with deep suspicion. Tears are dismissed as an infirmity of the nerves and readers are not invited to luxuriate in the moral or sentimental pleasures of illness and death. None of the mistreated children actually die, and the death of the young seamstress, Lucy, is narrated with resolute brevity and that of the "old idiot wretch" (4:62), her grandmother, with acid scorn. Although one might expect Marian or her child to expiate impurity and earn our forgiveness by dying, they remain in robust health. Barrett Browning would have preferred Mrs. Gaskell's Ruth, who bore an illegitimate child, not to have undergone the final purification of a self-sacrificing death, but she thought perhaps "the English public might not have borne it."[35] She herself refused to conciliate such prejudice except by having Marian raped rather than, as Ruth had been, seduced. In this poem weakness does not attract sympathy, edify onlookers, or signify virtue, and speaking what is not supposed to be spoken is a sign of strength and courage and a source of energy and pleasure. And the sense of God's nearness that had cramped Elizabeth

Barrett's imagination gives Aurora, whose father's death exempts her from pressures to remain a child, joyful confidence that she is fighting on God's side for the establishment of a new spiritual age.

The celebratory gusto which rejoices in vitality of all kinds, fine or sordid, joyful or malign, is essential to her triumph, both effect and cause. "Earth's crammed with heaven, / And every common bush afire with God" (7:821–22). To Romney's appalled humanitarianism, earth is old and bad, but Aurora is joyfully alive to "holy art and golden life" (2:250), and even her depictions of depraved and hostile mobs and the satirical presentation of the upper classes are full of relish for the abundant particularity of life. It may be true that (as some reviewers observed), the poem suffered because blank verse imposed less discipline than the strict rhyme schemes of *Sonnets from the Portuguese* and *Casa Guidi Windows*, and the last part was written under considerable pressure of time. But the effect is artful in its apparent artlessness.

Words overflow in great surges of energy, piling up images as if for the sheer fun of it, somewhat in the manner of the Metaphysical poets and in a way that has distressed some squeamish or fastidious readers. For Romney's wedding "The humours of the peccant social wound" "clogged the streets" and "oozed into the church / In a dark slow stream, like blood" (4:544–54). An epic simile doesn't want to stop even in depicting misery:

> What succeeded next
> I recollect as, after fevers, men
> Thread back the passage of delirium,
> Missing the turn still, baffled by the door;
> Smooth endless days, notched here and there with knives,
> A weary, wormy darkness, spurred i' the flank
> With flame, that it should eat and end itself
> Like some tormented scorpion.
>
> (1:215–22)

The characters are delineated with the same kind of loving attention: not just Aurora's aunt (a portrait singled out for praise and quotation by many reviewers, including George Eliot),[36] Lord Howe, and the sharp-tongued and alarmingly observant Lady Waldemar, but also such lesser figures as the conspicuously Catholic Sir Blaise (whose "ebon cross worn innermostly" is usually visible through "some unaware unbuttoned casualty / Of the under-waistcoat" [5:676–80]), a student who smugly parrots German rationalist dogmas and calls for "Reverence for the young" (5:713), or some women glimpsed at prayer in Florence.

The gusto, of course, reminds us of Browning's. The poem anticipates a marriage which will enhance the fictional poet's work, and it is the product of such a marriage. The poetry of both husband and wife had been enriched by their years together: Browning's had become emotionally deeper, more attuned to the normal range of human feelings, and more finely varied, while hers had acquired a new ease and freedom and a new delight in characterization, the material world, and ordinary life. We are reminded of Browning by the dramatic representation of the speaker: her idiosyncratic and disarmingly garrulous voice is placed in concretely realized settings and situations, and we are invited to infer feelings (especially jealousy and love) that she conceals from herself. Lady Waldemar, in her unshakeable self-complacency, is like Browning's monologuists too. And the aesthetic credo that by painting bodies one paints souls, enunciated at length in the seventh book but implicit everywhere, combines Swedenborg's visions with those of Browning's Fra Lippo Lippi. *Aurora Leigh* comprises a small tour of Italian artworks— not just the monuments of grandeur that are grandly evoked in *Casa Guidi Windows*, but what must have struck the Protestant Englishwoman as grotesque oddities, of the sort Browning had always delighted in: the Madonna pierced by seven swords (1:160–61), Saint Lucy carrying her eyes on a plate (5:683–84), the upside-down crucifixion of Saint Peter (3:6), all of which she could have seen in Florence.

Both Browning and Barrett Browning conceive of divinity as a principle of individuation expressing itself in a great rush of creation, a "golden spray of multitudinous worlds" (3:754), of which poetic creativity is the earthly analogue. The awareness of God's presence colors the poems of both, and its converse, the sense of a nightmarish life of deprivation in inanimate things for which the *locus classicus* is " 'Childe Roland to the Dark Tower Came'," appears in *Aurora Leigh*, too: "a meagre, unripe house: a line / Of rigid poplars elbowed it behind, / And, just in front, beyond the lime and bricks / That wronged the grass" (6:533–36).[37] And the division of characters into nearly absolute categories of good and evil, centering on girls who remain spotless despite the vilest contaminations of inheritance and experience (Pompilia in *The Ring and the Book* is in this respect Marian's sister), is common to both, as is—most appropriately—the idealization of married love as both physical passion and the union of souls. These qualities may have been latent or developing in Barrett Browning's earlier poetry, but they reached maturity only after her marriage.

The fertile intermingling of life and love and art for which Aurora longs and strives is exemplified by *Aurora Leigh* itself. Although the heroine is not, of course, Elizabeth Barrett Browning (who marked the distinction in all sorts of small ways, such as giving Aurora blonde hair and blue eyes), the author's life is essential not only to the poem's genesis but also to its public meaning. Since hers was the only example of such a life that her readers would have known (for which reason, Coventry Patmore complained, the subject was uninteresting),[38] the personal application could hardly have been avoided. It makes plausible, furthermore, what would otherwise seem fantasy or wish-fulfillment, her heroine's accomplishments being no more remarkable than her own. The fact of the Brownings' happy marriage assures us that Aurora will live happily ever after and—the poem being in that sense a self-fulfilling prophecy—continue to write. Had Barrett Browning not already done it, reviewers would have said it was impossible.

> The advent of *Aurora Leigh* can never be forgotten by any lover of poetry who was old enough at the time to read it. Of one thing they may all be sure—they were right in the impression that they never had read, and never would read, anything in any way comparable with that unique work of audaciously feminine and ambitiously impulsive genius. It is one of the longest poems in the world, and there is not a dead line in it.[39]

This is Swinburne's testimony; and although his estimate of the poem's impact is obviously exaggerated, it is not wholly absurd. Ruskin told Browning that it was "the greatest *poem* in the English language, unsurpassed by anything but Shakespeare" (and only by the plays, not the sonnets); in a second letter he asserted that "all the best people shout, with me, rapturously," and he encouraged the rapturous shouting by publishing the opinion that it was "the greatest poem which the century has produced in any language."[40] Reading it made Dante Gabriel Rossetti feel "something like a bug" in comparison: "an astounding work . . . . O the wonder of it!"[41] Leigh Hunt sent Browning a twenty-page letter stuffed with praise of this "unique, wonderful and immortal poem."[42] George Eliot, who reread it more than once with unabated admiration, called it in the *Westminster Review* Barrett Browning's "greatest poem."[43] Many lesser critics were equally excited—"the greatest poem ever written by a woman," said the *Daily News*[44]—and even those who deplored its aims or execution admitted its importance. Barrett Browning was amazed by the "extravagances written to [her] about that book" and the strange fact that "the daily and weekly press, upon which I calculated for furious abuse, has been, for the most part, furious the other way" (*LEBB* 2:249). A fortnight after publication it went into a second edition.

By no means all the responses were of the sort reported by Ruskin and Swinburne, but friendly or hostile, laudatory or scornful, reviewers were responsive to the issues the poet had raised, and on the whole the negative reactions did not disturb her. There were the usual complaints about carelessness, obscurity, and diffuseness, and a few critics saw a falling-back in that respect from *Casa Guidi Windows*.[45] Most, however, thought that over the years her style had improved. Even more than in *Casa Guidi Windows*, the poet's sex is essential to the poem, and reviewers responded to her direct challenge with less thoughtless condescension than past experience might have led her to anticipate. But several vigorously objected to what struck them as arrant feminism, and the most hostile complained about a picture of womanhood they found exceedingly offensive. The *Saturday Review*, which begins with the comment that "The negative experience of centuries seems to prove that a woman cannot be a great poet," saw nothing objectionable in the education provided for Aurora by her aunt, and *Blackwood's* declared Aurora "not a genuine woman" because she lacks "instinctiveness, which is the greatest charm of women" and disobeys the rule "that woman was created to be dependent on the man."[46] Such commentary, of course, reinforced Barrett Browning's conviction that the evils she addressed were real ones. Readers with any knowledge of the appalling depths of poverty and deprivation in Victorian England, however, will probably agree with critics who, attacking the poem where it is least defensible, assert the value of Romney's material assistance to the poor.[47]

Having deliberately courted accusations of indecency, Barrett Browning rejoiced in hearing both that "quite decent women" were "taking the part of the book in a sort of *effervescence* which I hear of with astonishment" (*LEBB* 2:252) and that "the 'mamas of England' in a body refuse to let their daughters read it" (*LEBB* 2:255). *Blackwood's* found Lady Waldemar's conversation "coarse and revolting," foresaw a rash of blank verse "conversations in the pot-house, casino, and even worse places," and warned that when poetry "attempts to descend to pits and charnel-vaults, it is stifled by the noxious exhalations."[48] Rape was objected to as a "harrowing and repulsive" subject, however delicately treated.[49] And the *Dublin University Magazine*, while otherwise favorably disposed, regretted "that the authoress has written a book which is almost a closed volume for her own sex."[50] All this was a little more painful than she had expected, and she was glad to be safely out of England when the reviews appeared:

> While I am away, I don't care to excess that the Dublin University Magazine, for instance, should [. . .] compare me to *'Afra Behn.'*! & talk of my book as "sealed to my own sex," though I should *hate* to hear the changes on it from a quantity of friendly persons sure to come to condole with one on that head. I should like to wait till all this dust has past a little—tho dust is beareable after all. There are worse things than dust.[51]

But a woman who had expected to be "put in the stocks and pelted with the eggs of the last twenty years' 'singing birds' as a disorderly woman and free-thinking poet" (*LEBB* 2:252)—a combination of Godiva and the runaway slave—could bear such insults, especially when she received "pretty pleasant letters from women [. . .] who write to thank me for 'help' . . for new views of 'love, truth, & purity.' "[52] Aurora is rather contemptuous of adulatory young women, but Barrett Browning found these letters comforting. *Aurora Leigh*'s reception was very similar to that of *Ruth*, which was praised by those whose opinions really mattered (including Barrett Browning) and reviled by the prudish and by much of the press.[53] She refused, of course, to change anything: "all the 'modern' passages, illustrations, are vitally necessary, she thinks," wrote Browning (who managed such affairs) to the publisher in regard to the second edition, although she did eventually make some small alterations.[54]

Along with offended prudery and distaste for assertive women there was the usual sentimental approbation for more acceptable portrayals of femininity. Aurora's self-consciousness was found repulsive in comparison to Marian's "artless and natural" story of her early life and her "shrinking, clinging, half reverence, half love" for Romney,[55] the woman as self-conscious artist being naturally less attractive than the "artless" and barely literate object of her story. The lush description of Marian's infant was particularly admired not only by Swinburne, who doted on babies, but by many reviewers, including (of course!) the satirical anti-feminist *Blackwood's*,[56] while maternal ambivalence and cruelty were ignored or, presumably, considered part of what should never have been written. Barrett Browning had a strong following among women, however, especially in America, where "many of the most cultivated of her sex" regarded her with an "ardor of admiration." "She speaks what is struggling for utterance in their own hearts, and they find in her poems the revelation of themselves."[57]

Early readers of the poem, like many later ones, were struck and often profoundly disturbed by its anomalousness, and in particular by its apparent transgressions of *two* boundaries: between poetry and fiction, and between masculine and feminine—the boundaries, that is, of genre and of gender. The *Dublin University Magazine* followed its rhetorical bewilderment about the "category" in which to "class" "this singular production" ("a poetic novel of real life, or a poetic romance . . . ?") with censure of the author's "effort to stand, not on a pedestal beside man, but actually to occupy his place": "She assumes as it were the gait and the garb of man, but the stride and the strut betray her."[58] Reviewers distinguished between poetic and novelistic aspects, whether or not they approved of the mixture; some admired the intensely poetical sections which others found strained and excessive, and some liked the pathos or the social satire. Many found large portions of it beneath the dignity of verse. Henry Chorley was simply bewildered:

> We have no experience of such a mingling of what is precious with what is mean—of the voice of clarion and the lyric cadence of harp with the cracked school-room spinet—of tears and small-talk—of eloquent apostrophe and adust speculation—of the grandeur of passion and the pettiness of modes and manners—as we find in these nine books of blank verse. Milton's organ is put by Mrs. Browning to play polkas in May-Fair drawing-rooms.[59]

"Milton's organ" (an expressive term for that exclusively male instrument the epic) in a lady's drawing room—transgressions of genre and gender go together, as Tennyson showed when he symbolized the relations of men and women in *The Princess* by the juxtaposition of narrative and lyric. The blurring of sexual boundaries in *Aurora Leigh* was remarked by reviewers with varying degrees of pleasure or distress. It was a matter not just of plot or setting or character, but of the gender characteristics of the poem as a whole. Leigh Hunt saw a wonderful mixture of "masculine power with feminine tenderness" in it, and George Eliot made the same point more fully: Mrs. Browning, she said, "is, perhaps, the first woman who has produced a work which exhibits all the peculiar powers without the negations of her sex; which superadds to masculine vigour, breadth, and culture, feminine subtlety of perception, feminine quickness of sensibility, and feminine tenderness."[60] While no doubt perfectly feminine in her life, said one reviewer politely, she is masculine in her aesthetics and philosophy—a quality he ascribes to the influence of a male teacher and more recently, her husband.[61] "She wields the lightnings of her genius with Jove-like freedom," said another[62]—an attribution of paternal force that must have impressed her.

Others, however, while equally excited, were less pleased. She tries to "prove her manhood" by the coarseness of her language and an "ostentation of strength."[63] Several thought Aurora herself disagreeably unwomanly. The phrase "brushed with extreme flounce / The circle of the sciences" was taken as an annoying example of the feminizing of masculine concerns: "Nothing assists her in a metaphysical argument like an illustration from a fashion-book."[64] Reviewers found transgressions of other boundaries, too: between the "universal element" and "the peculiarities of our time"[65] and between the beautiful and the repulsive, as well as in mixed metaphors, lines written by a woman not fit for women to read, and, in general, sins against taste and decorum that crossed the boundary between literature and parts of life that could not be written about. The mixing of autobiography and fiction was touched on by contemporary reviewers only delicately if at all, but years later Virginia Woolf heard the author's voice too clearly through her protagonist's and found (as one might with many poets in the middle of the nineteenth century) that her life impinges too much on her art.[66] Barrett Browning's urge to dissolve boundaries and reconcile opposites here receives its fullest play, and the multifarious transgressiveness was not only essential to the poem's meaning but meant to be provocative. Once the dust had settled, she was satisfied with the response she had provoked: she cared more for the praise of Ruskin and Hunt and the enthusiasm of the book-buying public than for the cavils of reviewers who represented precisely the conventionalities she was trying to destroy.

8

Poems before Congress, Last Poems

When the reviews of *Aurora Leigh* came out, the Brownings were back in Florence. Thereafter, aside from a few months in France in 1858, they remained in Italy, migrating in search of benign weather between Florence, Bagni di Lucca, Siena, and Rome until Barrett Browning's death in 1861. Except for a few spurts of poetic activity in response to the Italian political crisis at the end of the decade, she wrote relatively little during these years and seems to have had no specific plans for another major work. Spells of debility and illness became increasingly frequent and severe, exacerbated by a series of emotional shocks. John Kenyon died at the end of 1856, climaxing years of quasi-paternal kindness with a legacy of eleven thousand pounds that ended their financial worries. Her father's death in April 1857 left her prostrated for weeks. "Strange, that what I called 'unkindness' for so many years, in departing should have left to me such a sudden desolation" (*LEBB* 2:265). It startled her into unwonted querulousness that the house in Wimpole Street was almost immediately deserted, Arabel and her brothers going their separate ways as soon as they possibly could, and none of them—not even Arabel, who to her sister's bewilderment chose to live by herself in London—ever taking advantage of their freedom to visit her in Italy. The home she had loved and fled no longer existed. But in fact the withdrawal was on her side, too, as it had always been, and a family vacation in Le Havre with various Barretts and Brownings in the summer of 1858 made her cross and restless ("sequestration in the south [. . .] spoils me, I fear, for the common 'give & take' of English life").[1] Other troubles included the temporary madness of her old servant Wilson, now running a lodging-house in Florence, the unexpected

225

death of Mrs. Jameson in the spring of 1860, and—most dreadful and devastating—Henrietta's painful death from cancer in the fall of the same year.

Still, she had many sources of happiness, although most had their admixture of pain. The fruits of fame turned out to be considerably less ashen than she had anticipated in her premature renunciations of them, and the continuing popularity and scandal of *Aurora Leigh* afforded her amusement as well as satisfaction. The only problem was that she had so thoroughly outpaced her husband, who rejoiced in her success, she said, more than if it had been his own. Indeed he did, and he never stopped believing that her genius transcended his. But the contrast to the indifference with which his own work had been received could not but occur to him, especially in his dealings with Chapman, their publisher, about editions, payments, and reviews. Once, catching himself writing to Chapman about her poems from the point of view of "us," he burst out with an uncharacteristic revelation of pain: "*Us*—I am the church-organ-bellows' blower that talked about *our* playing, but you know what I do in the looking after commas and dots to i's."[2] He seemed to be acting the role of Romney to her Aurora. Her fame was in the ascendant, his hardly rising at all, and he seems to have lost heart.[3]

She was enraged at the stupidity of the British public (Americans were less obtuse) and grateful to anyone who recognized the superiority of his poetry to hers, and his eagerness to do almost anything rather than write distressed her very much. He apparently composed no poetry at all for four years after the publication of *Men and Women* in 1855, and not very much in the next few years either. He did not publish another book until 1864, three years after she died. He threw his energies into a series of other activities: drawing, riding, sculpture, evening parties (especially in the lively social atmosphere of Rome), and the care of his wife during her increasingly serious attacks of illness. On the subjects which divided them they had agreed to disagree, but the divisions did not cut very deep, as Browning explained to George Barrett not long before she died: "We differ *toto coelo* (or rather, *inferno*) as to spirit-rapping, we quarrel some-times about politics, and estimate peoples' characters with enormous difference, but, in the main, we *know* each other" (*LBGB* 256). Even when he was displeased with her, she said, he couldn't help "think[ing] aloud with" her; nobody understands his fits of depression "except me who am in the inside of him and hear him breathe" (*LEBB* 2:435).

Pen was still loving, happy, and good-natured, although less attentive to his lessons than his parents quite liked. He still wore velvet and embroidery, the thinnest leather shoes, and long golden curls, despite his occasional requests for ordinary trousers, heavy boots, or a haircut. But his father saw to it that he became a proficient swimmer and bought him a pony which accompanied them around Italy and eventually to England. His mother was prouder of him, she said, than of "twenty 'Auroras' "—a supererogatory comparison that casts an odd light, or shadow, on the poem's argument.[4] At the beginning of 1859 she was still his chief instructor: "he reads with me, German French & English, & Italian daily, & writes English & Italian *dictations*" (*LMO* 141). Later that year a gentle Abbe was engaged to induct him into the mysteries of Latin, arithmetic, and geography, but Pen still would not do his lessons without his mother, and his indisposition to apply himself continued for the rest of her life—indeed, for the rest of his undistinguished scholastic career.

She still expected an imminent spiritual revival—"in twenty years the probability is you will have no more doubters of the immortality of souls" (*LEBB* 2:289)—and her confidence in the proximity of the spirit world brought some comfort as deaths pressed close about her. The Swedenborgian conviction that souls continue to develop in the afterlife kept open the possibility of her father's posthumous forgiveness, and she was sure that Henrietta was "only in the next room—though for me I cannot see her or hear her—others might."[5] The doings of Home the medium continued to interest her, especially when he was taken up by her hero, Louis Napoleon. She was amused to hear that Homes' baby was an even greater medium than he was (*TTUL* 90). The visionary, otherworldly tendencies manifested in her earlier writings continued to cluster extra-poetically around her spiritualist beliefs, rarely impinging significantly on her poetry.

Browning remained unconverted, and the spirits that drew her a little apart from her husband became a link with women, especially Americans: Harriet Beecher Stowe, for instance, and the popular American novelist who wrote under the name of Grace Greenwood.[6] In America the spirits not only provided careers for women but endorsed women's rights.[7] Barrett Browning, however, was always a bit doubtful of female capability and was inclined, as exceptionally successful women often are, to underestimate the obstacles in the paths of others. She stayed aloof from the recently revived women's movement, of which her old friend Anna Jameson had become a leading patron and to which *Aurora Leigh* gave inspiration and encouragement, although she did sign a petition widely endorsed by literary women in support of a married women's property law.[8] Aurora Leigh denounces feminists because they assert their rights instead of demonstrating their abilities, and while she has male friends with whom to discuss art and life and the ways of the world she has no comparable female friend, the bond of sisterhood with Marian not including intellectual companionship. But women flocked around Barrett Browning, including some good writers and others whose literary pretensions were more dubious. Motherhood had made one bond with women, spiritualism made a second, and fame attracted others to her door.[9]

The strangest of these friendships was with Sophia Eckley, who presented herself as the finest flower of sentimental womanhood and eventually published several volumes of sugar-watery verse. Eckley was an American with an adoring husband, a great deal of money, some skill as a medium, and an insinuating gift for flattery, all of which she utilized to captivate the famous poet. The Brownings and the Eckleys met in 1857 and for periods of several months seem to have been together almost daily. Browning rather liked Mr. Eckley; and Barrett Browning responded to her dear, dearest, darling Sophie with a somewhat embarrassed sweetness of her own. "And I love you, dear. You have done me real good with your sweet pure harmonious spirit & by the grateful sense of its tenderness towards me. You exaggerate what I am, and what I can do for you."[10] Sophie is "so sympathetical to me, & so delicate & refined that there never is a jar for a moment. Her fault [is that] she over-rates & over-loves me to a most extravagant degree."[11] The Eckleys followed the Brownings around Italy, once even hiring a carriage to take them from Florence to Rome, and it required constant vigilance to ward off a shower of gifts. Eckley captured Barrett Browning's attention primarily with accounts of her spiritualist experiences, and she held it with further manifestations; when the Brownings and the Eckleys were travelling to Rome together, for instance, "the spirits made signs several times" to the two women (although not, apparently, to their husbands).[12] Together they practised automatic writing, and while Barrett Browning herself, who had observed the workings of her own mind and body too closely for self-deception in such a matter, was never successful at it, her friend received messages for her.[13]

But in 1859 the friend whose purity seemed too good to be true was revealed (it is not clear how) as "utterly false."[14] Browning said afterwards that she had "cheated Ba from the beginning," and his vituperation is impressive even for that virtuoso of hyperbolical contempt: "those inventions about spirits &c were not at all more prodigious than the daily-

sprouting toadstools of that dunghill of a soul,—lies about this, that &
the other."[15] He not surprisingly detested the woman who played so
blatantly on his wife's credulity and aroused such intimate ardor, and he
implies (no doubt with some exaggeration) that his warnings had caused
serious marital strife: "I cried 'poison' at first sniff—and suffered more,
from maintaining it, than from any incident in my whole life."[16] What
would most have offended Barrett Browning would have been falsifica-
tions of messages from her own dead. Sophie's unmasking retrospectively
cancelled the perfect, unstinting love through which Sophie must have
seemed to be making up in her own person, and no doubt by means of
mediumistic interventions as well, for the "mother-want" that fills *Aurora
Leigh,* providing the sisterly bond the poem celebrates and the all-
embracing love it longs for. Had she appeared on the scene a little earlier,
we might have thought her a prototype for the portrait of Aurora's mother—
first angelic, then witch and Lamia—and she inspired an astonishingly
venomous poem, "Where's Agnes?"

A parallel and even more engrossing drama of the apparent fulfillment
and betrayal of long-held desires—the paternal as opposed to the ma-
ternal version, one might say—was provided by the vicissitudes of the
Risorgimento, which seemed to have entered a final triumphant phase
(like spiritualism) and then suddenly to have been betrayed. Napoleon
III appeared ready to effect the liberation and unification of Italy: French
troops entered Italy in 1859, and as usual the Brownings were fascinated
and unafraid in the face of upheaval and armies. "We flourish in the air
of revolution, and are in the highest spirits, all of us, about the war."[17]
In Rome, Browning participated in the general excitement, Pen wished
he were old enough to fight, and Barrett Browning's happiness reached
the intensity of pain, punctuated by rage against England's inveterate
distrust of Napoleon and unwillingness to act decisively on Italy's behalf.
Henry James said of her impassioned partisanship at this time that "to
'care' . . . as she is caring is to entertain one's convictions as a malady
and a doom"; "we absolutely feel the beautiful mind and the high gift
discredited by their engrossment."[18] But James's opinion, although widely
shared, is based on a narrow idea of health and beauty. "Just now [March
1859] I am scarcely of sane mind about Italy. It even puts down the
spirit-subject. I pass through cold stages of anxiety, and white heats of
rage" (*LEBB* 2:308). The woman who wrote that not discreditable self-
description was at least healthy enough to laugh at herself. The singular
feature of her character, she rightly remarked, was her ability to care
about impersonal things. "Women don't generally break their hearts on

these exterior subjects. But I am otherwise made; & whatever small worth may be in me .. arises exactly from this earnestness & thoroughness of thought & feeling upon subjects which don't personally touch me."[19] Her earnestness no doubt sprang in part from the way the pattern of her experience recurred in the political arena, but that is not discreditable either.

What almost did destroy her balance of mind was Napoleon's unexpected withdrawal from the verge of victory, ending the war in July 1859 with the treaty of Villafranca. To most people this looked like betrayal, and although a day or so later Barrett Browning managed to call it statesmanship, the disappointment made her ill.

> Though it may sound absurd to you [her sister-in-law, Sarianna Browning], it was the blow on the *heart* about the peace after all that excitement and exultation, that walking on the clouds for weeks and months, and then the sudden stroke and fall, and the impotent rage against all the nations of the earth—selfish, inhuman, wicked—who forced the hand of Napoleon, and truncated his great intentions. Many young men of Florence were confined to their beds by the emotion of the news. As for me, I was struck, couldn't sleep, talked too much, and [. . .] at last this bad attack came on. (*LEBB* 2:320)

It was the worst attack she had ever had in Italy, with violent palpitations and cough and what felt like *angina pectoris*. She dreamed of "inscrutable articles of peace and eternal provisional governments" and of following a woman in white, with a white mask and "the likeness of a crown," whom she knew to be Italy but whose face she could not see. "Walking on the mountains of the moon, hand in hand with a Dream more beautiful than them all, then falling suddenly on the hard earth-ground on one's head, no wonder that one should suffer" (*LEBB* 2:321). Louis Napoleon and the mysterious woman with whom she walked in dreams, holding hands or following like a child, were the latest avatars of the quasi-parental figures that, although temporarily laid to rest in *Aurora Leigh*, continued to shape her imagination. The exhilarating prospect that this time, at last, the story would have a happy ending, the bitter disappointment, and the willed recovery of hope fuelled what was almost her last burst of poetry.

Of the eight poems in *Poems before Congress*, published in March 1860 and named for a meeting of nations that never took place, seven deal with current events in Italy. She and Browning had intended to publish a joint volume on Italian politics, but he abandoned his share of the project when Palmerston's accession to power made him think his strictures on England irrelevant. The little volume opens with "Napoleon III in Italy," an ode of over four hundred lines in celebration of a hero that is matched (if at all) in the Victorian period only by Tennyson's laureate ode on the death of Wellington. In its finely varied tone and meter, and especially its quiet, conversational moments and its delicately voiced questioning and wonder, it recalls Tennyson's *Maud*, which also celebrates martial valour and the hope that a dead woman (in Barrett Browning's poem, Italy) will revive and men be heroically redeemed.

> Now, shall we say
> Our Italy lives indeed?
> And if it were not for the beat and bray
> Of drum and trump of martial men,
> Should we feel the underground heave and strain,
> Where heroes left their dust as a seed
> Sure to emerge one day?
>
> (145–51)[20]

Everyone is heroic: the emperor who has been lifted "to the level of pure song" (72) by his selfless leadership; Italy reborn, "Pale and calm in her strength" (166); the soldiers poised to die for freedom; and the poet herself who meets Napoleon "at this height / At last, and [finds him] great enough to praise" (80–81). The return of the dead ("we feel the underground heave and strain" [149], like Hector stirring in the garden) is strange and solemn but not frightening. She overreaches only in the crudely conceived and painfully rhymed refrain, comically reminiscent of Poe's "The Raven": "Emperor / Evermore."[21]

Despite the limited subject matter the volume has remarkable variety of tone. Two poems about the eternal emperor written after Villafranca forget about heroic attitudes and try to make the best of an altered case. "A Tale of Villafranca" tells a tale for a child about a deed too great for earthly acceptance and therefore postponed by its grand projector. In "An August Voice" Napoleon ironically asks the Tuscans, in accordance with his agreement at Villafranca, to recall the grand duke.

> You'll take back your Grand-Duke?
> There *are* some things to object to.
> He cheated, betrayed, and forsook,
> Then called in the foe to protect you.
>
> (37–40)

This is like the urbane voice that had commemorated the first Napoleon years before in "Crowned and Buried." Fairy tale and irony combine in "Christmas Gifts," a caustic comment on the pope. And "Italy and the

World," which calls upon Italy to prefigure the "one confederate broth-
erhood" of nations ("For civilisation perfected / Is fully developed Chris-
tianity" [51–52]), rises through the rhetoric of a political pamphlet,
exhortation, and irony to a rich prophetic chant.

> Beautiful Italy! golden amber
>   Warm with the kisses of lover and traitor!
> Thou who hast drawn us on to remember,
>   Draw us to hope now: let us be greater
> By this new future than that old story.
>
> Till truer glory replaces all glory,
>   As the torch grows blind at the dawn of day;
> And the nations, rising up, their sorry
>   And foolish sins shall put away,
> As children their toys when the teacher enters.
>
> Till Love's one centre devour these centres.
>
>   (106–16)

In the meter and swiftness, the antithesis, repetition, and parallelism, the
sonorously elemental vocabulary, and the incantatory, prophetic tone, this
sounds astonishingly like Swinburne, Barrett Browning's great successor
as English laureate of Italian freedom.[22]

The other three poems are about women who display themselves
publicly as representatives of freedom. "The Dance," based like all the
other episodes in these extroverted poems on an actual event, tells an
anecdote about Florentine women who showed their gratitude to French
soldiers by dancing with them. "A Court Lady" refers to the fashion
among patriotic Milanese ladies of visiting military hospitals in formal
dress and open carriages: a beautiful woman has herself attired in silk
and diamonds, like a fairy princess and the incarnation of Italy, and goes
to the bedside of various wounded soldiers. This is a commentary both
on the proper behavior of great ladies and on the romantic aura that
Florence Nightingale's almost mythic popularity had given to the idea of
women as nurses, especially for soldiers. Barrett Browning's experience
of the sickroom and her exalted notion of women's proper work im-
munized her against the Nightingale glamor—it was only, she thought,
a reaffirmation of the old assumption that woman's highest function is
to bind men's wounds. "I do not consider the best use to which we can
put a gifted and accomplished woman is to *make her a hospital nurse*. If
it is, why then woe to us all who are artists! The woman's question is

at an end" (*LEBB* 2:189). The court lady's ministrations body forth Italy's grandeur in beautiful symbolic gestures, like the Florentine women's dance, and in gracious words, not in self-abnegating service.

And the book closes with an even more heroic woman: the poet. "A Curse for a Nation" stands at the end of *Poems before Congress* as a fiercely direct statement about women writers' place in politics. Barrett Browning's third and last poem concerning America, it was composed like "The Runaway Slave" at the request of the Anti-Slavery Bazaar in Boston and published in *The Liberty Bell*.[23] Once again America—which for the cultivated British represented everything that was rude, crude, and unpoetical about the rising tide of democracy, and so far as other Victorian poets were concerned scarcely existed at all—gave her an arena in which to express her angriest impulses and most outrageous convictions and prove her courage. Like "The Runaway Slave" and "Hiram Powers' 'Greek Slave,' " "A Curse for a Nation" pivots on the issues of slavery, speech, and self-exposure. Here, however, self-exposure is literally and explicitly identified with poems, and the poem itself is Godiva's ride. The woman exposing herself to public view and courting public obloquy is the poet speaking more or less *in propria persona,* and her speech is conceived as an offense (as a poem for the Anti–Corn Law League would have been in 1845) against male friends and relations.

The Prologue recounts, in the matter-of-fact tone of one who has read Blake and Swedenborg and lived among those who converse with spirits, how an angel commanded her to write at his dictation a curse against America. "I heard an angel speak last night, / And he said 'Write!' " (1–2). She made two essentially familial objections to undertaking this task: that the Americans were her brothers and that she could hardly curse another country when her own was not much better; but the angel reassured her that curses can manifest love and that her hatred of evil at home entitles her to curse it abroad. Her final objection was that it is unwomanly to curse. But the angel appealed to her sympathy with categories of women—Barrett Browning almost always thinks of slaves, like prostitutes, as women victimized by men—who are left out of account when womanliness is defined, firmly instructing her to curse on their behalf:

> "A curse from the depths of womanhood
> Is very salt, and bitter, and good."
>
> So thus I wrote, and mourned indeed,
>   What all may read.

> And thus, as was enjoined on me,
> I send it over the Western Sea.
>
> (49–52)

As in the Godiva story, the purity of her self-exposure is guaranteed by the fact that it is "enjoined," not chosen.

The conversation with the angel reenacts the old argument about the anti–Corn Law poem, but of course the time for yielding to fathers or brothers had long passed, and her husband thought she should publish whatever she pleased. The curse itself begins like "The Runaway Slave" with a denunciation of Americans for denying others the freedom they had won for themselves. The imagery is remarkably violent, like the story in the earlier poem, with chains, brands, thongs, "writhing bond-slaves" (63), the fiend, and strangled martyrs all in the first eighteen lines. And the curse is peculiarly appropriate for a poet whose courage had once failed her: it is that the Americans will be unable to denounce oppression elsewhere, that praise will shame them and taunts be unanswerable, and that they will "recoil" from cursing others' ill deeds lest they curse themselves. The curse is verbal impotence, the inability to curse. As she had told Anna Jameson in 1853, not to denounce slavery is to be oneself enslaved: "is it possible that you think a woman has no business with questions like the question of slavery? Then she had better use a pen no more. She had better subside into slavery and concubinage herself" (*LEBB* 2:110–11).

The storm of abuse that *Poems before Congress* provoked in England ranged her with those on whose behalf she was protesting. The "burning sympathy so vividly expressed," the "outpourings of a noble spirit," the "noble utterance" of "the greatest poetess our language has yet produced" helped some reviewers overlook political differences.[24] But others responded to the suavely ironical challenge of the preface ("if the verses should appear to English readers too pungently rendered to admit of a patriotic respect to the English sense of things [. . .]") by denouncing her as very unpatriotic indeed. The *Saturday Review* spewed forth insults against her "delirium of imbecile one-sidedness" and "denationalized fanatic protests."[25] Henry Chorley, who had been disappointed by *Casa Guidi Windows* and bewildered by *Aurora Leigh*, was now smarting under her friendly but candid response to his novel, *Roccabella*, which despite the fact that its villain is an Italian patriot he had unaccountably dedicated to her, and he finally lost patience with her deviation from the kind of womanliness he admired. Even friendly reviewers were outraged by the impression, which Chorley shared, that she was cursing England rather than America. This impression while careless was not entirely unreasonable, since in "Italy and the World" the poet also appears to speak in her own person, and in similarly denunciatory mood, against England. When she pointed out that "A Curse for a Nation" unmistakably addressed America, Chorley reported her explanation in the *Athenaeum*, but in such a way as to suggest that she was trying to wriggle out of responsibility for what she had said.[26] Browning was furious on her behalf, and she felt that she had been "dishonored" and made to look "ungenerous, cowardly, mean" (*LEBB* 2:374, 380), as she had accused herself of being in the matter of the Anti–Corn Law League—not like a Godiva. Of all the hard things that were ever said about her, this hurt most.

The attacks recapitulated publicly and on a much larger scale the objections that her male friends and relations (including Chorley) had made to the Anti–Corn Law project, especially their contemptuous assumption that women should not meddle in politics, and in fact her brother George was against her this time too. The reviewers' ridicule in effect reduces her to the condition of the enslaved women of the poems, subjecting her to public insult and depicting her as both unwomanly and powerless. One of them speaks of her "instinct of servility" and "servile and seditious platitudes,"[27] and others feminize and belittle the curse as mere "scold[ing]."[28] Her loyalty to Napoleon III encouraged accusations of servility: "It is base and unnatural . . . when the poet, except as a captive in fetters, follows the despot in his triumph."[29] But none of this surprised her. She had predicted that the English critics would "worry [her] alive" (*LEBB* 2:360), as if recalling the hunters who tracked down the runaway slave, or those in *Uncle Tom's Cabin* who hunt black women with dogs,[30] and she reverted to the image of the hunt later, when the *Athenaeum* made her look, she said, as if to "escape from the dogs in England" she "threw them the good name of America" (*LEBB* 2:380).

The issue that aroused the angriest attack on *Poems before Congress* was not Italy or England or America, but her indecorous behavior as a woman. *Blackwood's* opens with three paragraphs of heavy-handed ridicule and a pompous lecture on womanliness, which the reviewer takes to consist mostly in not exposing oneself in public, not cursing, and not interfering in politics. "To bless not to curse is woman's function," she is informed, and she is dismissed with the advice to ponder the example of Florence Nightingale (fully justifying, she must have reflected, her doubts about Nightingale's contribution to feminism).[31] All women, she said, should be "vexed on [their] own accounts" by *Blackwood's* attack

(*LEBB* 2:387). As with *Aurora Leigh*, however, she concluded that "the abuse of the press is the justification of the poems" (*LEBB* 2:376). "If [the book] had been otherwise received, its application would have been doubtful in my own opinion even" (*LBGB* 225). She emerged from the fray battered but cheerful: "it's only what I expected, and I have had that deep satisfaction of 'speaking though I died for it,' which we are all apt to aspire to now and then" (*LEBB* 2:387).

Poems before Congress was her last coherent book. Attacks of illness (presumably a recurrence of pulmonary tuberculosis), became more frequent and severe, and she grew steadily weaker. She had been accustomed to surviving what would have seemed hopeless debility in others and does not seem to have been seriously alarmed, but she gradually grew weaker and on June 29 1861, a few weeks after returning from Rome to Casa Guidi, she died. The contents of *Last Poems*, published by Browning eight months later from a list she had drawn up herself, are a mixed lot. A few pre-date her marriage. Several were prompted by political events since the publication of *Poems before Congress*, and others that are not about politics were evidently written in the last few years of her life. "A Song for the Ragged Schools of London" had appeared in 1854 with a poem by Browning as a pamphlet sold to raise money for one of Arabel Barrett's charities, the only joint publication they arranged together. There are also several translations. These poems acquire a somewhat factitious importance from being last, inviting us to look both for closure and for signs of what might have come next, and on the whole they are disappointing: they do little to exploit or expand her fame, nor do they clearly foreshadow new projects or an approaching end. Several, however, take a new kind of interest in maternity, femininity, sexuality, and death, and "A Musical Instrument" very powerfully adumbrates connections between sexuality and artistic creation. Certainly her powers were not waning, nor was her inspiration exhausted; some of her finest poems are among the latest written. Taken all together, they necessarily complete, however fortuitously or inconclusively, the pattern of her career.

Almost half of the twenty-eight poems (not counting translations) spring from the imaginative energies, here considerably attenuated, that produced *Poems before Congress*. Victor Emmanuel is hailed as "King of us all" ("King Victor Emanuel Entering Florence, April 1860") in verse that is never more than pedestrian, a pale pendant to the grand if uneven ode on Napoleon III. The satire on foreign prejudices ("Summing Up in Italy") is rather dull. As in *Poems before Congress* (and in the late writings of Tennyson and Browning), there is a tendency to the anecdotal, but the anecdotes are more sentimental and are recounted with less ingenuity and verve. Several celebrate varieties of heroism available to people who can't fight: a woman who sends her lover off to battle ("Parting Lovers"); the queen of Naples, "young and kind, and royally blind" ("Nature's Remorses," 7), to whom children and sunshine matter more than a lost throne (and who, although the poem does not say so, had won the poet's favor by smiling on Pen); Garibaldi's daughter, who fulfills Barrett Browning's girlhood desire by singing of freedom, pleasing both an heroic king and her own heroic father ("The King's Gift"); and an Italian youth impressed into service in the front lines of the Austrian army who gladly lets himself be shot in battle by the Italians ("The Forced Recruit"). She had become more fertile in ideas of heroism since her celebration of Riego's mute widow many years earlier, but nothing here has the gusto of comparable pieces in *Poems before Congress.*

The two best political poems, "A View across the Roman Campagna" and "Mother and Poet" (both dated 1861 and therefore among her very last works), do not celebrate heroism at all. "A View" is an extraordinary fusion of satire, visionary dreariness, and religious epiphany. The apparition of Christ on the Campagna is stated, not described, but it is a daring conception nonetheless (especially in the middle of a satire on the pope) even for someone whose friends used regularly to be distressed by her habit of mentioning sacred names and subjects in her verse.

> Over the dumb Campagna-sea,
>   Out in the offing through mist and rain,
> Saint Peter's Church heaves silently
>   Like a mighty ship in pain,
>   Facing the tempest with struggle and strain.
>
>   (1–5)

Over this sea "The Christ walks" (14). But:

> Peter, Peter! He does not stir;
>   His nets are heavy with silver fish;
> He reckons his gains, and is keen to infer
>   —"The broil on the shore, if the Lord should wish;
> But the sturgeon goes to the Caesar's dish."
>
>   (26–30)

The portent of a new Rome at the end of this grim comic apocalypse is a flight of vultures.

And "Mother and Poet" casts a harsh revisionary light on the incite-ments to political ardor which make up so much of Barrett Browning's later works. The speaker is Laura Savio, a poet of the Risorgimento whose two sons died fighting for Italy. She resents male condescension—she was "good at [her] art, for a woman, men said" (7)—and yet she bitterly asserts that a woman's art should be motherhood, which in images like those of *Aurora Leigh* she conceives as both self-immolation and destruction. Being a mother meant "hurting her breast / With the milk-teeth of babes, and a smile at the pain" [12–13]); and it also meant, as both mother and poet, teaching her sons the self-immolating patriotism they died for. Now she is sick of sacrifice, patriotism, and poetry: having seen the consequences of her song, she will sing no longer. "If in keeping the feast / You want a great song for your Italy free, / Let none look at *me*" (98–100). There is no simple opposition of "mother *or* poet," as in most of *Aurora Leigh*, since in both capacities she has sent her sons to death. She can imagine no resolution except one beyond poetry and country ("*your* Italy"), in the next world.

"Little Mattie" is another surprising variation on the theme of ma-ternal and filial relations. Addressed to a mother whose thirteen-year-old daughter has died, the poem considers what it would be like actually to communicate (as bereaved parents thought they did at seances) with a dead child. The first three stanzas, drafts of which appear in a notebook from the early 1840s,[32] describe the unresponsiveness—the "innocent revolt" (36)—of a child who, being dead, has attained strange knowledge: "Now she knows what Rhamses knows" (24). Like a girl who becomes a poet, she sees what is invisible to her mother and defies maternal standards and authority—she died at the beginning of puberty, the age when Aurora's feminizing education began. The four later stanzas imag-ine a coldly Christ-like response to maternal importunities. "Ay, and if she spoke, maybe / She would answer, like the Son, / 'What is now 'twixt thee and me?' " (37–39) She might look with "Grand contempt" (70) on the mother who once "survey[ed] her with sweet scorn" (62), or "Rise up suddenly full-grown" (80) to appall her into madness. "Show me Michael with the sword / Rather than such angels, Lord!" (83–84). She would terrify the mother as her mother's portrait had terrified Aurora Leigh, and the poet seems to gloat over the prospect of the mother's discomfiture. On the theme of mothers and daughters, "Little Mattie" provides—for the daughter—triumphant closure. But, like the ballads, it expresses so unexpected a sentiment that it passes unobserved.

The largest group of poems besides those about Italy (eight, or, if we include "Parting Lovers" from the political group, nine) deal with char-

acters of women and relations between women and men. In comparison
to the ballads of the 1830s and 1840s, they are more dramatic in pre-
sentation, more directly concerned with sexuality, and more overtly par-
tisan in the battle between the sexes. "My Kate," "Amy's Cruelty," "May's
Love," and "A False Step" are high-class album verse (the first two were
actually published in *The Keepsake,* and the others might as well have
been) which consider characters of women and inculcate a mildly feminist
point of view. "Where's Agnes?" is more interesting, a cry of revulsion
against a pretense of feminine virtue inspired, Browning said, by Sophia
Eckley's treachery, and falling into something of Browning's denunciatory
tone.[33]

> Her sweetness strained the sense
>   Of common life and duty;
> And every day's expense
>   Of moving in such beauty
> Required, almost, defence.
>
> (46–50)

The speaker has succumbed to a wholly conventional ideal of feminine
virtue as sweetness, softness, purity, weakness—the ideal of the knight
in "The Romaunt of the Page," for instance, or the angelic aspect of the
portrait of Aurora's mother—that she (or perhaps he) should have known
all along must be false. "She, who scarcely trod the earth, / Turned
mere dirt?" (86–87)

Agnes's sin is apparently sexual: she is a white rose that fell from the
branch not because it was plucked by force, but because it willfully let go.

> Then henceforth may earth grow trees!
>   No more roses!—hard straight lines
> To score lies out! none of these
>   Fluctuant curves, but firs and pines,
> Poplars, cedars, cypresses!
>
> (116–20)

The poem ends with this furious repudiation of feminine softness in
favor of "hard straight lines," exemplified both in the trees and in the
bare listing; and the final, appropriately abrupt off-rhyme shows Barrett
Browning's mature mastery of what had always been considered a defect
in her style, clearly aligning—as "Catarina to Camoens" had more ob-
scurely done—stylistic innovation with new ideas about feminine
attractiveness.

Detestation of sexual hypocrisy and the determination to "score lies out" also informs a group of poems in which women excoriate male treachery and speak with great frankness about sex. "Lord Walter's Wife," in fact, is so frank that Thackeray in some embarrassment rejected it for the *Cornhill Magazine*—and while Barrett Browning was good-humored about being "turned out of a room for indecent behaviour" she argued, as she had for *Aurora Leigh,* that if pure women did not ignore the existence of vice other women might not be afflicted by it (*LEBB* 2:445). Although Lord Walter's wife (like Riego's Widow in her first appearance) has no name of her own, she has considerable self-possession; when her husband's friend flirts with her, she acts the hackneyed role of temptress in order to demonstrate that his passion is a sham and his flattery an insult. The long polemic with which she berates him is a sensible denunciation of men who play the game of illicit sentiment without the courage to sin, but the self-righteous assertion of her own purity ("Understand, if you can, / That the eyes of such women as I am are clean" [47–48]) is less attractive. She does not manage to elude the peril that *Sonnets from the Portuguese* had shown to lie in wait for women who, for whatever reason, say "look at me" ("Look me full in the face!—in the face" [47]).

As in the *Sonnets,* however, problems of self-deprecation and self-praise do not arise when the speaker expresses her own desire rather than responding to another's. Affirming female desire makes good feminist politics and good poems, whereas "Bertha in the Lane" had long ago demonstrated the political and poetic dangers both of suppressing desire and of oblique self-praise. "Void in Law" and "Bianca among the Nightingales" portray the essential purity of maternal and sexual passion, in contrast to Agnes's false ostentation of chastity and Lord Walter's friend's equally conventional miming of illicit love, even in compromising circumstances and under the sting of jealousy and betrayal. (Male sensuality is another matter; to Lord Walter's wife, being "moved [. . .] / In the senses" is "a vice [. . .] common to beasts and some men" [37–38].) The speaker in "Void in Law" has been abandoned by the lover who tricked her into an invalid marriage, and like Marian Erle she has innocently borne an illegitimate child, but unlike Marian's, her child is the fruit of life. "Bianca among the Nightingales" rebels, as nineteenth-century women writers liked to do, against a fundamental cliché of literary portraiture: Bianca, a dark passionate southern woman who, like Corinne, has lost her lover to a cool golden-haired English beauty, is frankly sexual and frankly jealous, but she is also pure, white, "Bianca."[34]

Like "Void in Law," which mingles ferocious jealousy, memories of desire, and maternal tenderness, "Bianca" is a highly charged mixture of moods, its hysterical edge justified by the dramatic situation. It begins with remembered ecstasy, a bold image of sanctified desire, and a picture of nature cleansed, empowered, and unified by passion:

> The cypress stood up like a church
>   That night we felt our love would hold,
> And saintly moonlight seemed to search
>   And wash the whole world clean as gold;
> The olives crystallised the vales'
>   Broad slopes until the hills grew strong:
> The fire-flies and the nightingales
>   Throbbed each to either, flame and song,
> The nightingales, the nightingales!

(1–9)

This is a freer, swifter, less self-conscious version of the passionate intensities of *Sonnets from the Portuguese*: the reciprocally throbbing flame and song would serve very well to express two poets' love. But this mutual bliss was shattered by the sudden appearance of a beautiful Englishwoman whom Bianca's lover eagerly assisted when their boats bumped in the Arno: the irruption into their equal passion of a different kind of story.

Bianca excoriates her rival—the rescued damsel, the perfect English lady, everything Elizabeth Barrett had never wanted to be—in the vituperous tones of "Where's Agnes?":

> She lied and stole,
> And spat into my love's pure pyx
> The rank saliva of her soul.
> And still they sing, the nightingales.

(105–8)

Although Barrett Browning's refrains are usually more or less mechanical and annoying, this one is entirely functional, conveying the intolerable iteration of balked desire, and effectively varied (as in "I cannot bear these nightingales" [117]). Like "A View across the Roman Campagna," the poem fuses very different kinds of feelings, thoughts, and images in a common mood of poetic intensity, and its outspoken association of passion, pain, and song links it with "A Musical Instrument."

"A Musical Instrument" has always been the best-known of the *Last Poems*, frequently anthologized and never suspected of subversive tendencies. Written early in 1860, or possibly late 1859, it is Barrett Browning's final statement about the nature of poetic creativity and the one poem in the volume which may be felt to provide satisfactory closure for her career as a whole. T. S. Eliot—of all people—used often to quote it.[35] "Pan is dead" are the last words of the 1844 *Poems,* announcing the coming of a modernized, Christianized art, but in "A Musical Instrument" Pan *redivivus* is the presiding genius of poetry, at whose irredeemably pagan force the "true gods sigh" but do nothing (40). The poem describes how Pan with careless cruelty makes a flute by hollowing out a reed. Based on Ovid's *Metamorphoses,* it draws its suggestive power from what Barrett Browning never mentions and most readers do not think about: that in Ovid's story the reed is the nymph Syrinx, transformed in her flight from lustful Pan.

In "A Musical Instrument" the reed is a figure for the poet, and as such pronomially male (Barrett Browning always refers to poets with the generic "he," even in *Aurora Leigh*), but in the imagery, feeling, and action as well as in the well-known myth the reed is female. The sexual violation that lies in a well of silence at the heart of *Aurora Leigh* becomes emotionally explicit—is, in effect, described—through the descriptions of Pan's brutality which comprise almost the whole poem:

> Spreading ruin and scattering ban,
> Splashing and paddling with hoofs of a goat,
> And breaking the golden lilies.

> (3–5)

When he has knocked down everything in sight like a destructive little boy (the crudely masculine kind that Barrett Browning did not want Pen to resemble even by the thickness of his boots), he attacks the reed. He "tore" it out of its "deep cool bed" (7–8), "hacked and hewed [. . .] / With his hard bleak steel at the patient reed" (15–16),

> Then drew the pith, like the heart of a man,
> Steadily from the outside ring,
> And notched the poor dry empty thing
>   In holes, as he sat by the river.

> (21–24)

"Then, dropping his mouth to a hole in the reed, / He blew" (29–30), and the "Piercing sweet" (32) song restored the ruined landscape. Even without a consciousness of Ovid's story this is painful; when we think of Syrinx it is almost intolerable.

The precise, deliberate articulation of sexual assault goes far beyond Ovid's gentle statement that Pan was inspired by the sighing of the reeds to bind up "pipes, made of unequal reeds fitted together by a joining of wax," and significantly revises previous English versions of the myth as well. English poets had made Pan, not Syrinx, their symbol of the artist, and without bothering about the feelings of the reed had moralized on Pan's frustration when (as Marvell put it) "Pan did after Syrinx speed / Not as a nymph, but for a reed." In his "Hymn of Pan" Shelley presents the violator as (literally) the injured party: "I pursued a maiden and clasped a reed. / Gods and men, we are all deluded thus!— / It breaks in our bosom and then we bleed." The Romantic poets' Pan, god of inspiring nature as well as the representative of the poet himself in Shelley's and Keats's use of the Syrinx myth, combines in "A Musical Instrument" with the Romantic wind of poetic inspiration and becomes something entirely new. Making Syrinx the poet changes the meaning of sexual pain as the source of art; it also introduces into English poetry the idea of Pan as a sexually brutal creature that became commonplace afterwards but had rarely appeared before. This version of the banished pagan deity is the natural consequence of seeing the story from the woman's point of view, and the dark vision of the links between sexuality and art is the unacknowledged shadow-side of Barrett Browning's valorization both of sexual love in her later works and of passivity, weakness, and pain in her early ones. The two are not unconnected. Just as the poet's openness to inspiration is figured in *Aurora Leigh* as Danaë's openness to Jove (3:122–41), and rape released Marian from speechlessness into impassioned eloquence, so Pan's violence sums up the various kinds of desire, betrayal, and loss—filial, parental, political, sexual—that arouse the most poetically energizing emotions in *Last Poems*.[36]

And that the poet who had heralded the major period of her career by banishing Pan, and all Greek mythology with him, should record his reappearance at the very end of it is surprising only until we remember her early fears of self-confrontation and creativity and her association of Greece with self-assertion, excess, and Promethean defiance. For what, after all, was the pain of art as Barrett Browning, for whom writing poetry had been for years almost the only hope and pleasure, had experienced it? "The Tempest," "A True Dream," "A Sea-Side Meditation," and "The Development of Genius" show that it was the pain of self-recognition and self-suppression, both of which became in her apparently impersonal political works their obverse and counterpart, the naked self-presentation of Godiva's ride in which passivity and aggression are one. She had feared not only her self-assertive and aggressive impulses, but also her will to submission, what she called in "The Tempest" power and stooping unto power and which appears in *Aurora Leigh* as the temptation to prefer marriage to art. And the fact that she tells Syrinx's story as a detached narrator, entirely suppressing the character whose feelings generate the poem, suggests a similarly doubled identification and revulsion. The return to the classics is itself a self-confrontation: a recognition and a rereading of her earliest impulses to poetry.

Like the ballads, "A Musical Instrument" does not call our attention to the revisionary shift from a male to a female, or even feminist, point of view, and in fact it has gone almost entirely unnoticed. But Robert Browning saw it, and responded many years later in "Pan and Luna" by retelling Virgil's story about Pan's pursuit of the moon-goddess as a story of Pan's brutality and the violated woman's ambivalent response. Although Luna appears as a woman as well as a natural object, her plight is like that of Syrinx, "trapped, / Bruised to the breast of Pan, half-god half-brute, / Raked by his bristly boar-sword."[37] Browning's narrator identifies sometimes with Pan's lasciviousness, sometimes with Luna's revulsion, working toward the appalled recognition that when Pan called Luna, she "followed . . . / by no means spurning him" (99–100). The narrator's horrified identification with the goat-god may reflect Browning's recognition that much of his own poetry springs from the contemplation of physically or spiritually violated women, from Porphyria and the duke's last duchess at the beginning of his career to Pompilia in *The Ring and the Book*—that his theme is not just Perseus' rescue of Andromeda, but Andromeda's subjection to the monster. Browning seems to have been afraid that his wife's source of inspiration might have been the mirror image of his own. Even more than their versions of the romance of heroic rescue of which the myth of Pan is the antitype, the two poets' Pan poems have a dark and subtle reciprocity.

"A Musical Instrument" is an origin myth, and it rounds back both to Barrett Browning's childhood vision of Greece as the place of origins and the source of energy and delight and to the story of the damsel and the knight. She avoids the problem of situating herself within this paradigmatic story by moving outside it into the role of narrator, as she had done in the political poems, making the poet the main character in new versions of the old plot. The story itself is in process of transformation. There is no knight, but in a sense there is no damsel either, since her gender and even her presence are concealed. Except on the field of international politics knights had long been banished from her poetry, and she had repudiated the image of Italy as a helpless woman. But just as subjugated Italy and her avatars rise to heroic grandeur, and Marian Erle is empowered not by rescue but by violation, and Laura Savio— going a step further in the transformation of the plot—urges her sons so powerfully to heroic action that she destroys them and therefore herself too, so Syrinx makes her song not of waiting but of pain. In her linking of power with motherhood, her wanderings through strange byways of maternal and filial feeling, her unashamed articulations of desire, and her rewritings of myth and romance, Barrett Browning vastly enlarged the territory of women's poetry. And yet she had always been half afraid that the creative moment for a woman is the long moment in which rescue does not come. She had not wanted to speak from the place of the victim unless that place could be redefined, as in *Prometheus Bound* or the Godiva poems, as the locus of power, and *Aurora Leigh* rides triumphant over male domination of almost every conceivable kind. But "A Musical Instrument" is a reluctant acknowledgment that great poetry might, after all, come—as her own, including much of *Aurora Leigh* itself, had in the largest part come—not from participation in male superiority and cultural dominance, but from exclusion and pain. The erasure of Syrinx from the poem and the acceptance of its theme (which without her shrivels into a Romantic commonplace) by male as well as female poets show that this is not just a matter of gender.

Aftermath

Barrett Browning's death and the publication of *Last Poems* occasioned numerous reflections on her career and on women generally. She was agreed to have been the greatest of women poets— or at least, as one reviewer put it, "woman's nearest approach to a great poet."[1] She inspired "new ideas as to the capacities of her sex" and also demonstrated (since "no woman can hope to achieve what Mrs. Browning failed to accomplish") "the qualities and uniform limits of the female intellect."[2] "If she exceeded her sex in strength and aspiration, it was only to foreshadow what a woman may gain in her proper sphere,— not in another": her proper sphere in this case not including philosophy, in which she displays only "an acute and imitative handling of the tools of the masculine workman."[3] The *Dublin University Magazine,* which had found *Aurora Leigh* splendid but unfit for women to read, once again gave with one hand, took with the other:

> Well, she is dead, England's chief poetess—the rose, the con-
> summate crown, the rarer and stronger and more passionate
> Sappho of our time. . . . Her faults were of her womanhood:
> her great achievements were her own. . . . None can deny her
> greatness. But the blemishes which we see in her works, the
> spots which here and there obscure the solar disc of her fame,
> may teach us, may teach woman especially, a weighty lesson.
> The function of woman is—not to write, not to act, not to be
> famous—but to love.[4]

So much for *Aurora Leigh.*

In regard to *Last Poems* the usual objections were raised— irreverence, coarseness, negligent and undisciplined style, excessive and unpatriotic political fervor—although her recent death moderated their expression. But her purity and her

246

essentially "womanly" nature were unquestioned. Her character was held in particularly high esteem in America: "All things are pure to her"; "Mrs. Browning's character was well-nigh perfect."[5] The course of her life was frequently (and despite exaggerations of the severity and duration of her illnesses, reasonably accurately) described. *Aurora Leigh* was agreed to be her major work, and although the ballads and "The Cry of the Children" evidently retained their hold on readers, *Sonnets from the Portuguese* had begun to assume the importance it was later to hold as a personal expression of her love.

And to the very end, her life met contemporary expectations, culminating in one of the great deathbed scenes for which the Victorians are justly notorious. The story has been told and retold, first of all by Robert Browning. Browning sat up alone with her the last night.

> Thro' the night she slept heavily, and brokenly—that was the bad sign. But then she would sit up, take her medicine, say unrepeatable things to me and sleep again. At four o'clock there were symptoms that alarmed me,—I called the maid and sent for the Doctor.—She smiled as I proposed to bathe her feet "Well, you *are* making an exaggerated case of it!" Then came what my heart will keep till I see her and longer—the most perfect expression of her love to me within my whole knowledge of her—always smilingly, happily, and with a face like a girl's—and in a few minutes she died in my arms, her head on my cheek. . . . God took her to himself as you would lift a sleeping child from a dark, uneasy bed into your arms and the light. Thank God . . . . Her last word was—when I asked "How do you feel?"—*"Beautiful."*[6]

The richly experienced woman becomes in this account a trusting child, returned by her husband to the paternal embrace of God. Increased doses of morphine made her wander a little[7] (a fact Browning's reports usually do not mention) and no doubt had some part in her beatific state of mind. Not expecting to die, she had no last words for Pen.

She is depicted in letters and memoirs as quiet, gentle, and unassuming, attentive to others and speaking little of herself, the center of a cozy domestic circle: not at all the formidable bluestocking many expected. Everyone remembered how small she was, how low her voice. Thomas Trollope, brother of the more famous novelist, recalled his visits to Casa Guidi in true hagiographic style:

> I was conscious even then of coming away from those visits a better man, with higher views and aims . . . . such effect was not produced by any talk or look or word of the nature of preaching, or anything approaching to it, but simply by the perception and appreciation of what Elizabeth

Barrett Browning was; of the immaculate purity of every thought that
passed through her pellucid mind, and the indefeasible nobility of her
every idea, sentiment, and opinion .... I mean the purity of the upper
spiritual atmosphere in which she habitually dwelt; the absolute dissev-
erance of her moral as well as her intellectual nature from all those lower
thoughts as well as lower passions which smirch the human soul. In mind
and heart she was *White*—stainless.[8]

More acerbic opinions were expressed privately. Edward Fitzgerald's
was printed after his death, arousing Browning's fury:

Mrs. Browning's Death is rather a relief to me, I must say: no more
Aurora Leighs, thank God! A Woman of real Genius, I know: but what
is the upshot of it all? She and her Sex had better mind the Kitchen and
their Children; and perhaps the Poor: except in such things as little Novels,
they only devote themselves to what Men do much better, leaving that
which Men do worse or not at all.[9]

Harriet Hosmer, the young American sculptor who was on intimate terms
with the Brownings when they were in Rome, thought her "truly angelic,"
and yet read a more balanced image in her physiognomy: her "wonderful
dark eyes," Hosmer said, were "large and loving and luminous as stars,"
but her mouth "perhaps [gave] the key to some of [her] less delicate
verse, large, full-lipped, yet harboring always a sweet compensating
smile."[10] Trollope's blanched vision, however, predominated, and as the
virtues he eulogized fell out of fashion, so did Elizabeth Barrett Browning.

She was buried in Florence, mourned by the Anglo-American colony
and honored by Italian patriots. Browning, having immediately had Pen's
curls cut off and his beautiful clothes replaced by simpler ones, carried
him off to London to become a proper Englishman at last. Pen eventually
managed to get through Oxford, although in an unambitious fashion that
perennially disappointed his father; then he became a sculptor; and then,
having been married briefly to a rich American, he settled in a Venetian
palazzo, to which he summoned the old servants from Florentine days.
He spent his last years in Italy, never fulfilling his parents' hopes for him
but loyal to the memory of his childhood.

Browning died in Venice, never having returned to Florence. In 1867
he wrote of his married years, "The general impression of the past is as
if it had been pain. I would not live it over again, not one day of it. Yet
all that seems my real *life*,—and before and after, nothing at all: I look
back on all my life, when I look *there*." He felt, he said, like Homer's
Greeks, whose life was all in their ten years' suffering at Troy;[11] to him,

Elizabeth Barrett had been both damsel and knight, Homeric and heroic after all. He survived her for almost three decades, a solid citizen and ornament of dinner parties, increasingly venerated as poet and sage, what had once been derided as intolerable obscurity revered as riddling wisdom. His poetry resumed its flow, issuing in *The Ring and the Book* and some fine shorter works. But the garrulity that had been arrested by marriage grew on him again, and he never matched the spare and brilliant output of the years when he had his one right reader. His reputation quickly outstripped that of his wife, who soon lost the esteem of the cultural establishment on which she had never had more than a very shaky hold.

Except for Christina Rossetti and some lesser-known and inferior talents, no line of women poets sprang up to naturalize her anomalousness, which seemed if anything to increase as the decades passed. But the greatest female intellectual of the century, George Eliot, enormously admired her work, and the greatest woman poet, Emily Dickinson, was profoundly influenced by it. As a spokeswoman for female aspirations and discontents, she retained her readership for many years, and as a love poet, still longer. The virtues for which she was esteemed in her lifetime no doubt injured her literary reputation—could an exemplary wife and mother be a great poet?—is purity compatible with art? But women, at least, continued to read her books, and as a grandmother of poets her influence has been, although not always recognized, unending.

Notes

Introduction

1. Most quotations from Barrett Browning's works are identified parenthetically in the text. Unless otherwise specified, they are from *The Complete Works of Elizabeth Barrett Browning*, edited by Charlotte Porter and Helen A. Clarke (New York: Thomas Y. Crowell, 1900; reprinted New York: AMS Press, 1973). Poetry is identified by line number, prose by volume and page. Abbreviations are listed at the beginning of the bibliography.

Ellipsis points within quotations from Barrett Browning's letters and poems indicate the original punctuation unless enclosed in brackets. Elsewhere in the text ellipsis points indicate omissions.

2. Margaret Homans brilliantly analyzes the literalization of women's language, in its widest implications, in *Bearing the Word: Language and Female Experience in Nineteenth-Century Women's Writing* (Chicago: University of Chicago Press, 1986). Homans has also pointed out the political and conceptual weakness of recent feminist assertions "that poetry by women must report on the poet's experience as a woman, and that it must be true," the feminist version of the old expressive fallacy. No such simple relation between language and experience is possible, and "To place an exclusive valuation on the literal, especially to identify the self as literal, is simply to ratify women's age-old and disadvantageous position as the other and the object"; Homans, *Women Writers and Poetic Identity: Dorothy Wordsworth, Emily Brontë, and Emily Dickinson* (Princeton: Princeton University Press, 1980), 216, 218.

3. [H. N. Coleridge,] *Quarterly Review* 66 (1840): 374–75. Coleridge asserts that women writers are no longer discriminated against (375–76), but his essay belies his argument.

Chapter 1

1. *BC* 1:361. The editors date the manuscript by the handwriting as belonging to the early 1840s and note the clearly autobiographical references to Elizabeth Barrett's pony and the Malvern Hills; *BC* 1:360, n. The period described would be late 1816 or shortly thereafter, when she began learning Greek. There may be exaggeration as well as amusement in these reminiscences, but their basic truth is confirmed by the earlier essay.

2. "Of all natural relations," said Martineau, who published her first article in an attempt to find relief from her misery when her brother James returned to college after a vacation, "the least satisfactory is the fraternal. Brothers are to sisters what sisters can never be to brothers as objects of engrossing and devoted affection"; Harriet Martineau, *Autobiography*, 2 vols. (London: Virago, 1983), 1:117–18, 99. Branwell Brontë was sent to London to study art but only squandered money, while his sisters were expected to pay their own way. Christina Rossetti was not allowed to join the Pre-Raphaelite Brotherhood. As they grew older a brother who was a childhood companion with abilities inferior to his sister's was likely to take a father's part and react with wounding disapprobation, leading even to estrangement, against his sister's attempts to make a life for herself despite social convention: as Eliot's brother did, and Maggie Tulliver's, and Elizabeth Barrett's when she married Robert Browning—Bro had died by then, but for a while her other brothers ranged themselves against her. For an interpretation stressing the rivalry between them, see Betty Miller, "Elizabeth Barrett and Her Brother: 'For we were nursed upon the self-same hill,' " *Cornhill Magazine* 166 (1952): 221–28.

3. Translation from Anacreon: "Nature gave horns to bulls, & hoofs to horses," Armstrong Browning Library, Baylor University.

4. "On Ancient and Modern Literature," Armstrong Browning Library, Baylor University.

5. See Walter J. Ong, "Latin Language Study as a Renaissance Puberty Rite," *Rhetoric, Romance, and Technology: Studies in the Interaction of Expression and Culture* (Ithaca: Cornell University Press, 1971), 113–41; and Frank M. Turner, "Antiquity in Victorian Contexts," *Browning Institute Studies* 10 (1982): 8. The fullest treatments are those of Richard Jenkyns, *The Victorians and Ancient Greece* (Cambridge: Harvard University Press, 1980), and Frank M. Turner, *The Greek Heritage in Victorian Britain* (New Haven: Yale University Press, 1981).

6. "No woman could take the classics for granted. Starting Latin or Greek was a journey into alien territory and for some women the sense of strangeness never entirely wore off"; "The classics sometimes eluded women, sometimes infuriated them, but were inevitably both a symbol and an instrument of their rebellion"; R. Fowler, " 'On Not Knowing Greek': The Classics and the Woman of Letters," *Classical Journal* 78 (1983): 337, 348. On the appeal of the Greek alphabet, see Jenkyns, *The Victorians and Ancient Greece*, 155. Mary Moulton-Barrett took a mixed view of her sons' departure into the world of male instruction: she was intelligently critical of the way Latin was taught to them and was "mortified" that Bro forgot geography when he went to school but had to admit "the Classics for the present to be all in all" (*BC* 1:139)—for the boys.

7. Fowler points out that girls read for the sake of reading, boys for examinations; " 'On Not Knowing Greek,' " 337–38. George Eliot had a similar passion for Greek and was similarly self-educated, and when she quoted two lines of Greek in "Amos Barton," the *Quarterly Review* "pounced on a couple of mistakes in her accents"; Jenkyns, *The Victorians and Ancient Greece*, 114. Virginia L. Radley notes the tendency of critics to condescend to Barrett Browning's scholarship, in *Elizabeth Barrett Browning* (Boston: Twayne, 1972), 17. Percy Lubbock is a good example: "she never became a scholar, either in the meticulous sense of the grammarian and philologist, or in the wider sense of the man [sic] who makes the Greek spirit his own, and moves

naturally in its equal radiance"; *Elizabeth Barrett Browning in Her Letters* (London: Smith, Elder, 1906), 18.

8. See Jenkyns, *The Victorians and Ancient Greece*, 194. Browning described his early encounters with Homer in "Development." References to Browning's poetry are to *Robert Browning: The Poems*, ed. John Pettigrew and Thomas J. Collins, 2 vols. (New Haven: Yale University Press, 1981).

9. *Childe Harold's Pilgrimage* II.1xxxviii in Byron, *Poetical Works*, ed. Frederick Page, 3d ed. (Oxford: Oxford University Press, 1970). All references to Byron's poetry are to this edition. See Turner, *The Greek Heritage in Victorian Britain*, 135–36, 38, on Byron and Greece.

10. Jenkyns, *The Victorians and Ancient Greece*, 14–15; Turner, *The Greek Heritage in Victorian Britain*, 187–263.

11. "My Character and Bro's Compared!" (*BC* 1:357–58). She compares Greece and Rome and calls Virgil a plagiarist in "On Ancient and Modern Literature."

12. Warner Barnes, "The Sorrows of the Muses: An Early Poem by Elizabeth Barrett," *Books at Iowa* 4 (April 1966): 31.

13. *Childe Harold's Pilgrimage*," II:xc, 1xxxix.

14. Many of these are published in *Hitherto Unpublished Poems and Stories*, ed. H. Buxton Forman, 2 vols. (Boston: Bibliophile Society, 1914).

15. Barnes, "The Sorrows of the Muses," 29.

16. Gardner Taplin, "An Early Poem by Mrs. Browning," *Notes & Queries* 195 (10 June 1950): 253.

17. "The Enchantress" and "Leila" are published in *New Poems by Robert Browning and Elizabeth Barrett Browning*, ed. Sir Frederic G. Kenyon (London: Smith, Elder, 1914). Elizabeth Barrett sent one of these poems to Campbell and received a kinder, less discouraging reply than Charlotte Brontë got to a similar approach to Southey (*BC* 1:164–65, 169–70). The poems also resemble Shelley's *The Witch of Atlas*, published in 1824.

18. These poems appear in *Hitherto Unpublished Poems and Stories*.

19. The poem is printed and discussed by Kay Moser in "Elizabeth Barrett's Youthful Feminism: Fragment of 'An Essay on Woman,' " *Studies in Browning and His Circle* 12 (Spring–Fall 1984): 13–26.

20. The 1824–26 Notebook, 159, English Poetry Collection, Wellesley College Library.

21. Freud found that cases of hysteria almost always began with genuine somatic symptoms and described the typical hysterical woman's character in terms highly relevant to Elizabeth Barrett: "her giftedness, her ambition, her moral sensibility, her excessive demand for love which, to begin with, found satisfaction in her family, and the independence of her nature which went beyond the feminine ideal and found expression in a considerable amount of obstinacy, pugnacity and reserve"; Josef Breuer and Sigmund Freud, *Studies on Hysteria*, trans. James Strachey (New York: Basic Books, 1957), 161. (Anna O. was actually Breuer's patient.) Cora Kaplan assumes that Elizabeth Barrett's was an hysterical illness brought on by excessive self-restraint; see "Wicked Fathers: A Family Romance," *Sea Changes: Essays on Culture and Feminism* (London: Verso, 1986), 201–2.

22. Medical specialists whom I have consulted believe that the illness was organic: perhaps Potts's disease, tuberculosis of the spine. George Pickering, who studied

her later illnesses and concluded that she suffered from organic disease, most probably pulmonary tuberculosis, does not analyze this early episode; see *Creative Malady: Illness in the Lives and Minds of Charles Darwin, Florence Nightingale, Mary Baker Eddy, Sigmund Freud, Marcel Proust, and Elizabeth Barrett Browning* (New York: Oxford University Press, 1974).

23. Howard M. Feinstein defines the function of illness in mid-nineteenth-century America: illness "provided social definition, sanctioned pleasure [such as travel], prescribed leisure for health, protected from premature responsibility, forced others to care, and expressed inadmissible feelings while protecting vital personal ties. For the patient it was a compromise between the attainment of forbidden goals and punishment for that accomplishment"; Feinstein, *Becoming William James* (Ithaca: Cornell University Press, 1984), 205. Ellen Moers sees Elizabeth Barrett's later illnesses as providing freedom to read and to write (*Literary Women* [Garden City: Doubleday, 1976], 7), but she had such freedom anyway.

24. Georgina Battiscombe, *Christina Rossetti: A Divided Life* (New York: Holt, Rinehart, & Winston, 1981), 33, 36.

25. The 1824–26 Notebook, 51: "I never knew that woman was an *animal*, or peculiar to the summer season."

26. ["A Commonplace Book," HM 4934] 1, Huntington Library, San Marino, California.

27. Lionel Stevenson recounts the story of her popularity in "Miss Landon, 'The Milk-and-Watery Moon of Our Darkness,' 1824–30," *Modern Language Quarterly* 8 (1947): 355–63.

28. The 1824–26 Notebook, 140.

29. The 1824–26 Notebook, 141.

30. *Literary Gazette*, no. 389 (3 July 1824): 417. The attack appeared in the *Westminster Review* 3 (1825): 537–39.

Chapter 2

1. Preface to *Lyrical Ballads* (1802), *William Wordsworth*, ed. Stephen Gill (Oxford: Oxford University Press, 1984), 603. All references to Wordsworth's writings are to this edition.

2. Arnold's Advertisement to the second edition of his 1853 *Poems* (1854) offers a similar defense of his advocacy of poetic subjects taken from classical literature: "There is . . . an immortal strength in the stories of great actions; the most gifted poet, then, may well be glad to supplement with it [his] mortal weakness"; *The Poems of Matthew Arnold*, ed. Kenneth Allott (London: Longmans, 1965; 2d ed., ed. Miriam Allott, 1979), 673. All references to Arnold's writings are to this edition unless otherwise specified.

3. The 1824–26 Notebook, 57.

4. Kathleen Hickok traces the major themes of nineteenth-century women poets in *Representations of Women: Nineteenth-Century British Women's Poetry* (Westport, Conn.: Greenwood, 1984); on their ambivalence about fame, see 145–48. Such ambivalence was not a specifically Victorian phenomenon: Elizabeth Barrett suffered less from it, in fact, than did such notable female predecessors as Katherine Philips and Anne

Finch. Poems expressing male Victorian poets' fear that art precludes love include Tennyson's "Palace of Art," Arnold's "Tristram and Iseult," and many works by Browning, the most famous being "My Last Duchess."

5. See Leo Braudy, *The Frenzy of Renown: Fame and Its History* (New York: Oxford University Press, 1986), 126, 449, 403. Braudy does not raise questions of gender: he doesn't point out, for instance, that his list of those who ostentatiously withdrew is mostly female, although there are very few women in his book.

6. On women's fear of publishing, see Angeline Goreau, *Reconstructing Aphra: A Social Biography of Aphra Behn* (New York: Dial, 1980), 144–55.

7. "Prospectus of an Ethic Poem," Henry W. and Albert A. Berg Collection, New York Public Library, Astor, Lenox, and Tilden Foundations.

8. But she "names" him only by his relationship to her, as she does Bro, while a younger brother is identified simply as a child, and even the word "brother" disappears from "Memory" between the manuscript and the published version. In "Verses To My Brother" she says, "I will write down thy name" (1) and gaze on it, turning from the world, but she doesn't. Naming others in poems is an act of love and also, although she is too modest to say so, an attempt to immortalize them. But love and art are not so easily reconciled. In "To _____" she asserts that love is artless, even speechless, and then gets out of the apparent impasse by saying that she will write in response to the expressed desire of this particular beloved audience. The poem is elaborately self-contradictory, renouncing art in the most highly wrought stanzas in the book.

9. In the other poem on Byron, "Stanzas" (subtitled with explanatory thoroughness "Occasioned by a Passage in Mr. Emerson's Journal, which states, that on the mention of Lord Byron's name, Captain Demetrius, an old Roumeliot, burst into tears"), Bryon has become an object of such extreme love that he cannot be named—"Name not his name," the speaker adjures—without evoking tears. As usual when the subject of naming comes up in this volume, the poem half-contradicts itself, naming Byron not in the poem but only in the subtitle. And if Byron is named only to say that he cannot be named, Riga speaks only to say that he can no longer speak.

10. In the faults of her verse, as often in her tone and subjects, her early work astonishingly resembles Matthew Arnold's. In tone and technique, the most striking likeness is between "Isobel's Child" and Arnold's "Tristram and Iseult."

11. "The Development of Genius," 1:224–28; in *Hitherto Unpublished Poems and Stories.*

12. *The Letters of John Keats, 1814–1821,* ed. Hyder Edward Rollins, 2 vols. (Cambridge: Harvard University Press, 1958) 2:80. Wordsworth, "The Old Cumberland Beggar," 153 ("we have all of us one human heart"). Elizabeth Barrett's literalization of the image is characteristic.

13. Alexander Pope, "Essay on Man," 1:200. George Eliot, *Middlemarch,* ed. Gordon S. Haight (Boston: Houghton Mifflin, 1956), 144 (chap. 20).

14. Quotations are from her record of the scene, made the following day (*BC* 1:358–60).

15. Browning, "Andrea del Sarto," 97–98.

16. *Hitherto Unpublished Poems and Stories* 2:85.

17. [Anecdotes of Literary Persons,] "An acquaintance said to Dr. Adam Clarke . . . ," Armstrong Browning Library, Baylor University.

18. *Westminster Review* 3 (April 1825): 539.

19. On Romantic views of Prometheus and Aeschylus, see Jenkyns, *The Victorians and Ancient Greece*, 88–90.

20. *Shelley's Poetry and Prose*, ed. Donald H. Reiman and Sharon B. Powers (New York: Norton, 1977), 133. Further references to Shelley's writings will be to this edition.

21. Thomas McFarland, *Romanticism and the Forms of Ruin: Wordsworth, Coleridge, and Modalities of Fragmentation* (Princeton: Princeton University Press, 1981), esp. 20–26; and Marjorie Levinson, *The Romantic Fragment Poem: A Critique of a Form* (Chapel Hill: University of North Carolina Press, 1986), esp. 197–220.

22. These lines are strikingly proleptic of Meredith's "Lucifer in Starlight."

23. "To a Poet's Child" balances love against fame in the context of family relationships, like "Minstrelsy," pointing out in ironical tones that even a daughter's love for a dead poet (presumably Byron) does not amount to much—and it is hard to imagine what object Elizabeth Barrett, worshipper of Byron and devoted daughter, would have thought more certain to inspire a lasting affection. The speaker ironically wishes to this girl of little feeling the attention after death that she deserves: mild tears, not a "sculptured urn" (70). And yet this is not much different, after all, from the fate that the speaker of "Minstrelsy" quite solemnly asks for herself.

24. *LHSB* 176. See Ellen Moers, "Performing Heroinism: The Myth of Corinne," *Literary Women*, 173–210.

25. *Maud* 3:34–35, *The Poems of Tennyson*, ed. Christopher Ricks (London: Longmans, 1969). All references to Tennyson's works are to this edition.

26. "Lines Composed a Few Miles above Tintern Abbey," 122–23. Her (mis)quotation appears in *Essays on the Greek Christian Poets and the English Poets* (1863; reprinted Plainview, N.Y.: Books for Libraries Press, 1972), 222. All references to her prose essays are to this edition.

27. According to Gardner Taplin, the shorter poems as well as the translation were probably all written at Hope End; *The Life of Elizabeth Barrett Browning* (New Haven: Yale University Press, 1957), 48.

Chapter 3

1. *The Life of Mary Russell Mitford, Related in a Selection from Her Letters to Her Friends*, ed. A. G. L'Estrange, 3 vols. (London: Richard Bentley, 1870), 3:141. She told a friend in 1839, "Next to my father, she is the creature whom I best love"; *Letters of Mary Russell Mitford*, 2d Series, ed. Henry Chorley, 2 vols. (London: Richard Bentley & Son, 1872), 1:273. "Her sweetness of character is even beyond her genius"; 1:274.

2. "A True Dream" appears in *New Poems*, 112.

3. The paradigmatic significance of "A True Dream" is suggested by the fact that Christina Rossetti and Emily Dickinson also wrote poems—not influenced by this one, of course, since it was not published until the twentieth century—in which reptilian figures of sexuality and evil both attract and repel and are disavowed by the assertion that the story was only a dream: Rossetti, "My Dream"; Dickinson, "In Winter in my Room."

4. See A. Dwight Culler, *Imaginative Reason: The Poetry of Matthew Arnold* (New Haven: Yale University Press, 1966), 1–17.

5. Cf. Wordsworth's "Ode [Intimations of Immortality from Recollections of Early Childhood]," 76. This ode gives perhaps Wordsworth's fullest, if most ambiguous, picture of nature as mother.

6. Only three of the 1826 poems deal with nature: "Memory" simply uses it for allegory, "The Prayer" argues that grief is necessary for the spirit to be "weanëd from a world so fair" (26), and "The Dream" records that earth was Paradise before "Sin claimed [her as] his bride" (35). That is, earth is a woman whom the child must leave, whom a man has spoiled (as thunder spoiled the milk), whose beauty is a deceitful illusion. Many of the poems published in 1833, however, after the death of Mary Moulton-Barrett in 1828, associate nature with death and look beyond it to love and to God ("Earth," "Minstrelsy," "The Image of God," "Idols," "The Autumn," "The Tempest").

7. My discussion of the relationship of female poets to nature in the nineteenth century is deeply indebted to Margaret Homans's seminal (if one may use the word) study, *Women Writers and Poetic Identity: Dorothy Wordsworth, Emily Brontë, and Emily Dickinson* (Princeton: Princeton University Press, 1980).

8. Wordsworth, "A slumber did my spirit seal." The epigraph comes from Wordsworth's "Lines Left upon a Seat in a Yew-tree," an early work that warns, in fact, against withdrawal from life into nature.

9. Over and over again Arnold, for instance, says plaintively of the Romantic myths that they are not literally *true*. This is another of the characteristics of women's writing which also characterizes Victorian poetry as a whole.

10. It has been suggested that women, not forced to achieve such absolute separation from their mothers, have more fluid ego boundaries than men do. "From the retention of preoedipal attachments to their mother, growing girls come to define and experience themselves as continuous with others; their experience of self contains more flexible or permeable ego boundaries"; Nancy Chodorow, *The Reproduction of Mothering: Psychoanalysis and the Sociology of Gender* (Berkeley and Los Angeles: University of California Press, 1978), 169.

11. "The Idea of Order at Key West" is also, but of course more overtly, about the complex interrelation of speech and sea.

12. "Behold, with tears mine eyes are wet"—the words are Arnold's in "The Buried Life" (2), but the diction and sentiment are indistinguishable from Elizabeth Barrett's. Men wept more then, too; Maisie Ward says of Browning: "He always did cry easily: when listening to great music or watching tragedy, when hearing his wife's poetry read, when reading his own (and the audience cried with him), even when visiting the room where Petrarch died. [He was seen] blindly weeping in the London streets months after his wife's death"; *Robert Browning and His World: The Private Face (1821–1861)* (New York: Holt, Rinehart & Winston, 1967), 168. For Dickens, Fred Kaplan points out, "the tears of sentimentality can dissolve the barrier that destructive individual and social pressures have erected to prevent the free expression of feeling"; *Sacred Tears: Sentimentality in Victorian Literature* (Princeton: Princeton University Press, 1987), 41.

13. "Its faith is a poor thing, but its doubt is a very intense experience"; T. S. Eliot, "In Memoriam," *Selected Essays*, 3d ed. (London: Faber & Faber, 1951), 336.

14. On Elizabeth Barrett as a religious poet, see Hoxie Neale Fairchild, *Religious Trends in English Poetry* (New York: Columbia University Press, 1957), 4:49–60. Perhaps the most memorable depiction of the poet as God's child is that in George Herbert's "The Collar."

15. *Personal Reminiscences by Chorley, Planché, and Young,* ed. Richard Henry Stoddard (New York: Scribner, Armstrong, 1874), 49.

16. L'Estrange, *Life of Mary Russell Mitford* 3:76–77. For a later volume, the artist altered the picture to accommodate the poem (*LMRM* 2:382).

17. Tennyson never wrote poems to match pictures, although he did very reluctantly contribute to annuals edited by titled ladies. "To write for people with prefixes to their names is to milk he-goats," he grumbled; "there is neither honour nor profit." Quoted by Robert Bernard Martin, *Tennyson: The Unquiet Heart* (New York: Oxford University Press, 1980), 227.

18. For her comments on Mrs. Hemans, see *LMRM* 1:18, 2:88; on Landon, *LMRM* 1:18–19, 232–33, 235, 251. An earlier version of the title stresses both of the earlier poets: "Stanzas Addressed to Miss Landon, and Suggested by Her 'Stanzas on the Death of Mrs. Hemans' "; *New Monthly Magazine* 45 (September 1835): 82. The poem appeared two months after L.E.L.'s, in the same journal.

19. Laman Blanchard, *Life and Literary Remains of L.E.L.,* 2 vols. (Philadelphia: Lea & Blanchard, 1841), 2:230.

Chapter 4

1. *BC* 4:375; *Athenaeum,* 7 July 1838, pp. 466–68. Chorley's role on the *Athenaeum* is described by Leslie A. Marchand in *The Athenaeum: A Mirror of Victorian Culture* (Chapel Hill: University of North Carolina Press, 1941), 181–93 et passim.

2. *BC* 4:383; *Metropolitan Magazine,* August 1838, pp. 97–101; *BC* 4:385; *Monthly Review,* September 1838, pp. 125–30.

3. "Recent English Poetry," *North American Review* 55 (1842): 202–18.

4. *BC* 4:380; *Blackwood's Edinburgh Magazine* 44 (August 1838): 279–84.

5. See, e.g., *BC* 4:375; *Examiner,* 24 June 1838, p. 388; *BC* 4:383; *Metropolitan Magazine,* August 1838, pp. 97–101.

6. Shelley, *Julian and Maddalo,* 546 ("They learn in suffering what they teach in song").

7. This illness seems to have been quite different from her earlier one, beginning with a broken blood vessel in her chest; see Dorothy Hewlett, *Elizabeth Barrett Browning* (London: Cassell, 1953), 62. For a medical analysis, see George Pickering, *Creative Malady,* 245–65. Pickering's diagnosis is "a chronic lung affliction, beginning acutely in her early thirties, becoming dormant . . . and finally killing her at the age of fifty-three" (260).

8. According to Alethea Hayter, she showed few of the symptoms generally associated with opium addiction, except in the imagery of such poems as "A True Dream" and *The Seraphim,* and in the restlessness that doctors gave her more opium to cure; *Mrs. Browning: A Poet's Work and Its Setting* (New York: Barnes & Noble, 1962), 58–68. See also Hayter's *Opium and the Romantic Imagination* (Berkeley and Los Angeles: University of California Press, 1968), 297–99. Pickering agrees that she was a "well-balanced addict"; *Creative Malady,* 262.

9. Quoted, from a manuscript letter in the Pierpont Morgan Library, New York, 23 March 1844, by Ann Blainey in *The Farthing Poet: A Biography of Richard Hengist Horne, 1802–84: A Lesser Literary Lion* (London: Longmans, 1968), 119.

10. *Athenaeum,* 24 June 1843, pp. 583–84.

11. See Blainey, *The Farthing Poet,* 143. Much later, when he published her letters to him, Horne attributed her eagerness to conceal her participation (she did not tell Mary Russell Mitford, even, or her father) to the scathing reviews that the book received when it appeared in 1844, but his letters to her refer frequently to their mutual desire for secrecy.

12. *LMRM* 2:401; R. H. Horne to EBB [4 March 1844], Pierpont Morgan Library, New York. He blamed the inadequacy of his notice of her poems on an accident to the copy sent to the printer.

13. Mitford improved the story by reporting that Elizabeth Barrett had deliberately had her Plato bound to look like a novel: *Recollections of a Literary Life: or, Books, Places, and People* (New York: Harper & Bros., 1852), 172.

14. *Essays on the Greek Christian Poets and the English Poets,* 17, 11. Further references to this essay will be in the text. The tone is not that of Arnold's classicism, but of Walter Pater's.

15. See, e.g., Mitford, *Recollections of a Literary Life,* 174; L'Estrange, *Life of Mary Russell Mitford,* 3:63–64; Edgar Allan Poe, "The Drama of Exile and Other Poems," *The Complete Works of Edgar Allan Poe,* 17 vols., ed. James A. Harrison (New York; Thomas Y. Crowell, 1902), 12:15–19; *LEBB* 1:199. Margaret Fuller, "Miss Barrett's Poems," *Papers on Literature and Art* (New York: Wiley & Putnam, 1846), 2:24–26. Discussions of the contemporary reception of these poems as well as examples of the modern critical revulsion can be found in Taplin, *Life of Elizabeth Barrett Browning,* 61–64, 127–31, and Hayter, *Mrs. Browning,* 80–86. "It is almost impossible now," Hayter says, "not to dislike these poems very much indeed" (79).

16. L'Estrange, *Life of Mary Russell Mitford,* 3:63.

17. EBB to R. H. Horne, undated fragment, Pierpont Morgan Library, New York.

18. When she tried to help her friend through desperate financial straits by writing poems to be published under Mitford's name in a thumbnail-sized annual that had to be read with a magnifying glass, however, she had one of her rare failures, producing poems that were too elaborate, artificial, and clever. *Schloss's English Bijou Almanac for 1843, Poetically Illustrated by Miss Mitford* appeared in 1843; see *LMRM* 2:34 n.

19. *United Services Gazette,* 2 November 1839; quoted *LMRM* 1:166, n. 8.

20. Fuller, "Miss Barrett's Poems," 25.

21. "Poems by Elizabeth B. Barrett," *Blackwood's* 56 (November 1844): 625.

22. *BC* 4:33, 38, 102. L'Estrange, *Life of Mary Russell Mitford,* 3:63; [Forster,] *Examiner,* 28 October 1838, p. 667 (*BC* 4:405); *Athenaeum,* 20 October 1838, p. 758 (*BC* 4:402).

23. On the difference between Victorian and twentieth-century women poets' revisions of old stories, see Alicia Ostriker, "The Thieves of Language: Women Poets and Revisionist Mythmaking," *Signs* 8 (1982): 68–90. One imagines the tone in which Anne Sexton would have told these stories.

24. The 1824–26 Notebook, 147. The poem was written in 1840, when Napoleon's remains rested for four days in Tor Bay en route from Saint Helena to France (Hewlett, *Elizabeth Barrett Browning,* 69). In his letters to Elizabeth Barrett, Haydon

defended his hero, Wellington, while she attacked England's lack of chivalry. Napoleon was one of the subjects suggested to Elizabeth Barrett for an epic.

25. Transcripts of these poems are given by Phillip D. Sharp, "Poetry in Process: Elizabeth Barrett Browning and the Sonnets Notebook" (Ph.D. diss., Louisiana State University, 1985), 32–35, 41, 47–61, 18, 19. Sharp explains the relevant historical background, including a significant brother.

26. "And on the ground, which is my moodres gate, / I knokke with my staf, bothe erly and late, / And saye, 'Leeve mooder, leet me in!' "; "The Pardoner's Tale," 729–31, in *The Poetical Works of Chaucer*, ed. F. N. Robinson (Boston: Houghton Mifflin, 1933).

27. Chaucer, "The Pardoner's Tale," 737.

28. Surrounding Childe Roland at sunset, "The hills, like giants at a hunting, lay / Chin upon hand, to see the game [himself] at bay," and then "all the lost adventurers my peers" "stood, ranged along the hill-sides, met / To view the last of me, a living frame / For one more picture" ("Childe Roland to the Dark Tower Came," 190–91, 195, 199–201)—the viewer of a picture laid out on such a plane being, by implication, God. As in "The Lost Bower," the hills are seen as a brotherhood allied with God, hostile to the speaker.

29. It was first published in *Graham's American Monthly Magazine* 23 (October 1843): 208–9. The first draft is printed in *Diary*, 316–18. For evidence of Dickinson's and Melville's familiarity with the poem, see George Monteiro, "On First Looking into Strangford's Camões: Elizabeth Barrett Browning's 'Catarina to Camoëns,' " *Studies in Browning and His Circle* 8 (Spring 1980): 8.

30. Lord Viscount Strangford, *Poems from the Portuguese of Luis de Camoens: With Remarks on His Life and Writings, Notes, &c &c* (London: J. Carpenter, 1803), 40.

31. Strangford, 8.

32. Strangford, 11. In a review of Elizabeth Barrett's poetry Edgar Allan Poe remarks that "a woman and her book are identical"; *The Complete Works of Edgar Allan Poe*, 12:1.

33. Strangford, 13.

34. "Recent Poetry," *Tait's Edinburgh Magazine* 11 (1844): 725.

35. *National Quarterly Review* (New York) 1 (1860): 173.

36. Preface to *The Venetian Bracelet, The Poetical Works of L. E. Landon*, 2 vols. (Philadelphia: Jasper Harding, 1850), 2:102.

37. "Night at Sea," *New Monthly Magazine and Humorist* 55 (1839): 30–32. "L.E.L.'s Last Question" appeared on 26 January 1839.

38. *New Monthly Magazine* 55 (1839): 28–29.

39. *Athenaeum*, 5 January 1839, p. 14.

40. Kathleen Hickok notes the similarity between "A Romance of the Ganges" and Landon's "Hindoo Girl's Song" and between "Bertha in the Lane" and Landon's "The Secret Discovered"; *Representations of Women*, 172, 175.

41. Elizabeth Barrett got two seeds from Mary Russell Mitford that L.E.L. had sent from Africa and tried (with what result is not recorded) to get them to grow. "In spite of the miserably low standard of her literary morality," wrote Henry Chorley, who as a writer for the *Athenaeum* had frequently been the victim of her pen, "Miss Landon was made for better things"; *Personal Reminiscences by Chorley, Planché, and Young*, 9. Planché in the same volume refers more sympathetically to "that most

cruelly maligned lady" and her "miserable and unmerited fate" (84). That she was unfortunate, Chorley agreed: "of all the lives of literary women . . . that of L.E.L. seems to me the most sorrowful" (11–12).

42. *LEBB* 1:233; *LMRM* 2:392; see also *RB-EBB* 1:113–14. Patricia Thomson sums up the similarities between Elizabeth Barrett and the worldly and notorious Frenchwoman three years older than herself: "Both were warm, impulsive, emotional; both were Romantics, Byron-worshippers in their youth, radicals, moderate feminists; both were genuinely and effortlessly creative, enthusiastic reformers; and for both, literary creation came first. . . . Both were above all idealists, 'aspiring spirits' "; *George Sand and the Victorians: Her Influence and Reputation in Nineteenth-century England* (New York: Columbia University Press, 1977), 46. Her feeling for George Sand is something else that she and Matthew Arnold have in common; Browning did not share it.

43. Tennyson, "The Lotos-Eaters," 36. "Self-Expression" ends like Tennyson's "The Kraken," in which a primaeval sea monster is said to reveal himself only once, at the moment of death: "once by men and angels to be seen, / In roaring he shall rise and on the surface die" (14–15).

44. The reviewer was a woman, Sarah Flower Adams, in the *Westminster Review* 42 (1844): 387. Years later, Mary Russell Mitford said that rumors of scandalous love affairs had circulated about Elizabeth Barrett before her marriage. Whether or not this is true (it seems unlikely), it shows Mitford's belief in a poet's vulnerability to scandal. Barrett Browning dismissed it as an absurdity, remarking that she had seen George Sand twice and therefore "Now's the time for my reputation to go"; EBB to Julia Martin, 27 February [1852], English Poetry Collection, Wellesley College Library.

45. "If Shakespeare were alive now & went to Windsor, he w^d be admitted by the back stairs [. . .]. It is one of our disgraces through Europe"; EBB to Thomas Westwood, 9 April 1845, British Library.

46. The emphatic echo of Wordsworth's "Immortality" ode brings to mind the lines that follow, which are very much to the point: "We will grieve not, rather find / Strength in what remains behind; / In the primal sympathy / Which having been must ever be; / In the soothing thoughts that spring / Out of human suffering; / In the faith that looks through death, / In years that bring the philosophic mind."

47. Hayter, *Mrs. Browning*, 46.

Chapter 5

1. *Christian Examiner* 38 (1845): 206, 207.

2. Edgar Allan Poe, *Complete Works* 12:34–35. "She has had little of the mental discipline which comes from a familiarity with the actual life of men and women"; *Graham's American Monthly Magazine* 26 (1845): 46. See also S[arah] F[lower] A[dams], *Westminster Review* 42 (1844): 381–82.

3. [James Ferrier,] "Poems by Elizabeth B. Barrett," *Blackwood's* 56 (1844): 621.

4. *Graham's American Monthly Magazine* 26 (1845): 46.

5. Margaret Fuller, "Miss Barrett's Poems," 22.

6. *Some Reminiscences of William Michael Rossetti*, 2 vols. (New York: Charles Scribner's Sons, 1906), 1:232. The influence of these poems can be seen in Dante

Gabriel's "The Blessed Damozel," some of his sonnets, and many of his ballads. In 1848 Dante Rossetti and Holman Hunt drew up a list of artistic "Immortals" on which "Mrs. Browning" appeared, with one star (of nineteenth-century poets, only Landor, Shelley, Keats, and Browning were awarded two stars; Shakespeare had three, Jesus Christ four); *The P.R.B. Journal: William Michael Rossetti's Diary of the Pre-Raphaelite Brotherhood, Together with Other Pre-Raphaelite Documents, 1849–1853*, ed. William E. Fredeman (Oxford: Clarendon Press, 1975), 107.

7. *RB-EBB* 1:3. In this chapter letters from *RB-EBB* will usually be identified only by volume and page number.

8. EBB to R. H. Horne, 1 May 1843, Pierpont Morgan Library, New York. Horne, whose publication of Barrett Browning's letters was made with Browning's concurrence, left this passage out.

9. Janet Gurkin Altman, *Epistolarity: Approaches to a Form* (Columbus: Ohio State University Press, 1982), 196. Christopher Ricks point out how wonderfully like an epistolary novel, with their tension and drama, the letters are: "It is hard to think of a real-life correspondence which more suggests the scribbled breathlessness and anxiety of the Richardsonian novel"; *The Brownings: Letters and Poetry* (Garden City: Doubleday, 1970), 10. For extensive analysis of the letters, see Daniel Karlin, *The Courtship of Robert Browning and Elizabeth Barrett* (Oxford: Clarendon Press, 1985).

10. Poe, *Complete Works* 12:1; George Eliot, *Middlemarch*, 166 (chap. 22). For further discussion of this question see my essay, "The Damsel, the Knight, and the Victorian Woman Poet," *Critical Inquiry* 13 (1986): 64–80.

11. But he says that he can't write or sing his love; see 2:623, and "One Word More."

12. John Maynard, *Browning's Youth* (Cambridge: Harvard University Press, 1977), 150–51. The significance in Browning's life and poetry of the Perseus and Andromeda myth and its cognate, Saint George and the dragon, was first set forth at length by William C. DeVane, in "The Virgin and the Dragon," *Yale Review* 37 (1947): 33–46. In *Pauline*, Browning describes Andromeda, "quite naked and alone" (665), without Perseus.

13. Browning tells his story in many ways, none of them simple. In "Porphyria's Lover" monster and hero are one and the same: Porphyria comes to the gloomy den of her lover, and he kills her. No one rescues the duke's last duchess. The only early heroine who acts the part of Andromeda fairly directly is the narrator of "Count Gismond," and while Elizabeth Barrett evidently took that poem as a straightforward account of chivalric rescue, later critics have been inclined to doubt the narrator's veracity and suspect that the rescuer was duped. *The Ring and the Book* is devoted to affirming the heroine's innocence. "Pan and Luna" is haunted by fears of, among other things, the heroine's complicity.

14. Elizabeth Gaskell, *The Life of Charlotte Brontë* (Harmondsworth: Penguin, 1985), 491, 508.

15. It has usually been seen, in fact, in terms of Browning's imagination and male-centered stories. As William Irvine and Park Honan put it: "Robert Browning's greatest exploit was his own romance. . . . It was a stratagem against an ogre, the awakening of a sleeping princess in an enchanted palace, surrounded by a thicket, the wooing of a confirmed old maid by a confirmed bachelor, an Orphic descent into a region of shadows and the guiding of an Eurydice upward into the light"; *The*

Book, the Ring, and the Poet: A Biography of Robert Browning (New York: McGraw-Hill, 1974), 172. Daniel Karlin acutely remarks of the letters that she "did not have Browning's resource of incorporating whatever she said into a pre-determined scheme," and "his language constructed . . . an image of herself with which she could not identify"; *The Courtship of Robert Browning and Elizabeth Barrett*, 130.

16. And yet when she claimed to know *him* through *his* poetry he insisted that "what I have printed gives *no* knowledge of me" (1:17); despite his professed desire to write from himself, his urgent disclaimers suggest that he does not really want to attain, for himself, transparent subjectivity.

17. "There was always a great delight to me in this prolonged relation of childhood almost . . nay altogether [with his parents]. [. . .] I hope if you want to please me especially, Ba, you will always remember I have been accustomed, by pure choice, to have another will lead mine in the little daily matters of life. If there are two walks to take [. . .] you must say, '*This* one' and not 'either' " (2:960). Betty Miller regards this attitude as pathological and thinks that Elizabeth Barrett must have disliked it; see *Robert Browning: A Portrait* (New York: Charles Scribner's Sons, 1953), 117.

18. One thinks especially of Ovid's *Heroides*, the great French women letter-writers, and the epistolary fiction of France and eighteenth-century England. Janet Altman lists paradoxes of epistolary fiction, including letters as bridge and as barrier between writer and reader and as potentially both transparent and opaque; the writer as reader; the play between intimate self-revelation and the need for an audience; the attempt to make the absent (reader) present; the closure at the end of each letter within the continuity of a correspondence; the individual letter as self-contained unity and part of a larger whole; *Epistolarity*, 186–87. These and related issues are the subject of *Men/Women of Letters, Yale French Studies*, no. 71 (1986), and are outlined by Charles A. Porter in his "Foreword" (1–14). See also Karlin, *The Courtship of Robert Browning and Elizabeth Barrett*, 191–216.

19. EBB to Thomas Westwood, 16 April 1844, British Library.

20. After 1725, says English Showalter, Jr., "every literate French man or woman writing a private letter would have been aware of the possibility of publication, intended or not"; "Authorial Self-Consciousness in the Familiar Letter: The Case of Madame de Graffigny," *Yale French Studies*, no. 71 (1986): 115.

21. "One is familiar with correspondences which can thrive only upon absence (those of Kafka, Kleist, Rilke and others far more numerous than one might guess). Such letters allow two people to share a dream both have woven, as the words bring about the exact coincidence of two fantasy worlds. . . . Face to face the individuals do not know one another"; Mireille Bossis, "Methodological Journeys through Correspondences," *Yale French Studies*, no. 71 (1986): 69. Elizabeth Barrett was extremely sensitive to the danger of such mutual fantasy, and while she could not resist participating in it, she did not want to mistake it for love.

22. "Occasions of embarrassment arise when the self projected is somehow confronted with another self which, though valid in other contexts, cannot be here sustained in harmony with the first"; Erving Goffman, *Interaction Ritual: Essays in Face-to-Face Behavior* (New York: Doubleday-Anchor, 1967), 108.

23. *The Letters of Robert Browning and Elizabeth Barrett Browning, 1845–1846,* 2 vols. (New York and London: Harper & Bros., 1898), vol. 1, prefatory note. She

had kept his letters tied in ribbons. The fetishizing of letters is remarked on by Bossis, 64, and Altman, 19. Letters produced on computers have different qualities.

24. Mitford described her letters as a combination of de Sevigne and Cowper, a judgment endorsed by Chorley; *Letters of Mary Russell Mitford,* 2d series, ed. Henry Chorley, 2 vols. (London: Richard Bentley & Son, 1872), 1:192. At first, said Mitford, "her letters were rather too much like the very best books," but then her thoughts came to "flow as naturally as water down a hillside" (1:181).

25. As Percy Lubbock says (capturing the overtones of the illicit in the pleasure of reading other people's mail), they "admit one for a moment inside the doors of the house. They hold out a sort of personal intimacy, a sense of her presence, something altogether more seductive than the mere record of opinions and sentiments"; *Elizabeth Barrett Browning in Her Letters,* 48. English Showalter, Jr., remarks that "perhaps . . . the most engaging letters are those in which the literary impulse most effectively makes accessible the invisible private world of the writer and gives readers the feeling of having grasped secret allusions"; "Authorial Self-Consciousness in the Familiar Letter," 123. Bossis notes "the language of the suffering body" as a frequent characteristic of correspondences: "The other's physical troubles seem to provide a privileged if not unique way for the writer to show attention to and affection for the other's body. The status of illness is thus called into question"; Bossis 74.

26. Alethea Hayter quotes this image; *Mrs. Browning,* 210. It recalls among other things her memory of her own mother's milk spoiled by Jove's thunder and her sorrow on not being allowed to nurse her child.

27. Henry James, *William Wetmore Story and His Friends: From Letters, Diaries, and Recollections,* 2 vols. (Edinburgh and London: William Blackwood & Sons, 1903), 1:370. Her huge epistolary output suggests, as Raymond and Sullivan say, that she was "something of a compulsive writer" (*LMRM* 1:xxx), and they point out that she wrote to be read, and kept a diary only briefly and perfunctorily.

28. Sonnet 26. References to *Sonnets from the Portuguese* are by sonnet, rather than line, numbers. The imperative to choose life and human community rather than isolating, self-enclosed art is enacted in Tennyson's "The Palace of Art" and other poems. Browning's Fra Lippo Lippi, who makes this choice too, is a better person and a better artist than Andrea del Sarto, who doesn't. Matthew Arnold, more drastically, abandoned isolating, alienating poetry for the socially oriented activity of writing prose. William S. Peterson comments on the similarity to *In Memoriam* in *Elizabeth Barrett Browning's Sonnets from the Portuguese: A Facsimile Edition of the British Library Manuscript,* ed. William S. Peterson (Barre, Mass.: Barre, 1977), xvi.

29. The title was a disguise agreed on by the Brownings together; it suggests without actually saying so that the poem is a translation.

30. Porter and Clarke in their notes identify the allusion to the *Iliad* and other allusions in the opening sonnets.

31. *Essays on the Greek Christian Poets and the English Poets,* 142.

32. Ann Rosalind Jones notes that changing the gender of the speaker changes the referent of a conventional phrase: praise, for instance, of the beloved's beautiful skin; "Assimilation with a Difference: Renaissance Women Poets and Literary Influence," *Yale French Studies,* no. 62 (1981): 137. An "essential paradox" of women's lyrics in the old amatory conventions, Marianne Shapiro points out, is that "desire

must express itself as the wish to *be* possessed. . . . The desiring subject would be, *in potentia*, the desired object"; "The Provincial *Trobairitz* and the Limits of Courtly Love," *Signs* 3 (1978): 562.

33. Angela Leighton points this out, adding that the exalted object also fills the poet's need for a muse; *Elizabeth Barrett Browning* (Bloomington: Indiana University Press, 1986), 94.

34. Leighton notes in connection with sonnet 5 that both her love and her poetry are conceived as dangerous to him; *Elizabeth Barrett Browning*, 106.

35. In this respect the sequence resembles Spenser's *Amoretti*, which also presents courtship leading to marriage. Spenser urges an imitation of Christ: "So let us love, deare love, lyke as we ought, / Love is the lesson which the Lord us taught" (sonnet 68).

36. In Christina Rossetti's *Monna Innominata*, in contrast, the man is not a poet; rather, each sonnet has epigraphs from Dante and Petrarch, with whom there is no possibility of working out a new, equal relationship. *Monna Innominata*, unlike *Sonnets from the Portuguese*, ends in separation.

37. *Paradise Lost* 1:609–10; Shakespeare, sonnet 116. Porter and Clarke's notes identify the allusions to Milton and Homer and others in the opening sonnets.

38. "I will bury myself in myself," says the hero of *Maud* (1:75; in an early version he plans to bury himself in his books, which is equally to the point [1:75 n.]), but Maud's love restores him to life. The prince in *The Princess* has a similar experience. Such images recur in Victorian literature. Sandra M. Gilbert and Susan Gubar remark that men and women draw them from different contexts: "The distinction between male and female images of imprisonment is—and always has been—a distinction between . . . that which is both metaphysical and metaphorical, and . . . that which is social and actual"; *The Madwoman in the Attic: The Woman Writer and the Nineteenth Century Literary Imagination* (New Haven: Yale University Press, 1979), 86. This is one of the clearest examples of the metaphorical becoming literal in women's writing.

39. On her influence on the Pre-Raphaelites, see Hayter, *Mrs. Browning*, 231–33; Lionel Stevenson, *The Pre-Raphaelite Poets* (Chapel Hill: University of North Carolina Press, 1972), 130, 201; Florence Saunders Boos, *The Poetry of Dante G. Rossetti: A Critical Reading and Source Study* (The Hague: Mouton, 1976), 279–81.

40. Sidney, *Astrophel and Stella* 1, 1; Wordsworth, "Scorn Not the Sonnet," 2–3; Browning, "House," 40. For Elizabeth Barrett's comment on Sidney, see *Essays on the Greek Christian Poets and the English Poets*, 163.

41. Hayter, *Mrs. Browning*, 105. Hayter notes that the letters affect us quite differently.

42. *Robert Browning and Julia Wedgwood: A Broken Friendship as Revealed by Their Letters*, ed. Richard Curle (New York: Stokes, 1937), 99–100. He told the same story more briefly to Leigh Hunt in 1857; see *Letters of Robert Browning, Collected by T. J. Wise*, ed. Thurman L. Hood (New Haven: Yale University Press, 1933), 48. Barrett Browning told her sister Arabel: "I never showed them to Robert till last spring. . I felt shy about them altogether . . even to him. I had heard him express himself strongly against 'personal' poetry & I shrank back—As to publishing them, it did not enter my head. But when Robert saw them he was much touched & pleased—& thinking highly of the poetry, he did not like, . . could not consent, he said, that they should be lost to my volumes—so we agreed to slip them in under

some sort of veil [. . . .] In a loving fancy, he had always associated me with Catarina, and the poem had affected him to tears, he said, again and again"; EBB to Arabel Moulton-Barrett, 12 January [1851], Henry W. and Albert A. Berg Collection, New York Public Library, Astor, Lenox, and Tilden Foundations.

43. Edmund Gosse, *Critical Kit-Kats* (New York: Dodd, Mead, 1896), 2. Gosse's version and Browning's, interestingly enough, have in common a focus on the poet's physical gestures and appearance, which in Gosse's version she conceals. On Gosse's anecdote and Thomas Wise's forged edition of the *Sonnets*, which together form a fascinating incident in the history of sentimental responses to the poem, see John Carter and Graham Pollard, *An Enquiry into the Nature of Certain Nineteenth Century Pamphlets* (London: Constable, 1934). Gosse's account was frequently reprinted with the *Sonnets* and became part of their tremendous popularity; see Fannie Ratchford, ed., *Sonnets from the Portuguese: Centennial Variorum Edition* (New York: Philip C. Duschnes, 1950), 29. It appears even in the *Poetical Works of Elizabeth Barrett Browning*, ed. Harriet Waters Preston (1st ed., 1900; Boston: Houghton Mifflin, 1974), 214; this is still in print.

44. See, for instance, Ralph Rader, *Tennyson's Maud: The Biographical Genesis* (Berkeley and Los Angeles: University of California Press, 1963). Whether or not Arnold's *Switzerland* is based on actual experience (and if so, *what* experience) is still being debated. Park Honan pushes the issue most vigorously, in *Matthew Arnold: A Life* (New York: McGraw-Hill, 1981), 144–67. In *Modern Love*, Meredith retold the story of his wife's elopement with another man in a manner more flattering to himself than the actual event had been; see Dorothy Mermin, *The Audience in the Poem: Five Victorian Poets* (New Brunswick: Rutgers University Press, 1983), 127–31.

45. Hallam Tennyson, *Alfred Lord Tennyson: A Memoir*, 2 vols. (London: Macmillan, 1897) 1:305.

46. Suzanne Juhasz points out that a male "confessional" poet like Robert Lowell can "plug into a larger tradition—that of being a poet whose life and consciousness is in some sense and to some degree meant to typify the consciousness of his age," but for a female poet, "No such tradition exists"; *Naked and Fiery Forms: Modern American Poetry by Women, A New Tradition* (New York: Octagon, 1976), 58.

47. Loy D. Martin points out the doubling of public and private in *Browning's Dramatic Monologues and the Post-Romantic Subject* (Baltimore: Johns Hopkins University Press, 1985), 173. Martin considers the poem as a series of dramatic monologues, like *Men and Women* but, of course, "much simpler" (169).

48. *Maud* 1:804–8.

49. A recent biographer of Browning, for instance, says that these poems "in which Elizabeth had enshrined her adoration for her lover" are "rich in a devotion simply expressed"; Donald Thomas, *Robert Browning: A Life within Life* (London: Weidenfeld & Nicolson, 1982), 127. The first assumption clearly produced the second. Irvine and Honan despise the sonnets, of course, but at least they realize that they are not "simple": "though she expressed herself in . . . quaint or inflated metaphors, Elizabeth had experienced love"; *The Book, the Ring, and the Poet*, 261. The assumption about the poem's origin apparently determines the description of its qualities.

50. Robert B. Heilman notes that Goneril protests her love in very similar abstractions: "Dearer than eyesight, space, and liberty; / Beyond what can be valued, rich or rare, / No less than life, with grace, health, beauty, honour" (*King Lear,*

1:1:56–62). Heilman finds Barrett Browning's poem "embarrassing," relying on "personal sincerity" instead of images to prove her experience; "E. B. Browning's *Sonnets from the Portuguese* XLIII," *Explicator* 4 (1945), 3. William T. Going replies (if he does not exactly demonstrate) in a note of the same title that the abstractions recall earlier phrases or images in the sequence; *Explicator* 11 (1953), 58.

Chapter 6

1. Gerardine MacPherson, *Memoirs of the Life of Anna Jameson* (Boston: Robert Brothers, 1878), 228–29.

2. EBB to Julia Martin, 1 February 1847, English Poetry Collection, Wellesley College Library.

3. Browning, *Letters of Robert Browning,* 14.

4. The Corn Laws were tariffs on the import of grain, which made bread too expensive for workers to buy. Agitation to repeal them went on throughout the 1840s.

5. Martineau had not objected in advance to the publication, expecting it to be a scientific article in a medical journal. The episode is described by Valerie Kossew Pichanick, *Harriet Martineau: The Woman and Her Work, 1802–1876* (Ann Arbor: University of Michigan Press, 1980), 129–37, and by Gillian Thomas, *Harriet Martineau* (Boston: Twayne, 1985), 21–24.

6. EBB to Julia Martin [17 December 1844], English Poetry Collection, Wellesley College Library.

7. *Westminster Review* 42 (1844): 387. She quoted the phrase about Godiva to several other correspondents too. "Think of it," she exclaimed to Mr. Boyd, "Godiva of Coventry, and peeping Tom. The worst and basest is, that in this nineteenth century there are thousands of Toms to one"; *LHSB* 273.

8. Jay Leyda, *The Years and Hours of Emily Dickinson,* 2 vols. (New Haven: Yale University Press, 1960), 2:482. This sentence is quoted in Terence Diggory's discussion of the meanings of nakedness for the female poet, "Armored Women, Naked Men: Dickinson, Whitman, and Their Successors," *Shakespeare's Sisters: Feminist Essays on Women Poets,* ed. Sandra M. Gilbert and Susan Gubar (Bloomington: Indiana University Press, 1979), 141.

9. On Actaeon as a figure for the poet in Petrarch's poems (many of which Elizabeth Barrett translated), the hunter who having seen the naked goddess is himself hunted and dismembered, see Leonard Barkan, "Diana and Actaeon: The Myth as Synthesis," *English Literary Renaissance* 10 (1980): 317–59, and Nancy J. Vickers, "Diana Described: Scattered Woman and Scattered Rhyme," *Critical Inquiry* 8 (1981): 265–79.

10. Victorian feminists' interest in slavery is placed in perspective by Elizabeth K. Helsinger, Robin Lauterbach Sheets, and William Veeder in *The Woman Question: Society and Literature in Britain and America, 1837–1883,* 3 vols. (New York: Garland, 1983), 2:91–92. Barrett Browning may have been aware of the frequent sexual relations between Barretts and black women. Her grandfather (who had two different mistresses established in England while his wife was living in Yorkshire) also had a son by a "free woman of colour" (commended to the care of his sons in his will) in Jamaica, and a cousin provided in his will for the education and maintenance of a "mulatto daughter" named Elizabeth Grant Barritt; Jeannette Marks, *The Family of*

the Barrett: A Colonial Romance (New York: Macmillan, 1938), 318. Her uncle Samuel Barrett had given up his seat in Parliament to attend to the family's affairs in Jamaica, and two of her brothers (Bro and Sam, who died there), and perhaps her father, too, went for briefer stays; Hope End would have been constantly getting news from Jamaica, and from early childhood she heard stories of life there from her grandmother's companion, Miss Trepsack ("Trippy"), a staunch enthusiast for the slave system.

11. *RB-EBB* 2:1005; Maynard, *Browning's Youth*, 23–24. On Mr. Barrett and abolition, see Marks, *The Family of the Barrett*, 320, 416–21.

12. "The Greek Slave" is discussed in the following works: Sylvia E. Crane, *White Silence: Greenough, Powers, and Crawford; American Sculptors in Nineteenth-Century Italy* (Coral Gables: University of Miami Press, 1972), 203–22; William H. Gerdts, *American Neoclassic Sculpture: The Marble Resurrection* (New York: Viking, 1973), 52–54; Samuel A. Roberson and William H. Gerdts, " '. . . *so undressed, yet so refined* . . .': The Greek Slave," *The Museum*, n.s. 17, nos. 1–2 (Winter–Spring 1965): 1–29, which includes several other poems about it; Donald M. Reynolds, "The 'Unveiled Soul': Hiram Powers's Embodiment of the Ideal," *Art Bulletin* 59 (1977): 394–414; Peter Gay, *The Education of the Senses*, vol. 1 of *The Bourgeois Experience, Victoria to Freud* (New York: Oxford University Press, 1984), 396–98. Linda Hyman, "*The Greek Slave* by Hiram Powers: High Art as Popular Culture," *Art Journal* 35 (1976): 216–23, describes the responses of women writers such as Margaret Fuller as narcissistic identification (221). It was said to have been "by far the most famous sculpture produced by an American in the 19th century," "seen by more people than any other sculpture"; Gerdts, 52.

13. Joy S. Kasson in "Power and Powerlessness: Death, Sexuality and the Demonic in Nineteenth-Century American Sculpture" (paper given at the American Studies National Convention, San Diego, 3 November 1985) points out that contemporary reports of the statue's effect describe it, in effect, as taking the viewers captive.

14. See Roberson and Gerdts, " '. . . *so undressed,* ' " 53–54.

15. "She is too deeply concerned to be aware of her nakedness. It is not her person but her spirit that stands exposed, and she bears it all as Christians only can"; quoted in Roberson and Gerdts, " '. . . *so undressed,*' " 4. "The nude statue should be an unveiled soul," Powers explained to Barrett Browning in 1853; quoted in Reynolds, "The 'Unveiled Soul,' " 394. Barrett Browning was amused by her maid Wilson's embarrassment when she first saw nude statues in Florence (*LS*, 39), but contemporary responses to "The Greek Slave" almost invariably speak of (if only to deny) its nakedness, which is, after all, part of its subject.

16. Irvine and Honan, *The Book, the Ring, and the Poet*, 250.

17. One such comparison began by noting with pleasure the appearance of "two thick, close-printed green volumes, identical in their aspect, and bearing the same name: 'Mr. Browning's Poems, in two vols. [sic],' a new edition; 'Mrs. Browning's Poems, in two vols.,' a new edition"; "The Minor Poets of the Day," *Christian Remembrancer*, n.s. 21 (1851): 353. The other major poem published that year was Wordsworth's *Prelude*.

18. *American Whig Review* 14 (1851): 463. *Harper's New Monthly Magazine* called her, in a one-paragraph review, "the most remarkable poetess of modern times"; *Harper's* 1 (1850): 714.

19. She is called pure and womanly in the *Eclectic Review*, n.s. 1 (1851): 295.

20. *Spectator,* 25 January 1851, pp. 85–86; "The Minor Poets of the Day," *Christian Remembrancer,* n.s. 21 (1851): 376.

21. *Athenaeum,* 30 November 1850, pp. 1243, 1244. Comments on the laureateship, which went to Tennyson, appeared 1 June 1850, pp. 584–85; 22 June 1850, p. 662; and 23 November 1850, p. 1218. The *Athenaeum* was concerned to prevent Leigh Hunt from being appointed laureate; see Marchand, *The Athenaeum,* 79.

22. *Fraser's Magazine* 43 (February 1851): 177, 178 (the author, according to the Wellesley Index, was probably Charles Kingsley, as the muscularly Christian tone suggests); *Examiner,* 25 January 1851, p. 52; *English Review* 14 (1850): 323. These journals also praised *Sonnets from the Portuguese.* The *Guardian*'s approval was in a similar vein, admiring her exemption from most female weakness although deploring her diffuseness and display of learning; *Guardian,* 22 January 1851, pp. 55–56.

23. Lawrence Lipking, *The Life of the Poet: Beginning and Ending Poetic Careers* (Chicago: University of Chicago Press, 1981), 16, 18, 19. " 'Who is a poet?' Thomas Mann asked, and answered his own question under the spell of Goethe: 'He whose life is symbolic' "; Lipking, 113.

24. Even Hayter scorns her "Enthusiasm without judgement," *Mrs. Browning,* 135, and the contempt expressed by Irvine and Honan is extreme even for that extremely contemptuous book. Correctives have been offered in the introduction and notes to Julia Markus's edition of *Casa Guidi Windows* (New York: Browning Institute, 1977), to which my discussion is much indebted. Flavia Alaya has shown how Browning critics have defined his political views by denigrating hers in "The Ring, the Rescue, and the Risorgimento: Reunifying the Brownings' Italy," *Browning Institute Studies* 6 (1978): 1–41. Kenneth Churchill gives a brief but sympathetic discussion of her writings about Italy in his useful survey of English writers in Italy, *Italy and English Literature, 1764–1930* (Totowa, N.J.: Barnes & Noble, 1980), 99–104.

25. Julia Markus describes the English enthusiasm and Barrett Browning's reservations, *Casa Guidi Windows,* xix–xxv.

26. Arnold speaks of modern men as "Light half-believers in our casual creeds, / Who never deeply felt, nor clearly will'd, / Whose insight never has borne fruit in deeds, / Whose weak resolves never have been fulfilled"; prey to (among other things) "divided aims"; "The Scholar-Gipsy," 172–75, 204. The significant difference is that Barrett Browning does not attribute modern failures of energy and will to too much thinking. Unlike Tennyson, Arnold, and Clough, she does not imagine herself a kind of Hamlet, too intellectual to act. Only wicked Lady Waldemar thinks that women poets' hearts are "starved to make [their] heads" (*Aurora Leigh* 3:410).

27. See, for instance, *Maud:* "Why do they prate of the blessings of peace? . . . lust of gain" (1:21, 23); "Peace sitting under her olive, and slurring the days gone by, / When the poor are hovell'd and hustled together, each sex, like swine" (1:33–34); "better, war! loud war by land and by sea, / War with a thousand battles, and shaking a hundred thrones!" (1:47–48). As very often with similarities to Arnold, if Barrett Browning had not written first she would surely be thought to have borrowed. *Maud,* like *Casa Guidi Windows,* was unpopular because of its politics and blamed for hysterical warmongering. See also *King Lear,* 3:4:28–32 ("Poor naked wretches . . . That bide the pelting of this pitiless storm") et passim.

28. For Italy as Cybele and Niobe, see *Childe Harold's Pilgrimage* 4:2, 4:79. Markus's notes give the literary sources to which Barrett Browning alludes.

29. Sandra Gilbert suggests that their betrayal of Italy mirrored for Barrett Browning her father's of her and that England now appeared to her as "magisterial and patriarchal as Edward Moulton-Barrett"; "From *Patria* to *Matria:* Elizabeth Barrett Browning's Risorgimento," *PMLA* 99 (1984): 199.

30. This was augmented by the imaginative responses of Barrett Browning, Swinburne, Meredith, and others and grew during the 1850s until it helped to bring about the fall of Lord Derby's Cabinet in 1859. George Macaulay Trevelyan remarks that "The feeling for Italy spread from the poets to the Philistines"; *English Songs of Italian Freedom* (London: Longmans, Green, 1911), xxiv.

31. *Spectator,* 28 June 1851, p. 617; *Prospective Review* 7 (1851): 320.

32. *Prospective Review* 7 (1851): 320.

33. *Guardian,* 11 June 1851, p. 424.

34. "La Poesie anglaise depuis Byron," *Revue des deux mondes* 30 (1852): 349–64.

35. *Athenaeum,* 7 June 1851, pp. 597–98.

36. "I have lately read again with great delight Mrs. Browning's Casa Guidi Windows. It contains amongst other admirable things a very noble expression of what I believe to be the true relation of the religious mind to the Past"; *The George Eliot Letters,* ed. Gordon S. Haight, 9 vols. (New Haven: Yale University Press, 1954–78), 4:15 (19 February 1862 journal entry).

37. For tales of *il gran ciuco,* see Thomas Adolphus Trollope, *What I Remember,* 2 vols. (London: Richard Bentley & Son, 1887), 2:104–9. Tuscany had the least repressive rulers in Italy, as Giuliana Artom Treves points out; *The Golden Ring: The Anglo-Florentines, 1847–1862,* trans. Sylvia Sprigge (London: Longmans, Green, 1956), 194.

38. S. Musgrove, ed., "Unpublished Letters of Thomas de Quincey and Elizabeth Barrett Browning" *Auckland University College Bulletin,* no. 44, English Series no. 7 (1954), p. 34 [1859]. On Pen's life and character, see Maisie Ward, *The Tragi-Comedy of Pen Browning (1849–1912)* (New York: Sheed & Ward and Browning Institute, 1972). Barrett Browning's disregard for class distinctions in Pen's upbringing is one of the few points on which Ward is unambiguously critical of her (26), although to a modern American eye her attitude toward servants does not seem remarkably enlightened.

39. Ross D. Waller, ed., "Letters Addressed to Mrs. Gaskell by Celebrated Contemporaries, Now in the Possession of the John Rylands Library," *Bulletin of the John Rylands Library* 19 (1935): 143.

40. *LMO* 100, 112–13. Dorothy Hewlett notes the exaggeration of the usual limits of boys' dress; *Elizabeth Barrett Browning,* 270. The Brownings' disagreement on this subject had begun by the time Pen was two years old. He's "a sort of neutral creature, so far," she said, reporting Browning's request that she remove the caps that kept him from looking like a boy; EBB to Arabel Moulton-Barrett, 5 June [1851], Henry W. and Albert A. Berg Collection, New York Public Library, Astor, Lenox, and Tilden Foundations; quoted in Irvine and Honan, *The Book, the Ring, and the Poet,* 272. As for herself—Mary Russell Mitford spoke of "the very simple but graceful and costly dress by which all the [Barrett] family are distinguished"; Chorley, *Letters of Mary Russell Mitford,* 2d series, 1:180.

41. *LEBB* 2:227–28 (1856). Robert Coles suggests in his introduction to Maisie Ward's *Tragi-Comedy of Pen Browning* that "some of the hysteria [Barrett Browning]

conveys as she virtually sings the child's praises has to do with her own struggle to push out of mind the darker side of childhood" (xvi). This may well be true, but it probably has more to do with the dark side of motherhood: the repressed rebellion against maternal self-sacrifice and filial demands.

42. Waller, "Letters Addressed to Mrs. Gaskell," 143.

43. EBB to Sophia Eckley, 23 July [1858], Henry W. and Albert A. Berg Collection, New York Public Library, Astor, Lenox, and Tilden Foundations.

44. It has been pretty much taken for granted by critics that her views were extreme and foolish and caused serious marital conflict, but there is no real basis for these assumptions other than an unexamined belief that women do not understand politics and should not argue with their husbands. Her admiration for Louis Napoleon, as for Pio Nono and the grand duke, was limited, and there is no reason to believe that the Brownings' difference of opinion was a source of distress to either of them. Forceful rebuttals to the usual view of the Brownings' politics are given by Flavia Alaya, "The Ring, the Rescue, and the Risorgimento," 1–41, and by Leo A. Hetzler, "The Case of Prince Hohenstiel-Schwangau: Browning and Napoleon III," *Victorian Poetry* 15 (1977): 335–50.

45. *Times*, 2 July 1852, p. 7.

46. For a summary of the manifestations, see Katherine H. Porter, *Through a Glass Darkly: Spiritualism in the Browning Circle* (1958; New York: Octagon Books, 1972), 3.

47. Edward C. McAleer, "New Letters from Mrs. Browning to Isa Blagden," *PMLA* 66 (1951): 596. Her favorite of his works at that time was *Heaven and Hell*. The spell of Swedenborg's vision fell upon many other distinguished imaginations, including those of William Blake, Henry James, Sr., William Butler Yeats, Victor Hugo, Lamartine, George Sand, Balzac, and Baudelaire; see Inge Jonsson, *Emanuel Swedenborg*, trans. Catherine Djurklou (New York: Twayne, 1971), 186–91.

48. An odd connection between spiritualism and the Godiva story, and a reminder of the sexual element that was frequently connected with mesmerism, appears in an episode reported to the Brownings by Robert Lytton. Mrs. Catherine Crowe, a novelist, appeared naked in the streets of London carrying a fan and a cardcase, which, she explained to the magistrates, "the Spirits" had promised would render her invisible; *Letters from Owen Meredith (Robert, First Earl of Lytton) to Robert and Elizabeth Barrett Browning*, ed. Aurelia Brooks Harlan and J. Lee Harlan, Jr., Baylor University Browning Interests, no. 10 (Waco, 1936), pp. 70–71. Dickens, too, took an interest in this story; Porter, 17.

49. Browning's biographers concur in the assessment of the pain her spiritualism gave him. Mrs. Sutherland Orr says it caused the only serious disagreement between them; *Life and Letters of Robert Browning*, 2d ed. (London: Smith, Elder, 1891), 216. Betty Miller finds it the chief cause for what she sees as his sad disillusionment with his wife; *Robert Browning*, 180–83. Miller's proof of his alienation depends too much, however, on biographical interpretations of his dramatic monologues to be wholly convincing. Irvine and Honan acutely observe that spiritualism "reinforced the intense, dark inwardness of her nature. Ultimately, Browning feared it, as he feared her opium habit"; *The Book, the Ring, and the Poet*, 306. Such criticism treats belief in spiritualism as a rather disgraceful aberration, whereas in the 1850s it was very common among intellectually respectable people.

50. Ronald A. Bosco, "The Brownings and Mrs. Kinney: A Record of Their Friendship," *Browning Institute Studies* 4 (1976): 86. Browning would not have been pleased to foresee that after his death his own spirit would communicate a good deal of twaddle to Hiram Corson, professor of English at Cornell, who was among Browning's most influential American admirers. These messages are recorded in Hiram Corson, *Spirit Messages: With an Introductory Essay on Spiritual Vitality* (Boston: Christopher, 1911; new ed. 1919), 54–57, 97–101, 134–40, 210–14.

51. On mediumship as a career for women, exploiting the passivity and weakness thought desirable in Victorian women and allowing them opportunities not otherwise available, see R. Laurence Moore, *In Search of White Crows: Spiritualism, Parapsychology, and American Culture* (New York: Oxford University Press, 1977), 102–29.

52. Browning, *Letters of Robert Browning,* 48.

53. Irvine and Honan call it "a nightmare beyond [his] darkest fears"; *The Book, the Ring, and the Poet,* 343.

Chapter 7

1. Reviewers called it by several names, including "epic" or "domestic epic," but combinations of "novel" and "poem" were the most common. Arthur Hugh Clough in exuberant youth and Browning in the twilight of his long career wrote what might be called long short stories—Clough's *The Bothie of Tober-na-Vuolich* (a mock-heroic love story in hexameters), Browning's *Red-Cotton Night-Cap Country* and *The Inn Album.* Browning speaks of her project as a "romance" (*RB-EBB* 1:262, 493), and she sometimes uses the word, too (*RB-EBB* 1:496, *LEBB* 2:112). What it was called did not much matter to her. The Victorians wrote all sorts of generically anomalous poems—such as those we now call "dramatic monologues"—without worrying very much about naming them.

2. Sandra Gilbert points out the echo of Augusta Leigh, "From *Patria* to *Matria,*" 205–6. The cousinship between Aurora and Romney, who have the same surname, may well hint at the notorious relationship between Byron and Augusta Leigh. The name is clearly overdetermined, and her hesitation in choosing it (she had thought of "Laura," too) hardly detracts from its significance. And then there is Duchess May, who spurns her cousin, "Leigh of Leigh" (Romney Leigh lives in Leigh Hall).

3. For a sustained comparison, see Kathleen Blake, "Elizabeth Barrett Browning and Wordsworth: The Romantic Poet as a Woman," *Victorian Poetry* 24 (1986): 387–98. *Aurora Leigh* is much more interested than *The Prelude* is in the poet's relation to the world of money, employment, class, gender, friendship and enmity, jealousy and love, marriage and giving in marriage.

4. On sources, see Hayter, *Mrs. Browning,* 159–62. Cora Kaplan cogently argues that *Aurora Leigh* is among other things a rebuttal to Tennyson, Clough, and Kingsley; see her introduction to *Aurora Leigh and Other Poems* (London: Women's Press, 1978), 26–35. Patricia Thomson discusses similarities to various of Sand's novels, especially *Indiana* (*George Sand and the Victorians,* 58). As the portrait of a pure and noble artist torn between the love of an obsessively high-minded altruist and a great career, *Aurora Leigh* resembles *Consuelo* and *The Countess of Rudolstadt,* which were among Barrett Browning's favorite novels. The most important similarities are to

Jane Eyre: Romney first makes a proposal of marriage as partnership in service, like St. John Rivers, is rejected and then blinded (although not maimed) in the burning of his house, like Mr. Rochester, and finally accepted.

5. I take the Victorian "novel" in this context to mean a long and more or less realistic narrative, set more or less in the present, dealing with the concerns of people in society. Other Victorian poems with some of these characteristics (Meredith's *Modern Love* and perhaps Tennyson's *Maud*) are relatively short, and do not have the retrospective narrative structure which is usual for the Victorian novel. Tennyson's pastoral or idyllic narratives are closer to the world of Mary Russell Mitford's sketches in *Our Village,* and "Locksley Hall," as Barrett Browning said when she thought of it as a possible antecedent for her own projected work, has "no story, no *manners,* no modern allusion, [. . .] and no approach to the treatment of a conventionality" (*LEBB* 1:204). The only real precursor she found, other than Byron, was Crabbe (*LEBB* 1:204).

6. On her sources of knowledge of lower-class life, see Dierdre David, *Intellectual Women and Victorian Patriarchy: Harriet Martineau, Elizabeth Barrett Browning, George Eliot* (Ithaca: Cornell University Press, 1987), 124–27.

7. This passage foreshadows the most famous Victorian description of a painting, perhaps the most famous ever written, Walter Pater's reverie on *La Gioconda* as the paradoxical and everchanging sum of man's dreams and desires, "all modes of thought and life"; "Leonardo da Vinci," *The Renaissance: Studies in Art and Poetry: The 1893 Text,* ed. Donald L. Hill (Berkeley and Los Angeles: University of California Press, 1980), 99.

8. A similar education is described, with similar exasperation, in Charlotte M. Yonge's immensely popular *Daisy Chain.* Ethel, the heroine, has managed to learn some Latin and finds solace in cube roots, but her governess prefers her to answer questions about such matters as the invention of paper, the latitude and longitude of Otaheite, the component parts of brass, and the sources of cochineal; *The Daisy Chain: Or, Aspirations, A Family Chronicle* (1868; reprint edition, New York: Garland, 1977), 64. Since Yonge's theology and sexual politics (she was a disciple of John Keble and believed firmly in female subordination and self-sacrifice) were very different from Aurora Leigh's, this likeness is all the more striking.

9. The image of Marian's drowned face and the subsequent rescue recur (9:293–96) when Marian asserts her separateness again. Lady Waldemar may be seen as representing the mother as rival for the affections of the father: Romney is Aurora's father's nephew, his heir as head of the family and thus in a sense a figure for the father himself. The reappearance of a drowned face can hardly avoid reminding us of the drowned Edward Barrett, although it is hard to believe that Barrett Browning consciously drew on memories of her brother. "The maternal face that returns her gaze enables her to reinstate the mother in herself"; Dolores Rosenblum, "Face to Face: Elizabeth Barrett Browning's *Aurora Leigh* and Nineteenth-Century Poetry," *Victorian Studies* 26 (1983):327.

10. EBB to Anna Jameson, 17 October 1854, English Poetry Collection, Wellesley College Library.

11. Patricia Thomson points out these parallels and convincingly suggests that Aurora represents Sand as Barrett Browning would have liked her to be, purged of impurity; *George Sand and the Victorians,* 56.

12. *"Aurora Leigh," The Complete Works of Algernon Charles Swinburne*, ed. Sir Edmund Gosse and Thomas James Wise, 20 vols. (London: William Heinemann, 1925–27), 16:5.

13. Gaskell, *Life of Charlotte Brontë*, 43.

14. Angela Leighton finds at the heart of *Aurora Leigh*, Barrett Browning's quest for and release from the father whose love she still craved; *Elizabeth Barrett Browning*, 116–40.

15. *RB-EBB* 1:157. As Patricia Thompson points out, this evidently stung; *George Sand and the Victorians*, 56.

16. "One great . . . cry rises from a suffering multitude of women, saying, 'We want work.'" Barbara Leigh Smith Bodichon, *Women and Work* (New York: C. S. Francis, 1859), 13. Bodichon's epigraph is from *Aurora Leigh*. "The pernicious psychological and physical consequences of the cult of female idleness, reinforced by the real poverty of many redundant gentlewomen, were becoming topics of public concern. Bodichon's pamphlet was the first feminist articulation of the issue, igniting the public controversy which raged over the next two decades"; Sheila R. Herstein, *A Mid-Victorian Feminist, Barbara Leigh Smith Bodichon* (New Haven: Yale University Press, 1985), 125. Arthur Hugh Clough, like Romney, brought this imperative into his courtship, writing to his wife: "Love is not everything, Blanche; don't believe it, nor try to make me pretend to believe it. *'Service'* is everything. Let us be fellow-servants"; *The Correspondence of Arthur Hugh Clough*, ed. Frederick L. Mulhauser, 2 vols. (Oxford: Clarendon Press, 1957), 1:300.

17. Tennyson, *In Memoriam*, 124:15–16. This is an even more awkwardly literalized "heart" than those described by Barrett Browning.

18. "Rarely discussed in public before 1850," prostitution then began to provoke "sympathy for the victimized woman" rather than moral outrage, and in the 1870s and 1880s it was "the focus of a heated debate between doctors, legislators, and feminists"; Helsinger, Sheets, and Veeder, *The Woman Question* 2:150–51. At least one feminist, Caroline Dall, saw it as "the symbol of the low value placed on women's work"; Helsinger et al., 156.

19. Rossetti, "Jenny," 253–54, *The Works of Dante Gabriel Rossetti*, ed. William M. Rossetti, rev. ed. (London: Ellis, 1911).

20. Mr. Kenyon suggested that "Locksley Hall" was the sort of modern poem Elizabeth Barrett wanted to write when she first mooted the idea, but she replied that "there is no story, no *manners*, no modern allusion, except in the grand general adjuration to the 'Mother-age,' and no approach to the treatment of a conventionality"; *RB-EBB* 1:204. The repeated phrase recalls, then, Tennyson's approach to a poem like *Aurora Leigh*.

21. Leighton argues that Barrett Browning rejects mythologizations of landscape (*Elizabeth Barrett Browning*, 134), but Aurora affirms the life of nature as a subject for women to write about even though she turns away from it herself.

22. Sandra M. Gilbert gives a brilliant analysis of the significance of maternal, redemptive Italy, stressing its positive aspects, in "From *Patria* to *Matria*," 194–211.

23. Angela Leighton sees the quest for the sister, as represented by Marian, as the culminating quest of Barrett Browning's career; *Elizabeth Barrett Browning*, 141–57.

24. Margaret Homans argues that Dickinson made her poetry from the perceived necessity of such doubleness in women's language; *Women Writers and Poetic Identity*,

162–214. Barrett Browning may have seen, but did not choose to utilize, the possibilities of duplicity.

25. Jerome Hamilton Buckley, *Season of Youth: The Bildungsroman from Dickens to Golding* (Cambridge: Harvard University Press, 1974), 17–18. The sense of "origin" is deeper here, however; she returns both to England (in her conversation with Romney) and to Italy: the father's place and the mother's.

26. The attitude expressed here is very close to those that are used in Coventry Patmore's *Angel in the House* to support undisguisedly retrogressive social and political attitudes. Patmore celebrates married love, he suggests, partly because it provides a "theme unsung" for the poet of "these last days, the dregs of time" (1, Prologue, 3), and also because social and religious purification and love radiate from it.

27. "Taskmaster" (9:493) echoes Milton's "How Soon Hath Time" (14). "A mere bare blind stone in the blaze of day / [. . .] / As dark" (9:570–72) echoes "O dark, dark, dark, amid the blaze of noon"; *Samson Agonistes*, 80.

28. See Carolyn G. Heilbrun, "Women Writers and Female Characters: The Failure of Imagination," *Reinventing Womanhood* (New York: W. W. Norton, 1979), 71–92.

29. Tennyson, "The Passing of Arthur," 388.

30. They can be categorized and denigrated as "spasmodic"; see Jerome Hamilton Buckley, *The Victorian Temper: A Study in Literary Culture* (Cambridge: Harvard University Press, 1951), 62–63.

31. Virginia Woolf, " 'Aurora Leigh,' " *The Second Common Reader* (New York: Harcourt, Brace [Harvest], 1932), 190.

32. Hayter does this, and points out Barrett Browning's dislike for realism on the stage; *Mrs. Browning*, 173–74.

33. *The Poems of George Meredith*, ed. Phyllis B. Bartlett, 2 vols. (New Haven: Yale University Press, 1978); *Modern Love* 25:15–16.

34. This aspect of the poem is brilliantly elucidated by Cora Kaplan in her introduction to *Aurora Leigh*, especially 11–12, 15–16.

35. EBB to Anna Jameson, June [1853], Henry W. and Albert A. Berg Collection, New York Public Library, Astor, Lenox, and Tilden Foundations. See also Waller, "Letters Addressed to Mrs. Gaskell," 141.

36. *Westminster Review* 67, n.s. 11 (1857): 308. The simile above, on the other hand, was mocked for its obscurity.

37. Cf. the "starved ignoble nature" (56) in "Childe Roland," or the river: "All along, / Low scrubby alders kneeled down over it; / Drenched willows flung them headlong . . . / The river which had done them all the wrong, / . . . Rolled by" (115–20).

38. *North British Review* 26 (1857): 454. Patmore himself had admired and been influenced by Barrett Browning; see Lionel Stevenson, *The Pre-Raphaelite Poets*, 262.

39. *Complete Works of Swinburne*, 16:4.

40. *The Works of John Ruskin*, ed. E. T. Cook and Alexander Wedderburn, 39 vols. (New York: Longmans Green, 1903–12), 36:247, 36:253, 15:227 (*The Elements of Drawing*, Appendix II).

41. *Letters of Dante Gabriel Rossetti*, ed. Oswald Doughty and John Robert Wahl, 4 vols. (Oxford: Clarendon Press, 1965–67), 1:309.

42. "*Aurora Leigh*: An Unpublished Letter from Leigh Hunt," *Cornhill Magazine*, n.s. 3 (1897): 739. Hunt was sure it must be better than *The Prelude*, which he had

not gotten around to reading (739). The published letter is from a draft or copy found among Hunt's papers; for the length, see *LEBB* 2:253.

43. [George Eliot,] *Westminster Review* 67, n.s. 11 (1857): 306.

44. *Daily News*, 26 November 1856, p. 2. The *Globe and Traveller* spoke in a similar vein (20 November 1856), although judging from the inaccurate plot summary, its reviewer's reading had been extremely cursory.

45. See, e.g., *Spectator*, 22 November 1856, pp. 1239–40; *National Magazine* 1 (1857): 315; [Coventry Patmore,] *North British Review* 26 (1857): 462. The *Morning Post* complained that her writing, always obscure, had become "absolutely unintelligible" (15 December 1856, p. 3). The *Press*, annoyed by praise like the *Globe*'s, complained of "fine writing" and pointed out that although Aurora "declaims against conventionalism of all kinds," she in fact ends up with all the conventional good things of life (22 November 1856, pp. 1122, 1120). For comparisons to *Casa Guidi Windows*, see [Charles Carroll Everett,] *North American Review* 85 (1857): 415–41; [Coventry Patmore,] *North British Review* 26 (1857): 447.

46. *Saturday Review* 2 (27 December 1856): 776, 778. Coventry Patmore agrees with the second of these propositions and also, apparently, with the first; *North British Review* 26:451–52.

47. *Blackwood's* 81 (1857): 32–33. *Westminster Review* 68 (1857): 399–415. The *Globe and Traveller* thought Romney "an ideal man—made up of the best things in many of our public men" (20 November 1856).

48. *Blackwood's* 81 (1857): 33, 36.

49. *National Magazine* 1 (1857): 314; *Spectator*, 22 November 1856, p. 1240. The *National Magazine* also deplored the "abrupt invocation of sacred names"; 314.

50. *Dublin University Magazine* 49 (1857): 470. It is like the prostitute in D. G. Rossetti's "Jenny," a "book / In which pure women may not look."

51. EBB to Julia Martin, 10 March [1857], English Poetry Collection, Wellesley College Library. She admitted, however, to being a little vexed by the *Dublin University Magazine* review; EBB to Anna Jameson, 9 April [1857], English Poetry Collection, Wellesley College Library. Aphra Behn was a notoriously bawdy Restoration dramatist.

52. EBB to Julia Martin, 10 March [1857], English Poetry Collection, Wellesley College Library.

53. Winifred Gerin, *Elizabeth Gaskell: A Biography* (Oxford: Clarendon Press, 1976), 138–41. Mrs. Gaskell was much more sensitive than Barrett Browning to such censure.

54. *New Letters of Robert Browning*, ed. William Clyde DeVane and Kenneth Leslie Knickerbocker (New Haven: Yale University Press, 1950), 96; Musgrave, *Unpublished Letters of Thomas de Quincey and Elizabeth Barrett Browning*, 32–33.

55. *Westminster Review* 68, n.s. 12 (1857): 409.

56. Swinburne, *Works* 16:7; *Blackwood's* 81 (1857): 36–37; *National Magazine* 1 (1857): 315; *Literary Gazette*, 22 November 1856, p. 917; *Critic*, 1 January 1857, p. 14.

57. *North American Review* 85 (1857): 419. She had already "made her name a household word in the best and most cultivated homes of the Old World and the New," and the mark of her influence could be seen in the recent writings of many women, an American reviewer said in 1857; *Putnam's Monthly Magazine* 9 (1857): 33.

58. *Dublin University Magazine* 49 (1857): 469, 470.

59. *Athenaeum*, 22 November 1856, p. 1425.

60. Hunt, *Cornhill Magazine*, n.s. 3 (1897): 739; [Eliot], *Westminster Review* 67, n.s. 11 (1857): 306.

61. *John Bull and Britannia*, 27 December 1856, p. 827.

62. *Literary Gazette*, 22 November 1856, p. 917.

63. *Westminster Review* 68, n.s. 12 (1857): 401, 400.

64. *Press* 68 (1856): 1121.

65. *North American Review* 85 (1857): 441, 423; *Critic*, 1 January 1857, p. 13.

66. Virginia Woolf, " 'Aurora Leigh,' " 185.

Chapter 8

1. EBB to Sophia Eckley, 28 August [1858], Henry W. and Albert A. Berg Collection, New York Public Library, Astor, Lenox, and Tilden Foundations.

2. DeVane and Knickerbocker, *New Letters*, 97.

3. In 1859, say Irvine and Honan, he "seemed to have accepted defeat"; *The Book, the Ring, and the Poet*, 370.

4. Browning, *Letters of Robert Browning*, 50. She often spoke in this vein. "I am much vainer of him [. . .] than I ever was yet of a poem or review"; EBB to Thomas Westwood, 2 October [1849], British Library. And later: "I have a valuable sort of celebrity in Rome as the 'mother of the pretty boy.' It's the best laurel I ever heard of"; EBB to Julia Martin, 20 March [1854], English Poetry Collection, Wellesley College Library.

5. EBB to Arabel Moulton-Barrett [8 December 1860], Henry W. and Albert A. Berg Collection, New York Public Library, Astor, Lenox, and Tilden Foundations.

6. On Grace Greenwood, whom she had dreaded to meet but who "satisfied [her] to the utmost in the matter of Spiritualism," see *Letters to Robert Browning and Other Correspondents*, ed. Thomas J. Wise (London: printed for private circulation, 1916), 27.

7. Moore, *In Search of White Crows*, 117.

8. See Helsinger, Sheets, and Veeder, *The Woman Question* 2:14.

9. There seems to have been a tendency toward jealous dislike among them, however, and the poet was occasionally the object of some spiteful resentment. Julia Ward Howe, author of "The Battle Hymn of the Republic," was annoyed because the Brownings did not praise her poetry; she published one poem accusing Barrett Browning of writing under the inspiration of drugs ("One Word More with E.B.B.") and another ("Kenyon's Legacy") deriding their insufficient hospitality. An American who knew the Brownings better, Mrs. Kinney (evidently a thoroughly disagreeable woman, smug, self-satisfied, and intolerably condescending toward Browning), claimed that Barrett Browning needed morphine to sustain her animation; see Ronald A. Bosco, "The Brownings and Mrs. Kinney: A Record of Their Friendship," *Browning Institute Studies* 4 (1976): 62.

10. EBB to Sophia Eckley [June 1858], Henry W. and Albert A. Berg Collection, New York Public Library, Astor, Lenox, and Tilden Foundations. On their friendship see Taplin, *Elizabeth Barrett Browning*, 355–56.

11. EBB to Arabel Moulton-Barrett, February 1859, Henry W. and Albert A. Berg Collection, New York Public Library, Astor, Lenox, and Tilden Foundations.

12. EBB to Arabel Moulton-Barrett [25 November 1858], Henry W. and Albert A. Berg Collection, New York Public Library, Astor, Lenox, and Tilden Foundations. One of Barrett Browning's many notes to Sophie refers to something "very wicked" that they did, when they "both joked & laughed"—"was it naughty?—If so, you saw that first. My conscience has been lighter since then. I meant no harm, you meant no harm—now did you?" EBB to Sophia Eckley [1859], Henry W. and Albert A. Berg Collection, New York Public Library, Astor, Lenox, and Tilden Foundations. The echo of "A True Dream," in which similar language describes the bestowal of life on strange creatures ("I had not an evil end in view, / Tho' I trod the evil way") suggests what seems in any event most likely, that this refers to some summoning of spirits.

13. But when her credulity was waning in 1859, she noted in a letter of summation to Sophie that in the "long messages from spirits pretending to belong to me," transcribed by Sophie, "the form of expression [especially "Americanisms"] was distinctly unlike those beings—in fact, I should say, *impossible to them*!" She was forced to conclude that "my particular spirits were not present," and she rather pointedly reminded Sophie that they never heard any *sounds* from the spirits, "though with you alone, you said they were always occurring"; EBB to Sophia Eckley [September 1859], Henry W. and Albert A. Berg Collection, New York Public Library, Astor, Lenox, and Tilden Foundations.

14. EBB to Fanny Haworth, quoted in Porter, *Through a Glass Darkly*, 65. This friendship and its collapse are discussed by Porter, 57–69, and by William Askins, in "Women in the Woods: A Reconsideration of the Relationship between the Brownings and Their American Friends, David and Sophia Eckley," *Browning Institute Studies* 16 (forthcoming).

15. *Dearest Isa: Robert Browning's Letters to Isabella Blagden*, ed. Edward C. McAleer (Austin: University of Texas Press, 1951), 314; *Browning to His American Friends: Letters between the Brownings, the Storys, and James Russell Lowell, 1841–1890*, ed. Gertrude Reese Hudson (New York: Barnes & Noble, 1965), 123.

16. Browning, *Browning to His American Friends*, 133.

17. Wise, *Letters to Robert Browning*, 39.

18. James, *William Wetmore Story and His Friends* 2:53, 55. For a rebuttal to this generally accepted view, and to the assumption that Browning maintained cool common sense in the face of her frenzy, see Flavia Alaya, "The Ring, the Rescue, and the Risorgimento."

19. EBB to Mary Hunter, 31 December [1859], British Library.

20. When Barrett Browning heard Tennyson read *Maud* aloud in 1855, she was impressed both by the beauty of the poem and by the naïveté with which the poet kept stopping to admire it (*LEBB* 2:213).

21. She had thought "The Raven" ludicrous, "not [. . .] the natural expression of a sane intellect," when Poe sent it to her in 1845, but admitted that the "rhythm acts excellently on the imagination—and the 'nevermore' has a solemn chime with it"; *LRHH* 2:174–76.

22. A reader coming upon these lines without knowing whose they were would surely attribute them to Swinburne. Swinburne's *Songs before Sunrise* was published in 1871. Samuel C. Chew notes that Swinburne derived various themes from Barrett Browning, including "the *motif* of the tricolor . . . the dawn of democracy upon the

world . . . England's selfish isolation and . . . the insularity that refused to recognize the greatness of France"; *Swinburne* (Boston: Little, Brown, 1929; repr. Hamden: Archon Books, 1966), 120.

23. The question of why she included it in a book about Italy has caused some puzzlement. She said that it was at Browning's suggestion (*LEBB* 2:366–67). He said that it was in response to the proslavery "Ostend manifesto" of 1854; see David J. DeLaura, "A Robert Browning Letter: The Occasion of Mrs. Browning's 'A Curse for a Nation,' " *Victorian Poetry* 4 (1966): 210. But its multifarious bearings on the rest of the volume are clear enough.

24. *John Bull,* 7 April 1860, p. 218; *Observer,* 23 April 1860, p. 7; *Atlas,* 24 March 1860, p. 231. "Alas! alas! why does a lady who can sing like this," asked a reviewer plaintively after quoting a long section from "Napoleon III in Italy," "persist in writing leading articles?" *Chambers's Journal* 13 (21 April 1860): 253. The strangest attack was from a spiritualist, William Howitt, who accused her of having been "biologized from below," an idea confirmed for him by the fact that the curse is presented as a spirit-communication; "The Earth-Plane and the Spirit-Plane of Literature," *Spiritual Magazine* 1, no. 7 (July 1860): 293, 295.

25. *Saturday Review* 11 (31 March 1860): 403.

26. *Athenaeum,* 7 April 1860, p. 477.

27. *Saturday Review* 11:403.

28. *Athenaeum,* 17 March 1860, p. 371; *Blackwood's* 87 (1860): 494. The same frame of reference governs William Howitt's dislike for her "Samsonian vigour"; "The Earth-Plane and the Spirit-Plane," 293; and the *Examiner's* desire "to see her freedom of song subject to no fetters but those it has too long disdained, of rhyme"; *Examiner,* 24 March 1860, p. 181; and *Blackwood's* crudely ironical pretense of believing that she is hiding behind a fictitious persona; *Blackwood's* 87:493.

29. *Fraser's* 61 (1860): 820.

30. Harriet Beecher Stowe, *Uncle Tom's Cabin,* chaps. 39, 40. "I expect to be torn to pieces by English critics for what I have ventured to write," she said before the reviews appeared; *LEBB* 2:357.

31. "Poetic Aberrations," *Blackwood's* 87: 490, 494.

32. Printed by Phillip F. Sharp in "Poetry in Process," 38–40. "The Best Thing in the World," which seems an anomaly even in the extremely heterogeneous *Last Poems,* is from the same manuscript, 61–65.

33. Browning identifies Agnes with Eckley; Browning, *Dearest Isa,* 295.

34. Maggie in *The Mill on the Floss* vehemently protests against the convention by which Corinne loses her lover to her cool blonde English half-sister; *The Mill on the Floss,* ed. Gordon S. Haight (Boston: Houghton Mifflin, 1961), 290–91 (book 5, chap. 4).

35. He would quote, according to his wife, "the true gods sigh for the cost and pain, / For the reed which grows never more again"; Timothy Wilson, "The Wife of the Father of *The Wasteland,*" *Esquire* 77 (May 1972): 44. I am grateful to Professor Ephim Fogel for calling this article to my attention. "Meek as maid," Barrett Browning called it (*LEBB* 2:377), and sent it to the *Cornhill* in place of the boldly assertive "Lord Walter's Wife."

36. Ovid, *Metamorphoses,* with an English translation by Frank Justus Miller, 2 vols. (Loeb Classical Library, 2d ed. 1921), vol. 1, 1:711–12 ("disparibus calamis

compagine cerae / inter se iunctis"); Andrew Marvell, "The Garden," 31–32; Shelley, "Hymn of Pan," 31–33. For the history of Pan in English literature, see Patricia Merivale, *Pan the Goat-God: His Myth in Modern Times* (Cambridge: Harvard University Press, 1969); on the new conception of Pan that the Brownings introduced into English poetry, see Merivale, 82. The *Cornhill*, for which "Lord Walter's Wife" has been found unsuitable, published "A Musical Instrument" with an illustration by Frederic Leighton: a full-page drawing of Pan dominated by huge, bestial legs with hairy thighs and heavy hoofs arranged so as to draw the eye to the genital area (covered, of course) at the center of the picture; *Cornhill Magazine* 2 (July 1860), facing page 84. The speaker in "A Reed," published first in 1846 and then in *Poems* (1850), had asked to be left unplucked, to sing in response to the sighs of a "little maid or child"—but now Syrinx represents a more ambitious poetry.

37. "Pan and Luna," 82–84. To suggest that because elsewhere he called his wife his "moon of poets" ("One Word More," 188) he was saying something about their marital relations in this poem is patently absurd, but he seldom used classical mythology in his poetry, and he could hardly have forgotten that two of his wife's best-known poems about poetry were about Pan. When what seems like a rape is expressed as the wrapping of the moon in a cloud, Browning may have been recalling the metaphor for Aurora and Romney's mutual passion: "If a cloud came down / And wrapped us wholly" (9:740–41).

Aftermath

1. *North British Review* 36 (1852): 515; "in no previous age has such a singer been found among women," *Blackwood's* 91 (1862): 451; she was "unquestionably the first English poet of her sex," *Harper's New Monthly Magazine* 23 (1861): 556; "the greatest English poetess that has ever lived," *Athenaeum*, 29 March 1862, p. 421.

2. *British Quarterly Review* 42 (1865): 359. *Saturday Review* 12 (13 July 1861): 42, and 13 (26 April 1862): 473.

3. *North American Review* 94 (1862): 338, 345. "We have seen a tender-handed woman enter her husband's shop, and mimic his handicraft with femininely stern countenance, and little sinews resolutely strung, until, weary of the uncongenial work, she threw down the implements, and stood in the grace of her sex,—lovelier for the pantomime. . . . If we are a little startled at first by the careless way in which she lays about her with the edged tools of reasoning, we speedily have the satisfaction of seeing that they are harmless in her hands, and that we have our woman yet" (345).

4. *Dublin University Magazine* 60 (1862): 162.

5. *North American Review* 94 (1862): 340; *Atlantic Monthly* 8 (1861): 370.

6. Browning, *Letters of Robert Browning*, 64–65.

7. Browning, *New Letters of Robert Browning*, 138.

8. Thomas Adolphus Trollope, *What I Remember* 2:172–73.

9. *The Letters of Edward Fitzgerald*, ed. Alfred McKinley Terhune and Annabelle Burdick Terhune, 4 vols. (Princeton: Princeton University Press, 1980) 2:407. He had rather liked *Casa Guidi Windows;* ibid. 2:31–32. "Fitzgerald was no lover of women in public life," his most recent biographer says, "and he was thoroughly

unfair to such writers as Jane Austen, Mrs. Browning, Charlotte Brontë, and George Eliot"; Robert Bernard Martin, *With Friends Possessed: A Life of Edward Fitzgerald* (New York: Faber & Faber, 1985), 181.

10. Harriet Hosmer, *Letters and Memories*, ed. Cornelia Carr (New York: Moffat, Yard, 1912), 180, 49.

11. Browning, *Dearest Isa*, 267.

Bibliography

Abbreviations

BC   *The Brownings' Correspondence.* Edited by Philip Kelley and
            Ronald Hudson. 6– vols. Winfield, Kan.: Wedgestone Press,
            1984–.

Diary   *Diary by E.B.B.: The Unpublished Diary of Elizabeth Barrett
            Barrett, 1831–1832.* Edited by Philip Kelley and Ronald Hud-
            son. Athens: Ohio University Press, 1969.

IF   *Invisible Friends: The Correspondence of Elizabeth Barrett Barrett
            and Benjamin Robert Haydon, 1842–1845.* Edited by Willard
            Bissell Pope. Cambridge: Harvard University Press, 1972.

LBGB   *Letters of the Brownings to George Barrett.* Edited by Paul Landis
            with the assistance of Ronald E. Freeman. Urbana: University
            of Illinois Press, 1958.

LEBB   *The Letters of Elizabeth Barrett Browning.* Edited by Frederic G.
            Kenyon. 4th ed. 2 vols. London: Smith, Elder, 1898.

LHSB   *Elizabeth Barrett to Mr Boyd: Unpublished Letters of Elizabeth
            Barrett Browning to Hugh Stuart Boyd.* Edited by Barbara P.
            McCarthy. New Haven: Yale University Press, 1955.

LMO   *Elizabeth Barrett Browning's Letters to Mrs. David Ogilvy, 1849–
            1861, with Recollections by Mrs. Ogilvy.* Edited by Peter N. Hey-
            don and Philip Kelley. New York: Quadrangle/New York
            Times Book Co., and Browning Institute, 1973.

LMRM   *The Letters of Elizabeth Barrett Browning to Mary Russell Mitford,
            1836–1854.* Edited by Meredith B. Raymond and Mary Rose
            Sullivan. 3 vols. Winfield, Kan.: Armstrong Browning Library
            of Baylor University, Browning Institute, Wedgestone Press,
            and Wellesley College, 1983.

LRHH   *Letters of Elizabeth Barrett Browning, Addressed to Richard Hengist
            Horne, with Comments on Contemporaries.* Edited by S. R.

Townshend Mayer. 2 vols. London: Richard Bentley & Son, 1877.

LS   *Elizabeth Barrett Browning: Letters to Her Sister, 1846–1859.* Edited by Leonard Huxley. London: John Murray, 1929.

RB-EBB   *The Letters of Robert Browning and Elizabeth Barrett Barrett, 1845–1846.* Edited by Elvan Kintner. 2 vols. Cambridge: Belknap Press of Harvard University Press, 1969.

TTUL   *Twenty-Two Unpublished Letters of Elizabeth Barrett Browning and Robert Browning Addressed to Henrietta and Arabella Moulton-Barrett.* New York: United Feature Syndicate, 1935.

Alaya, Flavia. "The Ring, the Rescue, and the Risorgimento: Reunifying the Brownings' Italy." *Browning Institute Studies* 6 (1978): 1–41.

Altman, Janet Gurkin. *Epistolarity: Approaches to a Form.* Columbus: Ohio State University Press, 1982.

Arishshtein, Leonid M. " 'A Curse for a Nation': A Controversial Episode in Elizabeth Barrett Browning's Political Poetry." *Review of English Studies,* n.s. 20 (1969): 33–42.

Arnold, Matthew. *The Poems of Matthew Arnold.* Edited by Kenneth Allott. London: Longmans, 1965. 2d ed., edited by Miriam Allott, 1979.

Artom Treves, Giuliana. *The Golden Ring: The Anglo-Florentines, 1847–1862.* Translated by Sylvia Sprigge. London: Longmans, Green, 1956.

Askins, William. "Women in the Woods: A Reconsideration of the Relationship between the Brownings and Their American Friends, David and Sophia Eckley." *Browning Institute Studies* 16 (1988).

Auerbach, Nina. "Robert Browning's Last Word." *Victorian Poetry* 22 (1984): 161–73.

Bald, Marjory A. *Women-Writers of the Nineteenth Century.* New York: Russell & Russell, 1923.

Barkan, Leonard. "Diana and Actaeon: The Myth as Synthesis." *English Literary Renaissance* 10 (1980): 317–59.

Barnes, Warner. "The Sorrows of the Muses: An Early Poem by Elizabeth Barrett." *Books at Iowa* 4 (April 1966): 19–35.

Barrett Browning, Elizabeth. *Aurora Leigh and Other Poems.* Introduced by Cora Kaplan. London: Women's Press, 1978.

———. *Casa Guidi Windows.* Edited with an Introduction by Julia Markus. New York: Browning Institute, 1977.

———. *Essays on the Greek Christian Poets and the English Poets.* 1863. Reprinted, Plainview, N.Y.: Books for Libraries Press, 1972.

————. *Hitherto Unpublished Poems and Stories, with an Inedited Auto-biography.* Edited by H. Buxton Forman. 2 vols. Boston: Bibliophile Society, 1914.

————. *Letters to Robert Browning and Other Correspondents.* Edited by Thomas J. Wise. London: printed for private circulation, 1916.

————. *New Poems by Robert Browning and Elizabeth Barrett Browning.* Edited by Frederic G. Kenyon. London: Smith, Elder, 1914.

————. *The Poetical Works of Elizabeth Barrett Browning.* Edited by Harriet Waters Preston, with a new introduction by Ruth M. Adams. Boston: Houghton Mifflin, 1900, 1974.

————. *The Poets' Enchiridion.* Edited by H. Buxton Forman. Boston: Bibliophile Society, 1914.

————. *Sonnets from the Portuguese: Centennial Variorum Edition.* Edited by Fannie Ratchford. New York: Philip C. Duschnes, 1950.

————. *Sonnets from the Portuguese: A Facsimile Edition of the British Library Manuscript.* Edited by William S. Peterson. Barre, Mass.: Barre Publishing, 1977.

————. *A Variorum Edition of Elizabeth Barrett Browning's Sonnets from the Portuguese.* Edited by Miroslavia Wein Dow. Troy, N.Y.: Whitston, 1980.

Battiscombe, Georgina. *Christina Rossetti: A Divided Life.* New York: Holt, Rinehart, & Winston, 1981.

Besier, Rudolf. *The Barretts of Wimpole Street: A Comedy in Five Acts.* Boston: Little, Brown, 1930.

Biasi Vitali, Ippolita de. *Vita di Elisabetta Barrett Browning.* Milano: Gastoldi [1955].

Blainey, Ann. *The Farthing Poet: A Biography of Richard Hengist Horne, 1802–84: A Lesser Literary Lion.* London: Longmans, 1968.

Blake, Kathleen. "Elizabeth Barrett Browning and Wordsworth: The Romantic Poet as a Woman." *Victorian Poetry* 24 (1986): 387–98.

————. *Love and the Woman Question in Victorian Literature: The Art of Self-Postponement.* Totowa, N.J.: Barnes & Noble, 1983.

Blanchard, Laman. *Life and Literary Remains of L. E. L.* 2 vols. Philadelphia: Lea & Blanchard, 1841.

Bodichon, Barbara Leigh Smith. *Women and Work.* New York: C. S. Francis, 1859.

Boas, Louise Schutz. *Elizabeth Barrett Browning.* London: Longmans, Green, 1930.

Boos, Florence Saunders. *The Poetry of Dante G. Rossetti: A Critical Reading and Source Study.* The Hague: Mouton, 1976.

Bosco, Ronald A. "The Brownings and Mrs. Kinney: A Record of Their Friendship." *Browning Institute Studies* 4 (1976): 57–124.

Bossis, Mireille. "Methodological Journeys through Correspondences." *Men/Women of Letters. Yale French Studies,* no. 71 (1986): 63–75.

Boyce, George K. "The Brownings." *New Colophon* 3 (1950): 110–19.

Brandon, Ruth. *The Spiritualists: The Passion for the Occult in the Nineteenth and Twentieth Centuries.* New York: Alfred A. Knopf, 1983.

Braudy, Leo. *The Frenzy of Renown: Fame and Its History.* New York: Oxford University Press, 1986.

Breuer, Josef, and Sigmund Freud. *Studies on Hysteria.* Translated by James Strachey. New York: Basic Books, 1955.

Brown, Cheryl L., and Karen Olson, eds. *Feminist Criticism: Essays on Theory, Poetry, and Prose.* Metuchen, N.J.: Scarecrow Press, 1978.

Browning, Elizabeth Barrett. *See* Barrett Browning, Elizabeth.

Browning, Robert. *Browning to His American Friends: Letters between the Brownings, the Storys, and James Russell Lowell, 1841–1890.* Edited by Gertrude Reese Hudson. New York: Barnes & Noble, 1965.

———. *Dearest Isa: Robert Browning's Letters to Isabella Blagden.* Edited by Edward C. McAleer. Austin: University of Texas Press, 1951.

———. *Letters of Robert Browning, Collected by Thomas J. Wise.* Edited by Thurman L. Hood. New Haven: Yale University Press, 1933.

———. *New Letters of Robert Browning.* Edited by William Clyde DeVane and Kenneth Leslie Knickerbocker. New Haven: Yale University Press, 1950.

———. *Robert Browning and Julia Wedgwood: A Broken Friendship as Revealed by Their Letters.* Edited by Richard Curle. New York: Stokes, 1937.

———. *Robert Browning: The Poems.* Edited by John Pettigrew and Thomas J. Collins. 2 vols. New Haven: Yale University Press, 1981.

Buckley, Jerome Hamilton. *Season of Youth: The Bildungsroman from Dickens to Golding.* Cambridge: Harvard University Press, 1974.

———. *The Victorian Temper: A Study in Literary Culture.* Cambridge: Harvard University Press, 1951.

Byron, George Gordon. *Poetical Works.* Edited by Frederick Page (a new edition, corrected by John Jump). 3d ed. Oxford: Oxford University Press, 1970.

Camões, Luis de. *Poems from the Portuguese of Luis de Camoens, with Remarks on His Life and Writings, Notes, &c &c.* By Lord Viscount Strangford. London: J. Carpenter, 1803.

Carter, John, and Graham Pollard. *An Enquiry into the Nature of Certain Nineteenth Century Pamphlets.* London: Constable, 1934.

Chaucer, Geoffrey. *The Poems of Geoffrey Chaucer, Modernized.* [Edited by R. H. Horne.] London: Whittaker, 1841.

———. *The Poetical Works of Chaucer.* Edited by F. N. Robinson. Boston: Houghton Mifflin, 1933.

Chesterton, G. K. *The Victorian Age in Literature.* 1913. 2d ed. New York: Oxford University Press, 1966.

Chew, Samuel C. *Swinburne.* Boston: Little, Brown, 1929. Reprint ed. Hamden: Archon, 1966.

Chodorow, Nancy. *The Reproduction of Mothering: Psychoanalysis and the Sociology of Gender.* Berkeley and Los Angeles: University of California Press, 1978.

Chorley, Henry Fothergill, James Robinson Planché, and Julian Charles Young. *Personal Reminiscences by Chorley, Planché, and Young.* Edited by Richard Henry Stoddard. New York: Scribner, Armstrong, 1874.

Churchill, Kenneth. *Italy and English Literature, 1764–1930.* Totowa, N.J.: Barnes & Noble, 1980.

Clough, Arthur Hugh. *The Correspondence of Arthur Hugh Clough.* Edited by Frederick L. Mulhauser. 2 vols. Oxford: Clarendon Press, 1957.

Conway, Eustace. *Anthony Munday and Other Essays.* New York: privately printed, 1927.

Corson, Hiram. *Spirit Messages: With an Introductory Essay on Spiritual Vitality.* Boston: Christopher, 1911; new ed., 1919.

Crane, Sylvia E. *White Silence: Greenough, Powers, and Crawford, American Sculptors in Nineteenth-Century Italy.* Coral Gables: University of Miami Press, 1972.

Craven, Wayne. *Sculpture in America.* New York: T. Y. Crowell, 1968.

Creston, Dormer. *Andromeda in Wimpole Street: The Romance of Elizabeth Barrett Browning.* New York: E. P. Dutton, 1930.

Culler, A. Dwight. *Imaginative Reason: The Poetry of Matthew Arnold.* New Haven: Yale University Press, 1966.

David, Dierdre. *Intellectual Women and Victorian Patriarchy: Harriet Martineau, Elizabeth Barrett Browning, George Eliot.* Ithaca: Cornell University Press, 1987.

DeLaura, David J. "A Robert Browning Letter: The Occasion of Mrs. Browning's 'A Curse for a Nation.' " *Victorian Poetry* 4 (1966): 210–12.

———. "Ruskin and the Brownings: Twenty-Five Unpublished Letters." *Bulletin of the John Rylands Library* 54 (1972): 314–56.

DeVane, William C. "The Virgin and the Dragon." *Yale Review* 37 (1947): 33–46.

Diehl, Joanne Feit. " 'Come Slowly—Eden': An Exploration of Women Poets and Their Muse." *Signs* 3 (1978): 572–87.

Donaldson, Sandra M. "Elizabeth Barrett's Two Sonnets to George Sand." *Studies in Browning and His Circle* 5, no. 1 (Spring 1977): 19–22.

————. " 'Motherhood's Advent in Power': Elizabeth Barrett Browning's Poems about Motherhood." *Victorian Poetry* 18 (1980): 51–60.

Du Bos, Charles. *Robert et Elizabeth Browning, ou la plenitude de l'amour humain.* Paris: Klincksieck, 1982.

Eckley, Sophia May. *Minor Chords.* London: Bell & Daldy, 1869.

————. *Poems.* London: Longman, Green, Roberts, & Green, 1863.

Eliot, George. *Middlemarch.* Edited by Gordon S. Haight. Boston: Houghton Mifflin, 1956.

————. *The Mill on the Floss.* Edited by Gordon S. Haight. Boston: Houghton Mifflin, 1961.

————. *The George Eliot Letters.* Edited by Gordon S. Haight. 9 vols. New Haven: Yale University Press, 1954–78.

Eliot, T. S. *Selected Essays.* 3d ed. London: Faber & Faber, 1951.

Enfield, D. E. *L.E.L.: A Mystery of the Thirties.* London: Hogarth Press, 1928.

Erickson, Lee. *Robert Browning: His Poetry and His Audiences.* Ithaca: Cornell University Press, 1984.

Fairchild, Hoxie Neale. *Religious Trends in English Poetry.* Vol. 4, *1830–1880: Christianity and Romanticism in the Victorian Era.* New York: Columbia University Press, 1957.

Feinstein, Howard M. *Becoming William James.* Ithaca: Cornell University Press, 1984.

Fitzgerald, Edward. *The Letters of Edward Fitzgerald.* Edited by Alfred McKinley Terhune and Annabelle Burdick Terhune. 4 vols. Princeton: Princeton University Press, 1980.

Fowler, R. " 'On Not Knowing Greek': The Classics and the Woman of Letters." *Classical Journal* 78 (1983): 337–49.

Friedman, Susan Stanford. "Gender and Genre Anxiety: Elizabeth Barrett Browning and H. D. as Epic Poets." *Tulsa Studies in Women's Literature* 5 (1986): 203–28.

Fuller, Margaret S. *Papers on Literature and Art.* New York: Wiley & Putnam, 1846.

Gaskell, Elizabeth. *The Life of Charlotte Brontë.* Harmondsworth: Penguin Books, 1865.

Gay, Peter. *Education of the Senses.* Vol. 1, *The Bourgeois Experience: Victoria to Freud.* New York: Oxford University Press, 1984.

Gelpi, Barbara Charlesworth. *"Aurora Leigh:* The Vocation of the Woman Poet." *Victorian Poetry* 19 (1981): 35–48.

Gerin, Winifred. *Elizabeth Gaskell: A Biography.* Oxford: Clarendon Press, 1976.

Gerdts, William H. *American Neoclassic Sculpture: The Marble Resurrection.* New York: Viking, 1973.

Giartosio de Courten, Maria Luisa. *Ba (Elisabetta Barrett Browning).* Firenze: Sansoni [1956].

Gilbert, Sandra M. "From *Patria* to *Matria:* Elizabeth Barrett Browning's Risorgimento." *PMLA* 99 (1984): 194–211.

_____. "Life's Empty Pack: Notes toward a Literary Daughteronomy." *Critical Inquiry* 11 (1985): 355–84.

Gilbert, Sandra M., and Susan Gubar. *The Madwoman in the Attic: The Woman Writer and the Nineteenth Century Literary Imagination.* New Haven: Yale University Press, 1979.

Gilbert, Sandra M., and Susan Gubar, eds. *Shakespeare's Sisters: Feminist Essays on Women Poets.* Bloomington: Indiana University Press, 1979.

Gladish, Robert W. *Elizabeth Barrett and the 'Centurion': The Background to an Addition to the Elizabeth Barrett Browning Canon.* Baylor University Browning Interests, no. 23. Waco, 1973.

_____. "Mrs. Browning's 'A Curse for a Nation': Some Further Comments." *Victorian Poetry* 7 (1969): 275–80.

Goffman, Erving. *Interaction Ritual: Essays on Face-to-Face Behavior.* New York: Doubleday-Anchor, 1967.

Going, William T. "E. B. Browning's *Sonnets from the Portuguese* XLIII." *Explicator* 11 (1953): 58.

_____. *Scanty Plot of Ground: Studies in the Victorian Sonnet.* The Hague: Mouton, 1976.

Goldfarb, Russell M., and Clare R. Goldfarb. *Spiritualism and Nineteenth-Century Letters.* Rutherford, N.J.: Fairleigh Dickinson University Press, 1978.

Goreau, Angeline. *Reconstructing Aphra: A Social Biography of Aphra Behn.* New York: Dial, 1980.

Gosse, Edmund. *Critical Kit-Kats.* New York: Dodd, Mead, 1896.

Gridley, Roy E. *The Brownings and France: A Chronicle with Commentary.* London: Athlone Press, 1982.

Gubar, Susan. "Mother, Maiden, and the Marriage of Death: Women Writers and an Ancient Myth." *Women's Studies* 6 (1979): 301–15.

Hayter, Alethea. *Mrs. Browning: A Poet's Work and Its Setting.* New York: Barnes & Noble, 1963.

———. *Opium and the Romantic Imagination.* Berkeley and Los Angeles: University of California Press, 1968.

———. *A Sultry Month: Scenes of London Literary Life in 1846.* London: Faber & Faber, 1965.

———. " 'These Men Over-Nice': Elizabeth Barrett Browning's 'Lord Walter's Wife.' " *Browning Society Notes* 8, no. 2 (August 1978): 5–7.

Heilbrun, Carolyn G. *Reinventing Womanhood.* New York: W. W. Norton, 1979.

Heilman, Robert B. "E. B. Browning's *Sonnets from the Portuguese,* XLIII." *Explicator* 4 (1945): 3.

Helsinger, Elizabeth K., Robin Lauterbach Sheets, and William Veeder. *The Woman Question: Society and Literature in Britain and America, 1837–1883.* 3 vols. New York: Garland, 1983.

Herstein, Sheila R. *A Mid-Victorian Feminist, Barbara Leigh Smith Bodichon.* New Haven: Yale University Press, 1985.

Hetzler, Leo A. "The Case of Prince Hohenstiel-Schwangau: Browning and Napoleon III." *Victorian Poetry* 15 (1977): 335–50.

Hewlett, Dorothy. *Elizabeth Barrett Browning.* London: Cassell, 1953.

Hickok, Kathleen. *Representations of Women: Nineteenth-Century British Women's Poetry.* Westport, Conn.: Greenwood, 1984.

Hicks, Malcolm. "Elizabeth Barrett Browning's 'Lord Walter's Wife': Its Family History." *Browning Society Notes* 8, no. 3 (December 1978): 7–12.

Homans, Margaret. *Bearing the Word: Language and Female Experience in Nineteenth-Century Women's Writing.* Chicago: University of Chicago Press, 1986.

———. " 'Syllables of Velvet': Dickinson, Rossetti, and the Rhetorics of Sexuality." *Feminist Studies* 11 (1985): 569–93.

———. *Women Writers and Poetic Identity: Dorothy Wordsworth, Emily Brontë, and Emily Dickinson.* Princeton: Princeton University Press, 1980.

Honan, Park. *Matthew Arnold: A Life.* New York: McGraw-Hill, 1981.

Horne, Richard Henry, ed. *A New Spirit of the Age.* 2 vols. London: Smith, Elder, 1844.

Hosmer, Harriet. *Harriet Hosmer: Letters and Memories.* Edited by Cornelia Carr. New York: Moffat, Yard, 1912.

Howe, Julia Ward. *Later Lyrics.* Boston: J. E. Tilton, 1866.

————. *Words for the Hour.* Boston: Ticknor & Fields, 1857.

Hudson, Ronald. "Elizabeth Barrett Browning and Her Brother Alfred: Some Unpublished Letters." *Browning Institute Studies* 2 (1974): 135–60.

Hunt, Leigh. "*Aurora Leigh:* An Unpublished Letter from Leigh Hunt." *Cornhill Magazine* 76, n.s. 3 (1897): 738–49.

[Hutton, W. H.] "Novels by the Authoress of 'John Halifax.' " *North British Review* 29 (1858): 466–81.

Hyman, Linda. "*The Greek Slave* by Hiram Powers: High Art as Popular Culture." *Art Journal* 35 (1976): 216–23.

Irvine, William, and Park Honan. *The Book, the Ring, and the Poet: A Biography of Robert Browning.* New York: McGraw-Hill, 1974.

James, Henry. *William Wetmore Story and His Friends: From Letters, Diaries, and Recollections.* 2 vols. Edinburgh: William Blackwood & Sons, 1903.

Jenkyns, Richard. *The Victorians and Ancient Greece.* Cambridge: Harvard University Press, 1980.

Jones, Ann Rosalind. "Assimilation with a Difference: Renaissance Women Poets and Literary Influence." *Yale French Studies,* no. 62 (1981): 135–53.

Jonsson, Inge. *Emanuel Swedenborg.* Translated by Catherine Djurklou. New York: Twayne, 1971.

Juhasz, Suzanne. *Naked and Fiery Forms: Modern American Poetry by Women, A New Tradition.* New York: Octagon, 1976.

Kaplan, Cora, ed. *Salt and Bitter and Good: Three Centuries of English and American Women Poets.* New York: Paddington Press, 1975.

————. *Sea Changes: Essays on Culture and Feminism.* London: Verso, 1986.

Kaplan, Fred. *Sacred Tears: Sentimentality in Victorian Literature.* Princeton: Princeton University Press, 1987.

Karlin, Daniel. *The Courtship of Robert Browning and Elizabeth Barrett.* Oxford: Clarendon Press, 1985.

Kasson, Joy. "Power and Powerlessness: Death, Sexuality and the Demonic in Nineteenth-Century American Sculpture." Paper delivered at the American Studies National Convention, San Diego, 3 November 1985.

Keats, John. *The Letters of John Keats, 1814–1821.* Edited by Hyder Edward Rollins. 2 vols. Cambridge: Harvard University Press, 1958.

Kelley, Philip. [Reply to "Greek Slave Mystery."] *Notes and Queries* 212, n.s. 14 (1967): 194.

Kelley, Philip, and Betty A. Coley. *The Browning Collections: A Reconstruction, with Other Memorabilia.* Winfield, Kan.: Armstrong Browning Library of Baylor University, Browning Institute, Mansell Publishing, Wedgestone Press, 1984.

Kelley, Philip, and Ronald Hudson. *The Brownings' Correspondence: A Checklist.* Arkansas City, Kan.: Browning Institute and Wedgestone Press, 1978.

Korg, Jacob. *Browning and Italy.* Athens: Ohio University Press, 1983.

Landon, Letitia E. "Night at Sea." *The New Monthly Magazine and Humorist* 55 (1839): 30–32.

———. *The Poetical Works of L. E. Landon.* 2 vols. Philadelphia: Jasper Harding, 1850.

Leighton, Angela. *Elizabeth Barrett Browning.* Bloomington: Indiana University Press, 1986.

Levinson, Marjorie. *The Romantic Fragment Poem: A Critique of a Form.* Chapel Hill: University of North Carolina Press, 1986.

Leyda, Jay. *The Years and Hours of Emily Dickinson.* 2 vols. New Haven: Yale University Press, 1960.

Liberty Bell. By Friends of Freedom. Boston: National Anti-Slavery Fair, 1848; National Anti-Slavery Bazaar, 1856.

Lipking, Lawrence. "Aristotle's Sister: A Poetics of Abandonment." *Critical Inquiry* 10 (1983): 61–81.

———. *The Life of the Poet: Beginning and Ending Poetic Careers.* Chicago: University of Chicago Press, 1981.

Lohrli, Anne. "Greek Slave Mystery." *Notes and Queries* 211, n.s. 13 (1966): 58–60.

———. "Sonnets to Mrs. Browning." *Studies in Browning and His Circle* 6, no. 1 (Spring 1978): 71–73.

Loth, David. *The Brownings: A Victorian Idyll.* New York: Brentano's, 1929.

Lubbock, Percy. *Elizabeth Barrett Browning in Her Letters.* London: Smith, Elder, 1906.

Lupton, Mary Jane. *Elizabeth Barrett Browning.* Long Island: Feminist Press, 1972.

Lytton, Robert. *Letters from Owen Meredith (Robert, First Earl of Lytton) to Robert and Elizabeth Barrett Browning.* Edited by Aurelia Brooks Harlan and J. Lee Harlan, Jr. Baylor University Browning Interests, no. 10. Waco, 1936.

McAleer, Edward C. "New Letters from Mrs. Browning to Isa Blagden."
  PMLA 66 (1951): 594–612.

———. *The Brownings of Casa Guidi*. New York: Browning Institute,
  1979.

McFarland, Thomas. *Romanticism and the Forms of Ruin: Wordsworth,
  Coleridge, and Modalities of Fragmentation*. Princeton: Princeton Uni-
  versity Press, 1981.

McGhee, Richard D. *Marriage, Duty, and Desire in Victorian Poetry and
  Drama*. Lawrence: Regents Press of Kansas, 1980.

MacPherson, Gerardine. *Memoirs of the Life of Anna Jameson*. Boston:
  Roberts Bros., 1878.

Mander, Rosalie. *Mrs. Browning: The Story of Elizabeth Barrett*. London:
  Weidenfeld & Nicolson, 1980.

Marchand, Leslie A. *The Athenaeum: A Mirror of Victorian Culture*. Chapel
  Hill: University of North Carolina Press, 1941.

Marks, Jeannette. *The Family of the Barrett: A Colonial Romance*. New
  York: Macmillan, 1938.

Markus, Julia. " 'Old Pictures in Florence' through *Casa Guidi Windows*."
  Browning Institute Studies 6 (1978): 43–61.

Martin, Loy D. *Browning's Dramatic Monologues and the Post-Romantic
  Subject*. Baltimore: Johns Hopkins University Press, 1985.

Martin, Robert Bernard. *Tennyson: The Unquiet Heart*. New York: Oxford
  University Press, 1980.

———. *With Friends Possessed: A Life of Edward Fitzgerald*. Boston: Faber
  & Faber, 1985.

Martineau, Harriet. *Autobiography*. 1877. 2 vols. London: Virago, 1983.

Maynard, John. *Browning's Youth*. Cambridge: Harvard University Press,
  1977.

Meredith, George. *The Poems of George Meredith*. Edited by Phyllis B.
  Bartlett. 2 vols. New Haven: Yale University Press, 1978.

Meredith, Michael. "The Wounded Heroine: Elizabeth Barrett's Soph-
  ocles." *Studies in Browning and His Circle* 3, no. 2 (Fall 1975): 1–12.

Merivale, Patricia. *Pan the Goat-God: His Myth in Modern Times*. Cam-
  bridge: Harvard University Press, 1969.

Merlette, Germaine-Marie. *La Vie et l'oeuvre d'Elizabeth Barrett Browning*.
  Paris: Librarie Armand Colin, 1905.

Meynell, Alice. *The Wares of Autolycus: Selected Literary Essays*. Edited by
  P. M. Fraser. London: Oxford University Press, 1965.

Miller, Betty. "Elizabeth Barrett and Her Brother: 'For we were nursed
  upon the self-same hill.' " *Cornhill Magazine* 166 (1952): 221–28.

————. "Elizabeth and Emily Elizabeth." *Twentieth Century* 159 (1956): 574–83.

————. "Miss Barrett and Mr. Hunter." *Cornhill Magazine* 165 (1951): 83–96.

————. *Robert Browning: A Portrait.* 1952. New York: Charles Scribner's Sons, 1953.

————. "The Seance at Ealing: A Study in Memory and Imagination." *Cornhill Magazine* 169 (1957): 317–24.

Mitford, Mary Russell. *Correspondence with Charles Boner and John Ruskin.* Edited by Elizabeth Lee. London: T. Fisher Unwin, 1914.

————. *The Friendships of Mary Russell Mitford, As Recorded in Letters from Her Literary Correspondents.* Edited by A. G. L'Estrange. New York: Harper & Bros., 1882.

————. *Letters of Mary Russell Mitford,* 2d series. Edited by Henry Chorley. 2 vols. London: Richard Bentley & Son, 1872.

————. *The Life of Mary Russell Mitford, Related in a Selection from Her Letters to Her Friends.* Edited by A. G. L'Estrange. 3 vols. London: Richard Bentley & Son, 1870.

————. *Recollections of a Literary Life: or, Books, Places, and People.* New York: Harper & Bros., 1852.

Moers, Ellen. *Literary Women.* Garden City: Doubleday, 1976.

Monteiro, George. "On First Looking into Strangford's Camões: Elizabeth Barrett Browning's 'Catarina to Camoëns.' " *Studies in Browning and His Circle* 8, no. 1 (1980): 7–19.

Moore, R. Laurence. *In Search of White Crows: Spiritualism, Parapsychology, and American Culture.* New York: Oxford University Press, 1977.

Moser, Kay. "Elizabeth Barrett's Youthful Feminism: Fragment of 'An Essay on Woman.' " *Studies in Browning and His Circle* 12 (Spring-Fall 1984): 13–26.

————. "The Victorian Critic's Dilemma: What to Do with a Talented Poetess." *Victorians Institute Journal* 13 (1985): 59–66.

Musgrove, S., ed. "Unpublished Letters of Thomas de Quincey and Elizabeth Barrett Browning." *Auckland University College Bulletin,* no. 44, English series no. 7 (1954).

Nicoll, William Robertson, and Thomas J. Wise. *Literary Anecdotes of the Nineteenth Century: Contributions towards a Literary History of the Period.* 2 vols. London: Hodder & Stoughton, 1895.

Ong, Walter J. *Rhetoric, Romance, and Technology: Studies in the Interaction of Expression and Culture.* Ithaca: Cornell University Press, 1971.

Oppenheim, Janet. *The Other World: Spiritualism and Psychical Research in England, 1850–1914.* Cambridge: Cambridge University Press, 1985.

Orr, Mrs. Sutherland. *Life and Letters of Robert Browning.* 2d ed. London: Smith, Elder, 1891.

Ostriker, Alicia. "The Thieves of Language: Women Poets and Revisionist Mythmaking," *Signs* 8 (1982): 68–90.

Ovid. *Metamorphoses.* With an English translation by Frank Justus Miller. 2d ed. 2 vols. Loeb Classical Library, 1921.

Pater, Walter. *The Renaissance: Studies in Art and Poetry, the 1893 Text.* Edited by Donald L. Hill. Berkeley and Los Angeles: University of California Press, 1890.

Patmore, Coventry. *The Poems of Coventry Patmore.* Edited by Frederick Page. London: Oxford University Press, 1949.

Phelps, William Lyon. "Robert Browning on Spiritualism." *Yale Review,* n.s. 23 (1933–34): 125–38.

Pichanick, Valerie Kossew. *Harriet Martineau: The Woman and Her Work, 1802–1876.* Ann Arbor: University of Michigan Press, 1980.

Pickering, George. *Creative Malady: Illness in the Lives and Minds of Charles Darwin, Florence Nightingale, Mary Baker Eddy, Sigmund Freud, Marcel Proust, and Elizabeth Barrett Browning.* New York: Oxford University Press, 1974.

Poe, Edgar Allan. *The Complete Works of Edgar Allan Poe.* Edited by James A. Harrison. 17 vols. New York: Thomas Y. Crowell, 1902.

Porter, Charles A. Foreword. *Men/Women of Letters. Yale French Studies,* no. 71 (1986): 1–14.

Porter, Katherine H. *Through a Glass Darkly: Spiritualism in the Browning Circle.* New York: Octagon Books, 1972.

Rader, Ralph Wilson. *Tennyson's Maud: The Biographical Genesis.* Berkeley and Los Angeles: University of California Press, 1963.

Radley, Virginia L. *Elizabeth Barrett Browning.* Boston: Twayne, 1972.

Raymond, Meredith B. "E.B.B.'s Poetics, 1830–1844: 'The Seraph and the Earthly Piper.' " *Browning Society Notes* 9, no. 1 (April 1979): 5–9.

―――. "Elizabeth Barrett Browning's Poetics, 1845–1846: 'The Ascending Gyre.' " *Browning Society Notes* 11, no. 2 (August 1981): 1–11.

―――. "Elizabeth Barrett's Early Poetics: The 1820s, 'The Bird Pecks through the Shell.' " *Browning Society Notes* 8, no. 3 (December 1978): 3–7.

―――. "John Kenyon, the Magnificient Dilettante." *Studies in Browning and His Circle* 14 (1986): 32–62.

Reid, Martine. "Correspondences: *Stendhal en toutes lettres.*" *Men/Women of Letters. Yale French Studies*, no. 71 (1986): 149–68.

Reynolds, Donald M. "The 'Unveiled Soul': Hiram Powers's Embodiment of the Ideal." *Art Bulletin* 59 (1977): 394–414.

Rich, Adrienne Cecile. *On Lies, Secrets, and Silence: Selected Prose, 1966–1978.* New York: Norton, 1979.

Ricks, Christopher, ed. *The Brownings: Letters and Poetry.* Garden City: Doubleday, 1970.

Ridenour, George M. "Robert Browning and *Aurora Leigh.*" *Victorian Newsletter* 67 (Spring 1985): 26–31.

Roberson, Samuel A., and William H. Gerdts. " '. . . *so undressed, yet so refined . . .*': The Greek Slave." *The Museum*, n.s. 17, nos. 1–2 (Winter-Spring 1965): 1–29.

Robertson, Eric S. *English Poetesses: A Series of Critical Biographies, with Illustrative Extracts.* London: Cassell, 1883.

Rosenblum, Dolores. "*Casa Guidi Windows* and *Aurora Leigh:* The Genesis of Elizabeth Barrett Browning's Visionary Aesthetic." *Tulsa Studies in Women's Literature* 4 (1985): 61–68.

———. "Face to Face: Elizabeth Barrett Browning's *Aurora Leigh* and Nineteenth-Century Poetry." *Victorian Studies* 26 (1983): 321–38.

Rossetti, Christina. *The Complete Poems of Christina Rossetti: A Variorum Edition.* Edited by R. W. Crump. 2 vols. Baton Rouge: Louisiana State University Press, 1979–86.

Rossetti, Dante Gabriel. *Letters of Dante Gabriel Rossetti.* Edited by Oswald Doughty and John Robert Wahl. 4 vols. Oxford: Clarendon Press, 1965–67.

———. *The Works of Dante Gabriel Rossetti.* Edited by William Michael Rossetti. Rev. ed. London: Ellis, 1911.

Rossetti, William Michael. *The P.R.B. Journal: William Michael Rossetti's Diary of the Pre-Raphaelite Brotherhood, together with Other Pre-Raphaelite Documents.* Edited by William E. Fredeman. Oxford: Clarendon Press, 1975.

———. *Some Reminiscences of William Michael Rossetti.* 2 vols. New York: Charles Scribner's Sons, 1906.

Ruskin, John. *The Works of John Ruskin.* Edited by E. T. Cook and Alexander Wedderburn. 39 vols. New York: Longmans, Green, 1903–12.

Sanders, Valerie. " 'The most manlike woman in the three kingdoms': Harriet Martineau and the Brownings." *Browning Society Notes* 9, no. 3 (December 1979): 9–13.

Shackford, Martha Hale. *E. B. Browning; R. H. Horne: Two Studies.* Wellesley: Wellesley Press, 1935.

Shapiro, Marianne. "The Provincial *Trobairitz* and the Limits of Courtly Love." *Signs* 3 (1978): 560–71.

Sharp, Phillip D. "On the Composition of 'Little Mattie.' " *Browning Society Notes* 14, no. 2 (Summer 1984): 21–22.

———. "Poetry in Process: Elizabeth Barrett Browning and the Sonnets Notebook." Ph.D. diss., Louisiana State University, 1985.

Shelley, Percy Bysshe. *Shelley's Poetry and Prose.* Edited by Donald H. Reiman and Sharon B. Powers. New York: Norton, 1977.

Showalter, Elaine. *A Literature of Their Own: British Novelists from Brontë to Lessing.* Princeton: Princeton University Press, 1976.

Showalter, English, Jr. "Authorial Self-Consciousness in the Familiar Letter: The Case of Madame de Graffigny." *Men/Women of Letters. Yale French Studies,* no. 71 (1986): 113–30.

Springer, Marlene, ed. *What Manner of Woman: Essays on English and American Life and Literature.* New York: New York University Press, 1977.

Steinmetz, Virginia V. "Beyond the Sun: Patriarchal Images in *Aurora Leigh.*" *Studies in Browning and His Circle* 9, no. 2 (Fall 1981): 18–41.

———. "Images of 'Mother-Want' in Elizabeth Barrett Browning's *Aurora Leigh.*" *Victorian Poetry* 21 (1983): 351–67.

Stevenson, Lionel. "Miss Landon, 'The Milk-and-Watery Moon of Our Darkness,' 1824–30." *Modern Language Quarterly* 8 (1947): 355–63.

———. *The Pre-Raphaelite Poets.* Chapel Hill: University of North Carolina Press, 1972.

Stowe, Charles Edward. *Life of Harriet Beecher Stowe.* Boston: Houghton Mifflin, 1889.

Swedenborg, Emanuel. *Heaven and Its Wonders, and Hell: From Things Heard & Seen.* Swedenborg Society translation, revised by F. Bayley. London: Everyman, 1909.

Swinburne, Algernon Charles. *The Complete Works of Algernon Charles Swinburne.* Edited by Sir Edmund Gosse and Thomas James Wise. 20 vols. London: William Heinemann, 1925–27.

Taplin, Gardner B. "*Aurora Leigh:* A Rehearing." *Studies in Browning and His Circle* 7, no. 1 (Spring 1979): 7–23.

———. "The Brownings and the Reverend William Ware." *Browning Newsletter,* no. 7 (Fall 1971): 3–8.

———. "An Early Poem by Mrs. Browning." *Notes & Queries* 195 (10 June 1950): 252–53.

———. *The Life of Elizabeth Barrett Browning.* New Haven: Yale University Press, 1957.

Tennyson, Alfred. *The Poems of Tennyson.* Edited by Christopher Ricks. London: Longmans, 1969.

Tennyson, Hallam. *Alfred Lord Tennyson: A Memoir.* 2 vols. London: Macmillan, 1897.

Thomas, Clara. *Love and Work Enough: The Life of Anna Jameson.* Toronto: University of Toronto Press, 1967.

Thomas, Gillian. *Harriet Martineau.* Boston: Twayne, 1985.

Thomas, Donald. *Robert Browning: A Life within Life.* London: Weidenfeld & Nicolson, 1982.

Thomson, Fred C. "*All* and *Light:* A Note on the Vocabularies of Elizabeth Barrett Browning and Matthew Arnold." *Browning Society Notes* 8, no. 2 (August 1978): 2–5.

―――――. "Elizabeth Barrett Browning on Spiritualism: A New Letter." *Victorian Newsletter,* no. 31 (Spring 1967): 49–52.

Thomson, Patricia. *George Sand and the Victorians: Her Influence and Reputation in Nineteenth-Century England.* New York: Columbia University Press, 1977.

Thorpe, James. "Elizabeth Barrett's Commentary on Shelley: Some Marginalia." *Modern Language Notes* 66 (1951), 455–58.

Trevelyan, George Macaulay, ed. *English Songs of Italian Freedom.* London: Longmans, Green, 1911.

Trollope, Thomas Adolphus. *What I Remember.* 2 vols. London: Richard Bentley & Son, 1887.

Turner, Frank M. "Antiquity in Victorian Contexts." *Browning Institute Studies* 10 (1982): 1–14.

―――――. *The Greek Heritage in Victorian Britain.* New Haven: Yale University Press, 1981.

Vann, J. Don. "Elizabeth Barrett's *Poems* (1844)." *Studies in Browning and His Circle* 12 (Spring-Fall 1984): 27–31.

Vickers, Nancy J. "Diana Described: Scattered Woman and Scattered Rhyme." *Critical Inquiry* 8 (1981): 265–79.

Waller, Ross D., ed. "Letters Addressed to Mrs. Gaskell by Celebrated Contemporaries, Now in the Possession of the John Rylands Library." *Bulletin of the John Rylands Library* 19 (1935): 102–69.

Ward, Maisie. *Robert Browning and His World: The Private Face (1812–1861).* New York: Holt, Rinehart & Winston, 1967.

―――――. *Robert Browning and His World: Two Robert Brownings? (1861–1889).* New York: Holt, Rinehart & Winston, 1969.

―――――. *The Tragi-Comedy of Pen Browning (1849–1912).* With an introduction by Robert Coles, M.D. New York: Sheed & Ward and the Browning Institute, 1972.

Weaver, Bennett, ed. "Twenty Unpublished Letters of Elizabeth Barrett to Hugh Stuart Boyd." *PMLA* 65 (1950): 397–418.

Whiting, Lilian. *The Brownings: Their Life and Art.* Boston: Little, Brown, 1911.

———. *A Study of Elizabeth Barrett Browning.* Boston: Little, Brown, 1900.

Wilson, Timothy. "The Wife of the Father of *The Waste Land.*" *Esquire* 77 (May 1972): 44–50.

Winwar, Frances. *The Immortal Lovers: Elizabeth Barrett and Robert Browning: A Biography.* London: Hamish Hamilton, 1950.

Wise, Thomas J., ed. *Letters to Robert Browning and Other Correspondents.* London: printed for private circulation, 1916.

Woolford, John. "EBB: The Natural and the Spiritual." *Browning Society Notes* 8, no. 1 (April 1978): 15–19.

———. "EBB: 'Woman and Poet.'" *Browning Society Notes* 9, no. 3 (December 1979): 3–5.

Woolf, Virginia. *Flush: A Biography.* New York: Harcourt, Brace, 1933.

———. *The Second Common Reader.* New York: Harcourt Brace/Harvest, 1932.

Wordsworth, William. *William Wordsworth.* Edited by Stephen Gill. Oxford: Oxford University Press, 1984.

Yonge, Charlotte. *The Daisy Chain: Or, Aspirations. A Family Chronicle.* 1868; reprint ed. New York: Garland, 1977.

Zimmerman, Susan. "*Sonnets from the Portuguese:* A Negative and a Positive Context." In *Be Good, Sweet Maid: An Anthology of Women and Literature,* pp. 69–81. Edited by Janet Todd. New York: Holmes & Meier, 1981.

Index

299